C0-CFF-597

LEADERSHIP AND DISCIPLESHIP

A Study of Luke 22:24-30

SOCIETY OF BIBLICAL LITERATURE

DISSERTATION SERIES

Number 138

LEADERSHIP AND DISCIPLESHIP
A Study of Luke 22:24-30

by
Peter K. Nelson

Peter K. Nelson

LEADERSHIP AND DISCIPLESHIP
A Study of Luke 22:24-30

Scholars Press
Atlanta, Georgia

LEADERSHIP AND DISCIPLESHIP
A Study of Luke 22:24-30

Peter K. Nelson

Library of Congress Cataloging in Publication Data
Nelson, Peter K., 1958
Leadership and discipleship : a study of Luke 22: 24-30 / Peter K. Nelson.
p. cm. — (Dissertation series / Society of Biblical Literature ; no. 138)
Includes bibliographical references (p.) and indexes.
ISBN 1-55540-900-8 (cloth : alk. paper). —ISBN 1-55540-901-6 (paper : alk. paper)
1. Bible. N.T. Luke XXII, 24-30—Criticism, interpretation, etc.
2. Leadership in the Bible. I. Title. II. Series: Dissertation series (Society of Biblical Literature) ; no. 138.
BS2595.2.N45 1994
226.4'06—dc20 94-26261
CIP

Printed in the United States of America
on acid-free paper

To my parents
Ken and Connie Nelson

Table of Contents:

CONCLUSION

Acknowledgements:

I owe a debt of gratitude to John Nolland, my primary supervisor, who read numerous drafts of this study and gave countless hours to discuss the work with me. His patience and kindness toward me throughout this research project has been deeply appreciated. David Wenham, my external supervisor, uncovered problems with the work that had escaped me and provided encouragement along the often-trying Ph.D. trail. Of course, I am responsible for any weaknesses which remain in the work.

I am also thankful for the guidance of former teachers. Robert Stein helped me understand the nature and importance of redaction criticism, and Tom Schreiner encouraged me in the study of Greek. And my former pastor, John Piper, has conveyed the value of biblical scholarship for the service of the church.

The importance of my family's support throughout this project could not be overstated. My wife, Cheryl, has shown her love and given encouragement with remarkable constancy while I have labored over Luke 22. She sacrificed *much* to make this study possible. And my sons, Elliot and Jeremy, have been my best buddies day in and day out, and have provided their father with countless refreshing diversions from academic work. The love of these three is appreciated beyond words!

I dedicate this work to my parents, Ken and Connie Nelson, as but a small token of my deep gratitude for their massive and continual support—monetary and otherwise—through too many years of education: without their support this project would never have even been imagined, not to mention accomplished.

Scholarship funding from the following organizations is gratefully acknowledged: Tyndale House Council, Cambridge; Bethel Theological Seminary, St. Paul, Minnesota (Karl J. Karlson Post-Graduate Scholarship); Sykes Charitable Trust, Harrogate, North Yorkshire.

Permission to include in the present volume material closely related to writings I have published elsewhere is gratefully acknowledged: "The Flow of Thought in Luke 22:24-27," *JSNT* 43 (1991): 113-23 [cf. sec. 6.3 of the present work]; "Luke 22:29-30 and the Time Frame for Dining and Ruling," *TynBul* 44.2 (1993): 351-61 [cf. sec. 7.4.4 below]; "The Unitary Character of Luke 22:24-30," *NTS* 40.4 (1994, forthcoming) [cf. secs. 1.1, 4.1, 4.6, 7.3.1 and 8.2 below].

Forward:

The aim of this study is to discern the Lukan significance of Luke 22:24-30. Limited scholarly work on the text and the importance of its context and content justify an extended analysis. Background studies of authority patterns (ch. 2), table (ch. 3) and reversal motifs (ch. 4), and the testamentary genre (ch. 5) constitute Part One and provide a multi-faceted platform upon which the direct and detailed analysis in Part Two of 22:24-27 (ch. 6), 22:28-30 (ch. 7) and 22:24-30 as a literary whole (ch. 8) is based. The interplay of looking closely and stepping back permitted by this two-part structure facilitates the quest for the text's meaning, as does an emphasis on redaction- and literary-critical priorities.

The work seeks to demonstrate a Lukan unitary conception for 22:24-30, contrary to the orientation of much tradition-critical study. The pericope's unity is evidenced in its overarching, full-circle reversal form (the great are to serve; loyal "servants" will be "great") as a pattern for discipleship which increases motivation for perseverance in adversity. Also unifying the text are a pervasive interest in authority which presents a challenge to conventional ideas of power and greatness (elevation comes to those who lead "from below"), and a keen concern for the solidarity of the apostles with Jesus during his earthly life and in the eschatological age.

Certain specific assertions of Part Two which undergird the above claims are these: the contrast structure of 22:25-27 with Jesus' self-description as "the servant" (v 27) paints the apostles' quarrel over greatness (v 24) not as an innocent rivalry but as a sharply negative event, and, despite a recent claim to the contrary, it portrays the kings and benefactors (v 25) as distinctly negative examples; the chief expression of Jesus' servant leadership (v 27) is his humble and benefit-giving death; Jesus recalls his "trials" (v 28) from the time of his public ministry during which the apostles persevered with him; the conferral of kingship and the promise of exaltation (vv 29-30) anticipate fulfillment not in the church age but in the eschaton.

Conventions and Abbreviations:

In the case of chapter and verse references in the MT or LXX which conflict with the numbering in English translations, English conventions are followed unless specified otherwise.

References to and translations of classical sources, Philo, Josephus and the Apostolic Fathers are from the Loeb Classical Library editions unless otherwise indicated.

Citations are by author only, or by author and short title when more than one work by a given author is included in the bibliography. See the bibliography for full documentation.

The abbreviations for primary sources and translations, periodicals, series and reference works set out by The Society of Biblical Literature are adopted in the present study (see *Journal of Biblical Literature* 107 [3, 1988]: 579-96; also see the 1993 AAR/SBL *Membership Directory and Handbook,* 383-400). Abbreviations for classical works, papyri and inscriptions, and other sources not listed by SBL follow the conventions of F. Blass and A. Debrunner, *A Greek Grammar of the New Testament and Other Early Christian Literature* (trans. and edt. R. W. Funk; Chicago: University, 1961), xvii-xxiv. Additional abbreviations are as follows:

AAnth	*American Anthropologist*
Adv. Haer.	*Adversus Haereses* (Irenaeus)
Alex.	*De Alexandri Magni fortuna aut virtute* (Plutarch)
Alex.	Alexander Rhetor
Andr.	*Andromanche* (Euripides)
Ann.	*Annals* (Tacitus)
Ap.	*Apologia Socratis* (Xenophon)
Aph.	ἀφορισμοί (Hippocrates)
BMI	*Ancient Greek Inscriptions in the British Museum* (Oxford: University, 1874-1916)
Cont.	*De Vita Contemplativa* (Philo)
Deip.	*Deipnosophists* (Athenaeus); or *Deipnosophists* (Lucian)
Det.	*Quod Deterius Potiori insidiari solet* (Philo)
Dinner	*The Dinner of the Seven Wise Men* (Plutarch)
FF	Foundations and Facets

Forum	*Foundations and Facets Forum*
Frag.	*Fragmenta* (Euripides)
GP	Gospel Perspectives
Hist.	*Histories* (Polybius)
Hp.	Hippocrates
IE	*Die Inschriften von Ephesos,* edt. Hermann Wankel, et al. (Bonn: Habelt, 1979-84)
IESS	*International Encyclopedia of the Social Sciences,* edt. David L. Sills (New York: Macmillan, 1968)
Inscr. Prien.	*Die Inschriften von Priene,* edt. F. Hiller von Gaertringen (Berlin: Reimer, 1906)
Inst.	*Institutes* (Gaius)
Jos. As.	*Joseph and Asenath* (OT Pseudepigrapha)
Nat. Hist.	*Natural History* (Pliny the Elder)
NIDNTT	*New International Dictionary of New Testament Theology,* edt. C. Brown (Grand Rapids: Zondervan, 1975-78)
NLNTC	New London Commentary on the New Testament
OBS	Oxford Bible Series
OBT	Overtures to Biblical Theology
PC	Proclamation Commentaries
PD	Parole de Dieu
Pol.	*Politica* (Aristotle)
PRS	*Perspectives in Religious Studies*
SNTSU	Studien zum Neuen Testament und seiner Umwelt
StBib	Stuttgarter Bibelstudien
Symp.	*Symposium* or *Convivium* (Lucian); or *Symposium* (Plato); or *Symposium* (Xenophon)
Table Talk	*Quaestiones Convivales* (Plutarch)
TI	Theological Inquiries
TNTC	Tyndale New Testament Commentaries
TPINTC	Trinity Press International New Testament Commentaries
T. 3 Patr.	*Testaments of the Three Patriarchs* (OT Pseudepigrapha)

Luke 22:24-30:

24a 'Εγένετο δὲ καὶ φιλονεικία ἐν αὐτοῖς,
24b τὸ τίς αὐτῶν δοκεῖ εἶναι μείζων.
25a ὁ δὲ εἶπεν αὐτοῖς·
25b οἱ βασιλεῖς τῶν ἐθνῶν κυριεύουσιν αὐτῶν
25c καὶ οἱ ἐξουσιάζοντες αὐτῶν εὐεργέται καλοῦνται.
26a ὑμεῖς δὲ οὐχ οὕτως,
26b ἀλλ' ὁ μείζων ἐν ὑμῖν γινέσθω ὡς ὁ νεώτερος
26c καὶ ὁ ἡγούμενος ὡς ὁ διακονῶν.
27a τίς γὰρ μείζων, ὁ ἀνακείμενος ἢ ὁ διακονῶν;
27b οὐχὶ ὁ ἀνακείμενος;
27c ἐγὼ δὲ ἐν μέσῳ ὑμῶν εἰμι ὡς ὁ διακονῶν.
28 'Υμεῖς δέ ἐστε οἱ διαμεμενηκότες μετ' ἐμοῦ ἐν τοῖς πειρασμοῖς μου·
29 κἀγὼ διατίθεμαι ὑμῖν καθὼς διέθετό μοι ὁ πατήρ μου βασιλείαν,
30a ἵνα ἔσθητε καὶ πίνητε ἐπὶ τῆς τραπέζης μου ἐν τῇ βασιλείᾳ μου,
30b καὶ καθήσεσθε ἐπὶ θρόνων τὰς δώδεκα φυλὰς κρίνοντες τοῦ 'Ισραήλ.

24a A quarrel even arose among them
24b as to which of them seemed to be the greatest.
25a He said to them,
25b "The kings of the Gentiles rule over them,
25c and those in authority over them are called 'benefactors.'
26a But not so with you!
26b Rather, let the greatest among you become like the youngest,
26c and the leader like the servant.
27a For which is greater, the diner or the table servant?
27b Surely it is the diner, is it not?
27c Yet I am among you as the servant.
28 But you are in fact those who have been persevering with me through my trials.
29 And so, as my Father conferred kingship on me, I confer kingship on you,
30a that you may eat and drink at my table in my kingdom;
30b and you shall sit on thrones ruling the twelve tribes of Israel."[1]

---

[1]My translation (see further chs. 6 and 7).

INTRODUCTION

Chapter 1:
Preliminary Considerations

1.1 Rationale

There are three major factors which justify a new, extensive and detailed study of Luke 22:24-30. They have to do with the volume and orientation of previous scholarship, the degree to which previous work has recognized the importance of the context of 22:24-30, and the degree to which the passage's content has been appreciated.

First, despite the existence of a vast body of literature on Luke-Acts and a sizeable scholarship on the Lukan Passion Narrative and Last Supper, until recently the literature focusing directly on 22:24-30 has been relatively sparse. This gap is highlighted by Metzger's *Index* (1966) which does not include a single entry under 22:24-30 in the section, "Critical and Exegetical Studies of Individual Passages in Luke." In recent years the field of literature on 22:24-30 has seen some significant contributions (see sec. 1.5 below), but the passage remains one that has received comparatively little direct attention. The only monograph to present an extended analysis of 22:24-30 is Schürmann's third volume in his series of tradition-critical works on Luke 22:7-38 (*Jesu Abschiedsrede Lk 22,21-38*, 1957), though even here our text is not made the center of attention. Furthermore, Schürmann's interest in tradition-historical issues has kept him from portraying 22:24-30 as a literary piece in and of itself. On the whole, then, both periodical and monograph literature have, especially before the 1980s, provided comparatively little on the text at hand.

Second, the context of 22:24-30 would suggest that the text is of considerable importance for Luke. In terms of the broader strokes of Luke's pen, the arrival in Jerusalem (19:45ff)—the Lukan Jesus' city of destiny—and the reinvigorated activity of Satan (22:3) lead to the climactic episode in Jesus' journey to God and the apostles' course of discipleship. Events and sayings in the Passion Narrative thus take on a distinctive nuance and significance in the Lukan story. Further, Luke is the only synoptic evangelist to offer a collection of Jesus' sayings in the form of a farewell discourse, a generic framework that is rich with implications for the interpretation of our text (farewell words are, by nature, climactic and pivotal).[1] Moreover, the presence of the Last Supper Narrative (vv 15-20) in the discourse lends to the whole of the farewell address something of its own christological, eschatological and ecclesiological significance.[2]

Third, in terms of content, a number of key themes of Luke-Acts surface in 22:24-30. These include a rebuke for the attitude of self-importance and a call for humility, a perspective on civil authorities, a commendation of endurance in trials, the promise of elevation for the humble, table imagery, the kingdom of God, and the place of Israel in salvation history. Thus a number of important ideas converge here in these seven verses. This suggests that 22:24-30 has a contribution to make to a number of larger Lukan strands of thought, and it also implies that our study of 22:24-30 will be aided by analysis of a wide array of material elsewhere in the Lukan corpus. The important content of 22:24-30 alone would suffice to warrant a new and in-depth examination of that text.[3]

Not all of the above factors, however, justify work on 22:24-30 only. Why not do a study of the whole farewell discourse (vv 14-38) or a portion of it larger than 22:24-30? To be sure, a thorough analysis of 22:14-38 with balanced attention to all sections of the discourse would be a worthwhile undertaking. Reasons for limiting the scope of the present work, however, include the following. First, 22:15-20 has been subjected

---

[1]See ch. 5 on the testamentary genre. John 13-17 also constitutes a farewell discourse, yet one that differs markedly from Luke 22:14-38 in length and content.

[2]And Luke 22:24-30 has important points of conceptual and verbal contact with the Last Supper.

[3]This is not to imply that the content of certain other texts in Luke is unimportant. On the contrary, an assumption of this work is that all parts of Luke's finished work are included because Luke wants them there. Still, it is useful to recognize the relative importance of certain texts in Luke in terms of their role for uncovering the plot of the story, the thought or theology of the writer, etc.

to extensive and meticulous study, and continues to receive a great deal attention in the literature (not least because of the complicated text-critical problem in vv 19-20).[4] Second, the desired depth of analysis for the present work together with limitations on space would seem to prohibit a focus on all of 22:21-38. Third, although there are certain lines of thought running through other sections of 22:14-38 and the discourse as a whole, the combined weight of arguments for the unified character of 22:24-30 offers a compelling invitation for a study of that unit in and of itself. It is to the issue of the text's unity that we now turn.

Although Luke's Last Supper discourse is sometimes characterized as a collection of sayings—a string of pearls—in which vv 24-27 and 28-30 are commonly thought to contain separate if not even contradictory sayings,[5] a strong case can be made for the unitary conception of 22:24-30. In the present study that argument will be developed primarily in two parts. Here we will draw attention to the verbal/ conceptual features that link vv 24-27 with 28-30, and also note a structural tie. In section 8.2 we will go on to develop the argument by uncovering certain logical, thematic and other unifying features of 22:24-30.[6] This element of the case for unity in vv 24-30 is saved for section 8.2 because it will be most clear and convincing when familiarity with the detailed analysis of vv 24-30 in chapters 6 and 7 can be assumed.[7] The points made here for taking 22:24-30 as a coherent unit, however, provide an adequate provisional basis for undertaking a study restricted and yet extended to 22:24-30.

An important verbal/ conceptual link of vv 24-27 and 28-30 consists of the language of authority and subordination (see further ch. 2). Note the following vocabulary for authority figures and their actions: οἱ βασιλεῖς (v 25b), κυριεύουσιν (v 25b), οἱ ἐξουσιάζοντες (v 25c), εὐεργέται[8] (v 25c), ὁ ἡγούμενος (v 26c), ὁ ἀνακείμενος[9] (v 27a, b), διατίθεμαι/

---

[4]See e.g., two articles in volume 37 (1991) of *NTS* (Maccoby and Petzer).

[5]E.g., Creed, 268.

[6]Secs. 4.1 and 4.6 also point to aspects of the text's unity (cf. sec. 7.3.1).

[7]Significant engagement with scholarship on the question of unity in vv 24-30 will be presented in sec. 8.2.

[8]εὐεργέτης appears in inscriptions as a title for rulers (e.g., Augustus, Nero, and certain of the Ptolemies and Selucid kings [Fitzmyer, *Gospel*, 2:1417; T. W. Manson, *Sayings*, 338]). See further secs. 2.2.2 and 6.5.1 on the title "benefactor" and its strong connections with concepts and positions of authority.

[9]ὁ ἀνακείμενος here connotes ideas of authority and social superiority by its

διέθετο (v 29), βασιλείαν (v 29), τῇ βασιλείᾳ (v 30a), θρόνων (v 30b), κρίνοντες (v 30b). Further, the nature of Jesus' response to the quarrel over "greatness" and the place of μείζων in the antithetical structure of vv 26-27 imply that μείζων carries connotations of authority. Conversely, people in subordinate roles or their actions are described in both vv 24-27 and 28-30: τῶν ἐθνῶν and αὐτῶν (v 25b, c), ὁ νεώτερος[10] (v 26b), ὁ διακονῶν (vv 26c, 27a, c), ὑμῖν and μοι (v 29), τὰς δώδεκα φυλὰς ... τοῦ Ἰσραήλ (v 30b). Clearly, there is a pervasive motif of authority and subordination extending through both subsections of 22:24-30. One notes, however, that this motif does not have nearly such a strong presence in either vv 15-23 or 31-38.

Table language also serves to unify vv 24-30 (cf. ch. 3).[11] Note the vocabulary: ὁ ἀνακείμενος ἢ ὁ διακονῶν (v 27a), ὁ ἀνακείμενος (v 27b), ὁ διακονῶν (v 27c), ἔσθητε καὶ πίνητε (v 30a), ἐπὶ τῆς τραπέζης (v 30a). Although it is true that the narrative setting for all of 22:14-38 is at table, it may be clarified that, apart from the Last Supper itself (vv 15-20) and ἐπὶ τῆς τραπέζης in v 21, only in vv 24-30 are table customs and table fellowship made a topic for discussion and reflection.[12]

A structural link (which is also a vocabulary link) may be noted here as well. Lull argues that vv 27c and 28 are connected by the parallel construction with ἐγὼ δὲ ... εἰμι and ὑμεῖς δέ ἐστε.[13] The importance of this framework is highlighted when one notes that a common feature of 22:24-30 as a whole is the union of Jesus and the apostles, a discipleship which joins them through the injunction to follow Jesus' model of leadership through service (vv 25-27), the shared experience of enduring trials (v 28), the conferral on them of kingship as the Father conferred it on Jesus (v 29), and the sharing of celebration and rule in the coming kingdom (v 30) (cf. chs. 6-9). The solidarity of Jesus and the Twelve, however, is not similarly emphasized in vv 21-23 or 31-38.[14]

---

antithetical relation to ὁ διακονῶν. See further chs. 2 and 3.

[10]Cf. sec. 2.4.2 on children and youth in the family authority structure.

[11]Cf. Hooker, *Son of Man*, 145.

[12]Fitzmyer draws attention to another possible unifying feature here, namely plural "you" in v 27c and v 28 referring to the apostles as a vocabulary link favoring the unitary conception of the Lukan paragraph (i.e., 22:24-30) (*Gospel*, 2:1412). It is difficult to be sure of the importance of this observation, however, since the plural pronoun "you" is common throughout the speech (see vv 15, 16, 18, 19, 20, 31, 35, 37), and is natural in an exhortatory discourse to an audience of more than one.

[13]Lull, 299-300.

1.2 Aims

The primary aim of the present study is to discern the meaning of Luke 22:24-30. This statement requires clarification in a number of respects: What is the definition of "meaning"? Is the locus of meaning in the finished text, the intention of the author behind the text, the thinking of earlier figures whose speech is reported, the audience that receives the text, or elsewhere?

"Meaning" is understood broadly here so as to embrace contributions from various theories. Our aim is not restricted in terms of a narrow idea of meaning as concerned with identifying the object to which a word refers, nor is the study concerned only with the semantic content of words or even larger linguistic units.[15] In the present work "meaning" is an umbrella term for the sum of various contributions made by linguistic building blocks in a text, both large and small,[16] to the formation of that text's line or field of thought and expression. Further, the interplay of these building blocks (through proximity, logical connections, thematic associations, etc.) makes an important contribution to meaning. A given term, then, may clarify or be clarified by portions of text that precede or follow it. Thus the big picture involves discerning a text's thought and expression, but a wide assortment of linguistic units play a part in this task. At any given point in the analysis of Luke 22:24-30, then, we will be concerned not only to ask what a given word or clause itself means, but also what role it plays in shaping the meaning of other units and the text as a whole, or what role other parts play in relation to 22:24-30.

---

[14]By way of clarification, the case for unity in vv 24-30 advanced here does not overlook the important factors that distinguish vv 24-27 from 28-30 in terms of temporal focus, tone (i.e., humiliation is juxtaposed with exaltation), and tradition history. It is not claimed that the seam between vv 24-27 and 28-30 is smooth in every respect. These distinguishing features, however, give color and emphasis and an attention-catching paradoxical quality to the sense of 22:24-30 as an organic whole, and are not sufficient to undermine the case for unity. See further esp. chs. 4 and 8.

[15]See Thiselton's discussion ("Meaning," 435-8) of referential, semantic, ideational and functional theories (cf. Cotterell and Turner, 38-42; Fowl, 73-5). Thiselton (ibid., 438) cautions against focusing on one theory to the exclusion of others: "No single theory of meaning is valid for every kind of question. Each offers some contribution within the terms of certain purposes."

[16]E.g., from suffixes and prefixes to words to clauses to sentences to paragraphs, and beyond. See Cotterell and Turner (77-82).

It must still be asked, however, *whose* thought and expression we are after, for there are layers of meaning in or associated with a text like this. The aim of this study will be to identify the meaning attendant to the final form of the Lukan text. Therefore, if there was any kind of proto-Luke, its meaning is not our chief concern. Further, the meaning of Luke's sources—written or oral—in their pre-Lukan settings is not our primary concern. Additionally, the focus is not on the meaning of the relevant logia in the period of the historical Jesus. The object of investigation is the finished text of Luke 22:24-30 as it stands in the Greek NT.[17]

This emphasis on the final form of Luke, however, does not make the pre-history of the text irrelevant for this work. On the contrary, information that can be gleaned as to the layers of tradition is potentially important for the study of Luke 22:24-30. Although we focus on the meaning of the text as it stands and as it represents the final stage of Lukan literary activity, it is quite improbable that Luke sought totally to transform what meaning the traditional elements of the text may have had. In short, pre-Lukan stages of tradition are of value in our study because they can shed some light upon the text in its final Lukan form (see further below on methods, sec. 1.3).

Having attached the meaning which is sought to the finished Lukan text, however, it remains to be clarified whether the author's or the reader's meaning is in view. Both are associated with the text at the time of its composition, and both play a part in allowing the text to "have its say." There are, however, reasons to be cautious on both fronts, and for avoiding an "either/ or" approach to author and reader.

It is here maintained that in an ideal circumstance (i.e., when one can consult with a text's author as to the thrust and desired impact of the writing) an author's intentions would be determinative for the meaning of a text. To be sure, this is not to say that the literature of living writers is slavishly tied to authorial intention. Texts do "come alive" in the process of reading, and they come to mean many things to many different people. The point here is merely that most authors would not, in all likelihood, concede that every such "meaning" could rightly be thought of as "the meaning" of a text for which they bear responsibility.

Our problem, of course, is that Luke is not available for consultation, so if we are to ascertain his meaning for a given portion of his writ-

[17] I.e., K. Aland et al., eds., NA26 and UBS3. The text-critical problems of Luke 22:24-30 will be taken up in chs. 6 and 7.

ing, it must be inferred from the text itself, the input of the rest of the Lukan writings and other relevant backgrounds.[18] Further, the multi-layer nature of Luke's Gospel complicates the task of discerning his intentions; at a given point we may wonder whether it is Jesus or a pre-Lukan writer/ editor or Luke that is "speaking." The difficulty of gaining access to Luke's meaning is heightened further by the great distance (in terms of time, culture, language, *Weltanschauung* generally, and other factors) which separates us from his writings. So it is necessary to admit that, even if an author's intentions would in theory be the basis for a text's meaning, the difficulty at points in determining Luke's intended meaning is great.[19] This dilemma confronts us with the need to be cautious in the present study when attempting to discern Luke's meaning.[20]

It is also necessary to be cautious about the reader's role in relation to meaning. It is no easier to reconstruct the situation and characteristics of Luke's first audience than it is to pinpoint the intentions of the author in forming the final text of Luke-Acts.[21] Further, an overemphasis on

[18]Cf. Morgan and Barton, 6-8.

[19]Cf. Cotterell and Turner, 42.

[20]The drift of recent scholarship has been away from making any intended meaning of biblical authors the focus of investigation (see the discussions in S. Moore, e.g., 12-13, 54-5, 120-3—this reflects the orientation of secular literary-criticism, which is said to have exposed the quest for an author's intentions as a fallacy [the pivotal essay by Wimsatt and Beardsley is often cited in this connection, though its concentration on poetry would limit its relevance for the study of a narrative text such as Luke 22:24-30]). Fowl proposes the substitution of "interpretive interests" for "meaning" as a focus for biblical studies (70-5), thus allowing the agenda for biblical scholarship to be set by modern pluralism. The only criterion then for pursuing a particular interpretative interest would be that it interests enough interpreters to allow for a conversation (75). By contrast, in a recent literary-critical study, Tyson (*Death of Jesus*, 19-21) follows Hirsch cautiously and makes it his aim to determine the meaning the author of Luke-Acts intended to convey to his readers. Despite the many limitations on the availability of a NT author's intention, it is not totally inaccessible (21). C. Black (238-9) maintains that, although redaction criticism has overemphasized authorial intent, it still ought to be given an "accent" in interpretation. According to S. Moore's assessment of gospel studies (12), the aim of recovering an author's intentions, though now often left implicit, is the unbroken link of "narrative criticism" with traditional biblical criticism. Similarly, Alter's study of OT narrative implicitly has the intentions of authors in view (188-9).

[21]See Tuckett (143) on the potential problems involved in attempting to reconstruct the situations of the evangelists and their communities, and in determining the degree to which such reader-based factors may have influenced the writing of texts.

the activity of the reader as one who engages with a text subjectively and creatively thereby developing new meanings[22] invites a radical relativism and ultimately undermines interpretation: saying that a text can mean many different things is tantamount to saying that it means nothing. One who holds that an author's role is at least of some importance in establishing meaning will see in this kind of subjectivity the deterioration or disintegration of such meaning. We may not choose to make the identification of authorial intent all-important in the quest for meaning, but neither should it be jettisoned. For this reason it will be important not to overemphasize reader-based factors in the quest to discern the meaning of Luke 22:24-30.

Therefore, in the present study an effort will be made to consider the roles of both author and readers in the quest to establish the meaning of Luke's finished text.[23] To the degree that grammar, word choice, context, Lukan themes, etc., make Luke's thought and expression reasonably clear, such factors will form a crucial element in our quest for meaning. And to the degree that an awareness of the knowledge, presuppositions, situations, etc., of the Lukan readers can be determined with probability, such factors will also be important for discerning the meaning of our text.

Meaning, then, is understood broadly here, it is associated with the finished Lukan text, and both reader and author perspectives offer windows to it. In the end, the sense most commonly given the term in the present study centers on the thought and expression of a text on its various micro- and macro-levels: what is the probable impact (i.e., on readers) the text was to have (i.e., by the author)?[24] The study, therefore, will be presented so as to lay the groundwork for and move finally toward the discerning of meaning understood in this way.[25]

---

[22]So the orientation of reader-response theories. S. Moore (120-1) observes that even a moderate reader-centered approach resettles the Bible's locus of meaning in the consciousness of the reader/ hearer: "Prior to the interpretive act there is nothing definitive in the text to be discovered" (121). Alter (179) does not argue for a fixed, absolute meaning of biblical texts, but neither does he accept the "contemporary agnosticism about all literary meaning."

[23]Cf. the description by Cotterell and Turner of "discourse meaning " being rooted in the shared knowledge of writer and readers (71-2). This is a nuanced adaptation of Hirsch's position. Cotterell and Turner maintain (59-71) that certain of the stock criticisms leveled against Hirsch are not sound or appropriate.

[24]The terms "impact" and "argument" and "thrust" and "point" in the present work are all to be seen in the light of the interfacing of author and audience.

Having stated that this study will focus on the finished Lukan text, it is still to be clarified whether we are seeking to understand the probable perception by Luke's readers of the inner workings of the narrative with its events and sayings (i.e., the story line), or the "message" Luke proclaims to his audience by means of that narrative. In fact, it will not be necessary to eliminate either perspective,[26] though the focus of attention will be on the narrative world of Luke 22:24-30 rather than an implicit message behind the text.

The reason for this priority on the narrative is that it is only there that we are given a full presentation of settings, characters, events and the actual content of direct speech. On the level of the Lukan proclamation to his contemporary readers, however, there are many large gaps in our knowledge. To be sure, the Lukan text provides a few explicit comments as to author, readership and occasion (e.g., 1:1-4), and a number of implicit clues as to the particulars of the Lukan *Sitz im Leben* as well.[27] Nevertheless, we still know far less about the Lukan congregation as readers of Luke 22:24-30 than we do about the Lukan apostles as hearers of that text's content. And we know a good deal more about the Lukan Jesus as a communicator than we do about Luke himself as a speaker. For such reasons we chiefly seek an analysis of the inner workings of the Lukan text; only secondarily will we probe the possibilities for Luke's distinctive proclamation to the church of his day.

---

[25]It is not implied that we will be able to discern such meaning with absolute certainty, for every interpreter brings an element of subjectivity to the task. This is where the advantage of interaction with scholarship is so important for the present work—it can count against or open up possibilities for meaning.

[26]Evidently Luke felt a necessity to present a story that was coherent in and of itself, yet he also had a particular message to convey along with and through that narrative that cannot be reduced to a mere restatement of the story. Understanding Luke's writings, then, involves a perception of these levels on which they were to function. Further, the thrust of the text as either an internally coherent narrative or a proclamation to the Lukan readership may sometimes be a single thrust (e.g., are Jesus' command to become like a servant [22:27] and his commendation of persevering allegiance [22:28] virtually transferable to Luke's readers as words to them?).

[27]See e.g., Brawley, Esler, Nolland (*Luke's Readers*) and York on discerning characteristics of Luke's audience which are implicit in his narrative.

1.3 Methods

A brief consideration of methodology will clarify how the present study is intended to achieve its aims. We will first consider the method of presentation (i.e., the organization of the work) and then discuss the role of traditional and newer methods of biblical criticism in the present study.

The present work, apart from its introduction and conclusion (chs. 1 and 9), is divided into two complementary parts. Part One offers a series of studies on backgrounds which are deemed relevant to Luke 22:24-30. Each chapter in Part One focuses on a background field that makes connections to *both* vv 24-27 *and* 28-30.[28] It is maintained that a significant familiarity with the background fields of authority and subordination patterns (ch. 2), table motifs (ch. 3), reversal motifs (ch. 4), and testamentary genre (ch. 5) constitutes a valuable platform upon which to stand in Part Two when making a more focused attempt to discern facets of meaning in 22:24-30.

Part Two then turns directly to the text—the progression from Part One may be thought of as being from "context" to text—and it offers a detailed and thorough analysis of vv 24-30 with a view toward achieving the aims of this study. Chapters 6 and 7 analyze at length vv 24-27 and 28-30 respectively, and it is there that the focus of study is often on the text in its detail rather than on broad strokes of thought. Chapter 8 steps back from this close work and analyzes 22:24-30 as a literary whole. It is initially here, yet finally only in chapter 9, that the dissertation offers some assessment of the *overall* thrust of the text at hand. By way of clarification, however, it is to the findings of each of chapters 6 through 8, with due regard to the contributions of chapters 2 through 5, that the discussion of leadership and discipleship in chapter 9 appeals.

Before turning to methods of biblical criticism, it will be useful to specify more precisely *how* the background studies of Part One are to function in this work. The background fields of Part One may be thought of as types of "contexts" (i.e., broad historical, literary and formal frameworks against which our text may be seen). For such contexts to affect the writing and reading of a text, its author and first readers obviously

---

[28]It is for this reason that there is no attention in Part One given to, say, the kingdom of God in Luke, or Luke's view of Israel. Some analysis of such backgrounds, however, will be offered in Part Two at the appropriate points.

would have to have been aware of them. It is assumed, for example, that Luke and his audience would have had some knowledge of Hellenistic symposia and certain Jewish table traditions.[29]

Awareness, in turn, is a building block of reader expectations. For instance, if Luke's readers were aware of Passover traditions, they would have built up a set of related expectations, and they would have even been able to detect allusions to the Passover if they were made with sufficient clarity. Readers might then have supposed that topics which resonated with what they knew of the Passover (e.g., slaughter of the lamb, recollection of the Exodus story, etc.) were intended to call that context to mind. And once such expectations are established, subsequent material may be fitted with them quite readily.

With the expectation grid in place, Luke can present material against it and thus invite assessments ranging from direct correspondence to comparison to contrast.[30] If a Lukan text and a given background grid are similar in every important respect, the reader would naturally align new data with existing expectations. If, however, similarities are extensive but not total, the reader may presume that Luke wishes the text to be compared with the grid, points of departure to be overshadowed by agreement, and the text to be read as having a sense similar to that of the grid. Alternatively, substantial dissimilarity may reveal the author's desire to jar the readers' categories and draw a contrast with background data. Moreover, there could be various combinations of comparison and contrast that backgrounds invite; reader expectations may be confirmed in certain respects and yet challenged in others.

Regarding Luke 22:24-30, our aim in considering backgrounds is to allow significant similarities and differences between the multi-faceted expectation grid of Luke's readers (involving their likely awareness of various background data) and the particulars of 22:24-30 to be detected. In short, the studies of "context" (i.e., Part One) are to create a framework which enables one to trace Luke's manipulation of readers' expectations to achieve alignment with, departure from, or some intermediate

[29]Even post-Lukan sources, however, have a certain relevance for Part One in that they may reflect earlier ideas or practices which were current in the Lukan period, although such sources (e.g., John, the Rabbis) are appealed to only with much caution.

[30]E.g., a given speech may be presented as a pure instance of the farewell genre, it may depart from the pattern only slightly and thus invite comparison, or it may depart from it dramatically and warrant contrast.

connection with their knowledge of backgrounds. It will be left to Part Two actually to turn to the details of Luke 22:24-30 and propose at various points just how a determination of the meaning of the text is influenced by the relevant background perspectives.

We now turn to the roles of the various methods of biblical criticism in the present work. To the degree that any available method makes it possible to gain insight as to the meaning of Luke 22:24-30, it will be employed. The fact that this study centers on the final form of the Lukan text naturally limits the contributions from approaches which center on the layers of tradition behind that text (e.g., form and tradition criticism). Still, when it is possible to recover relevant pre-Lukan material, noting what Luke has done with it may provide valuable clues as to the meaning of the finished text. Therefore, the present work avoids the tendency of some newer literary-critical and reader-based approaches to jettison historical-critical perspectives.[31]

The methodological heart of this work, however, consists of a hybrid of redaction and literary criticism. The redaction-critical aspect comes out most clearly in the commitment to understanding the author's distinctive communication, and the literary-critical aspect comes out most strongly in the emphasis on the final text of Luke as forming a whole and coherent literary piece regardless of its pre-history.

An excess accompanying redaction criticism, perhaps most common in the earlier years of its development, was that departures from sources were overvalued as indicators of a writer's theology. This approach tends to yield an eccentric theology, a caricature of an evangelist's true outlook.[32] Literary criticism has sometimes also been given to excess by making texts into free-floating, self-contained literary units that become detached from the world in which they came to be. The present study seeks to avoid both of these extremes, and to develop a balanced approach which retains "the best" of what redaction and literary criticism can offer. Luke's departures from sources offer crucial clues as to his thinking and theology, but their importance must not overshadow the clues presented by his total finished work.[33] So a balance is favored

[31]Tuckett (2-4, et al.) is similarly cautious.

[32]Cf. C. Black's helpful critique of redaction criticism as applied to Mark (e.g., 233-40).

[33]As is sometimes said, and quite rightly, Luke never expected his audience

here, one that allows redaction and literary criticism to remove each other's rough edges.

It may be added that some newer approaches which give special attention to sociological and anthropological concerns will be drawn upon in this study. These will not, however, be used with an ultimate aim of establishing the characteristics of the Lukan community or situation, for to do so is to fall into the trap of other criticisms that dwell upon the extra-textual layers of tradition and spheres of experience and yet fail to give an analysis of the meaning of Luke's final text.[34] Rather, they will be utilized, like any other method of biblical criticism, in the course of seeking the meaning Luke wished to convey to his audience.[35]

The employment of redaction criticism of course assumes some knowledge of the sources Luke drew upon. Markan priority is accepted here as a relatively firm working hypothesis, though other reconstructions are not ruled out.[36] The existence of a sayings source, "Q," however, is accepted more cautiously. It still seems more likely than not that Luke and Matthew independently had access to such a source, but it is very difficult to prove this.[37] Luke also includes a great deal of material without parallel in Mark or Matthew (i.e., "L"), though the degree to which such material has been taken over from sources or is Luke's own composition is often uncertain. In the case of either Markan or Q or L texts, however, it is important to keep in mind that all elements in Luke's final text are there because Luke wanted them there—no source can hold Luke's arm behind his back.[38] In short, though the two/ four source the-

---

to read his Gospel in a synopsis.

[34]To uncover the occasion for a text (e.g., if the presence of poor people in the congregation is said to occasion harsh words toward the wealthy) is not the same as explicating its meaning. Esler seems to be among those who may overvalue the role of Luke's community and his situation in determining the content of his writings (e.g., 200).

[35]Textual criticism will also be employed when called for.

[36]Note e.g., the recent work of J. Wenham (proposing the sequence, Matthew, Mark, Luke), and those advocating the Griesbach hypothesis (esp. Farmer).

[37]Goulder (*Luke*, 1:1-194) points up certain shortcomings of the Q theory, but seems less able to demonstrate his alternative thesis, i.e., Luke's knowledge of Matthew (cf. my review of Goulder's work in *Anvil* 7 [1990]: 256-7).

[38]Perhaps this is a bit of an exaggeration: if Luke had wanted to omit such a sacred and pivotal gospel tradition as, say, the resurrection of Jesus, it is doubtful that his Gospel would have survived. But given the decision to write a Gospel with its attendant requirements (i.e., including the passion and resurrection), Luke is still able to exercise a great deal of freedom in deciding what to include or exclude, how to order his account, etc.

ory has its shortcomings, it is sufficiently well established to warrant a cautious appeal to it in this work.

1.4 Clarifications

It will be helpful to point out a few features of this study that will surface repeatedly and that may invite confusion if they are not clarified here. First, "Luke" is used in this study as the name of the writer of Luke-Acts, though no case is being marshalled for the identity of that author as the traveling companion of Paul or as anyone else.[39] Further, the use of masculine pronouns for the author is owing to the choice of the name "Luke," and does not depend on any argument concerning the actual author's gender.

The Lukan "reader(s)" are referred to frequently in this work. It is recognized, however, that many in Luke's audience probably encountered the Lukan writings as its hearers.[40] For the sake of convenience, however, "reader(s)" will be made to stand for "reader(s)/ auditor(s)."

The Lukan "community" (or "church," etc.) is a term that may give the impression of greater precision than is actually intended. Its use does not imply any specific view on the nature, location, social or economic or religious contours, etc., of Luke's audience, nor is its singular form to imply that there could not have been many communities for which Luke wrote.[41] The use of the term in this work, however, does reveal a presupposition that even if Theophilus (1:3) was an individual, Luke would have wished his writings to be given more than one person's private use.

Luke-Acts is taken to be a two-volume work by a single author. Dawsey[42] and others rightly observe that the unity of the two parts is sometimes overstated. Aspects of discontinuity between Luke and Acts, however, are probably due mostly to the differing roles of tradition in the composition of the two volumes, the difference of subject matter (i.e., Jesus totally dominates the Gospel, but he departs the narrative scene in

[39]Cf. Fitzmyer (*Gospel*, 1:35-53) and Goulder (*Luke*, 1:129-46) on this question.

[40]Cf. S. Moore, 84-8; York, 164, n. 1.

[41]To speak of the Lukan community seems to have become conventional in recent years when much study of the NT has been centered on establishing the situation and social aspects of authors and their audiences ("community" has a stronger social connotation than "audience").

[42]Dawsey, "Unity," 48-66.

Acts 1), and perhaps the passage of some time. The strong lines of linguistic, thematic and structural similarity, the presence of plot features that extend through both volumes, plus the very similar prologues, however, together imply that Luke-Acts may be properly thought of as a single literary work. Accordingly, material in Acts has a unique relevance for a study of a text in Luke's Gospel, one not shared by other NT documents.

Reader-based theories of biblical interpretation raise the question as to which reading is assumed for a given analysis of a text.[43] Logically, the prospect of a first reading of Luke 22:24-30 comes up, one which would involve no acquaintance with the rest of the Gospel and all of Acts, and a limited knowledge of the anterior context as well. To be sure, such a stage in the earliest reading of Luke-Acts probably did exist. But a careful analysis of the Lukan writings reveals a number themes, forms, plot features, etc., which run through the writings and which allow the Lukan whole to shed light on its parts. It is hard to imagine, for instance, that Luke would not have wished his readers to read the Gospel with the awareness that the course of the apostles in Acts would in many respects come to replicate the journey of Jesus.[44] The present study, then, is based on the assumption that it is no violation of the author's desire nor of natural reading practices (and it is in line with the possible liturgical use of Luke's writings) to allow for reflection on a text in light of both preceding and succeeding contexts. Indeed, the quest to discern the meaning of Luke 22:24-30 is facilitated by approaching the text in this way.

1.5 Survey of Literature

As noted above (sec. 1.1), 22:24-30 constitutes a corner of Lukan studies that has not been as well researched as most other areas. In recent years the situation has improved somewhat, but it remains demonstrable that there is room for new scholarly work in the area. The following survey will move through the different types of works[45] which

[43]See e.g., the discussion in S. Moore (78-81).

[44]Nolland maintains, "Only the reader who already has Acts in hand will do full justice to the subtle literary foreshadowings which Luke from time to time employs" (*Luke*, xxxiv; cf. O'Toole, "Parallels," 195-212).

[45]Since many works cross categories and cannot be neatly placed under a given "type," the classifications are only in general terms.

make a contribution to the study of 22:24-30 (it is limited to those which are most noteworthy).[46]

The commentaries, of course, have not been able to overlook this text as the periodical literature used to do. The nature of the analysis of 22:24-30 in many older commentaries, however, is heavily oriented toward the text's tradition history, allowing for rather little explication of 22:24-30 as a literary piece in and of itself. Naturally, there are works which look beyond this emphasis (e.g., the works of Creed, Grundmann, Lagrange and Schmid). More recent commentaries have been less preoccupied (though still quite concerned) with the text's prehistory, and have given greater scope to literary and theological issues (e.g., Ernst, Evans, Fitzmyer, I. H. Marshall and G. Schneider).[47] The commentaries have tended, however, to offer only minimal attention to possible lines of unifying thought in 22:24-30 (by contrast, see ch. 8 below).[48] Further, their format necessitates a brief, if densely packed, analysis of our text, thus making it impossible to pursue in depth some of the issues to be taken up in the present study (e.g., the nature of the apostles' "discussion" in v 24, Jesus' self-description in v 27 and his action in v 29). Nonetheless, the commentaries do provide an important foundation for the present study.

There is a sea of works on the Gospels or certain logia written mostly between the fifties and the seventies, many in English and even more in German, which center on the tradition history of texts like Luke 22:24-30. Although this is not the orientation of the present work, it should be made clear that these many works, several done in great detail, have provided many clues as to the meaning of our text. The leader of the pack, as noted above (sec. 1.1), is Schürmann's meticulous work, *Jesu Abschiedsrede*.[49] Among the many useful works of this "genre" are

[46]See further the notes in each of the chapters to follow. Two recent bibliographies on Lukan scholarship have been extremely useful for locating studies that give significant attention to 22:24-30, or to the themes which surface in that text (Van Segbroeck [1989] and Wagner [1985]; also see Bovon's *Vingt-cinq ans* [1988] and *Thirty-three years*[1987]).

[47]Fitzmyer and Marshall have provided particularly useful bibliographies. On a different note, it is worth mentioning that L'Eplattenier's commentary offers some keen insights, albeit in a short space and a popular format.

[48]G. Schneider (2:451) and Grundmann (402) are exceptions, though their comments on the unity of 22:24-30 are very brief. By contrast, I. H. Marshall (814) stresses the disunity of vv 24-27 and 28-30. Fitzmyer discusses the matter, but claims that it is of "minor importance" (2:1412). For the present study, however, the paradoxical unity in 22:24-30 takes on major importance.

[49]One notes from the subtitle that it is a "*quellenkritischen Untersuch-*

those by Bammel ("Das Ende"), Broer, Bultmann (*History*), Jeremias (*Sprache*), Page, Schlosser, Schmahl, Soards,[50] Taylor (*Passion*) and Trautmann. Others that have frequently looked beyond tradition-critical concerns and have been particularly helpful in opening the way for an analysis of the finished text of 22:24-30 are those by Dupont ("Ministerès" and "Trônes"), Feuillet, Hoffmann and Eid, Howard (*Das Ego*), Lohfink (*Sammlung*), Roloff ("Anfänge") and Theisohn. Even these works, however, give little attention to the thought and expression of 22:24-30 as a unified piece.[51] Further, the lack of a scholarly consensus as to the relation of Luke 22:24-27 to Mark 10:41-45 and Luke 22:28-30 to Matt 19:28 makes one hesitant to build on the findings of these tradition-critical works.[52] Their chief asset for the present study would seem to be a rigorous attention to certain of the text's details.

Of the studies with a redaction-critical orientation, S. Brown's discussion of 22:28-30[53] offers a useful reply to the rather selective treatment of the Last Supper sayings by Conzelmann (*Theology*, 80-3), yet Brown mistakenly aligns 22:28-30 with the church era (see sec. 7.4.4 below) and overstates Luke's positive portrayal of the disciples. Jervell's essay on "The Twelve on Israel's Thrones" (*Luke*, 76-102) does not center on 22:30 only, but a good deal of attention is given to that verse. Jervell, however, shows little interest in the sense of 22:28-30 as a whole, not to mention 22:24-30, and his viewpoint on the place of Israel in the Lukan framework is contested by many. Broader redaction-critical works on Luke show only a very limited interest in 22:24-30; there is the occasional reference to v 27c (commonly to ponder the omission of Mark's ransom saying) or Jesus' temptations (often to interact with Conzelmann) or the thrones saying, but extended, significant discussion of the passage is a sparse commodity.[54]

---

ung." See Schürmann's *Ursprung* for a less technical analysis.

[50]Though a very recent work (1987), Soards's study is heavily oriented toward establishing the tradition history of Luke 22, even if some observations as to Luke's tendencies and purposes are presented (e.g., 124-5).

[51]E.g., Hoffmann and Eid restrict their treatment to 22:24-27, and Lohfink centers on 22:28-30.

[52]See further chs. 6 and 7 below.

[53]S. Brown, 62-5 (see also 66-74; cf. 5-19 on the πειρασμός of Jesus). Also see Garrett (41-3) for a critique of Conzelmann's understanding of Jesus' temptations.

[54]Flender's work gives very little attention to 22:24-30; even in his section on "The Table Scenes" (80-4), only 22:31-38 receives any extended discussion (83-4). The monograph by Maddox offers only brief and scarce comments on 22:24-30, and

Works on Luke which reflect the current interest in literary criticism have sometimes offered important contributions for the present study of 22:24-30. Tannehill's narrative analysis (*Unity*, 1986) picks up on a theme in Luke concerning rivalry over rank (254-7), and offers extended discussions of Lukan reversal motifs (26-32, 109-10). Moessner's literary-critical study of the Lukan travel narrative (1989) emphasizes the hospitality motif in Luke, and accordingly offers a useful analysis of the passion meal in 22:7-38 (176-82).[55] Neither work, however, analyzes 22:24-30 in much depth, and Moessner's study is perhaps excessively concerned to uncover links between the travel section and the Last Supper.[56]

In recent years a number of studies on the synoptic or Lukan Passion Narratives have appeared, some of which show a new measure of interest in 22:24-30 (though not an interest exceeding that shown to other passion texts). These works commonly give minimal attention to, or bypass altogether, the layers of tradition upon which Luke's text lies,[57] and focus on theological and literary features of the final written work. The works of Senior (1989 [with an interest in discipleship]), Neyrey (1985 [conscious of table motifs and testamentary genre]), Matera (*Passion*, 1986 [explaining the testamentary form of 22:14-38]) and LaVerdiere ("Passion," 1986)[58] are particularly worthy of mention. There is a drift in these studies, however, toward identifying the promises of vv 29-30 with the church era (contrast the analysis in sec. 7.4.4 below). Further, the literary-critical orientation common in these works produces analyses with only minimal attention to the details of our text.

The ever-growing field of works on the NT world has provided a plethora of helpful background information to give color and texture and concreteness to the content of 22:24-30. Various aspects of life in the Greco-Roman world of interest here include the many-faceted mentality

Franklin's work provides only slightly more. I. H. Marshall (*Historian*, esp. 87-90, 170) offers a bit more attention, and he maintains that 22:29-30 is "an important passage peculiar to Luke" (90), but the discussions are still very brief. To be sure, the many redactional studies on Luke's theology or themes or purposes are of great value for the present work, but chiefly for their portrayals of the Lukan whole as a backdrop and not for their analysis of the details of 22:24-30.

[55]Talbert's narrative commentary, *Reading Luke* (1982), also may be noted here. Although the concern to follow the broad strokes of Luke's thought is important, the result in this case is minimal attention to the text's details.

[56]Further, Moessner treats 22:24-27 and 22:28-30 as separate saying units.

[57]Exceptions include Green (*Death*) and Soards.

[58]LaVerdiere, however, offers precious little on 22:24-30 in particular.

and practices of benefaction,[59] authority patterns such as slavery[60] and political rule,[61] and domestic life and the experience of children and youth.[62] Studies on the ancient world with a sociological or anthropological drift have also proven quite helpful, including those on patron-client relations,[63] shame and honor,[64] and characteristics of the peasant economy and mentality.[65] Although the standard works in these areas offer virtually no direct analysis of Luke 22:24-30, a familiarity with them plays an important role in forming a historically and socially appropriate platform for a thorough analysis of that text.

Scholarship on Hellenistic symposium traditions comes together with Lukan studies, particularly as regards 7:36-50 (Delobel), 11:37-54 (Steele) and 14:1-24 (de Meeûs). Smith (1987) ably distills certain key themes within Luke's literary motif of table fellowship, and Barth (1987) provides a valuable essay on the implications of Luke's meal motif. Further, both writers comment significantly on the Last Supper and the text before us.[66] Nevertheless, their useful analyses of 22:24-30 are brief and are limited by their interpretative framework (i.e., their pursuit of the Lukan meal motif).

Studies of reversal in Luke-Acts have also been of use for the present work. The new monograph by York (1991) is most important here, for it covers the issues taken up in prior studies of the topic,[67] yet goes beyond them as well. In particular, York is interested not in isolated sayings or parables removed from their Lukan context, but in the purpose or

[59]See e.g., Danker, *Benefactor* (some attention is given to Luke 22:25); Kötting; P. Marshall; Veyne; B. Winter, "Benefactors."

[60]See e.g., Barclay; Bartchy's works; Finley's works; Hoffmann and Eid; Laub, *Sklaverei*; Vogt; Wiedemann, *Greek* and *Slavery*.

[61]See e.g., Badian's works; Sandmel; Sherwin-White; de Vaux.

[62]See e.g., Gnilka; Légasse's and Rawson's works; Weber; Wiedemann, *Children*.

[63]E.g., Elliott, "Patronage"; Levick; Saller, *Patronage*; Wallace-Hadrill.

[64]E.g., Daube; Malina's works; Moxnes, "Honor."

[65]E.g., Foster; Gregory; Malina, *World*; Pitt-Rivers's works.

[66]Quite profitable are the studies by Bösen, Guillaume, Karris ("Food"), Minear ("Glimpses"), Moxnes ("Meals"), Neyrey and Wanke, though their value is greater for an understanding of table motifs in Luke generally than for the study of 22:24-30 in particular. Esler takes up the issue of table fellowship in Luke-Acts (71-109), but only as pertains to the Jew-Gentile question.

[67]E.g., Danker, *Luke*; Hamel; Schottroff; Tannehill, *Unity*. Unfortunately, these works are closely connected to discussions of the Magnificat (particularly 1:52-53), are chiefly concerned with a two-party reversal (contrast the study in ch. 4), and offer little or nothing on 22:24-30.

function of reversal in Luke's Gospel as a whole (10). As will be elaborated below (ch. 4), however, York is concerned with the "bi-polar" reversal which in fact involves two reversals in opposite "directions" (e.g., first to last and last to first) (42), while the primary form of reversal in Luke 22:24-30, it will be argued, is a single course for one party from "high" to "low" to "high." This distinction limits the importance of York's work for the present study, though his analysis remains both relevant and instructive.[68]

Some of the literature on the testamentary genre or specific farewell discourses offers a measure of close attention to Luke 22:14-38. The most significant work here for study of the text at hand is the essay by Kurz ("Luke 22:14-38," 1985) with its discussion of functions as well as components of farewell speeches.[69] Kurz's treatment of 22:24-30, however, is scattered through a comparison with OT discourses, and he does not recognize unifying features in 22:24-30.[70] Léon-Dufour also presents some very useful studies on the Lukan Last Supper discourse as a farewell speech ("Jésus," "Letzte Mahl," "Testament" and "Tradition"). Léon-Dufour mentions but does not develop a symbolic unity of 22:24-27 and 22:28-30 (these sections symbolize Jesus' death and resurrection);[71] his works are to some degree limited by the approach to our text as part of a farewell discourse.[72] Further, a limitation of this genre perspective

[68]Regrettably, York offers precious little in the way of comment on Luke 22:24-27, and vv 28-30 are bypassed altogether. Another angle on the "reversal" (or antithetical or chiastic) form of Luke 22:24-30 is discussed and depicted by Meynet (*Parole*), though his architectonic findings may be rather inventive. Certain concepts of reversal have an important background in Jewish martyr theology (cf. Fox; Lebram; Pobee; Schweizer, *Erniedrigung*).

[69]See also Kurz's recent and somewhat more popular work on farewell speeches (*Farewell*).

[70]Other works seem to offer little on the contribution of discourse form to the role or meaning of a text (though LaVerdiere ["Discourse"] makes some brief comments here). The scholarship on the speeches in Acts tends to focus on questions of authenticity and comparisons with Paul's theology in his letters (e.g., Dibelius; Gempf; Hemer, *Acts* and "Miletus"), having little to say on the importance of form for meaning in the Lukan context.

[71]Léon-Dufour, "Testament," 273, and "Letzte Mahl," 47. See the discussion in sec. 8.2 below.

[72]Also helpful are the studies of Berger (*Formgeschichte*), Collins, Kolenkow, Michel and especially von Nordheim. These are among the standard works on the farewell genre, and though they offer very little on Luke 22 in particular, they are of use in constructing our platform for investigation. Neyrey and Matera (*Passion*) bring the testamentary genre and Luke 22:14-38 together (but see above

is that there is some uncertainty in scholarship as to the place of Luke 22:24-30 (or parts of it) in the testamentary framework.[73]

A variety of works focusing on a wide assortment of themes in Luke-Acts have provided valuable perspectives for the study of 22:24-30. These themes include eschatology,[74] the kingdom of God,[75] the place of Israel/ the Jews in Luke's theology,[76] discipleship,[77] and the apostles.[78] Of course, there is considerable debate on certain of these issues.[79] Additionally, in each area the existing scholarship offers little direct attention to 22:24-30; instead it expands our background perspectives for an analysis of the text. Fitzmyer's extended introduction to his commentary on Luke (*Gospel*, 1:3-283) has proved to be quite useful in terms of introducing these and other noteworthy issues, and pointing to important relevant works.[80]

Sellew's recent essay (1987) on Luke 22:21-38 for the Jesus Seminar examines vv 24-30 at length (in fact, vv 21-23 and 31-38 are virtually bypassed). He approaches the text from many angles (e.g., in terms of sources [comparisons with Mark 10:41-45 and Matt 19:28 figure heavily here], genre [i.e., the farewell discourse form], literary and theological connections with Luke-Acts, and matters of historical authenticity), and provides four pages of bibliography (91-5). This article, however, amounts to a survey of research that collects a host of critical views on the text, and thus it comes up short in terms of making an original contribution to scholarship.

---

in this sec. on shortcomings of their works).

[73]E.g., Matera (*Passion*, 164-5) sees in 22:24-30 Jesus' recollections of his past, while Berger (78) isolates the issue of leadership. To be sure, the various allocations of 22:24-30 to different testamentary components/ functions are not mutually exclusive, but their existence invites further attention to the role of our text in its testamentary setting.

[74]See e.g., Chance; Conzelmann, *Theology*; Ellis, *Eschatology*; Franklin; Geiger; Kaestli.

[75]See e.g., Carroll; George, "Royauté"; Merk; Polag; Völkel; Winton.

[76]See e.g., Brawley; Chance; Dahl, "Abraham"; George, "Israël"; Jervell, *Luke*; Lohfink, *Sammlung*; J. Sanders; Tiede, "Glory"; Tyson, ed., *Jewish People*.

[77]See e.g., Beck, *Character*; Conzelmann, *Theology*; Fitzmyer, *Theologian*; R. Martin; Thysman.

[78]Consider e.g., A. Clark; Lohfink, *Sammlung*; Lohse, *Ursprung*; Roloff, *Apostolat*.

[79]E.g., consider the differences of J. Sanders and Jervell on the Jews in Luke-Acts.

[80]Similar comments could be made regarding Bovon's surveys.

Perhaps the most important analysis of 22:24-30 is Lull's recent essay (1986), a work that has provided many valuable insights for the present study. Lull focuses on the finished text of 22:24-30 without ignoring the value of research which attends to antecedent stages in the text's tradition history, he seeks to reveal the coherence and unity of the text as a literary piece (though some arguments here are questionable), and he does offer some original and constructive contributions to scholarship. Regrettably, however, Lull's reconstruction of the flow of thought in vv 24-27 is flawed (see sec. 6.3 below), a problem that undermines certain crucial claims of the article.

In summary of the literature on or relevant to Luke 22:24-30, two general points may be made: 1) There are many works in many different areas of Lukan and NT studies that have, in spite of their shortcomings, provided useful perspectives and insights for the study of the text at hand. These have drawn attention to important issues and questions raised by the text, and have set the stage for further research. 2) It is clear, however, that there is room in scholarship for a new monograph on Luke 22:24-30 that balances and integrates methodological approaches to the text, that brings together and synthesizes findings of previous research, and that seeks to discern the meaning of the finished Lukan text in its parts and as a coherent literary whole.

PART ONE:

BACKGROUND PERSPECTIVES FOR THE STUDY OF LUKE 22:24-30

Chapter 2: Authority and Subordination

2.1 Introduction

The present chapter is the first of four background studies which make up Part One. By opening up as well as weighing against certain possibilities for Lukan thought and reader expectations, and by illuminating and bringing to life some of the Lukan Jesus' vivid and concrete imagery, Part One is to constitute a platform that will significantly enhance our "view" of the text and thus inform the direct analysis of Luke 22:24-30 provided in Part Two.

That some attention should be devoted to the task of surveying patterns of authority and subordination familiar to the writer and readers of Luke 22:24-30 becomes readily apparent when one recalls the pervasive presence of authority language and concepts in that text (cf. sec. 1.1). Patterns of authority and subordination in four arenas will be surveyed: the Greco-Roman world (sec. 2.2); the history of Israel (2.3); the ancient household (2.4); and the Lukan writings (2.5). While these divisions are convenient for presentation, it will quickly become clear that they overlap substantially, so it will be possible at points to generalize as to the overarching climate of authority and subordination which constitutes a broad background for 22:24-30.[1]

[1]The present chapter is limited strictly to backgrounds which are alluded to by the language and concepts of vv 24-30. This means we will only scratch the surface of a vast field of study, and many important facets of the fabric of authority and subordination in antiquity will be left untouched. Further, this chapter will provide only an overview, so it will not be possible to go into great depth at any

"Authority" has been defined in many ways.[2] In the present study the term corresponds not to a personal attribute (e.g., as a synonym for "expert" and implying competence), nor is Weber's concept of the "charismatic" authority in view.[3] Further, we do not wish here to equate "authority" with "power," or even align the two concepts very closely. To be sure, the possession of power is a key aspect of authority, but authority is something quite distinct from the mere ability to force one's will on others. J. Schütz provides a definition that rightly identifies the sphere of our interest when he speaks of authority as the *right* to power, legitimate power.[4] Legitimacy is what distinguishes authority from sheer force or influence: a shared perception of social constraint inclines both superiors to claim a right to issue commands and subordinates to perceive an obligation to obey.[5] Thus authority requires a social milieu within which legitimacy may be discerned.[6]

Since legitimate power can be the possession of either the leader who wins obedience as a result of his or her charismatic personality[7] or the person who holds a recognized position or office within a social structure, it remains necessary to clarify further our definition of "authority." The nature of the terms and concepts of Luke 22:24-30 (e.g., king, table servant, father, judge, throne) tilts our emphasis toward the latter understanding, namely toward an idea of authority that is fixed not primarily in people but in positions as specified by prevailing views within a social milieu. For our purposes, then, authority is a right to

one point.

[2]See the helpful discussion and bibliography in Peabody, 473-7.

[3]See the discussion in Gerth and Mills, 245-9. The charismatic authority is the "natural leader" and not (necessarily) the expert or office holder. As results of possessing charisma, inner determination and not official status drive a leader, and others are drawn to him and willingly obey him (245-6).

[4]J. Schütz, 10.

[5]Peabody, 474; cf. Holmberg, 131.

[6]To be sure, subordinates may rebel and throw off the status of subjection, but if such actions are clearly those of a minority, the legitimacy of authority is not altered and the true standing of the rebel as a defiant subject is not changed.

[7]So Weber's emphasis. Holmberg's claims that "Authority rests upon the ability to issue communications capable of reasoned elaboration" (131), and that authority ceases to be legitimate and ceases to exist if it clashes with objective reason (133), seem to conflict with his contention that the leadership relation is voluntary while the authority relation is not (129). Perhaps Holmberg is closer here to Weber's view (that leadership is to be equated with authority [i.e., charismatic authority]) than he seems to concede (128; cf. Peabody, 474 [leadership involves the capacity to influence followers]). Cf. sec. 9.1 on "leadership" in the present study.

power acquired and maintained by virtue of a person's socially approved accession to and possession of a recognized superior office.

2.2 The Greco-Roman World

Luke and his readers, despite their extensive exposure to Judaism, lived and breathed in a world keenly aware of the powerful and pervasive rule of Rome, and they were familiar with the Greek culture and language that had dominated the known world since the time of Alexander the Great. The vast field of Greco-Roman backgrounds can only be touched on here, though it constitutes a broad and important backdrop for the study of Luke 22:24-30.

2.2.1 The Power of Rome

The language and concepts of Luke 22:25 ("kings of the Gentiles," "rule," "those in authority" and "called benefactors") beckon one to scan the subject of Roman rule and consider the pervasive power of Rome in the civil/ political sphere. We may begin with the emperor. Modern western forms of monarchy make useful the clarification that the Roman emperor was no figure-head king. In fact, he exercised tremendous power, and, in practice, was answerable to no one. The ascription of deity—a practice tolerated by some emperors and promoted by others—only served to extend the emperor's powers. Perhaps we may best get a feel for the authority of the emperor by glancing at the careers of a few who held the crown.

Octavian (or "Augustus," "Princeps" from 27 BCE to CE 14) became a disguised constitutional monarch, and though he shared many functions with the senate, his power came to be nearly unlimited.[8] In 27 BCE the senate gave him the greater part of the army, and Spain, Gaul and Syria (in addition to Egypt which he had wrested from the hands of Mark Antony in 31) as his province.[9] In the following years other provinces swore allegiance to him, his power in the senate was increased dramatically (including absolute right of veto and complete control of the state),[10] and a cult of Augustus began to arise in the East.[11] Growth of

[8]Scullard, 930.

[9]Momigliano, "Augustus," 149-50.

[10]Vestiges of city-state democracy from earlier Greece thus gave way to the

the ruler cult served both to unify the empire[12] and, in most quarters, to enhance the perception of Augustus' increasing legitimate power.

The example of Gaius (or "Caligula," who ruled from CE 37 to 41) is as striking as it is significant. There is no shortage of tales about his autocratic rule, his acts of terror rooted in insecurity and megalomania, and, in short, his abuse of power.[13] What is important to note here is that even the dreadful deeds of Caligula were made possible by the vast scope of power duly granted him by the Roman senate.[14] Caligula expressed his lust for power by presenting himself as one of the gods[15] and actively seeking divine titles.

Among the additional tales to be told of the power of Rome is the increasing advance toward absolute monarchy under the Flavian emperors (Vespasian and his sons Titus and Domitian, CE 69-96).[16] By Luke's day it had become crystal clear: Rome ruled the known world with an iron fist, a fact vividly highlighted by the crushing of the Jewish rebellion and the destruction of Jerusalem in CE 70.

If we step back and look into the world of the Roman empire at another level, that of the provincial governor (before Claudius *praefectus*, later *procurator*), additional insights as to the nature of the prevailing patterns of authority may be obtained. Sherwin-White ably demonstrates that not only governors of senatorial rank (*legates*), but also equestrian governors in Judea and elsewhere held the *imperium*.[17] To be sure, the emperor had the overriding power to cancel a governor's decisions, and a governor only held the *imperium* for the duration of an appointment by the emperor.[18] Nevertheless, especially in the Julio-

---

pressures of monarchy—so the end of the Roman Republic (Roetzel, 73).

[11]Momigliano, "Augustus," 149-50. Though Augustus discouraged divine ascriptions from his countrymen, for political reasons he accepted them from elsewhere (Roetzel, 74).

[12]Scullard, 930.

[13]See e.g., Philo's portrayal (*Leg. ad Gaium* 22-65); cf. Balsdon's summary of Caligula's career noting many executions owing to his paranoia ("Gaius," 452-3).

[14]Philo admits that Gaius came to power within the law (*Leg. ad Gaium* 8).

[15]Philo *Leg. ad Gaium* 93-97; Jos. *J.W.* 2.184. He even attempted to introduce the imperial cult in the temple of Jerusalem (cf. Jos. *J.W.* 2.185). M. Charlesworth (113-14, 131) maintains that, by the middle of the second century, qualities such as *providentia* and *aeternitas* were thought to be inherent in the emperor.

[16]Scullard, 931; Sherwin-White, 2.

[17]Sherwin-White, 1-12. "Imperium" was "... the supreme administrative power, involving command in war and the interpretation and execution of law..." (Balsdon, "Imperium," 542-3).

Claudian period, the provincial governors were relatively independent figures who felt no compulsion to consult the senate or the emperor about problems they faced. "Having the *imperium*, the proconsul had the total power of administration, jurisdiction, defence ... and the maintenance of public order."[19] For the purposes of this study, then, it is noteworthy that the long arm of Rome reached into the provinces in a firm and effective manner; for the average citizen, Roman rule was not a distant or intangible reality.[20]

In summary, the *imperium* held by Roman emperors and provincial governors in the NT era enabled them to exercise virtually absolute rule. Further, within the Roman framework, this became a legitimate rule, a power (ordinarily) gained and exercised within the limits of the law. Democratic ideals of earlier times had given way to the pressures of monarchy, and the Hellenistic impulse to ascribe deity to the king helped allow monarchy to acquire increasing legitimacy. The emperor and his governors were not unopposed, to be sure, but their power to subjugate opponents was not seriously challenged. Through its hierarchy of rule (emperor, governors, and various local officials), Rome was able to exercise substantial authority and ensure the subjugation of those within its vast territories.

2.2.2 Patronage and Clientism

Here we continue to focus on general, widespread features of life in the Greco-Roman world, but our attention now turns to what may be termed an "unofficial" pattern of authority and subordination. Although an unofficial pattern, however, it is as if patronage and clientism were prescribed by an unwritten social "law" for virtually all relationships; whether one was senator or slave, landlord or peasant, relations with non-family members were heavily influenced by each party's relative status as patron or client.[21]

---

[18]Sherwin-White, 9.

[19]Sherwin-White, 2. The same can be said for the equestrian governors of Judea (5-12). Only the law against extortion limited the governor's power (2-3).

[20]The average citizen of a Roman province felt the domination of Rome in at least three ways: by permanent military occupation, regular taxation and Roman supervision of public order (so Sherwin-White, 12, citing Tacitus *Ann.* 11.18.3; 15.6.6; cf. Caesar *BG* 2.1.3; 5.41.5; 7.77.14-16).

[21]Cf. Meeks, *Moral World*, 34.

Elliott provides a helpful description: The patron-client relationship "... is a personal relation of some duration entered into voluntarily by two or more persons of unequal status based on differences in social roles and access to power, and involves the reciprocal exchange of different kinds of 'goods and services' of value to each partner."[22] Elliott postulates that modern attachment to the principle of equality has kept analysts of ancient society from perceiving the prevalence of this pattern of dependency relations in private and public life.[23]

It should be stressed that the patron-client relationship was characterized by personal honor and obligation: the patron was obliged to protect or provide for his dependent client, and the client was obliged to offer service to and enhance the reputation of the patron.[24] The mind-set attuned to honor and shame was heavily influenced by the expectations of significant others; one was not "free" to act autonomously.[25]

The powerful impulse always to act within the constraints of honor and shame justified and, in a sense, "enforced" this widespread system of dependency relations. Further, the provision of reciprocal benefits enhanced the ideology of hierarchical authority patterns—when inferior clients can gain valuable benefits and superior patrons can obtain useful services, they may not be inclined to welcome a transformation of the social status quo. Thus, although the system was built on the presupposi-

[22]Elliott, "Patronage," 42; this is a very useful summary article with bibliography (also see the bibliography in Wallace-Hadrill, 12-13). On the subject also see Badian; Clarke, 137-8; Levick; D. Martin, 22-30; Momigliano, "Cliens" and "Patronus"; Saller, *Patronage;* Veyne (note the distinction between patronal gift giving and alms [19-20]). A freedman was ipso facto a client to his former owner (Momigliano, "Cliens," 252; cf. Barclay, 169).

[23]Elliott, 40. Veyne (70, 103) argues that the acceptance of patronal gifts would have signified a promise of obedience. This reveals something of the extent to which the social system of patron-client relations was saturated with significance for authority and subordination within a social sphere. Moxnes (*Economy*, 157-9) maintains that Luke rejects this key dimension of the patronage system: benefaction is no longer to be used to form a power base of clients; greatness is not to be transformed into privilege and power.

[24]Elliott, 42-43. A keen consciousness of honor and shame seems to be reflected in the apostles' question as to who *seemed* to be greatest (Luke 22:24b; cf. sec. 6.4).

[25]Malina (*World*, 44, 67) argues that this mind-set was prevalent in first century Mediterranean societies. On the importance of honor in the ancient world see also Meeks, *Moral World*, 32-8, 51-2; Moxnes, "Honor"; J. Schneider, 170-1; on the place of honor and shame in peasant societies, see especially the works by Pitt-Rivers. Cf. also sec. 6.4.

tion of human inequality, within that framework all parties generally benefitted in some sense.[26]

Glancing back to Luke 22:24-30, it is primarily the reference to rulers being called "benefactors" in v 25 that prompts us to consider the place of patronage and clientism in the Greco-Roman world, for the term εὐεργέτης was common in ascriptions made by clients to honor their patrons.[27] The role contrasts of vv 26-27, however, also represent relationships between people of unequal status in which patronage and clientism could be expected to flourish.

The client kings of the Roman "patron-empire" illustrate this pattern in the political arena, thus demonstrating that patron-client social relations were not restricted to the private sphere and small scale relations. The Herodian kings, for example, were permitted to retain substantial powers in exchange for repeated expressions of loyalty to and support for Rome. Consider the following examples:[28] Herod the Great opposes Antigonus, an enemy of Rome. Antony executes Antigonus after receiving a large bribe from Herod. After Augustus defeats Antony, Herod accuses Hyrcanus II of disloyalty to Rome and has him killed; Augustus consequently confirms Herod's royal rank. Herod builds the harbor city of Caesarea and erects a theater in Jerusalem in honor of Caesar. Two of Herod's sons are sent to be educated in Rome. Herod Antipas founds Tiberias in Galilee in honor of Augustus' adopted son and heir to the throne. Agrippa I becomes a protégé of the heir apparent, Caligula, and is given the tetrarchy of Philip when Caligula comes to the throne. After the murder of Caligula, Agrippa is helpful in the ascent of Claudius to the throne, and in turn his territories are expanded to include Judea. Agrippa II, being always on the side of Rome, has his territories increased by Nero and again later by Vespasian. So we see the ongoing patron-client interplay of support from below and favors from above.[29]

Figures like the client kings and Roman provincial governors provide a relevant background for the study of Luke 22:24-30 not only be-

---

[26]Veyne, 5; cf. Clarke, 138.

[27]See e.g., the many inscriptions in Danker, *Benefactor* (cf. also references in Kötting, 848-9; Nock, 725-30; B. Winter, "Benefactor," 88-92); cf. sec. 6.5.1.

[28]Distilled from Sandmel, 585-94.

[29]Braund (5) notes that "in one way or another all of the provinces of Rome had been, wholly or partly, monarchies before the Roman conquest." Had Rome failed to maintain "friendships" with these client kingdoms, her empire would not have survived unchanged.

cause they illustrate a facet of the field of ideas surrounding the term "benefactors," but also because they are "middle-men." That is, like the apostles in Luke 22:24-30 who are called to adopt the posture of servant (vv 26-27) and yet are delegated power to rule (vv 29-30), client kings and governors stand both in and under authority (cf. sec. 2.5.2 below). Being both patrons and clients, they represent secular models of middle links in a hierarchical chain of command.

2.3 The History of Israel

While it is probable that the background of Jewish kings and rulers is not directly relevant to the description in Luke 22:25, vv 29-30 may presuppose a Jewish model (see the discussion in sec. 7.4.3). The act of ruling "the twelve tribes of Israel" (v 30b) points in this direction, as could the idea of a king receiving his sovereignty from God (v 29).

The uniform conception of the OT is that rulers—whether a prophetic figure like Moses, or the judges, or later the kings—were subordinate to the sovereign God. Thus all leaders in Israel, no matter how "great," were in theory only mediators of the superior authority of the God who governed his theocracy. So, as with the client kings, here too we may have a basis for analyzing the juxtaposition in Luke 22:24-30 of a call to a subordinate status with a promise of authority.

2.3.1 Judges

A glance at the role of judges in pre-monarchy Israel may be useful. The description of Othniel's judgeship is brief (Judg 3:7-11) but representative: the people of Israel forget their God and turn to idols (v 7); God punishes Israel by empowering the king of Mesopotamia to subdue them (v 8); the people of Israel cry to the Lord for deliverance (v 9a); the Lord raises up Othniel to deliver Israel (v 9b); in "judging" Israel Othniel leads them into war, and they defeat the forces of Mesopotamia (v 10); Israel has "rest" for forty years (v 11a); Othniel dies (v 11b). The reader of Judges repeatedly finds this apostasy-repentance-deliverance sequence in which a "judge" leads Israel in a military conquest of its oppressors.

Correspondingly, in contrast to the sense of "to judge" in English, OT usages do not necessarily focus on hearing cases and passing sentence, and may emphasize a kind of judging that more broadly involves leading and governing. To be sure, where judicial proceedings are described in the OT, the root used repeatedly in Judges (שׁפט) often appears (e.g., 2 Sam 15:4; 1 Kgs 3:28). Nonetheless, an important sense for the term is the one commonly exemplified in Judges where governing rather than performing forensic duties is primarily in view.[30]

It is appropriate, however, to be cautious when attempting to distinguish the roles of judges and kings or the actions of seeking justice and governing, for at several points in the OT these terms and concepts come together.[31] A number of texts in Isaiah illustrate this interplay: in 16:5 the prophet envisions the end of oppression by Moab when a throne will be established "in the tent of David" (i.e., the king), and the one to sit upon it will "judge" and "seek justice"; in 32:1 it is prophesied that "a king will reign in righteousness, and princes will rule in justice"; Isa 33:22 portrays the Lord as a saving "judge," "ruler" and "king."[32]

Another feature of the pattern of authority and subordination exhibited in Judges is the regular (if not fully consistent) attribution to God of the basis for a judge's rise to power and right to rule.[33] This reveals the link between religious authorization and political authority, the hallmark of theocracy. It is ultimately God who rules over Israel (Judg 8:23), though this divine activity is expressed through subordinate agents who execute God's rule. Similarly, the appointment of the apostles to "judge" the twelve tribes of Israel (Luke 22:29-30) stems ultimately (through Jesus' intermediate role) from the conferral of authority by "the Father" (cf. secs. 7.4.2-3).

[30]Bright (178-82) describes the role of OT "judges" in terms of military leadership; judicial functions are not mentioned. Both Malamat and Speiser argue on the basis of evidence from the Mari texts that, as early as the 18th century BCE, the etymologically equivalent root of שׁפט did not have "to judge" as its primary meaning (Malamat, 131; Speiser, 280-3; Speiser [282] similarly claims that שֹׁפֵט is not unlike the Mesopotamian term for "governor" in that its authority was divine and not human). Speiser asserts in summary that the semantic range of שׁפט "... is by no means oriented toward the legal concept 'to judge.' The strictly judicial aspect is here [i.e., in the OT] tangential or incidental at best" (282).

[31]Trautmann's caution (197) that there is "... nicht immer eine scharfe Grenze..." between "judging" and "ruling" in the OT is well taken (her claim [198] that ruling and judging are distinguished in Jer 23:5, however, seems dubious).

[32]Here יְהוָה is the subject of שֹׁפֵט, חֹקֵק and מֶלֶךְ. In Ps 97:2 the Lord's throne is associated with "judgment/ justice" (מִשְׁפָּט), and in v 1 the Lord's "reign" is clearly in view (יְהוָה מָלָךְ). Judging, ruling and kingship all come together in Wis 3:8.

[33]See e.g., Judg 2:16; 3:9, 15; 6:11-24.

"Judging" and "thrones" (cf. Luke 22:30b) appear together at points in the OT in addition to Isa 16:5 (see above). In Ps 9:4, 7, God is the judge who sits on his throne. There the probable sense is that of judging as ruling and leading in battle.[34] In Ps 122:5a we read of multiple "thrones for judgment" (cf. Dan 7:9; sec. 7.4.3), so it is not, or not only, God's throne that is in view. As to the nature of the "judging," Ps 122:5b clarifies that it is kingly thrones that are in view (i.e., they are "of the house of David"). Since it can be difficult to draw a line between ruling and judging, and since Jewish kings did exercise judicial functions (so e.g., 2 Sam 15:1-6; 1 Kgs 3:16-28), it would perhaps be best here to envision a broad idea of "ruling" that could nonetheless encompass judicial functions.[35]

2.3.2 **Kings**

The references to *βασιλεία* in Luke 22:29-30a invite some consideration of OT kingship. Further, the implication of v 30a that Jesus is a king (cf. sec. 7.4.3) may increase our interest in Jewish monarchs. Having already surveyed certain forms of monarchy in the Greco-Roman world, the focus here will be on points where kingship in Israel seems to differ from that in the Greco-Roman sphere.

Such a point of difference is the refusal in the OT and Jewish religion to ascribe deity to the king or any human ruler.[36] The OT portrays kings in Israel (during the united and divided monarchies) as subordinate rulers under the final authority of God. There is only one God (Deut 6:4), and no other gods were to be put on a par with the one God (Exod 20:3).[37] Although some monarchs in the Greco-Roman world opposed the attribution of deity to them, others approved or even sought it (see sec. 2.2.1 above). Most importantly, in the world of the Roman empire there was no widely accepted religious framework which upheld a normative view on the matter.

---

[34]Note the emphasis on or appeal for God's active intervention to protect his people and defeat their enemies (vv 1, 3, 5-6, 9, 12-14, 16). Vv 19-20, however, seem to refer to forensic judgment.

[35]Trautmann (198) points out the linking of "justice" or "judgment" with "throne" in Ps 89:14; Isa 9:7; Prov 20:8. In the last two verses reference is made to kingly thrones, and in the first it is God's throne; none of these texts draw attention to a throne for judgment.

[36]Bright, 226. Even if Ps 45:6 contradicts this claim, it remains a very unusual exception to the "rule" (cf. the discussion in Dahood, 272-3).

[37]For Luke's view on the attribution of deity to monarchs, see Acts 12:22-23.

It also seems that in the OT, generally speaking, a greater measure of restraint was placed on kings than was typical in the Roman world. This was probably due to the fact that kings in Israel were to be subject to God and to the biblical directives attributed ultimately to God.[38] By contrast, in spite of the fact that the Roman emperor held a seat in the senate and (theoretically) shared authority with that body, after Augustus absolute rule by a monarch answerable to no one was typical.

Another point of difference seems to be the degree of openness to monarchy itself. Although Roman monarchy was not welcomed by all, the influence of Hellenistic kingship and Egyptian deification of rulers led to an ever more heavy-handed form of rule in the NT era. By contrast, in the OT Gideon objects on theological grounds to calls for him to become a king: "I will not rule over you,... The Lord will rule over you" (Judg 8:23; cf. 1 Sam 8:6; 12:17).[39] In reaction to this tension between the rule of God and that of a king, Israel developed a concept of the king as Yahweh's adopted son and vicegerent who ruled by divine election and yet was subject to Yahweh's prophets and their rebukes.[40] Thus a system of "checks and balances" was to keep kings firmly under the rule of God.[41]

The verb "to anoint" (MT מָשַׁח, LXX χρίω) appears often in the OT in connection with "king,"[42] and the initiative of God in sending a human agent to anoint someone as king is noted at times.[43] A priestly figure like Samuel may act as God's mediator to perform the anointing (1 Sam 10:1; 15:1; 16:12).[44] When David decided that Solomon would succeed him as

[38]See e.g., Deut 17:14-20; 2 Sam 7:4-17 (cf. Bright 228; Talmon, 3-10). There is no suggestion here that Jewish kings consistently lived up to these and other biblical standards (indeed, see 1 Kgs 11:1-8 in light of Deut 17:14-20; and cf. the many references to wicked kings in 1 and 2 Kgs). Other "systematic" OT statements on kingship include 1 Sam 8:11-18; Judg 8:22-23; 9:7-20 (so Talmon, 3).

[39]Talmon (5-10) seems to understate this perspective.

[40]So Bright, 226.

[41]Perhaps the rule of OT kings appears at times to have been as much an absolute rule as that of pagan monarchs or later Roman emperors, but at least in theory the Israelite king exercised his great power only as God's delegate. Further, Stager (25) notes that there was a sense in which monarchs in Israel shared a measure of their power with "little chiefs" who ruled in various regions of the segmentary state.

[42]E.g., Judg 9:8, 15; 1 Sam 15:1, 17; 2 Sam 2:4, 7; 5:3, 17; 12:7; 1 Kgs 1:34, 45; 5:1; 19:15.

[43]E.g., 1 Sam 10:1; 15:1; 16:12; 1 Kgs 19:15-16; Ps 45:7 (cf. the role of "the Father" in Luke 22:29).

[44]Such a figure does not himself possess royal power or status (contrast the

king (1 Kgs 1:30), the actual anointing—the formal conferral of kingship—was performed by Zadok the priest (1:39). Thus there is at least a rough parallel between an OT pattern of anointing kings and the chain of events in Luke 22:29: divine activity underlies the process and a mediating figure officially imparts kingship.[45]

2.4 The Household

We now turn to a brief survey of patterns of authority and subordination in the ancient household. Our attention will not be restricted to either Jewish or Greco-Roman households since both provide useful perspectives and they seem to be similar in many respects. At points, however, there will be a concentration in one area or the other. It is useful to clarify that in many ways ancient households do not resemble modern Western nuclear families.[46] For instance, the ancient household typically included husband and wife, unmarried children, slaves, perhaps freedmen and foster children.[47]

2.4.1 *Paterfamilias*

Consideration of the role of the *paterfamilias* is prompted by the description in Luke 22:24-30 of God as "the Father" (v 29), and by references in vv 26-27 to persons and roles in the household ("the youngest" [i.e., children], "the servant") which imply the presence of a *paterfamilias*. The *paterfamilias* was the oldest living male ascendant in a family, and he was recognized formally as head of the household.[48] The measure of power held by a *paterfamilias* was indeed very great: like the *imperium* of Roman rulers, in practice his *patria potestas* was nearly unlimited.[49]

---

role of Jesus in Luke 22:29-30).

[45]The OT pattern, however, does not involve conferring kingship on more than one person at a time (contrast Luke 22:29-30). For a discussion of OT texts on the importance of dining at a king's table (e.g., 2 Sam 9:1-13; 1 Kgs 2:7; 2 Kgs 25:27-30) as a background for Luke 22:30a, see sec. 3.3.

[46]So e.g., Gnilka, 229-31; Laub, *Sklaverei*, 29; Meeks, *Urban Christians*, 75.

[47]See Laub, *Sklaverei*, 28-29; Rawson, "Family," 7-8; de Vaux, 20-23. It was more common in Jewish than Roman spheres for extended families to dwell together (so Rawson, "Family," 7; de Vaux, 20).

[48]Matthews, 67-8; Rawson, "Family," 7; Stager, 19-20.

[49]So Lacey, 131; cf. Daane, 285; Hunt, 280; Matthews, 68-9; Rawson, "Family,"

As ruler of the house, the Christian *paterfamilias* acted as teacher of family members, and manager of the household in every respect.[50] In the Israelite setting the father acted as family "priest," being responsible for its religious life,[51] and represented the family in the village assembly of elders.[52] In short, the *paterfamilias* was the dominant figure who sat atop the household's hierarchical structure.[53]

There seems to be little background for the act of "conferring" ruling status or power by a father upon his son(s) (cf. Luke 22:29) prior to the time when the father's death is imminent (cf. ch. 5 on the testamentary genre), and even then the transfer of authority to the oldest male ascendant seems to be more or less automatic (i.e., it did not necessitate a deliberate conferral). Precedent has not been uncovered for the idea of household "rule" shared by father and son(s). On the contrary, the *paterfamilias* typically remained the dominant authoritative figure of the household until his death, even in relation to his wife and adult children.[54]

In sum, the *paterfamilias* functioned as household monarch-priest-teacher; in every respect he was the unquestioned household ruler. Although his wife would commonly have exercised a subordinate rule over children and domestic servants,[55] the fact remained that the *paterfamilias* governed the household hierarchy in antiquity.[56] And while harsh treatment of family subordinates was not a standard pattern, the *paterfamilias* had power over the very lives of household members.[57]

16; de Vaux, 20-3. See also Gnilka (230) on the dominant position of the "Hausvater." Laub (*Sklaverei*, 28-31) favors the designation "Hausherr" for the man of the house as οἰκοδεσπότης.

[50]Laub, *Sklaverei*, 28-9; cf. Hunt, 280.

[51]So Hunt, 280. Consider the Rabbis' description of the father's role in family observance of the Passover (*m. Pesaḥ.* 10.4).

[52]Matthews, 68-9.

[53]Gnilka, 230-1.

[54]Rawson, "Family," 7, 16-18; cf. Matthews, 68; de Vaux, 20. Rawson (ibid., 7) claims, however, that the authority of the *paterfamilias* could be legally dissolved prior to the time of his impending death, though this is seen as the exception to the rule, and circumstances which might give rise to such a transaction are not discussed.

[55]Gnilka, 236-7.

[56]So Laub, *Sklaverei*, 29; Meeks, *Urban Christians*, 76, 127. Indeed, Lacey contends (123, 131) that the Roman institution of *imperium* was derived from the *patria potestas* of the *paterfamilias*; public life followed the assumptions of private life, not vice versa.

[57]De Vaux (20) cites Gen 38:24, though in "later times" certain (minimal) limitations of family authority were introduced (Deut 21:18-21).

2.4.2 Children and Youth

For three reasons it is in order to consider the role of children and youth in the ancient household. First, ὁ νεώτερος in Luke 22:26 introduces "the youngest" into the text at hand.[58] Second, elsewhere in Luke (Luke 9:46-48 [par. Matt 18:1-5 par. Mark 9:33-37]) Jesus' teaching on greatness is explicitly connected with the child image. Third, a logical implication of the use of "father" is the existence of a child or children.

In the ancient Near East the aged were shown great respect or even veneration,[59] but children were usually held in very low regard.[60] To be sure, it was important to bear children, for they provided free labor and care in old age, and they represented the continuation of the family name.[61] Further, in the Jewish sphere children were seen as a blessing from God; they represented the continuation of God's covenant faithfulness (e.g., the case of Isaac), and to have many was an honor.[62] Such reasons for valuing children, however, were typically rooted in advantages they brought to adults and not in the inherent worth of children.[63]

The parent-centered outlook of the Greco-Roman world made possible certain harsh attitudes and practices: the death of a child was seen as a tragedy for the parents (not the child); under Roman law, abortion was a crime against the father; a father had the right to decide whether a newborn would live; it was even thought that a child itself could not have gotten anything worthwhile out of life if it died before

---

[58]On the translation "youngest" for comparative νεώτερος, see sec. 6.5.3.

[59]So Liefeld, 1028; Tiede, *Luke*, 385; et al.

[60]So Beare, *Matthew*, 376; Gundry, 361; Weber, 5-9. Gnilka maintains, "In der Antike hatte man den Kindern gegenüber weitgehend eine neutrale oder sogar negative Einstellung" (237, n. 13; it may be noted that the rediscovery of the child in Hellenistic poetry and art was but an episode). Note the low view of children at Qumran (1QM 7.3; cf. also the fragment from 4QD[b] cited by Légasse [*Jésus*, 284-5; cf. Milik, 114] which aligns children with the insane) and in the rabbinic literature (*m. ʾAbot* 3.11b [cf. Achtemier, 182; Jeremias, *Theology*, 227, n. 2]; *m. Git.* 2.6; *Ter.* 1.1; *Ketub.* 2.3; *Ber.* 7.2; [cf. Légasse, *Jésus*, 284; Str-B 1:105, 279, 607]). It is not insignificant that the παῖς word group denotes both "child" and "servant" (BAGD, "παῖς κτλ.," 604-5).

[61]De Vaux, 41; Wiedemann, *Children*, 39.

[62]De Vaux, 41; Weber, 8-9; cf. Ps 127:5.

[63]This was the case in the Roman world (so Wiedemann, *Children*, 9, 35-42; Weber, 5) as well as Israel (so Weber, 8-9: the child *as such* had no special importance).

reaching adult status.[64] There was, in fact, a sense in which the child was thought not to be truly human.[65] Of course, the love and affection of parents for their children was common in the ancient world,[66] but it did not undermine the categorical distinction thought to exist between children and adults nor the consequent low esteem in which children were typically held.

The harsh reality in antiquity of high infant mortality rates was an important reason for the low view of children:[67] people had to find a way to come to terms with the probability that some if not most of their children would not live to adulthood. The practice of exposing (usually female) children in the Greco-Roman world is relevant here, however, for it shows that high infant mortality rates were not entirely inevitable, and it gives evidence that an underlying problem was that children could be seen as insignificant and even disposable.[68]

A related perspective on children in the ancient world highlighted their weakness, smallness and dependence on adults.[69] As such, the child constituted an ideal candidate for God's purely gracious saving initiative. It is arguable, however, that a more directly relevant background for the study of Luke 22:24-30 is the low esteem and often negative social valuation of children in antiquity. This seems to be so since vv 25-27 present role contrasts that are striking precisely because of the dramatic shift of social position called for (cf. secs. 6.3 and 6.5).[70]

---

[64]See the well-documented discussion in Wiedemann, *Children*, 7-42.

[65]Wiedemann, *Children*, 176-86. Note Wiedemann's claim that it was precisely this not-truly-human status of the child that played a key part in placing the child in a special role in the mystery cults. Because the child only marginally belonged to the human community and was in a sense "not there" as a citizen, its speech could be taken as an ominous mediation of the divine word (186).

[66]E.g., consider the implied attitude of Jairus toward his daughter (Luke 8:40-42).

[67]Wiedemann, *Children*, 204.

[68]Weber, 5-7. The exposure of infants by the wealthy demonstrates that the practice was not owing merely to poverty; rather it signified the low status of children (6-7). Another common perspective on children in antiquity was that they were the embodiment of ignorance (Wiedemann, *Children*, 17-23; Weber, 10). Weber points out rightly that the OT does not, however, present children as innocent (9-10; cf. Gen 8:21, etc.).

[69]Légasse recognizes the significance of this background for the wider teaching of Jesus concerning children ("L'enfant," 420-1; on the vulnerability of children, cf. Wiedemann, *Children*, 17).

[70]The smallness and weakness of children can figuratively connote a low social standing, and accordingly it can be merged with the perspective of the infer-

2.4.3 Domestic Servants

The very brief parable in Luke 22:27a-b with its contrast between ὁ ἀνακείμενος and ὁ διακονῶν invites us to consider the background of domestic servanthood (as does the promise in v 30a against the backdrop of Luke 12:37). Because chapter 3 focuses on table motifs, here we will concentrate on the role and status of servants within the household with minimal attention to meal-related factors.

A matter of terminology must be addressed first, namely the distinction, if any, between "servant" and "slave." Such a clarification is necessary because sometimes (e.g., Luke 12:37; 17:7-10; cf. Mark 10:43-44) the terms typically translated "servant" and "slave" (διάκονος and δοῦλος and cognates) appear to be used interchangeably. Do these words have significantly different meanings?

It is possible and necessary to draw some distinctions between "servant" and "slave." While the former would ordinarily denote one who is employed to render a form of assistance to another, particularly domestic duties, the latter would correspond to a person who, as the property of another,[71] is entirely subject to that master. Thus the extent of a master's authority over slaves would exceed that of an employer over servants.[72] Luke's apparent special interest in διακονέω for table

ior status of slaves/ servants.

[71]The slave's status as chattel is often associated with Aristotle's view of the slave as an animate tool (*Pol.* 1.2.2-7; see the discussion in Laub, *Sklaverei*, 32-4; cf. Finley, 74-5; Stambaugh and Balch, 113). Mendelsohn (122) claims that the legal status of a slave as property was characteristic in the Near East during the two millennia preceding the Common Era. De Vaux cautions, however, that despite the slave's legal status as chattel, it was never quite forgotten in the ancient East that slaves were human and had certain rights (84-5). If a man blinded or broke the tooth of his slave, Jewish law required that he be manumitted (Exod 21:26-27; cf. 21:2), and a master who beat his slave to death was to be punished (21:20). Further, slaves joined in the family worship, rested on the sabbath and shared in sacrificial meals and religious feasts (e.g., Exod 20:10; 23:12; 12:44; Deut 12:12, 18; 16:11, 14). Nevertheless, the killing of a slave was not murder, and if a slave was mortally wounded by his master's beating but survived for a day or two, the master was exonerated of any punishment (save the loss of his chattel) (Exod 21:21). On the whole, then, it seems that Jewish law and practice oscillated on the personhood of the slave.

[72]Beyer, 81. The absolute power of owners over slaves is documented by Wiedemann, *Greek*, 23-28 (cf. Gaius *Inst.* 1.25 [a slave cannot make a will nor have anything willed to him]; 1.52 [owners have the power of life and death over

service[73] may also imply that a difference of nuance can distinguish these terms and concepts.

It is useful also to recognize that OT and NT writers sometimes use servant or slave language in technical, symbolic or other distinctive ways: the Servant in Isaiah stands in a special relationship to God and performs a redemptive service (e.g., 52:13-53:12); Paul seems to find a certain honor in being δοῦλος Χριστοῦ Ἰησοῦ (e.g., Rom 1:1); Paul depicts civil "authority" (ἐξουσία) as God's "servant" (διάκονος) (Rom 13:1-4). In spite of the wide range of ideas such examples provide as a backdrop to our text, however, the nature of the role contrasts in Luke 22:26-27 favors the more basic idea of servanthood involving low status, the loss of rights and full subjection to one's master (cf. secs. 6.3-5).

Hoffmann and Eid caution that modern notions of "civil service" and "social service" can dull one's perception of ancient servanthood's sharp edges.[74] Although the διάκονος may not have been wholly lacking freedom as the δοῦλος was, as a servant he was still bound to devote his energies and abilities to meeting the wishes of another. Moreover, the root sense of διακονέω (and cognates) had to do with table service, and in the Judaism of the NT era that did not amount to a position of dignity.[75]

The closeness of "servant" and "slave" may also be seen from the other direction, i.e., that despite the status of a slave as property, his or

---

slaves]; 2.86-91 [a slave's possessions are legally the owner's property]; Strabo, 7.3.12 [a slave can have no name but what his master gives him]); cf. Barclay, 167 (he cites Seneca *De Beneficiis* 3.19.1 [a slave does not have the right to refuse his master's orders]). It may be added, however, that owners did not always fully exercise these powers (e.g., D. Martin [7-11] notes that some slaves possessed money and property, even though by law they could not own anything).

Although the shift from ὑμῶν διάκονος to πάντων δοῦλος in Mark 10:43-44 signifies an escalation to a more radical subordination, Mann maintains that that shift is due chiefly to the difference between ὑμῶν and πάντων; δοῦλος here may carry the same sense as διάκονος and replace it merely for stylistic variation (414). From a different angle, Roloff sees "eine gewisse Verschiedenheit der Nuancierung" between διάκονος and δοῦλος in Pauline usage, the latter being unique as a "Beschreibung eines *absoluten* Dienstverhältnisses gegenüber Gott..." (*Apostolat*, 121, emphasis added).

[73]Luke's Gospel introduces διακονέω and cognates for service *at table* four times (10:40; 12:37; 17:8; 22:27a) without parallel in Mark and Matthew (see also Acts 6:1-2). On the importance of table service for Luke, see further ch. 3.

[74]Hoffmann and Eid, 196-7 (referring to both διάκονος and δοῦλος).

[75]Hoffmann and Eid, 197-8; cf. Cranfield, 341 (the "ignoble ring" of the term to Greek ears is documented from Plato *Gorg.* 518A); Shepherd, 786. Beyer (82) makes a similar claim for the Greek perspective.

her lot was not always as bad as one might imagine. Vogt notes that skilled slaves were sometimes entrusted with crucial household tasks, and were even asked to look after the master and his family when they were vulnerable (e.g., as nurse or tutor to the master's children, or as physician to an aging master).[76] Additionally, tolerable treatment for slaves was the norm in the ancient world[77] (despite glaring exceptions); the shrewd, pragmatic strategy of owners was to cultivate a positive attitude among slaves and thereby maximize their productivity.[78]

Related to the fact that the duties and treatment of slaves were not usually intolerable is the fact that some slaves found themselves not only under authority but in subordinate positions of authority.[79] Such was the case of the enslaved husband who remained the *paterfamilias* over his wife and children.[80] Luke himself can envision a household servant being entrusted with considerable responsibility and authority (Luke 12:41-48; 16:1-9; 19:11-27; cf. sec. 2.5.2 below). Accordingly, when we turn to Luke 22:24-30, the image of a slave which includes the possession of some limited authority cannot be ruled out.[81]

In the end, then, it seems inappropriate to draw a bold line between "servant" and "slave."[82] In fact, it appears that slaves often did duties we might expect of hired servants, and free servants were not above very menial chores. Thus it seems appropriate to allow the concepts of serv-

[76]Vogt, 104-20 (the ancient aristocrat entrusted to the slave as much work as was practicable to free himself for creative spiritual achievements [120]); cf. D. Martin, 1-49.

[77]Finley, 122; Flory, 87; de Vaux, 85. This is far from saying that *good* treatment was common. Indeed, Bartchy (*1 Corinthians 7:21*, 69) rightly notes that close slave-master relationships and expressions of outstanding kindness to slaves were not at all typical; conversely, severe cruelty was also quite unusual. The best and worse cases, however, stand out because they depart from the norm (cf. Barclay, 167).

[78]Laub, *Sklaverei*, 36-9; cf. Bartchy, *1 Corinthians 7:21*, 69-72. The prospect of manumission was among the major incentives held out to slaves (so Laub, *Sklaverei*, 37; cf. Barclay [168] on the importance of gaining freedom), an event that male slaves in the first century could expect by age thirty according to Roman law (Bartchy, "Slavery," 545; cf. Flory, 89; Wiedemann [*Slavery*, 28], however, claims that manumission of Roman slaves was not as common or as early as some have supposed).

[79]Bartchy, "Slavery," 544; D. Martin, 15-22.

[80]Gnilka, 238.

[81]Cf. also the servant with servants in 2 Sam 9:9-10.

[82]Wolf, 291.

anthood and slavery to come together to a degree, and in reading Luke 22:24-30 to keep both in mind.

Although it is important to consider both slavery and servanthood backgrounds, however, it is the status of the slave that will allow the most revealing light to be shed on 22:24-30. As noted above, the slave's ascribed status—even a beloved slave or one entrusted with great responsibility—was that of property. In Roman thought, a household consisted of two elements, people and possessions, and slaves fell into the latter category.[83] Slaves, like children, were seen as inferior to free adults, and in this sense were thought to be outside the fully human community of citizens.[84] It is this low view of slaves that made possible the instances of harsh treatment and abuse which did occur.[85] Further, this low estimation of slaves accents the breadth of the gulf between the positions contrasted in Luke 22:25-27, and underscores the radical nature of the directive to "become like a servant" (v 26).

Becoming like a servant or slave—indeed, actually becoming a slave—was a commonplace in the NT world, for there were many paths that led to enslavement. Unlike the case of slavery as practiced in the West in recent centuries, in the ancient world defaulting on one's debts was a common basis for enslavement.[86] Further, the grinding realities of poverty led some to opt for slavery in the household of one sufficiently well off to provide food and shelter, despite the need to perform menial or trying tasks, the consequent bondage of children born in slavery, and a loss of rights.[87] Also, captives of war were routinely forced to become slaves.[88] So the command of Luke 22:26 (which is also implicit in v 27) to become like a slave was not an empty symbol or abstract notion; it was a vividly real prospect, a path known to all of Luke's readers and surely traveled by some. Most importantly, it was a path that was followed

[83]Laub, *Sklaverei*, 34; cf. nn. 71 and 72 above. The departure from this standard at the Saturnalia feast when the master waited on his slaves (so Nilsson, 205) was but a token exception to the usual practice (cf. Luke 22:27c; sec. 6.5.3).

[84]Wiedemann, *Slavery*, 25.

[85]See e.g., Laub, *Sklaverei*, 39. A later rabbinic view asserted that a dog was more valuable to God than a slave (*Midr.* Exod 22:30 [cited in Rengstorf, "δοῦλος," 271, n. 84]).

[86]Mendelsohn, 122; de Vaux, 83.

[87]Barclay, 168; Bartchy *1 Corinthians 7:21*, 71. An "advantage" of slavery is that it was a preferred alternative to death (Wiedemann, *Slavery*, 26; this is clearly the case with exposed infant raised as slaves).

[88]De Vaux, 80-1.

almost always in unfortunate circumstances. Slavery may have offered the prospect of survival to a peasant who could not otherwise provide for his destitute family, but even then it was a momentous and desperate step to sell one's free status and accept the position of mere property.

2.5 Backgrounds in Luke-Acts

Finally we turn to a brief survey of certain strands of language and thought in Luke-Acts reflecting patterns of authority and subordination. While still pursuing background perspectives for the study of Luke 22:24-30, here we move a step closer to gaining insights that have a direct bearing on the task of discerning Luke's thought and expression in that text.

2.5.1 "The Apostles"

Consideration of "the apostles" in Luke-Acts and its possible importance as a title for people in or under authority is prompted here by the identification of Jesus' hearers in Luke 22:15-38 as "the apostles" (v 14).[89] It is noteworthy that neither Mark nor Matthew have a parallel usage of ἀπόστολος. Further, while Mark and Matthew together have only three usages of the term, Luke's Gospel contains six (four are unparalleled) and Acts has twenty-eight. Evidently Luke has something to say about the apostles that is absent in the Markan and Matthean traditions.[90]

As to the identity of the apostles in Luke-Acts, it seems quite clear that they are to be equated with the Twelve (Luke 6:13; Acts 1:26).[91] The usage in Acts 14:4, 14, which identifies Paul and Barnabas as apostles, is exceptional. It is arguable that if Luke wished to rank Paul among the apostles, one would expect to find the term used of him on at least a few occasions in the long story about Paul in Acts 16-28, but it is not.[92] Per-

[89]As Via (42-3) observes, we are also told that Jesus plans to observe the Passover with his "disciples" (v 11). In dependence on Quesnell (69-71), Via argues that this finding supports the notion that women disciples were present in the upper room (42, n. 18). The correspondence of the twelve apostles to the "twelve tribes" (v 30), however, would seem to weigh against that claim. More likely is the view that v 11 simply refers to those disciples who were also apostles (cf. the identification of the apostles as a subgroup of disciples in 6:13 and perhaps 17:1, 5).

[90]So e.g., Schmithals, *Apostle*, 247.

[91]So Lake, 55; Lohse, "Ursprung," 272-3; Roloff, "Apostel," 442; *Apostolat*, 169; G. Schneider, "Zwölf," 41; against M. Mills (115), who includes Paul among the apostles in Acts.

haps, then, the usage of ἀπόστολος in Acts 14:4, 14 reflects a pre-Lukan understanding of the term involving a less restricted application.[93]

The function of the Lukan apostles may be considered as well, and on two levels. First, what do the Twelve *do* in the Lukan story? Second, what does Luke *do with them* in his two-part work? As to the first question, the apostles in Acts perform "signs and wonders" (Acts 2:43; 5:12), devote themselves to "prayer and the ministry of the word" (6:1-6), serve as teachers (2:42) and exercise authority with "the elders" in Jerusalem concerning matters of church practice and policy (15:2-16:4). That they are recognized as central authority figures in Acts 1:1-16:4 is apparent (e.g., 4:35, 37; 5:2; 6:6; 8:18; 15:2-16:4). In the Gospel there are fewer descriptions of the apostles' actions, but we may note that there too, even when Jesus is present on the narrative scene, the apostles exercise power to heal, cast out spirits and preach the kingdom of God (9:1-10 cf. Mark 6:30).[94] Yet despite their possession of authority, it is clear that they stand under Jesus' authority, for he formed the apostolic band and authorized the Twelve to carry out his mission (Luke 6:12-16; 9:1-6; 24:46-49; Acts 1:8).

If we step back and ask what the writer of Luke-Acts does with the apostles, it appears that he bridges from Jesus to the church: "The apostles connect together in their own persons the period of the ministry of Jesus and the time of the church, and serve to guarantee the total transfer into the life of the church of the significance of the ministry of Jesus."[95] The apostles in Luke-Acts are the authorized delegates of Jesus (so the comparatively frequent occurrence of ἀπόστολος in the Gospel) who are uniquely appointed to carry on his mission in the first stage of the life of the emerging church (thus the heavy usage of the term in Acts 1:1-16:4).

[92]And if Paul does not truly qualify as an apostle according to Luke, neither does Barnabas.

[93]Luke may be influenced by Pauline thinking here. That this passage exhibits a sense different than Luke's usual idea of an "apostle" is maintained by Lohse, "Ursprung," 273; Nolland, *Luke*, 268; Roloff, *Apostolat*, 169; et al.

[94]The usage in 11:49, unique to Luke, links the apostles with "prophets" and thus serves to lay a foundation for their authoritative role in Acts as divinely appointed emissaries to the people of God. It is probable, then, that Luke means more by "apostle" than the etymological sense of "sent one, missionary" (cf. Barrett, "Apostle," 101; Evans, 318; Nolland, *Luke*, 267-8; Fitzmyer [*Gospel*, 1:617] makes too little of the authority dimension here).

[95]Nolland, *Luke*, 268. He continues, "The apostles are in this way transitional figures, as may be seen by the way they are allowed to drop from sight as the Acts account unfolds,..." (ibid.). Cf. Roloff, *Apostolat*, 170.

One more question about the Lukan apostles may be raised here, namely the degree to which they function as models for the Lukan reader. Although this study centers on the story line of Luke 22:24-30 rather than its implicit "message" to the Lukan community, the claim that uncovering the text's meaning requires attention to both author- and reader-based factors justifies some reflection on the "distance" readers of the Gospel may have sensed between themselves and the Lukan apostles (cf. sec. 1.2).

Here it seems fitting to navigate between two extremes. On the one hand, the apostles have a unique and temporary "bridging" function, so not every instruction or promise to them could be equally relevant to all later Christian disciples. On the other hand, it seems impossible that Luke would devote so much space to the activities of the Twelve if their role were utterly unique. Between these extremes lies the view that for Luke the apostles have a role as representative leaders.[96] To be sure, the apostles are also disciples (6:13), and we may suppose that Luke would have any Christian reader gain some personal input from the account of the Twelve. There seems to be an important interest, however, in portraying the apostles as paradigmatic leaders for future generations of Christian leaders to follow. Jesus' teaching to the Twelve and the account of their ministry in Jesus' stead provide guidelines for how to understand and exercise authority in the church.[97]

2.5.2 Stewardship Motifs

In this final section we turn to stewardship motifs in Luke-Acts and the key texts upon which they are based. It will only be possible to present an abbreviated overview, and other authority motifs and texts must be bypassed.[98] We will, however, focus on a few vitally important lines of Lukan thought that may provide helpful perspectives for developing an interpretation of Luke 22:24-30.[99]

[96]Cf. Roloff, "Apostel," 442-3; Wanke, 70.

[97]Dupont, "Ministères," 147.

[98]Some other Lukan texts relevant to the theme of authority and subordination are the mission mandates and reports (e.g., Luke 9:1-6; 10:17-20; 24:46-49; Acts 1:8), commissioning texts (e.g., Acts 6:6; 13:1-3), the ecclesiastical judicial scene in Acts 15, the portrayal of the lowly slave in Luke 17:7-10, and the rule of Peter in Acts 5:1-11. Frequently in these and other texts Luke draws attention to the importance of faithful leadership or service in an intermediate role within a hierarchical framework of authority.

Luke 12:35-48 (vv 41-46 in particular) is a key text contributing to the stewardship motif. Since there are a number of points of similarity between this text and 22:24-30[100] (e.g., Jesus as "servant," delegation of authority as a reward for responsible stewardship, table fellowship as a reward for faithful service), 12:35-48 deserves careful consideration. The sayings of Jesus in Luke 12:35-40 and 41-48 have in common the theme of "slaves/ servants" (δοῦλοι) waiting faithfully for the return of their master (vv 37, 43).[101] The actions of the servants differ, however, in these two subsections. In the first case their waiting is characterized by watchfulness, anticipating the sudden return of the master (i.e., the Son of man, v 40). The servant found watching for his master can expect to be rewarded with the striking reversal of roles in which the master serves him at table (cf. 22:27). In the second case the time of waiting for the master's return is one in which responsible leadership in and care for the household are marks of faithfulness. The servant who is found exercising proper stewardship (v 42) within the household will be rewarded with additional subordinate authority (v 44; cf. the link between 22:28 and 29-30 [sec. 7.4.1]).

Peter's question in v 41 is unique to Luke: "Lord, are you telling this parable for us or for all?" While it is difficult to be sure whom "us" and "all" represent,[102] the content of 12:42-46 implies a shift of focus to leadership roles. This is apparent not only from the two usages of καθίστημι with ἐπί (vv 42, 44 par. Matt 24:45, 47), but also from the unparalleled use of language revealing a hierarchy among the master's subordinates.[103] Luke makes it explicit that the household consists not only of master and servants, but of master, steward and inferior servants. Perhaps most

[99]Cf. sec. 8.3, which expands on Lukan stewardship for its place in "pivot-point" discipleship.

[100]So Moessner, 181; D. Wenham, *Rediscovery*, 132-3.

[101]The blessing formula repeated in vv 37 and 43 also unifies 12:35-48.

[102]Although Fitzmyer's view (*Gospel*, 2:989) that "us" refers to the disciples and not just the Twelve (cf. 12:1, 22), and "all" recalls the crowds (12:1, 13, 54) has the merit of fitting well with the nearest named antecedents for the terms, it overlooks the function of v 41 in turning attention to authority roles not held by all disciples (contrast Dupont, "Ministères," 149-50). I. H. Marshall (*Gospel*, 540) links "us" with the apostles at this point in Luke's story.

[103]Matthew shows no hierarchy with δοῦλος and σύνδουλος. Luke, however, alternates οἰκονόμος and δοῦλος, and uses παῖς and παιδίσκη where Matthew has σύνδουλος. This is in contrast to Luke 12:35-40 where no exercise of authority is involved in faithful waiting; no distinction is made there between the "servants" (note the plural).

important for this study is the focus of Luke 12:41-46 on the intermediate role of the one under yet in authority (cf. the apostles in 22:24-30).[104]

An interest in a subordinate figure entrusted with authority while his master is away recurs in the Parable of the Pounds (19:11-27 par. Matt 25:14-30) and the Parable of the Unrighteous Steward (16:1-9).[105] Both parables commend wise (in the latter case, shrewd) stewardship during the period of the master's absence, and both portray the returning master as one who would settle up with his servant on the basis of his performance. It seems that, for Luke, this would have implications as to the nature of responsible discipleship for Christian leaders. In the Parable of the Pounds, Luke, in contrast to Matthew, has the first two servants rewarded by being given "authority over" cities.[106] Thus they become subordinate rulers entrusted with authority to govern people, not merely caretakers of property. In this way the link of faithful service with the reward of leadership responsibilities is brought to the attention of the Lukan reader (cf. 22:29-30).

This glance at stewardship reveals that the theme is of special interest to Luke; he has a particular concern that the apostles, and other leaders as well, see themselves as standing both under and in authority, and as bearing a responsibility to set aside self-important concepts of authority, meet the needs of followers and thereby please their master. Further, the texts surveyed reveal a direct link between faithful stewardship and future reward from the returning master. The presence of these ideas elsewhere in Luke sheds a certain light on 22:24-30 and conveys something of that text's importance in the Lukan framework.

2.6 Conclusion

In summary of this survey of patterns of authority and subordination familiar to the writer of Luke 22:24-30, a few observations may be made. The great degree to which the ancient world was saturated with

---

[104]The striking reversal of v 37 would remind church leaders, however, that to rule is not to be above the duties of service. Here connections between 12:35-48 and 22:24-30 become quite apparent. Also noteworthy are the similar priorities for Christian leadership set out in 1 Cor 4:1-5 and 1 Pet 5:1-4.

[105]Consider too the centurion (7:8) who is both in and under authority.

[106]The servant is given ἐξουσίαν "over" (ἐπάνω) cities (v 17; v 19 has ἐπάνω only). In Matthew (25:21, 23) the servants are rewarded by being "set over much." Cf. 12:44.

and influenced by authority structures has been highlighted. Modern western notions of human equality, and the (often unspoken) expectation of many that in today's societies all people have inherent worth and ought to possess extensive personal liberties, seem to be largely lacking the NT world. Instead we find pervasive networks of power—official and unofficial—that were seen and felt by all, and which kept each man, woman and child in his or her place.

The preceding survey has also underlined the great distance between top and bottom in the prevailing structures of authority in antiquity. Emperors and governors and client kings, Jewish kings and judges, and the *paterfamilias* did not chair governing committees within participatory democracies. Far from it, they had access to far-reaching powers and could do virtually anything they wished to those subject to them.[107] The very lives of subjects and slaves and children were in the hands of their kings and masters and fathers. Considering the extent of power held by ancient rulers also gives one a feel for the stark, concrete realities of life in the sphere of such a broad spectrum of power and impotence. When we consider the contrasts in Luke 22:25-27 and the injunction to turn from greatness to youth and leadership to service, then the background of ancient authority patterns reminds us that such a call was profoundly radical, and that such a condescending step crossed a wide and deep gulf. Correspondingly, the dramatic elevation in the conferral of kingship and the promise of thrones (vv 29-30) stands out in bold relief against the backdrop of various patterns of authority and subordination surveyed in the present chapter.

A feature that has come to the fore again and again in the present chapter is the role of "middle-men." Whether in the case of Roman governors, client kings, Jewish judges and kings, or household servants entrusted with significant responsibilities, subordinate rulers take a prominent place in authority networks as they rule over inferiors, yet do so in such a way as to please their superiors. Authority is not necessarily something one simply possesses or lacks; it exists on a continuum and people hold greater or lesser degrees of it.

Jewish and OT backgrounds draw attention to the role of God as ruler over rulers, particularly the importance of divine involvement in

[107]OT conceptions of authority that placed all human rulers under the superior rule of God constitute a noteworthy wrinkle in this fabric of raw power, but the theocratic outlook did not prevent human leaders from exercising great power.

the selection, raising up and anointing of kings or judges. Thus the Jewish concept of authority clearly places God at the head of the chain of command: he has the ultimate right to power, so all human rulers become middle-men in the divine economy.

Attention to Lukan backgrounds appears to reveal an interest in the authority figure who is also subordinate to higher powers (both the apostles and stewards in the Lukan story fit this description). Luke may have a special concern to show that Christian leaders are to rule in such a way as to please their soon-to-return master (12:40). Further, if the master would one day return to serve his servants (12:37), then it may be implied that Christian stewards and apostles could not stoop too low in caring for those under their charge (cf. sec. 8.3).

Chapter 3: Table Motifs

3.1 Introduction

In the present chapter various table motifs will be examined with a view toward discovering their possible value as elements of a platform upon which to build an interpretation of Luke 22:24-30.[1] The broader contexts of Hellenistic symposia (3.2), Jewish banquets and meal traditions (3.3) and Pauline table motifs (3.4) are considered first, followed by an examination of table motifs in Luke-Acts (3.5).

A chapter on table backgrounds is warranted in light of the prevalence of table images in Luke 22:24-30 (see sec. 1.1). Since the setting for sayings and events in 22:14-38 is at table—Jesus "reclined" (ἀνέπεσεν, v 14) with the Twelve for a Passover[2] meal—and vv 24-30 come on the heels of the theologically poignant interpretation of the meal (vv 19-20)[3] (a table backdrop which may have important links with our text), we are all the more inclined to discern the possible importance of table backgrounds for an understanding of 22:24-30.

---

[1]"Table" is used loosely here; it connotes food, meals, special feasts, etc.

[2]Note (τὸ) πάσχα in 22:1, 7, 8, 11, 13. Although it is debated whether or not the historical Last Supper was a Passover meal (Jeremias [*Words*, 15-88] discusses the issues), it is obvious the Luke portrays it as a Passover meal.

[3]On the text-critical problem in 22:19-20, see sec. 6.5.3, n. 209.

3.2 The Hellenistic Symposium

The symposia of Plato and Xenophon are regarded as the archetypes of a widespread literary form.[4] In these banquet discourses the table context is made a vehicle for the transmission of wisdom uttered by a chief guest. That this genre was still recognized and used in the first century CE is apparent from the works of Philo and Plutarch.[5] Since some argue that certain table scenes in Luke's Gospel are fashioned on a symposium model,[6] we might wonder if the same could be true for the Last Supper.[7]

This possibility, however, must be evaluated in light of the claims of chapter 5. There it will be argued that Luke 22:14-38 is cast in the literary form of the farewell testament. Is it reasonable to suppose that Luke has adapted and formed material to suit the "requirements" of two genres?[8] A description of the symposium literature should help us weigh the likelihood of such seemingly extraordinary compositional constraints.

Features of the symposium genre may be distilled from Delobel's study:[9] A respected central figure displays his wisdom and insight at a

[4]So Mau, 1208; et al. Smith (614) and de Meeûs (856) note the literary as well as social character of the tradition. De Meeûs (856, n. 49) lists many of the literary works in the symposium genre.

[5]Philo criticizes features of the symposium practice, and contrasts the table practices of the Therapeutae (*Cont.* 40-62, 64). Plutarch employs the symposium genre (*Dinner*) and recalls the content of symposium dialogues (*Table Talk*). That the tradition extends into the second century CE and beyond is evidenced by Lucian's parody (*Symp.*) and Athenaeus (*Deip.*). Hug ("Symposion-Literatur," 1276) asserts that the first century BCE was "besonders fruchtbar" for the literary symposium.

[6]E.g., Luke 7:36-50 (so Delobel), 11:37-54 (so Steele) and 14:1-24 (so de Meeûs).

[7]Steele sees no prima facie reason why Luke could not have been influenced by the genre in shaping 22:14-38 (394).

[8]Kurz ("Luke 22:14-38," 253 and n. 8) allows for some influence of the symposium tradition on this farewell address. Luke never loses sight of the fact that the dialogue is at table: "Greco-Roman symposium discussions probably also influenced Luke 22:14-38" (253). Smith (620, n. 22), who favors the symposium over the farewell model, is inclined against Kurz's testamentary interpretation, "... although clearly Jesus' 'table talk' on this occasion is also a farewell address." Smith asserts, "... our theories are not fundamentally opposed,..." (n. 22). Berger sees here a combination of testamentary and symposium elements (*Formgeschichte*, 79; cf. Danker, *Jesus*, 344; R. Pesch, "Last Supper," 64).

[9]Delobel, 459.

banquet through dialogue and dispute. Other typical characters are host, comic, intruder, doctor, drunk and lovers.[10] Some *fait divers* triggers a dialogue in which there is often a conflict involving the chief guest.[11] Places at table are perceived to be important and can provoke conflicts between guests.[12] Steele adds two points to Delobel's description: 1) The chief guest regularly triumphs in arguments or has the wisest things to say; 2) Not all guests speak in some examples of the genre,[13] and the length of speeches can vary greatly. Smith's observation that symposia often have an "anecdotal character" may be noted here as well.[14]

Regarding dialogue content, Coffey claims that the symposium literature represents a loosely defined genre in which unconnected questions serve as a vehicle for miscellaneous learning and lore.[15] Plutarch sees a *very* wide spectrum of acceptable table topics,[16] though the classic symposia of Plato and Xenophon center on philosophical concerns.[17]

The "looseness" of the genre enables Steele to contend that Luke 11:37-54 is a modified Hellenistic symposium.[18] De Meeûs similarly

---

[10]The "intruder" may be a welcome guest (e.g., Plut. *Dinner* 160Cff). An entertainer such as a flute girl (e.g., Plato, *Symp.* 176E) may also be present.

[11]The attempt of de Meeûs (858-9, 863) to liken the conflict-based dialogues in Plato *Symp.* and Luke 14:1-24 seems to underestimate the intensity of conflict in Luke 14; Jesus claims to utter more than philosophical opinions.

[12]A lively concern about position at table is seen in many of the symposia (e.g., Plato *Symp.* 175C, 177D-E, 213A-C; Lucian *Symp.* 8-9; Petronius *Satyricon* 70 [so Danker, *Jesus*, 269]). Cf. Dio Chrys. *Or.* 30.29; Plut. *Table Talk* 1.616F-617E. See also Aune, "Septem," 73; Karris, "Food," 62-3; de Meeûs, 864-5; Smith, 617, 620.

[13]De Meeûs (863) notes, however, that it is typical for each participant to speak. The lack of speeches by characters other than Jesus in Luke 7:36-50, 11:37-54 and 14:1-24 may be due to Luke's concern to be brief (Steele, 386, 390; so Plato, *Symp.* 180C).

[14]Smith, 620, n. 22. Steele (380-1) boils the dramatis personae down to host, chief guest and other guests; the structure consists of invitation (often not explicit), *fait divers*, discourse. One wonders if this constitutes an overly general common denominator.

[15]Coffey, 1028-9. So also Aune, "Septem," 53, 74.

[16]Topics in his *Table Talk* include "Should the host seat guests or let them choose their own seats?" (1.615C); "Why are people hungriest in autumn?" (2.635A); "Which came first, the chicken or the egg?" (2.635D); "Is wrestling the oldest sport?" (2.638A); "What is the suitable time for sex?" (3.653B); "Who is the god of the Jews?" (4.671C).

[17]In Plato's *Symposium* each guest offers an encomium to love (177A-E), while in Xenophon's *Symposium* each tells of his most valuable knowledge or possession (3.1-3). Cf. J. Martin, 136-7.

[18]Steele, 394.

argues for Luke's use of the genre in 14:1-24, but concedes that it is only a framework which Luke adapts liberally.[19] Could it be that Luke's Last Supper discourse also represents an adapted usage of this genre?

In answer to this question it may be noted that neither de Meeûs nor Steele consider the lack of shared discourse in Luke 14:1-24 and 11:37-54 problematic for their theses.[20] In both texts, however, Jesus totally dominates the dialogue; only 14:15 and 11:45 contain *any* direct speech by parties other than Jesus, and then only to trigger additional sayings of Jesus. For all practical purposes these texts are in monologue form, a fact that is in stark contrast to the lively dialogues of Plato and Xenophon, and so many other symposia.

Even if it were to be conceded, however, that Luke follows this genre elsewhere, is it evident that 22:14-38 conforms significantly to the pattern?[21] Points of general correspondence include the following: 1) The discourse setting is at table. 2) Jesus, the chief figure at table, speaks with profound wisdom. 3) Some of Jesus' table talk is on table matters (vv 15-21, 27, 30), a feature not uncommon in symposia (cf. Plutarch's *Table Talk*). 4) There is some dialogue at the Last Supper (in vv 31-38). 5) Some of Jesus' sayings are rooted in conflict with others at table (e.g., vv 21-22, 25-27, 34-35). 6) Luke 22:14-38 exhibits what Smith labels an "anecdotal character."[22] 7) The Last Supper discourse conforms roughly to the order of meal followed by teaching.[23]

On the negative side are the following points: 1) There is no taking turns at giving discourses, a hallmark of the classic symposia. 2) A related point is that there is no sense that Jesus' table companions are in a position to offer words on a plane with his. 3) Jesus foreshadows his imminent death (see sec. 5.3), a feature without parallel in symposia. 4) Two of Steele's "essential aspects" of the symposium structure are absent, namely the invitation and *fait divers*.[24] 5) The characters in vv 14-

[19]De Meeûs, 854. Delobel (462) makes similar claims for 7:36-50.

[20]De Meeûs, 863; Steele, 386, 390.

[21]Smith (620, n. 22) is inclined to say, "Yes" (cf. Berger, *Formgeschichte*, 79). J. Martin (314) concedes some influence here, though finally designates the Johannine Last Supper as "das erste christliche Symposion" (317).

[22]Smith, 620, n. 22. Cf. also Aune, "Septem," 53.

[23]Note μετὰ τὸ δειπνῆσαι in v 20. Still, vv 15-20 also contain Jesus' teaching. In a sense there is no point in vv 14-38 at which Jesus is not "teaching."

[24]Steele, 380-1. One may attempt to construe 22:8 as an invitation of sorts, but that idea breaks down when one considers the obligatory character of the Passover meal. The *fait divers* of v 24 does function as the point of departure for the sayings about greatness (vv 25-27), though it does not give impetus for the dis-

38 do not match well with the typical symposium dramatis personae.[25] 6) Jesus' teaching does not have the abstract, philosophical quality characteristic of many symposia.[26] 7) The atmosphere of the Last Supper is radically solemn and sober in contrast to that of many symposia.[27]

By weighing these positive and negative correspondences it becomes apparent that the case against Luke 22:14-38 as a clear example of a symposium dialogue is strong. On the one hand, some of the positive points seem flawed or rather general;[28] only points 3 and 6 appear to have much weight.[29] Yet on the other hand, all of the negative points contribute to a weakening of the symposium hypothesis (perhaps especially points 1 and 2). Therefore, the case for a definite adherence to the symposium genre in 22:14-38 is not persuasive.

In spite of this assessment, however, the fact that 22:14-38 bears some resemblance to that tradition requires further reflection. The points of similarity may not be sufficient to sustain the case for definite adherence to the genre, but alternatively it seems improbable that the convergence here of all seven features would be wholly coincidental. Perhaps it is sufficient to support the view that Luke unconsciously reflects a familiarity with the symposium genre, or that he mirrors it consciously yet sporadically. Another possibility is that it is more the customs of symposia than a literary genre from which Luke draws. Any such view would explain the poor quality of 22:14-38 as a "pure" literary symposium, but it

course as a whole.

[25]None of Delobel's character types noted above (host, joker, intruder, doctor, drinker, lovers) appear in Luke 22.

[26]Cf. e.g., Plato *Symp.* and Xen. *Symp.* The subject matter of Jesus' discourse is personal and urgent. Additionally, the injunctions and predictions of Luke 22:14-38 are not typical of symposia.

[27]The drunkenness common in symposia (see e.g., the parody of Lucian [*Symp.*] and Philo *Cont.* 40-47) is absent in Luke 22, as is the festive spirit, the priority on entertainment and the burlesque atmosphere of some symposia.

[28]Regarding 1) we note that Luke records non-symposium table talk of Jesus elsewhere (10:38-42; Acts 1:4-5); 2) Jesus is the central figure and bearer of wisdom in all of Luke as in the gospel tradition generally; 4) the dialogue at the Lukan Last Supper is little more than a device to introduce Jesus' sayings; 5) many of Jesus' sayings in Luke and the gospel tradition are rooted in conflicts with others; 7) this point is debatable (see above, n. 23).

[29]Further, much of Luke's Gospel exhibits an anecdotal character, and talk on table matters also fits well elsewhere (e.g., 6:21, 25; 11:9-13; 12:22-34; 20:46). Still, though the table features of 22:15-21 are traditional, the brief parable in v 27a-b and the promise in v 30a are without parallel in the Synoptics.

would also provide an explanation for points of similarity with the genre or practice which appear in 22:14-38.[30] In any case, it would seem improper totally to dismiss the symposium backdrop when in Part Two we turn to the task of analyzing 22:24-30.

3.3 Jewish Banquet and Meal Traditions

Although Jewish table traditions did not produce a literary genre (contrast the symposium), as religious and social patterns they nonetheless provide some valuable perspectives for an interpretation of Luke 22:24-30. The following survey is not intended to cover, even briefly, all of the table motifs in the OT and Jewish sources; that would be a massive undertaking well beyond the scope of this study.[31] Instead, attention is restricted to motifs which appear to have some similarities to the Lukan Last Supper Narrative. The Passover meal is thus the obvious starting point (see 22:1, 7, 8, 11, 13).[32]

The Rabbis insisted that even the poorest Israelite must recline to eat the Passover as a symbol of having passed from slavery to freedom.[33] This viewpoint and practice reflects the customary estimation in antiquity of reclining as a posture of privilege.[34] Since Jesus and the apostles are portrayed as reclining at the Passover table (22:14),[35] it is possible that an allusion is made to the free status of those present at the Last Supper. The difficulty here of course is in determining the relevance of later rabbinic sources for the study of NT texts. That the Hellenistic practice of reclining at formal meals had been adopted in Jewish life by the NT era seems apparent not only from NT occurrences of ἀνάκειμαι,

[30]To be sure, I do not concede as much of a connection as Steele does when he speaks of a "Modified Hellenistic Symposium." However, when we consider how an awareness of various table motifs influences one's interpretation of 22:24-30 (see Part Two), it will be necessary to keep in mind Luke's loose and/ or limited association with symposium backgrounds. Nonetheless, Hellenistic sources of any genre or type are arguably more "distant" from Luke 22:24-30 than the OT and Jewish sources, Paul's letters, and the context formed by the rest of Luke-Acts itself.

[31]On Jewish table/ food/ feast motifs, note Feeley-Harnik, 71-106; Mussner, 92-3; Navone, *Themes*, 32-4; Patsch, *Abendmahl*, 139-42; de Vaux, 484-517.

[32]Although the Passover setting is traditional (cf. Mark 14:1-16 par. Matt 26:1-19), it still appears to the Lukan reader as a protruding feature.

[33]See *b. Pesaḥ.* 108a; cf. texts cited by Jeremias (*Words*, 49); *m. Pesah.* 10.1; see also Dalman, 114-15.

[34]Büchsel, "κεῖμαι," 654-5.

[35]Similarly Mark 14:18; Matt 26:20.

ἀναπίπτω (etc.), but also from other sources.[36] What is difficult is determining when the custom of reclining came to be seen in Israel as a symbol of Exodus freedom. In any case, the practice would have been understood in Luke's time at least as an expression of privilege and relative "greatness," as the double rhetorical question in 22:27a assumes.

Another noteworthy dimension of table experience in Jewish life was a keen consciousness of rank at formal meals.[37] A diner's placement at table symbolized his level of importance in the group.[38] Considering, then, that both the position and posture of banquet guests amounted to expressions of status, the believability in context of the apostles' quarrel (v 24) may be enhanced.[39] Further, the fact that the Passover event on the most basic level commemorates deliverance from bondage casts a distinctive light on Jesus' call to servanthood (v 27).

The Passover perspective also involves an awareness of the role of death—the lamb must be slaughtered and its blood spread on the doorposts to secure the Lord's deliverance (Exod 12:7, 13). The many allusions in Luke 22:14-38 to Jesus' imminent death (especially vv 19-20; cf. sec. 5.3) at a meal repeatedly identified as the Passover (vv 1, 7, 8, 11, 13) would then seem to imply that some form of deliverance is to be accomplished

[36]E.g., Philo *Cont.* 67; cf. *Ep. Arist.* 183. The practice of reclining at table may be traced back to much older non-Jewish sources (e.g., Hdt. 9.16; Plato *Symp.* 175A-C; Xen. *Symp.* 1.8; cf. Mau, 1205).

[37]Dalman, 115. Concern over table rank is well attested in Jewish sources: A Qumran community meal participant was seated "in the order of his rank" (1QS 6.22; cf. 2.22-23; 6.8-9; 1QSa 2.11-22; also see Jos. *J. W.* 2.8.5 on meals at Qumran). The Therapeutae reclined at table in a sequence reflecting their time with the order (Philo *Cont.* 67). The seventy LXX translators were seated at Ptolemy's banquet according to age (*Ep. Arist.* 187; note that *Ep. Arist.* constitutes a Jewish borrowing of the symposium genre [Hug, "Symposion-Literatur," 1276-7]). Later rabbinic sources provide banquet regulations for the order in which diners were to wash their hands, take food, and regarding which guest was asked to pray (*b. Ber.* 46b, 47a; *Der. Er. Rab.* 6 [19b]; cited in Str-B, 4:621-37). On table position in Judaism as a sign of worth, see Schürmann (*Ursprung*, 138; cf. Ernst, *Evangelium*, 593). De Meeûs (849) notes that a Jewish host guarded his honor by inviting to a banquet only guests of his social class (cf. Grassi, 51).

[38]To be sure, this attitude was not unique to Judaism (cf. n. 12 above), nor to the Passover meal.

[39]Was Passover freedom (if this custom dates back to the NT era) overvalued by the Twelve with the result that an undue regard for their "distance" from slavery arose—a love for Passover freedom that could kindle a resistance to deeds and attitudes of service? Is the atmosphere of Luke's Last Supper charged for a conflict that needs only a spark to set it off (see sec. 6.4)?

through Jesus' death. If the service of Jesus described in v 27 were to encompass his death (see the discussion in sec. 6.5.3), the Passover backdrop could offer a useful perspective for the interpretation of our text.[40]

Although the Passover is recognized as a memorial of Jewish deliverance from bondage in Egypt, "... also associated with this reliving of their historic liberation was an anticipation of an eschatological, even messianic, deliverance. In this sense the second part of the Hallel was sung, especially Ps 118:26, 'Blest be the one who comes in the name of the Lord.'"[41] In this way the Passover takes on a historiographical function of marking out a middle era between decisive periods in history (cf. ch. 5 and the similar functions of testaments); it recalls a past deliverance and anticipates a future, final salvation.[42] The bi-directional aspect of Luke 22:15-20 is apparent,[43] but similar features of vv 24-30 are sometimes overlooked (see esp. sec. 9.3). Keeping this Passover feature in view may thus be of use for interpreting those verses.

Messianic or eschatological hope in Judaism, however, extends well beyond the Passover context. A facet of such hope is portrayed in Jewish sources by the expectation of an eschatological banquet marking the final restoration of Israel.[44] In Isaiah 25:6-8 the prophet anticipates a lavish feast one day when the Lord will swallow up death and wipe away all tears. In 65:13-14 a feast of food and drink is set parallel to the joy envisioned for the servants of the Lord (cf. 55:1-2; Zeph 1:7).[45]

[40]The significance of the Lukan omission of the ransom saying (cf. Mark 10:45b) would be affected by such an understanding of Luke 22:27 (cf. sec. 6.2 on Luke's relationship to Mark 10:41-45; cf. also sec. 6.5.3).

[41]Fitzmyer, *Gospel*, 2:1390.

[42]Although the harsh reality of Roman occupation in Palestine would give a hope for future deliverance a sharp edge, the reference in v 20 to the New Covenant would seem to conjure up images of a more-than-political redemption (cf. Jer 31:31-34 on the inward orientation of New Covenant blessings).

[43]I.e., Passover reflections and recollections (v 15—and throughout, by virtue of the context) and eschatological expectations (vv 16, 18).

[44]Behm, "ἐσθίω," 691 (cf. *Exod. Rab.* 25 on 16:4); Trautmann, 161.

[45]Lohmeyer, 79. One also notes that in *1 Enoch* the righteous elect will be saved and the Lord will abide over them, and they shall eat and rest and rise forever with the Son of Man (62:13-14; cf. *2 Enoch* 42:5 on the banquet as an image of heavenly joy [see also Str-B 4:1154-6]). At the end-time the earth will yield fruit in abundance and all the hungry will enjoy it, and manna will fall again (*2 Apoc. Bar.* 29:5-8). To be sure, these sources are rather late and may show traces of Christian influence, but they would still have some importance in documenting a Jewish hope of eschatological celebration which is expressed in images of a final joyous feast.

The Rabbis have a different angle on the theme of the eschatological banquet, for a connection is made between the feast and judgment. Rabbi Akiba is credited with the saying, "... the judgement is a judgement of truth; and all is made ready for the banquet" (*m. ᵓAbot* 3:17). Similarly Isa 65:13-14 correlates eschatological blessing with judgment: the Lord's servants shall eat, but those who forsake the Lord (v 11) shall go hungry (v 13) and cry out for pain of heart (v 14; cf. Luke 6:21, 25). The motif of a banquet for judgment or the combination of feasting and judging could offer a useful backdrop for Luke 22:30 (cf. sec 7.4.3).

In Jewish life table fellowship was a symbol of interpersonal union. De Meeûs argues that sharing food created a special intimacy between people.[46] This outlook is reflected in Ps 41:9: "Even my bosom friend in whom I trusted, who ate of my bread, has lifted his heel against me." To turn against one's table companion was to breach a profound trust. In Ps 101:5 the psalmist reflects a similar principle by speaking of the refusal to eat with the haughty and arrogant.[47] The importance in Jewish thought of the table as a tangible expression of earnest friendship and solidarity may shed light on the expressions of Jesus' union with the apostles (Luke 22:27-28, 30) as well as the divisive actions of the Twelve (vv 21, 24, 34).

Correspondingly, being invited to dine with a king may reveal his desire to secure or reward a subject's loyalty or friendship. A backdrop for the meal with king Jesus (v 30a) may be seen in 1 Kgs 2:7 where David instructs Solomon to reward the loyalty of the sons of Barzillai by letting them "be among those who eat at your table." Similarly, in 2 Sam 9:1-13 David honors Mephibosheth with table fellowship out of his desire to show kindness to the line of Jonathan (vv 1, 3, 7).[48]

3.4 Pauline Table Motifs

A consideration of Pauline table motifs seems to be warranted for at least three reasons: 1) The Lord's Supper at the church of Corinth evidently had become an occasion for divisiveness (1 Cor 11:17-22; cf. Luke

[46]De Meeûs, 849; cf. LaVerdiere, "Testament," 17; Mánek, "Umwandlung," 64; Mussner, 92-3; Trautmann, 161. The banquet was also a symbol of communion with God (Navone, "Banquet," 155-6).

[47]The RSV translation of אֹתוֹ לֹא אוּכָל as "I will not endure [him]" seems to lose some of the force or feel of the original. Cf. also *m. Ned.* 4.4.

[48]Note also Jehoiachin's elevation to table fellowship with the king of Babylon (2 Kgs 25:27-30; Jer 52:32-33).

22:24), a problem for which teaching such as that of the Lukan Jesus on service (22:27) would be apt. 2) The Lukan Institution Narrative (22:19-20) is at many points similar to the version in 1 Cor 11:23-25.[49] 3) Acts presents an implicit Lukan claim of familiarity with the basic contours of Paul's life and teaching, suggesting the possibility of some influence of Paul upon Luke.[50] Further, the importance of the Lord's Supper and table fellowship in Pauline thought is not easily overestimated. Accordingly, three key Pauline table topics will be considered.

First, in Gal 2:11-14 Paul describes an encounter with "Cephas" at Syrian Antioch. Although Peter had been eating with Gentile believers, after the arrival of emissaries from James he withdrew from such table fellowship for fear of the circumcision party. Paul sternly opposed this hypocrisy and rebuked Peter publicly because of it, for his withdrawal had constituted a failure to be "straightforward about the truth of the gospel" (οὐκ ὀρθοποδοῦσιν πρὸς τὴν ἀλήθειαν τοῦ εὐαγγελίου). So we see that crucial theological principles were symbolically at stake in relation to Jew-Gentile table fellowship (cf. Acts 10:1-11:18), and to break fellowship was to repudiate such truths.[51] In Luke 22:24 the problem is not Jew-Gentile table conflict, but the clash over greatness may reflect a similar superiority complex which threatens important symbols of table unity.

Second, 1 Cor 10:14-22 and 11:17-34 provide a window to Paul's understanding of the Lord's Supper. In 10:16 it is conveyed that the cup and bread are more than tokens of remembrance; they are also a κοινωνία in the blood and body of Christ. Correspondingly, since there is only one bread, those who partake of it are thereby unified as one body (v 17). Threats to table unity are later confronted (11:18-21): divisions and factions at table, and the problems they cause, reduce the community meal to something less than "the Lord's Supper" (v 20). Paul has harsh words about such conduct (vv 21-22; cf. Luke 22:25-27).

---

[49]Note the following terms and phrases which are absent in Mark and Matthew: εὐχαριστήσας; τὸ ὑπὲρ ὑμῶν (ὑπέρ does appear in Mark 14:24); τοῦτο ποιεῖτε εἰς τὴν ἐμὴν ἀνάμνησιν; μετὰ τὸ δειπνῆσαι; and καινή with ἡ διαθήκη.

[50]This is not to suggest that there are no differences of perspective or even substance between the Paul of Luke and the Paul of his letters (Vielhauer ["Paulinism"] discusses such issues). For a recent defense of of the view that the author of Luke-Acts was a companion of Paul, see Goulder (*Luke*, 1:129-46).

[51]The juxtaposition of 2:11-14 with 2:15-21 may then imply that the practice of exclusivism at table amounted to an attempt to be justified by works (v 16). Cf. Mussner (95-6), who maintains, "Das συνεσθίειν hängt also mit der Rechtfertigung zusammen!".

In 11:23b-25 Paul presents the proper practice for observing the Lord's Supper (cf. Luke 22:19-20) as it was "received from the Lord" (11:23a). This account is followed by an ominous warning of danger accompanying that meal: one who eats or drinks "in an unworthy manner will be guilty of [profaning (so RSV)] the body and blood of the Lord" (11:27), an action that brings judgment upon oneself (v 28). Here again, then, inappropriate table conduct brings a firm rebuke (cf. Luke 22:25-27), and an implication is that weighty theological freight is symbolically associated with the Lord's Supper.

Third, in both Rom 14:1-15:6 and 1 Cor 8:1-13; 10:14-11:1, Paul comments on how to relate to "the weak" at table.[52] In both letters Paul concedes that there is no *inherent* quality of foods which would make some of them unacceptable (Rom 14:14; 1 Cor 8:4). Nonetheless, because there is a profound symbolism associated with what one eats, Paul urges the more liberal in his congregations to err on the side of caution, i.e., abstinence. Diners ought not elevate their own self-interest (cf. Luke 22:24) so as to damage their table companions. Indeed, at stake in clashes of strong and weak is the risk of "injuring," "ruining" and "destroying" (Rom 14:13, 15, 20; 1 Cor 8:11) the weaker Christian. Thus there is a vulnerability which accompanies table fellowship (cf. the Lukan motif involving the disclosure of one's thoughts at table [sec. 3.5.1 below]), and Paul would protect those most susceptible to harm. By so doing he follows the loving, serving model of Christ (15:3; cf. Luke 22:27).

With each of these Pauline table topics, then, meal settings or food symbolize profound theological or spiritual realities. On the physical level, food is food (e.g., Rom 14:14), but there is so much more than the literal in Paul's use of table motifs: Jew-Gentile table fellowship symbolizes both a break from bondage to law and a mission which embraces all people; the Lord's Supper symbolically involves a "fellowship" with the risen Christ and an attendant unity among the members of Christ's body; consideration of conscience recognizes a strong symbolic value of foods that can even lead to the demise of a weak person's faith.[53] Further, it

[52]To be sure, one must compare these texts cautiously, for the version in Romans does not mention ὁ εἰδωλόθυτος (cf. 1 Cor 8:1) (so Ziesler [322], though he opts for the view that idol worship is behind the Romans passage as well [326]). Nevertheless, similar elements of Paul's table theology and table ethics arise in these two contexts.

[53]Cf. Lohmeyer (79-82) on the early Christian communal meal as both metaphor and reality.

seems that in each case the pursuit of or excessive attention to self-interest clashes with the profound symbolic dimensions of table experience and merits harsh rebukes (cf. Luke 22:24-27).

3.5 Lukan Table Motifs[54]

By overviewing table motifs in Luke-Acts we continue a progression through concentric circles of context and move nearer to the target text. Minear observes that "Luke is especially fond of arranging strategic conversations about the table."[55] Indeed, Jesus appears in several meal scenes in the Lukan narrative, he describes meals in his teaching,[56] and numerous images of eating and drinking appear in the Lukan writings.[57] Particularly noteworthy is the measure by which the motif in Luke's Gospel extends beyond traditional material in Mark and as reflected in Matthew. According to Neyrey, thirteen of the nineteen references to meals in Luke are unique in the Gospels.[58] It is even maintained that the motif expresses Luke's central theological themes.[59] Keeping 22:24-30 in mind, then, we may survey the major contours of this Lukan motif.

---

[54]Works which focus on or address this subject include: Aune, "Septem"; Barth, 142-72; Bösen; Davis; Delobel; Dumm, 231-4; Esler, 71-109; Flender, 80-4; Guillaume; Karris, "Soteriology" and "Food"; Leonard; Mánek, "Umwandlung"; Marshall, *Historian*, 138-9; de Meeûs; Minear, "Glimpses"; Moxnes, "Meals"; Navone, *Themes*, 22-37; Neyrey, 8-11; Smith; Steele; Tyson, "Food."

[55]Minear, "Note," 128; cf. Feldkämper, 207. Karris ("Food," 47) goes too far by saying, "... the aroma of food issues forth from every chapter of Luke's Gospel." "Most," perhaps, but not "every."

[56]In narrative (texts unique to Luke's Gospel in italics): Luke 5:27-32; 7:36-50; 9:10-17; *10:38-42*; *11:37-54*; *14:1-24*; 22:14-38; *24:28-35, 41-43*; Acts 1:4. In Jesus' teaching: Luke *12:35-38*; *13:29-30*; *15:22-24*.

[57]See e.g., Luke *1:15, 53*; *2:7, 12, 16, 37*; *3:11*; 4:1-4, *25*, 39; 5:33-39; 6:1-5, *21, 25*; 7:31-35; 8:11; 10:2, 7-8; 11:3, *5-8*, 9-13; 12:1, *13-21*, 22-34, 41-48; *13:6-9*, 20-21; *15:1-2*; *16:19-31*; *17:7-10*; *18:12*; 20:46 (texts unique to Luke's Gospel in italics). In Acts: 2:42, 46; 6:1-6, 7:11; 9:9, 19; 10:1-11:18; 14:17; 15:20, 29; 16:34; 20:7, 11; 23:12, 21; 27:31-38. Karris ("Food," 50) claims that "Luke uses a minimum of forty-five different words to refer to the theme of food,..." including many that are unique to Luke in the NT.

[58]Neyrey, 8.

[59]E.g., Minear, "Glimpses," 325; cf. Smith, 638.

3.5.1 Material in the Gospel

One of the most prominent building blocks of Luke's table motif, that of Jesus practicing or promoting table fellowship with "sinners," is attested to by a number of texts.[60] "Sinners" here signifies a variety of types including tax collectors, prostitutes and other outcasts. The depiction of Jesus at table with sinners is not merely passed on by Luke from gospel traditions; at points it is added to the traditions (e.g., 7:39; 15:1-2).[61] The references in the Last Supper discourse to the betrayal and denial of Jesus (22:23, 34) and the apostles' quarrel (v 24) may suggest that there are significant connections between the theme of table fellowship with sinners and the text before us.[62]

Jesus' unconventional table fellowship is roundly condemned by the Pharisees and scribes (5:30; 15:1-2) and "this generation" (7:34), for it threatens their definition of legitimate table boundaries.[63] As noted above (sec. 3.3), in Judaism sharing a meal is an expression of mutual acceptance and solidarity, so it is no surprise that Jesus' eating habits cause such alarm (cf. the scenario in Gal 2:11-14). Jesus' defiance of Jewish custom, however, does not amount to a rejection of the principle that sharing a meal means sharing community. Rather, his break with convention is a statement about the boundaries or size of that community. The Lukan Jesus calls into question the supposition that the people of God excludes sinners.[64]

---

[60]See 5:27-32; 7:34, 36-50; 14:12-24; 15:1-2. Many (e.g., Barth, 156, 170; Bösen, 32; Delobel, 460; Dumm, 232; Guillaume, 140-1; Karris, "Food," 66; Koenig, 88, 115; Leonard, 127-30; Moessner, 222; Moxnes, "Meals," 162; Navone, *Themes*, 29) include 19:1-10 as well, but this distorts the sense of μένω (v 5), ὑποδέχομαι (v 6) and καταλύω (v 7), and it forces the table into Luke's text. On the theme of Jesus at table with sinners, see e.g., Flender, 81; Guillaume, 140-1; Hofius; Karris, "Soteriology," 347-8, "Food," 57-64; Marshall, *Historian*, 138; Minear, "Glimpses," 322-31; Moxnes, "Meals," 160-1; Mussner, 96; Neyrey, 8-9.

[61]Jesus' injunction to dine with the poor, blind, maimed and lame (14:13) reveals a similar overturning of conventional table boundaries; the principle of reciprocity is not to govern hospitality.

[62]Minear ("Glimpses," 327-8; see esp. v 37) and Karris ("Food," 69-70) align 22:14-38 with the Lukan motif of table fellowship with sinners.

[63]Moxnes, "Meals," 161; cf. de Meeûs, 849; Parkin, 251. Trautmann (398-9) maintains that Jesus' meal fellowship with tax collectors and sinners has "keine Analogien in den Handlungen der atl und frühjüdischen Profeten."

[64]Trautmann (162-3) argues cogently that the Lukan Jesus sees all people as

What then does Jesus do for sinners whom he welcomes to his table? While the sinful woman who anointed Jesus (7:36-50) is not properly a table companion, in her contact with Jesus at table it is made explicit that she is "saved,"[65] though nothing similar is said of the Pharisee host. More broadly speaking, it is arguable that the Lukan Jesus' act of eating with sinners constitutes a call to conversion and an offer of salvation;[66] his acceptance of extraordinary sinners demonstrates God's extraordinary love and forgiveness for them.[67] In this way the table becomes a place of celebration and is characterized by joy.[68]

It is in order to temper the claims of some who see salvation for *all* in the image of Jesus at table with sinners. To be sure, Jesus' departure from the narrow limits of the strict Judaism attributed to the Pharisees and scribes is extensive, and it does portray a regard for all kinds of sinful people. But many[69] fail to see the implied limits of Jesus' welcome to his table (13:26-27; 14:24; 22:22). Minear rightly notes that "such meals are no insurance against final rejection."[70]

How is it, then, that table fellowship with Jesus brings salvation for some but not for others? Mussner observes, "In Lk 15,1 wird bermerkt,

---

sinners. This, however, does not take away the striking aspect of Jesus' table fellowship with the despised and socially rejected who came to be called "sinners."

[65]To be sure, her faith is instrumental (ἡ πίστις σου σέσωκέν σε) and not solely the fact of having encountered Jesus at table.

[66]Guillaume, 157; Trautmann, 162. Luke is not without a soteriology; it involves the "with-ness" of Jesus and sinners at table (Karris, "Soteriology," 346-8; cf. Parkin, 253). Guillaume (145, n. 5) sees bread, wine and water in biblical and rabbinic sources often as metaphors for the nourishment of God-given spiritual life.

[67]Trautmann, 163; cf. Flender, 81; Guillaume, 140-4, 149, 156-7; I. H. Marshall, *Historian*, 138. Stated negatively, to decline to dine with Jesus is to refuse the fellowship of Jesus himself (Mánek, "Umwandlung," 65; cf. Barth, 158).

[68]Barth (146-7, 166-9) develops the idea of the Lukan table as a setting for joy (cf. Cousar, 62; Koenig, 114-19; Minear, "Glimpses," 329; Navone, *Themes*, 24; Smith, 626).

[69]E.g., Karris, "Food," 58-9, "Soteriology," 346-8; Neyrey, 8-9. Note that Matthew makes no mention of eating or drinking in 7:22-23 par. Luke 13:26-27. Barth rightly argues that Luke does not portray all table fellowship as positive (148-9).

[70]Minear, "Glimpses," 326; cf. Barth, 156. Moxnes is aware of the problem 13:26 presents to a fully inclusive view of salvation in Luke, but he skirts the issue nonetheless ("Meals," 162-3). Also, the obdurate Pharisees and scribes themselves are often overlooked (e.g., again Karris, "Food," 58-9, "Soteriology," 346-8; Neyrey, 8-9); does an inclusive salvation portrayed at table include even these who oppose the inclusiveness of salvation? Minear ("Glimpses," 324) argues that the Pharisees in the Lukan table scenes are themselves depicted as sinners, though they are blind to their sins.

daß »alle Zöllner und Sünder« sich Jesus nahten, ἀκούειν αὐτοῦ, das heißt sie kommen nicht »irgendwie« interessiert zu ihm, sondern heilsbegierig."[71] Koenig similarly highlights the necessity of a readiness to repent on the part of Jesus' table companions,[72] a claim supported by the unparalleled εἰς μετάνοιαν in 5:32. Receptivity to Jesus and his message is thus a crucial element in Luke's table soteriology.

Proper table attitudes are clarified further in Luke's unparalleled instructions to banquet guests in 14:7-11: one should abandon the widespread convention of seeking the highest position at table and choose the lowest seat (cf. 20:46),[73] for the way of humility leads to a greater elevation (i.e., by God) (14:11; cf. the reversal structure of 22:24-30 [see sec. 4.1]).[74] Thus the thrust of 14:7-10 seems to be against self-exaltation, not the basic hope for elevation or reward (cf. sec. 8.4). If self-exaltation is the problem in view in 22:24, then the pattern in 14:7-11 may provide an important perspective for understanding 22:24-30.[75]

The Lukan table is frequently the setting for controversy and conflict, a circumstance which Jesus often seizes as an opportunity for teaching:[76] Simon the Pharisee's dismay at Jesus' toleration of the sinful woman's conduct (7:39) becomes the occasion for teaching on sin and forgiveness (vv 40-50). Martha's complaint about Mary's failure to help with serving (10:40)[77] leads to a lesson on choosing what is most needful (vv 41-42). A Pharisee's astonishment at Jesus' failure to wash before dinner (11:38) occasions teaching on internal cleanliness (vv 40-41) and

---

[71]Mussner, 99.

[72]Koenig, 91, 114-19; cf. Navone, "Banquet," 158-9. Mussner remarks, "Denn Jesu συνεσθίειν ist nicht wegzudenken von seiner μετάνοια-Forderung" (99).

[73]Moxnes, "Meals," 163; Schürmann, *Ursprung*, 138. A keen consciousness of rank at table and the function of seating patterns which reflect a diner's status were noted above in the discussions of the Hellenistic symposium and Jewish table traditions (secs. 3.2 and 3.3).

[74]It is probable that 14:10 does not commend the worldly wisdom of taking the low seat at banquets precisely so that one can be seen being ushered to a higher seat. The point of the parable rather seems to involve humble living now in anticipation of final elevation by God (so the divine passive in v 11).

[75]I.e., lower yourself to serve and you will be brought up (cf. chs. 4 and 8).

[76]Ford, 115-16; cf. Borg, 82.

[77]Guillaume (142) observes, "Bien qu'en ce passage il n'y ait pas mention explicite du repas, les termes διακονία et διακονεῖν (v 40) indiquent, à n'en pas douter, un service de table." Cf. 12:37; 17:8; 22:26-7; Acts 6:2 for the dominant Lukan meaning of διακονέω as involving a table context. See also Hoffmann and Eid, 198.

other features of true piety (vv 42-54). Jesus' healing on the sabbath of a man with dropsy (14:3-4) and his defense of the act to the silently disapproving Pharisees (vv 1, 4, 5-6) leads into a series of illustrations implicitly critical of attitudes and actions ascribed to the Pharisees (vv 7-24). In 22:25-27 Jesus again confronts his table companions (this time the quarreling apostles) with corrective teaching.[78]

A close look at the content of Jesus' table teaching exposes a pattern of self-revelation.[79] At Levi's feast Jesus discloses the purpose of his "coming," namely to call not the righteous but sinners to repentance (5:32; cf. 19:10). At the home of Simon the Pharisee Jesus reveals that he has authority to forgive sins and confirm a person's salvation (7:47-50).[80] Jesus' clashes with the Pharisees in 11:37-54, and 14:1-24 further reveal his identity as one who claims authority over the law, or strict interpretations of it. The Last Supper of course offers profound christological revelation: Jesus is one who can give his body and blood *on behalf of* (ὑπέρ) his disciples (22:19-20)—his death is, in some sense, beneficial to his people.[81] Further, descriptions of Jesus as "servant" and "king" (22:27, 30) would seem to have christological significance (cf. chs. 6 and 7). Jesus' teaching in 24:25-27 precedes the table scene with Cleopas and the other disciple (vv 28-31), but when "their eyes were opened and they recognized him" (v 31) it was his teaching they recalled (v 32). This Lord's Supper[82] thus triggers the revelation and knowledge of Jesus.[83]

[78]An effect of the Luke's repeated linkage of table scenes with Jesus' instruction is that teaching may be thought of as a sort of food. As human life is impossible without food, so life as a child of God is impossible without wisdom (Navone, "Banquet," 157). Instruction and food can be interchangeable symbols, for both offer forms of vital nourishment, commodities which would have special value on the eve of Jesus' passion and in anticipation of an era of conflict (22:36) (so Neyrey, 11; Senior, 55).

[79]So e.g., Barth, 163; Leonard, 133-5; Navone, *Themes*, 27-30, and "Banquet," 158. The term "revelation" here is used not concerning simply any disclosure of information about Jesus, but more specifically concerning the disclosure of distinctive aspects of Jesus' identity.

[80]It has already been disclosed in 5:17-26 that Jesus forgives sins, but the motif is emphatic in 7:47-50 (cf. Mark 14:9).

[81]Hoffmann and Eid (198) note that a commitment to the welfare of another was an important aspect of what it meant in the first century to be a διάκονος.

[82]That the meal at Emmaus is to be understood as the Lord's Supper seems apparent from the echo of verbs in 24:30 (took bread, blessed, broke, gave) and 22:19 (took bread, gave thanks, broke, gave; cf. 9:16); see Guillaume, 143. Note also the possible eucharistic references in Acts 2:42, 46; 20:7, 11; 27:31-38. See further sec. 3.5.2 below.

The feeding of the five thousand (9:10-17) also illumines Jesus' identity: he is one with an exceptional ability to care for the masses. The unique Lukan sandwiching of the feeding story between Herod's question, "Who is this about whom I hear such things?" (v 9), and Peter's confession (vv 18-20), however, gives it a sharp Christological focus.[84] The Lukan portrayal of Jesus as Messiah is inextricably linked to Jesus' practice of nourishing those who come to him (cf. Ezek 34:11-16, 23-24). Moreover, the eucharistic vocabulary in 9:16[85] may imply that Jesus *himself* is nourishment for the people (cf. John 6:35). In fact, three times it is mentioned that the one who would reign forever as king over the house of Jacob (1:32-33) actually occupies a feeding trough (2:7, 12, 16).[86]

Minear correctly observes that revelation at Jesus' table functions not only to disclose the identity of Jesus but also to expose the secrets of his table companions' hearts.[87] This is true especially in connection with table conflict: Simon the Pharisee is portrayed as ungrateful for forgiveness (7:36-50), Martha is preoccupied with unimportant things (10:38-42), the Pharisees are characterized as shallow and corrupt (11:37-54) and self-centered (14:7-24). It may also be noted that it is at table that Jesus uncovers those who were about to betray (22:21-23) and deny (22:33-34) him (and cf. v 24). The truth comes out at table; meal companions cannot conceal sin from Jesus.

When turning to the Last Supper, it is necessary to keep the broader Lukan meal motif in view. Verbal connections of 22:19-20 with other

---

[83]So Smith, 629; cf. Barth, 151.

[84]Nolland, *Luke*, 448. Cf. 8:25, "Who then is this, ..." The question of Jesus' identity is a primary concern in 8:22-9:20 (ibid., 399, 430-1). Flender (81) detects a christological aspect in the hospitality motif in Luke.

[85]Guillaume,143 (note the verbs: took, blessed, broke, gave). Cf. above, n.82.

[86]Fitzmyer (*Gospel*, 1:408) notes that, whether in an enclosure or under the open sky, a φάτνη would have been a feeding place of some kind (similarly Ellis, *Gospel*, 79; Leaney, *Gospel*, 93; I. H. Marshall, *Gospel*, 106; Nolland, *Luke*, 105; so MM, 665). The association of φάτνη with drinking in Luke 13:15 implies a similar idea. On Jesus in the manger as a symbol of sustenance, see R. Brown, *Birth*, 420; Grassi, 104; Karris, "Food," 49. Although one may claim that Luke's references to the manger originally made a point about identifying the baby, it could be argued that this would be inadequate for such a purpose since there surely would have been more than one manger in Bethlehem. Further, how many newborns could there have been on a given night in Bethlehem? The more probable understanding is that the manger has mostly symbolic significance, perhaps to highlight Jesus' humble "origins" as well as his role of nourishing the people of God.

[87]Minear, "Glimpses," 330; cf. Barth, 165.

Lukan meals (9:10-17; 24:28-35; Acts 2:42, 46; 20:7, 11; 27:31-38) clearly show that the Last Supper is related to a larger whole. When we see the Last Supper in the light of the wider meal motif,[88] it is prevented from being thought of as an isolated cultic ceremony. Instead, it is seen as providing a footing for a Lord's Supper that is saturated with ethical and spiritual implications for Christian living.[89]

Bösen makes a related point when he identifies the Lord's Supper as being in a sequence of Lukan suppers that bridge the ages and portray the progressive fulfillment of salvation.[90] Bösen summarizes:[91]

> So wird das eucharistische Mahl für Lk zum verbindenden Symbol:
> - Es verbindet nach rückwärts mit der "Jesuszeit", für die Jesu heilwirkende Mahlgemeinschaften charakteristisch waren.
> - In ihm realisiert sich endzeitliches Heil für die "Zwischenzeit".
> - Es weist erinnernd nach vorne auf die "Endzeit" hin, die mit dem Endzeitmahl die Erfüllung des Heiles bringen wird.

Thus with the meal symbol Luke creates an important soteriological continuity: salvation is given to God's people progressively in connection with meals that mark the stages of history.[92] One may detect here a reflection of the function of the Passover as a meal which both recalls and anticipates the Lord's saving actions.[93]

The expectation of an eschatological banquet surfaces in a number of Lukan texts in addition to those which may be found in the Last Supper context (6:21; 12:37; 13:29; 14:15; cf. 22:16, 18, 30).[94] In 12:37 it is made clear that the meal following the return of the Son of man (v 40) will bring the return of table fellowship with Jesus (cf. 22:30).[95] Further,

[88]Guillaume (158) and Minear ("Glimpses," 330-1) emphasize the need to do so.

[89]Schürmann, *Ursprung*, 149.

[90]Bösen, 75-7. See Guillaume (140-159) for a similar depiction (cf. Bovon, *Thirty-three years*, 381 [discussing the work of Davis]; Patsch, 141).

[91]Bösen, 76.

[92]Bösen (76-7) adds, "Jesu Erscheinen war also nicht nur einem Kometen gleich, hell and leuchtend bei seinem Aufgehen and jäh verblassend am Kreuz, sondern sein Leuchten hält an bis zum Ende der Zeit."

[93]Some maintain that the Lukan Last Supper appears to constitute something of a table motif convergence point in Luke-Acts (so Barth, 142-3; Karris, "Food," 66; Smith, 628, 630; cf. Moessner, 178). This may be conceded, but it is difficult to demonstrate that it is a more important convergence point than, say, Luke 12 or 14.

[94]Cousar, 60. This is emphatic in contrast to Mark's and Matthew's portrayals (Barth, 142). See sec. 7.4.4 on the time frame for the meal in v 30a.

[95]This is not to minimize the "fellowship" element in the Lord's Supper.

Jesus will serve his servants (12:37; cf. 22:27) at this eschatological feast. The fact that the eschatological banquet receives a special emphasis in Luke may be important for determining the "timing of conferral" in 22:29-30 (cf. sec. 7.4.4).[96]

3.5.2 Material in Acts

Luke's table motif continues in Acts, but it is less prominent than in the Gospel.[97] The change is probably due in large part to Jesus' departure from the narrative scene in Acts 1:9, and no figure is presented to take Jesus' place. To be sure, the apostles provide a bridge from Jesus to the church (cf. sec. 2.5.1) and observe community meals (2:42, 46; 6:1-2; cf. 20:7, 11), but none of them adopts the role of table teacher, dispenser of forgiveness, etc. The role of table master belonged to Jesus, and it would not be passed on.[98]

In Acts the eschatological banquet disappears from view (cf. Luke 6:21; 12:37; 13:29; 14:15; 22:16, 18, 30)[99] while the eucharistic meal remains (see Acts 2:42, 46; 20:7, 11; 27:31-38).[100] That salvation is associated

[96]It may be observed that the table motif in Luke has a certain very practical dimension. The many references to the poor and hungry in Luke (e.g., 1:52-53; 3:11; 6:21; 14:13, 21; 16:19-31), though they are not without figurative significance (see e.g., L. Johnson, *Possessions*), reveal a concern for sharing with those in need (Moxnes, "Meals," 164-5). The Lukan table is not only for teaching and revelation and salvation, etc.; it is also for eating. The increased attention to this issue in Luke as opposed to Mark and Matthew suggests a high priority of the evangelist.

One additional feature of the Lukan table motif may be noted, namely the prominence of the "eat and drink" formula (Luke uses πίνω twenty times, and only three times is it not paired with ἐσθίω). It is sometimes a redactional element (e.g., 5:30, 33; 10:7; 17:28), and is more frequent in Luke than in the other Gospels. Cf. Bösen, 136; Guillaume, 145, n. 5.

[97]Roughly speaking there are only about one fourth as many table motif texts in Acts as there are in Luke's Gospel. Dawsey ("Unity," 53) maintains that there is an avoidance of table language in Acts.

[98]Cf. Barth, 168. The shift in Acts may prompt one to suppose that Luke was heavily indebted to the Jesus tradition for the table motif in his Gospel. As observed above (see nn. 56 and 57, however, a great number of the table texts in Luke are without parallel in Mark or Matthew. It is quite probable that Luke himself sees this motif as being central to the message of his Gospel.

[99]A possible reason for this could be that predictions or descriptions of the eschatological banquet were thought to be exclusively in Jesus' domain; the meal was still in view, but only a prophet like Jesus could speak authoritatively on such future exigencies. Cf. sec. 7.4.4 on the time frame for 22:29-30.

[100]In 2:42, 46 the characteristic term from meals in Luke 9, 22 and 24 (κλάω /

with the Lord's Supper seems likely from the "saving" encounters in the immediate literary contexts of 20:7, 11 and 27:35.[101] Nevertheless, the prominence of the theme of salvation in meal contexts is significantly less than in Luke's Gospel.

In Acts 6:2 διακονέω (cf. Luke 22:26-27) has the narrow sense, "to serve tables." Such duties are depicted as drawing the apostles away from the work of "preaching the word of God" (v 3), so a new band of people is appointed to the task of table service (vv 3-6). That such duties are vitally important not only for practical reasons but also for their religious significance is suggested by the need for servants who are reputable, wise (v 3) and "full of faith and the Holy Spirit" (v 5). Our assessment of Jesus' "service" in Luke 22:27 may be informed by the sidelight of Acts 6:1-6.

In Acts the motif of table fellowship with sinners takes a new form in which the issue of Jew-Gentile table fellowship comes to the fore.[102] The opposition toward such union constitutes the chief objection of the circumcision party in the Jerusalem church to Peter's visit in the home of Cornelius (11:3; cf. Gal 2:11-14). Again the Jewish perspective is described as limiting the boundaries of table fellowship, but God himself prompts Peter and the Christian community in the other direction (11:17). The Gospel principle of a table open to all outsiders carries through in Acts;[103] indeed, it is probable that Jesus' meals with "sinners" find a logical extension in the table fellowship of Jewish and Gentile Christians accompanying the expansion of the early church. The absence of Jesus from the narrative scene, however, may suggest that inclusive table

---

κλάσις) reappears; an echo of the Last Supper and first Lord's Supper (Luke 24:30) seems apparent. Acts 20:7, 11 is similar, and 27:35 reproduces three of the four verbs in Luke 22:19 (took bread, gave thanks, broke).

[101]I.e., the raising of Eutychus from the dead (20:10), and the predictions of the sailors being saved (σωθῆναι) and not perishing (ἀπολεῖται).

[102]On this issue see Esler, 71-109. Esler contends that the legitimating of Jew/ Gentile table fellowship is at the center of Luke's effort to legitimate the sectarian separation of the believing community from Judaism (72, 96-7). This view, however, depends on a prior conclusion that Luke does intend to portray the church as fundamentally separate from Israel, a view that is dubious (see sec. 7.4.3). Esler further speculates that with the table fellowship theme in Acts Luke would affirm Jewish and Gentile Christians in his community who were being criticized for eating together (105), but one may equally suppose that Luke wished to correct these parties for refusing to eat together.

[103]See also the hospitality/ meal scenes in Acts 16:15, 34; 18:7.

fellowship in Acts has greater ecclesiological or ethical than soteriological significance.

In summary of the Lukan table motif in the Gospel and Acts two points may be made: 1) The motif is complex[104] and cannot be reduced to a single point or idea. 2) There are, however, recurring table subthemes that together form an integrated motif: Jesus defies custom and dines with sinners thereby signifying the acceptance and salvation of those who are receptive to him. Although Jesus favors an unrestricted guest list and dines with "sinners" as well as upright figures, it seems to be mostly social outcasts who are receptive to his salvation. Inclusive table fellowship in Acts involves a general shift of focus from soteriological to ecclesiological or ethical concerns. The Lukan Jesus also undercuts the impulse to exploit the table as a stage for pride and ambition. The table is often a scene of conflict within which Jesus finds opportunities for teaching. His words and actions give crucial insights into his identity, and they also reveal the sinful secrets in people's hearts. Meals in Luke-Acts serve as a vital backdrop for the Last Supper and the Lord's Supper: eucharistic meals recall the many vivid and practical features of Jesus' suppers, and anticipate a great messianic banquet. In this way the Lukan meal motif provides a salvation-historical perspective.

3.6 Conclusion

In summary, it may be noted that in many Jewish, Pauline and Lukan backgrounds, table scenes and food language are highly symbolic; they are riddled with associations which extend beyond physical realities. The fact that Jesus' practice of dining with "sinners" was so upsetting to his opponents also reveals just such a symbolic aspect of table fellowship. When focusing on 22:24-30, then, it will be important to recall that table motifs potentially go beyond what "meets the eye."

A familiarity with table traditions also reminds the interpreter of the social character of the meal setting. Table practices and teachings routinely involve or address groups, not isolated individuals. This is not to minimize the value of Jesus' table teaching for the individual, but only

[104]This fact is evidenced by the various ways in which interpreters have sought to outline the Lukan table texts (see e.g., Barth, 147-72; Bösen, 76-7; Karris, "Food," 48; Guillaume, 140-57; Neyrey, 8-11; Smith, 616-7, 638).

to emphasize the fact that the table context itself puts a certain focus on community life and experience.[105]

Although the discourse in Luke 22:14-38 was not, in all likelihood, fashioned throughout on the model of the Hellenistic symposium (sec. 3.2), the prevalent symposium tradition gives Luke's table talk a general aura of appropriateness—teaching (e.g., 22:25-30) is fitting at meals. The symposium backdrop also cultivates a reader's expectation of controversy and conflict at table (e.g., 22:24),[106] and of resolution through decisive words of wisdom from the chief guest (cf. Jesus' teaching and example in vv 25-27). To be sure, one could make similar points on the basis of Jewish or Lukan contexts. Further, these general observations leave one far from the point of being able adequately to discern the meaning of 22:24-30. Nevertheless, the existence of the symposium tradition does cause aspects of our text to be seen in a particular light.

More may be said on the basis of Jewish banquet and meal traditions. The nature of the Passover as a feast that looks back and ahead, that recalls and anticipates God's deliverance of his people associated with the shedding of blood, may prepare the reader to see similar dimensions in 22:24-30 (cf. chs. 6 and 7). The prominent Jewish expectation of a messianic banquet marking the age of Israel's final and ultimate restoration may also reinforce this historiographical conception.

Additionally, an awareness of the importance in Judaism of friendship and unity shared by those at table, and of the horror associated with the violation of such ties, may shed some light on the gravity of the breaches of table fellowship in Luke 22. Surely vv 21-23 and 33-34 stand out in this respect, but the quarrel of the apostles in v 24 may also be a serious threat to table solidarity (cf. sec. 6.4).

Paul's letters provide a perspective on Luke 22:24-30 which would heighten the interpreter's awareness of table symbolism. In particular, Paul emphasizes the great importance of fellowship involving unbroken and ongoing union among table companions and with the Lord (contrast 22:24). Self-centered pursuits, however, clash with this ideal. The table is an arena in which the love of Christians for one another—regardless of race, lifestyle, etc.—is to be displayed. In so doing diners follow the example of their serving Master (Rom 15:3; cf. Luke 22:27).

---

[105]See Flender (81-2) on table and the community context (cf. Mánek, "Umwandlung," 65).

[106]A preoccupation with table rank is a common feature of symposia (cf. n. 12 above).

Turning to material in Luke-Acts, the prominence of the theme of Jesus at table with "sinners" may be noted first. Luke emphasizes Jesus' challenge to the limits of conventional hospitality, and it is not surprising that those who represent a stricter tradition disapprove (e.g., 5:30; 15:1-2). Even the Last Supper may be connected with this theme; table talk highlights the sins of the betrayer and Peter (22:23, 34), but the quarrel of the apostles (v 24) should be noted too (see sec. 6.5.3).[107] In Acts the theme extends to Jew-Gentile table fellowship (e.g., Peter and Cornelius). The inclusive table has symbolic importance: in the Gospel meal fellowship with Jesus is symbolic of salvation for those who are receptive to his teaching; in Acts it represents ethical and ecclesiological priorities for the church with its mission to all peoples.

The Lukan Jesus resists table conventions which emphasize the relative honor of diners. Instead, his banquet etiquette commends the rejection of self-important attitudes and the selection of the lowest seat (14:7-10), for only the humble will ultimately be exalted by God (v 11) (cf. the reversal structure of 22:24-30 [see chs. 4 and 8]). Also, a concern for one's superiority over table companions is at odds with the important Lukan priority on table unity and solidarity.

On a number of occasions Jesus turns table conflict or controversy into opportunities for teaching (e.g., 7:39; 11:38; 15:1-2). The event-response sequence of 22:24-27 may be aligned with this theme. Jesus' table teaching often reveals important information as to his identity and mission (e.g., 5:32; 7:47-50; 9:9-17; 24:31-32), a feature which is also present in the Last Supper Narrative (22:19-20). Indeed, Jesus' messianic identity is closely tied to his role as one who cares for and nourishes the masses who receive his teaching (9:9-20). A special interest in table revelation may help account for Jesus' self-description in the text before us as "servant" (22:27) and (implicitly) as king (vv 29-30). Revelation at table, however, works two ways; meals are also a scene for the disclosure of the sinful secrets in the hearts of Jesus' companions (consider v 24).

The Last Supper takes its place in the larger Lukan table motif—it is not an isolated event. Among other features, it has a backward- and forward-looking orientation; it recalls its Passover and Lukan roots, and anticipates eschatological fulfillment. Correspondingly, the Lord's Sup-

[107]In 22:37, however, the Lukan Jesus looks ahead to contact with "transgressors" other than the Twelve (the statement of what must happen is in the context of prophecy [v 36]), i.e., probably the two thieves crucified beside him.

per provides a way for saving solidarity with Jesus in the center time between the meals shared during his life and public ministry, and the reunion at his messianic table of final salvation. The temporal perspectives of 22:24-30 and the importance there of union with Jesus (cf. chs. 6, 7 and 9) take on a certain emphasis when seen against this backdrop.

Chapter 4: Reversal Motifs

4.1 Introduction

The present chapter introduces a shift of the perspective in Part One. Whereas the preceding chapters have grown out of the content of Luke 22:24-30, here we concentrate on backgrounds with similarities to the form of the passage (see also ch. 5).[1] After a brief examination of reversal in 22:24-30, the present chapter is concerned to explore reversal motifs in classical (sec. 4.2), Jewish (4.3) and NT (4.4) literature—especially the Lukan corpus (4.5)—so as to establish a reader expectation grid which will allow our text to be seen in a particular light. Section 4.6 will briefly draw attention to the main features of that grid and its potential importance for the direct analysis of the text in Part Two.

Luke 22:24-30 exhibits the following complex reversal pattern: the apostles want to be great but Jesus tells them to serve; they have continued in his trials and Jesus promises them exaltation.[2] Thus we observe a full-circle progression from lofty ambitions to lowly roles and back to a final elevation.[3]

This reversal may be specified further by noting that both admonition and promise are involved.[4] Jesus admonishes the Twelve to make

[1]The content of the text, however, remains in view, for verbal or conceptual features of the text serve at points to narrow the field of reversals which are considered.

[2]Regarding features of 22:24-30 which invite an analysis of that text as constituting a unified literary piece, see sec. 1.1 (verbal, conceptual and structural factors) and sec. 8.2 (esp. logical and thematic factors).

[3]Many Lukan reversals share a similar unifying progression (see sec. 4.5).

a downturn from their interest in greatness and adopt the status of servants (vv 24-27), but he also promises them an upturn involving future exaltation to seats of honor and authority (vv 28-30). This gives a particular twist to the issue of agency, for the downward motion is motivated by a "push" against the demonstrated disposition of the apostles, but the upward one involves a "pull" toward a distinctly desirable goal. In any case, throughout 22:24-30 it is not merely that the apostles themselves follow a reversal course, but that Jesus urges and then draws them along one.

This reversal may be further described in terms of the degree of movement. The combined downward and upward motions in vv 24-30 constitute a course from high to low to high ("360 degrees"), from power and prestige (i.e., the prizing of greatness) to humble subordination and perseverance in trial to final positions of honor and authority. This may be contrasted with many Lukan (and other) reversals of 180 degrees.[5] Although Luke 22:24-27 alone would amount to a 180-degree downward reversal from the preoccupation with greatness to the adoption of serving roles, and 22:28-30 alone would amount to a 180-degree reversal in an upward direction,[6] when vv 24-27 and 28-30 are taken together we see a 360-degree high-low-high progression.[7]

By way of clarification, however, the text does not follow a perfectly neat circular motion. Although both the starting and ending positions for the apostles are lofty, the former is a negative ambition or preoccupation while the second is a positive actual assignment to prestigious authority positions.[8] Further, the seam between the two 180-degree units is not as smooth as it could be: servanthood links with perseverance in trials, and urged behavior is aligned with already approved conduct.

---

[4]Cf. G. Schneider, *Evangelium*, 2:451.

[5]E.g., Luke 12:13-21; 16:15 (cf. n. 56 below). York's "bi-polar" reversal involves two 180-degree movements in opposite directions (see further sec. 4.5 below on York's significant contributions to the study of reversal in Luke).

[6]The endurance of trials (v 28) may itself seem to connote a downward progression, but within vv 28-30 we are not told of any "higher" starting point than this sharing of adversities with Jesus.

[7]Certain other reversals have the appearance of taking a 360-degree course, but consist in fact of twin 180-degree reversals experienced by two distinct parties moving in opposite directions (e.g., Luke 1:52-53; 6:20-26; 16:19-31).

[8]York (42) similarly clarifies that some bi-polar "opposites" in Luke may better be described as "contraries" since their elements are not exact opposites (e.g., rich and hungry in 1:53).

To be sure, the various arguments for the unitary conception of 22:24-30 (cf. secs. 1.1 and 8.2) as well as other factors (see sec. 7.3.1) bring the service urged and the commended perseverance very close together, but there remains a measure of imprecision in the 360-degree reversal description. Nonetheless, it is demonstrable that, in terms of the general flow of the narrative, 22:24-30 follows a high-low-high course.

The timing of movement is also an important feature. In the Lukan story the downturn of vv 25-27 is commended to the apostles for immediate reception, but the upturn of vv 28-30 is held out as a promise which is yet to be fulfilled. Thus the apostles' reversal is in progress; the discipleship[9] portrayed in 22:24-30 follows a path through present-time condescension yet in anticipation of future elevation.

We may also clarify the matter by noting the object that is reversed. In the case of certain other texts in Luke, many point to the theme of reversal of *fortunes*[10] (especially in the Magnificat [1:52-53], the Beatitudes [6:20-26] and the Parable of the Rich Man and Lazarus [16:19-31]).[11] Here we anticipate the future exchange between two parties of their respective lots. Elsewhere one may detect a reversal of *values* in which a new outlook prizes what was formerly scorned (e.g., 14:7-11; 16:15). This involves a radical transformation of customary ways of thinking. There is also a reversal in terms of *definition* in which one quality is said to be equivalent to its supposed opposite (e.g., 9:48).[12] More possibilities could be offered,[13] but these suffice to show that, for Luke, reversal can have its effect in a variety of spheres (see further sec. 4.5 below).

The reversal in Luke 22:24-30 is a complex one involving certain elements from the preceding types, though it may not be properly described as falling only into a single category. Especially in 22:28-30 there is an element of reversal of fortunes in which the trial-laden apostles are promised that they will become lofty rulers over Israel, though we may note that this does not involve an exchange with another party going through reversal in the opposite direction. In vv 24-27 a reversal of val-

---

[9]On "discipleship" in 22:24-30, see esp. chs. 8 and 9.

[10]From the reader's point of view, this would be a reversal of expectations.

[11]E.g., Danker, *Luke*, 47-57; Mealand, 41-50; Tannehill, *Unity*, 27-30; also see Hamel.

[12]Cf. the similar case of power *through* weakness in 2 Corinthians (see Savage's analysis).

[13]E.g., Jesus' reversal of relationships evidenced by his table fellowship with "sinners" (Luke 5:30; 15:2; cf. 19:7).

ues is apparent in the unconventional preference for humble positions and menial duties over roles of power and prestige. There is also a sense in which definitions are reversed here: greatness can no longer be taken to mean being high and mighty; rather, it involves leading from a position of servanthood.

Other facets of reversal could be discussed,[14] but the above analysis highlights the most prominent features of 22:24-30 as a reversal. The complexity of the text's structure along with the variety of forms in background contexts (see further below) make it inadequate to speak in simple terms about the nature of reversals—even those in Luke-Acts—and extrapolate from them as to aspects of meaning in 22:24-30. This fact, however, should not prevent us from thinking that an examination of many reversals in various background[15] contexts will be useful in developing an informed, nuanced frame of reference from which to approach our text. Accordingly, an eye to points of contact with Luke 22:24-30 will be maintained in the following sections. By way of clarification, the following is not presented as an exhaustive survey, especially in the broad fields of classical and Jewish literature. An attempt will be made, however, to analyze representative texts and themes which have verbal, conceptual or formal similarities to 22:24-30.

4.2 Reversals in Classical Sources

A great number of diverse reversal motifs appear in the classical literature.[16] Danker maintains that the theme of *peripetia* involving altered or reversed fortunes is prominent among them, its classic treatment being Sophocles' tragic story of King Oedipus.[17] Aristotle speaks at length of *peripetia* in his *Poetica* (see 10.1-11.7). He tells of a certain Lynceus who was to be executed and escaped, while a man named Danaus who sought to kill Lynceus was himself killed (11.3). Diodorus Siculus tells of an unexpected and tragic "reversal of fortune" (περιπέτια) involving a boy named Actaeon who died at the hands of the one who

[14]E.g., the role of "the Father" (v 29) in effecting reversal, etc.

[15]"Backgrounds" is understood loosely, for a few of the items considered would be antedated by Luke-Acts.

[16]See e.g., the summary treatment in Danker, *Luke*, 47-8; Hamel, 58-60; Schottroff, 298-300; York, 173-82.

[17]Danker, *Luke*, 47. Luke's mastery of *peripetia* gives evidence of his literary skill (ibid.).

had helped him the most, namely his father, who was too vigorous in attempting to protect the boy from a molesting intruder (8.10).[18]

Reversals which have some conceptual or verbal similarity to Luke 22:24-30 may also be noted. Euripides declares that divinity often abases the greatest, only later to elevate them again (*Frag.* 706).[19] This 360-degree movement for a single party to a positive end (cf. Luke 22:24-30) leaves the agency entirely in the hands of divinity. Elsewhere Euripides observes how the gods elevate lowliness and bring down greatness (*Troades* 612-13). Hesiod similarly contends that Zeus is able to topple the proud and lift up the humble (*Opera* 1-5). Many other examples involving reversal of the proud and the humble, of great and lowly, could also be cited.[20]

We note in these examples attention to the social position of the parties involved, and a recurring sentiment that those atop the pyramid will not always remain there and those at the bottom will one day be elevated. Similarly, Luke 22:24-27 reflects a keen awareness of a social context with lowly and lofty roles, but it differs from the above classical models in that the Lukan Jesus commends rather than predicts the humiliation of the great.

York maintains that with the decline of traditional Greek religion in the fifth and fourth centuries BCE, the gods' role in reversals of fortune was gradually replaced by the capriciousness of "chance" (τύχη).[21] By the third and second centuries, *Tyche* became personified as a powerful yet arbitrary goddess who controlled human destinies.[22] This development contributed to the secularization of Hellenistic religion, and it played a part in shaping a popular first-century expectation in the Greco-Roman world that capriciousness characterized the actions of the gods in effecting human reversals of fortune.[23] Lukan reversal motifs, and aspects of 22:24-30 in particular, may take on a distinctive sense when seen against the background of such an outlook.

---

[18]See also the reversals described in Hdt. 8.20; Eur. *Andr.* 982. On περιπέτια as a term in literature for sudden changes of plot, note LSJ, "περιπέτια," 1382.

[19]Cited in Hamel, 59.

[20]E.g., Xen. *An.* 3.2.10; Diog. L. *Lives* 1.69; Cicero *De officiis* 1.26.90 (cf. York, 79-80). One of the fables attributed to Aesop (*Two Roosters and an Eagle*; see Hausrath, 85-6 [no. 266]) offers the moral, ... Κύριος ὑπερηφάνοις ἀντιτάσσεται, ταπεινοῖς δὲ δίδωσι χάριν (a verbatim parallel to Prov 3:34 in the LXX; cf. Jas 4:6).

[21]York, 176-7 (citing Hdt. *History* 1.32).

[22]Cf. Pliny the Elder, *Nat. Hist.* 2.5.22; Polyb. *Hist.* 39.8.2.

[23]York, 178-81.

4.3 Reversals in Jewish Sources

There is a wide array of potentially relevant material (i.e., reversals which bear some resemblance to the language, concepts or form of Luke 22:24-30) in several strains of Jewish source material: the canonical OT, the OT Apocrypha and Pseudepigrapha, the scrolls of Qumran and rabbinic literature.[24] Further, there is a wide assortment of reversal types in these sources. While allowing for breadth, however, it is necessary to guard against describing reversals too loosely and, for instance, labeling nearly any striking turn of events in narrative or any antithetical parallelism in poetry a reversal.

The OT contains several vivid *narratives* in which characters go through reversal. The Joseph story is perhaps the most outstanding example of a pattern involving descent into humiliation and adversity followed by ascent to vindication and prosperity (Gen 37-50). The grueling plight of Job followed by the eventual restoration of his health, family and riches represents a similar story line. A comparable progression through trial to final victory surfaces in the stories of Daniel in the den of lions (Dan 6), and Shadrach, Meshach and Abednego in the furnace (Dan 3). The daring appeal of Esther to Ahasuerus and its successful outcome follows a similar narrative course (Esth 4:1-9:19). The exodus story also, particularly the passage through the Red Sea, exhibits a related reversal image.[25] Other examples could surely be added to this list, but these suffice to show a rich Jewish tradition of 360-degree reversals with positive outcomes.

An important feature of these OT reversal stories is the role of God as an active agent. Although the downturn is often the doing of antagonists (though note Job 1:8), protagonists regularly prevail only with the help of God.[26] The role of Jesus in elevating the apostles in Luke 22:28-30 is not without some likeness to this motif, especially in light of the reference in v 29 to "the Father." Different from the Lukan form, however, is the lack of a downward side of reversal based on admonition in these OT contexts. With the exception of Esther (for whom Mordecai's

---

[24]For summary treatment, see Hamel, 60-5; Hoffmann and Eid, 202-8; Mealand, 41-4; Schottroff, 299-300.

[25]Note the use of ἔξοδος in Luke 9:31 (cf. Mánek, "Exodus").

[26]Even if unstated, this is often implied (cf. Hamel, 60).

admonition is not corrective anyhow), external forces bring the downturn upon the characters involved.

Here we shift to reversal *sayings and teachings* in the OT and other Jewish sources relating to themes seen in Luke 22:24-30 (e.g., lowliness and reward). Hannah's song (1 Sam 2:1-10; cf. Luke 1:46-55) emphasizes the agency of God in effecting reversal, even the downward side: "The Lord kills and brings to life; he brings down to Sheol and raises up. The Lord makes poor and makes rich; he brings low, he also exalts" (1 Sam 2:6-7).[27] Later, however, stress falls on the Lord's exaltation of the lowly (2:8).[28] Elsewhere humility and subsequent honor are connected: "Before destruction a man's heart is haughty, but humility goes before honor" (Prov 18:12; cf. Luke 22:24-30).

The Servant of Isaiah 53 follows a descending path of vicarious suffering to the point of death (53:5-7, 12). An element often overshadowed by interest in the importance of the Servant's suffering, however, is the ascent of reward which results from his affliction. In 53:12 it is stated that, because of the Servant's sin-bearing death, "I will divide him a portion with the great, and he shall divide the spoil with the strong" (cf. vv 10-11).[29] Thus the full reversal sequence includes both serving condescension and consequent elevation (cf. Luke 22:24-30).[30]

The hope of a final rescue for God's suffering people is voiced in Wis 2:19-24. This is a hope that even death does not eliminate (3:1-4), and which yields an ultimate vindication in which the righteous "... will judge nations, rule over peoples, and the Lord will be their king forever" (3:8; cf. Dan 7:22).[31] Here there are some noteworthy parallels with Luke 22:28-30 along the lines of endurance of trials,[32] judging and ruling as rewards, and the overarching kingship of the Lord, though the lack of an active role for the righteous in following a path of descent is in contrast to the commendation in 22:24-27. Further, the intermediate position of the righteous both in and under authority (Wis 3:8) appears to be re-

[27]Cf. Deut 32:36-39; Ps 75:7; Prov 3:34; Wis 3:1-6; Sir 7:11; 20:11; *Ep. Arist.* 363.

[28]Cf. Job 22:29; Ps 147:6; Sir 10:14-15; 11:5-6.

[29]Whybray says regarding v 12, "Yahweh now announces the reward which the prophet is to have for his faithfulness" (182; cf. Westermann, 268; Young, 358).

[30]In contrast to the pattern in Luke 22:24-30, the descent of the Servant is not based on admonition and it does involve an element of divine agency (53:10).

[31]Pobee, 41-2; cf. sec. 7.4.3 on parallels between Dan 7:22 and Luke 22:28-30.

[32]Note the endurance-reward connection in Wis 3:5.

stricted to the afterlife, while the apostles in Luke 22:24-30 are leaders in the narrative's present era as well as a future age.

A reversal saying with a likeness to the whole of Luke 22:24-30 is found in Sir 3:18: "The greater you are (ὅσῳ μέγας εἶ), the more humbly you should behave, and then you will find favor with the Lord." Not only do both texts share the theme of greatness being expressed in humility, they also link condescension and subsequent reward. Further, both mingle the reversal participants' actions with the consequent work of Jesus/the Lord. A difference, however, is the lack in Sir 3:18 of a stated flaw which prompts the commendation of downturn.[33]

The martyrdom of Eleazar and the woman with her seven sons (2 Macc 6:18-7:42) illustrates some noteworthy reversal motifs in Jewish martyr traditions. Each figure is tortured and executed publicly for refusing to comply with the order of Antiochus IV to eat pork. Their devotion to the law is praised and they are held up as examples of courage and virtue (6:31). The tragic turn of events is offset by the martyrs' confident expectation of resurrection from the dead (7:9, 14, 23, 29);[34] thus there is a path of reversal through suffering to glory.[35] Lebram compares the martyr accounts of 2 Macc 6-7 with the rescue legends in Dan 3 and 6, and notes general similarities of each with "Weisheitserzählungen" in which exemplary figures are rescued from difficulty through their wisdom (e.g., the Joseph, Tobit, Job and Esther stories).[36] All share the overarching structure of "Erniedrigung und Erhöhung": "Gott lässt den Frommen in tiefste Bedrohung geraten und wird ihn gegen allen Augenschein erretten."[37]

---

[33]It may also be possible that "finding favor with the Lord" is not so much an actual elevation as a redefinition of lowliness as a favorable position, though a concrete concept of reward is predominant in Sir (so the drift of μίσθος usages). Skehan and Di Lella (83-6) maintain that the writer does not conceive of reward or punishment in the afterlife, a view that may support a tangible form of reward in 3:18. Cf. also Sir 22:23.

[34]Lebram, 92-4; Pobee, 44-5. On the hope for resurrection from the dead, see also Jos. *J.W.* 1.33.3; 4 Macc 10:15; 16:25. Note also the hope of Akiba in *b. Ber.* 61b: "Blessed are you, Rabbi Akiba, for your portion is life in the Age to Come!" (cited in Cartlidge and Dungan, 184-5). Pobee (39-43) discusses aspects of reward for the martyr in addition to resurrection itself. On Jewish martyr traditions, see Fox, 436-7; Frend, 31-78; Lebram; Nickelsburg, *Resurrection*, 38-42; Pobee, 13-46; Ruppert; Schweizer, *Erniedrigung*, 38-43; Talbert, "Martyrdom," 104-5.

[35]Cf. the similar line of thought in 1 Macc 2:50-51, where the sons of the dying Mattathias are urged to give their lives for the covenant and so receive great honor and an everlasting name. See also *1 Enoch* 103:1-4.

[36]Lebram, 95.

Although such themes and structures bear significant resemblance to the reversal in Luke 22:24-30, a difference is that condescension to death is forced upon the martyrs. To be sure, the mother of the seven sons commends a martyr's death rather than survival in disobedience to the law (2 Macc 7:29), but external constraints motivate her definition of virtue and her consequent advice. For this reason the pursuit of martyrdom is not on a plane with the pursuit of greatness in lowly service in Luke 22:24-27.[38] A distinction may also be drawn between the apostles as culpable (22:24; cf. sec. 6.4) and the martyrs as innocent of wrongdoing. Nonetheless, the structural and thematic similarities between the martyr traditions and our text are significant.

The literature of Qumran also contains some reversal motifs.[39] A portrayal of God as one who overpowers the strong and lifts up the weak and poor is seen in 1QH 2:34-35 and 1QM 11:13. A similar reversal exalting "the congregation of the poor" and condemning "the wicked of Israel" appears in 4QpPs 37:21-22. Despite the general "shape" of reversal here comprising fall and rise, however, in each case there are two parties in view, and each undergoes only a 180-degree reversal (contrast the 360-degree sequence in Luke 22:24-30).

The OT Pseudepigrapha constitutes the last sector of Jewish backgrounds to be discussed here. A reversal theology runs through *1 Enoch* 92-104 in which fierce resentment is directed at wealthy persecutors.[40] Hoffmann and Eid examine this theme in depth noting the repeated emphasis on the end-time reversal of present conditions.[41] God will judge those who trust in wealth and commit oppression (94:8-9). The tables will be turned and persecutors will be persecuted (95:7; cf. 46:4-8). The powerful who coerce the righteous will be destroyed (96:8; 99:11-16). This vision of a reversal brought to fulfillment at the end-time may shed some light on the temporal dimension of Luke 22:29-30 (cf. sec. 7.4.4). A difference from Luke 22:24-30 is that the reversal in *1 Enoch* consists of two 180-degree reversals in opposite directions.[42]

---

[37]Lebram, 97; cf. 95-9; see also Nickelsburg, *Resurrection*, 42.

[38]The later Christian practice of "volunteering" for martyrdom (see Fox, 442-9) contrasts with Jewish opposition to any such overeagerness (so Talbert, "Martyrdom," 105, citing *Gen. Rab.* 82). (1 Macc 2:50-51 presupposes a persecution context [2:49].)

[39]See the discussion in Mealand, 42-4.

[40]Mealand, 113, n. 46.

[41]Hoffmann and Eid, 205.

The Joseph story is recalled in *T. Jos.* 17:8-18:4 in a way that emphasizes reversal features.[43] A striking likeness to Luke 22:27c is seen in *T. Jos.* 17:8b: ἀλλ' ἤμην ἐν αὐτοῖς ὡς εἷς τῶν ἐλαχίστων.[44] This statement follows Joseph's claim that he, as a ruler in Egypt, did not exalt himself over his brothers, but identified with them and loved them. He then asserts, "If you live in accord with the Lord's commands, God will exalt you with good things forever" (18:1),[45] after which he enumerates his blessings.[46] So we see a 360-degree reversal course for one party from greatness to being "one of the least" to final exaltation. Further, the downward motion is self-imposed while the elevation is given by God.[47] For the reader the stress on the rewards of humility would seem to offer incentive for condescension (cf. sec. 8.4).[48]

4.4 Reversals in the New Testament

A survey of reversals in the NT uncovers some interesting "parallels" to Luke 22:24-30.[49] The idea of condescension to the position of "servant" (δοῦλος) is seen in Phil 2:7, and the depth of this humiliation is highlighted by the prior standing of Christ Jesus "in the form of God" (v 6). It is also noteworthy that this humble service leads to exaltation (vv 9-11). Moreover, the whole reversal paradigm is presented in conjunction with the admonition to have a humble, self-giving disposition like that of Jesus (vv 3-5); as such it may be thought of as a commended pattern for discipleship.[50] Although an upward aspect of reversal is not explicitly promised to the Philippian Christians, the clear link between the humiliation and exaltation of Christ (διό, v 9) probably justifies the hope of reward.

---

[42]So too with the vision of the son of Rabbi Jehoshua ben Levi, who sees a reversed world in which rulers are subordinated and subordinates rule (*b. Pesah.* 50a, cited in Hoffmann and Eid, 206-7)

[43]The writer of *T. Jos.* is not recalling here the reversal seen in the larger story of Joseph's life (cf. Gen 37-50), though the structure is comparable.

[44]The possibility of Christian influence on *T. Jos.* here is not ruled out.

[45]Kee's translation ("Testaments," 823).

[46]*T. Benj.* 5:4b seems to duplicate this reversal pattern, as does *T. Jos.* 10:1-3.

[47]Hollander, 47 (cf. Hollander and de Jonge, 403-6). A humiliation-exaltation thread runs through the Testaments (Hollander, 48).

[48]The shift in 18:1 to the second person supports this claim (cf. 10:1-3).

[49]Synoptic reversal texts will be noted in sec. 4.5.1.

[50]Cf. Hurtado, 125.

The service theme is present again in John 12:26 (this time with διακονέω), though it corresponds only to the follower of Jesus and not Jesus himself.[51] The one who serves and follows Jesus will be honored by the Father (a 360-degree sequence with a positive end).[52] The likelihood that "service" is not merely a figurative expression which lacks social "rough edges" is supported by the reversal aphorism in v 25b ("... he who hates his life in this world will keep it for eternal life"). V 25 may also imply that the honor from the Father in v 26 is an eschatological gift (cf. the role of the Father and the time frame in Luke 22:29-30).

In Rom 8:17 Paul explains that "[we are] fellow heirs with Christ, 'provided' (εἴπερ) we suffer with him 'in order that' (ἵνα) we may also be glorified with him." As in Luke 22:24-30, both fall and rise involve association with Christ; discipleship follows his path.[53] The ἵνα clause closely links descent with ascent, making the latter the aim of the former. Although an imperative admonishing one to follow this reversal course is lacking (cf. Luke 22:26), the εἴπερ ... ἵνα sequence with the very positive end of glorification with Jesus surely has the force of an exhortation. Rom 8:17 has a thematic likeness to 2 Tim 2:11-12a: "If we have died with him, we shall also live with him; if we endure, we shall also reign with him." As in Luke 22:28-30, endurance is here linked with the reward of shared reign.[54] Both Rom 8:17 and 2 Tim 11:12a differ from Luke 22:24-30, however, in lacking a stated fault which prompts the commendation of reversal.[55]

Sayings about humbling oneself merit some attention: "Humble yourselves before the Lord and he will exalt you" (Jas 4:10; cf. 4:6; 1 Pet 5:6, 9-10). Here we see a self-imposed fall and a God-given rise, much as in Luke 22:24-30. It appears that the expectation of exaltation would serve to motivate the downward movement. It is difficult to specify the timing of exaltation in view in these texts, but the sense of 1 Pet 5:9-10 may suggest an eschatological end in 5:6.

[51]Contrast the exemplary value of the symbolic footwashing in John 13 (cf. sec. 6.5.3 on the possible relationship of John 13:1-20 with Luke 22:27).

[52]Cf. Boulton, 418.

[53]Cf. 1 Pet 4:12-13 (also note the baptism imagery in Rom 6:3-5 and Col 2:12).

[54]Cf. Rev 3:21; Wis 3:8 (also see sec. 8.3).

[55]Others of Paul's letters offer some reversal concepts as well (notably 2 Cor with its two-party substitution statements [5:21; 8:9] and the motif of power in weakness [e.g., 12:9-10; cf. Savage]), but the "shape" of these structures is significantly different from that in Luke 22:24-30.

4.5 Lukan Reversals

It has often been noted that reversals are prominent in Luke-Acts.[56] While some of this material is paralleled in other Gospels, much of it is unique to the Lukan writings. The suspicion thus arises that reversals, and more broadly a mentality or theology of reversal, may be of special interest to the author of Luke-Acts. Additionally, it is noteworthy that the prevalence in Luke-Acts of 360-degree reversals adds weight to the case for the unitary conception of 22:24-30 (cf. secs. 1.1 and 8.2). Following a few reflections on York's recent study, we will survey some of the contours of Lukan reversal which resemble those of 22:24-30.[57]

York's work on the rhetoric of reversal in Luke is a thorough and well-documented study of the prevalent "bi-polar" form (i.e., involving two parties whose fortunes or circumstances are replaced by opposite ones). Among York's more important findings is a Lukan emphasis on the role of God in effecting reversal, and on the eschatological content of reversal.[58] The form of 22:24-30, however, is not bi-polar (cf. sec. 4.1), so many of York's findings as to the purpose and function of reversal in Luke's Gospel are not directly pertinent to the present study.

[56]Attention is commonly drawn to the Magnificat (see 1:52-53), the Beatitudes and Woes (6:20-26) and the Parable of the Rich Man and Lazarus (16:19-31). On these and other texts and themes, see e.g., Braumann, 129; Carroll, 84-6; Cosgrove, 188-9; Danker, *Luke*, 47-57; Grassi, 38-50; Hamel; Hoffmann and Eid, 201-14; Koenig, 90-1; Mealand, 44-49; Minear, *Heal*, 19-23; Moxnes, "Meals"; Schottroff; Tannehill, *Unity*, 26-32; York (and note Flender's antithetical comparisons [27-35]). Koenig (90-1) sees a connection between Lukan reversals and Jesus' table sayings and actions (cf. Barth, 166). Also, many works which examine "the poor" and possessions in Luke-Acts see in that theme an aspect of Lukan reversal thought (see e.g., Fitzmyer, *Gospel*, 1:247-51; Tannehill, *Unity*, 101-40; on the poor and possessions in Luke-Acts generally, see also Bammel, "πτωχός," 905-7; Beck, *Character*, 28-54; Degenhardt; L. Johnson, *Possessions*; Karris, "Poor"; Koch; Mánek, "Umwandlung," 67-70; Pilgrim; T. Schmidt; Seccombe; Thériault).

[57]Many of these are reversals of 360 degrees for (at least) one party with a positive outcome. Reversal texts in Luke-Acts following various other patterns include Luke 1:36-37, 52-53; 6:20-26; 7:28; 10:21, 25-37; 11:43; 12:1-3, 13-21; 51-53; 13:25-30; 16:15, 19-31; 17:12-19; 18:15-17; 19:26; 20:45-47; 21:1-4; Acts 8:9-13; 13:46; 18:6; 28:28. Also note the reversal of values implied in Jesus' association with "sinners" and outcasts (e.g., 5:29-32; 7:37-39; 15:1-2; 19:1-10). Conversions, healings, exorcisms and raising the dead may also be seen as reversal types (e.g., Luke 7:11-17; 8:40-56; 9:37-43; 13:10-17; Acts 3:1-10; 8:1-10; 9:34; 11:19-21; 14:8-10). The Lukan use of "paradox" (i.e., reversal) is distinctive in the variety of ways it is expressed (Evans, 101).

[58]York, e.g., 61, 71, 74, 77, 80, 93, 181-2.

One of York's claims may, however, be pursued here: "The most important reversal portrayed in the Gospel is that which takes place in the life of Jesus."[59] After noting Jesus' lofty origins (i.e., he is conceived by the Holy Spirit), and stating that his self-humiliation and shameful death prepare for God's great exaltation by resurrection and ascension, York declares, "Jesus thus becomes the model to be followed (9.22ff.; 14.26ff.; 17.25ff.) for those wishing to experience the exaltation side of God's bi-polar reversal."[60] This explanation is problematic for two reasons: 1) For York "bi-polar" routinely corresponds to the opposite movements of two parties,[61] but here it is connected to the successive stages of Jesus' own descent-ascent course. 2) Luke 14:26ff and 17:25ff have only the downward motion in view (see sec. 4.5.1 below on 9:22-24) and do not speak of an "exaltation side." If one is going to focus on the reversal experience of the Lukan Jesus, it would be crucial to note the writer's numerous passion-resurrection predictions and recollections (9:22; 18:32-33; 20:17; 24:26, 46; Acts 2:23-24, 36; 3:15; 4:10-11; 5:30-31; 10:39-40; 13:27-30; 17:3; 26:23), for they have the 360-degree course in view. It may thus be more appropriate to reflect on Jesus' reversal course in the following survey of Lukan texts resembling the form in 22:24-30 than it would be in connection with the bi-polar pattern.

4.5.1 Material in the Gospel

Here we note texts which have substantial verbal, conceptual and/or structural similarities to 22:24-30—many of which are unique to Luke in part or in whole—by moving through the Gospel in roughly canonical order. Only Luke 2:34 preserves Simeon's prediction, "Behold, this child is set 'for' (εἰς) the fall and rising of many in Israel, and 'for' (εἰς) a sign that is spoken against,..." Although some envision two groups behind "fall and rising,"[62] a balanced antithetical parallelism of the εἰς phrases results from seeing a single group falling and then rising.[63] On this reading the first phrase would describe people who accept the Messiah (v

---

[59]York, 171.

[60]York, 171-2.

[61]York, 23-4, 42, 92, 150, 160, etc.

[62]E.g., Chance, 70; Schürmann, *Lukasevangelium*, 128; Tannehill, *Unity*, 152, 169, 190; York, 114. Typically the two groups are thought to be Jews and Gentiles respectively.

[63]So I. H. Marshall, *Gospel*, 122; cf. Caird, *Luke*, 64; Goulder, *Luke*, 1:263.

26)—i.e., disciples who follow the passion-resurrection course of Jesus (cf. 9:23-24)—and the second those who reject Jesus.[64]

In 6:35 the Lukan Jesus commends love for enemies involving the hardship of lending without being repaid, and attaches to it the hope of great reward.[65] It is probable that this reversal sequence of admonition and promise anticipates eschatological compensation and not only the reward of being "sons of the Most High" amidst one's sacrificial lending, for v 35 repeats ὁ μισθὸς ὑμῶν πολύς from v 23 where it is modified by ἐν τῷ οὐρανῷ. Further, even if the reward were to be equated with being sons of the Most High in the present, the use of "reward" modified by "great" prompts the reader to imagine some kind of significant "ascent" resulting from descending to love one's enemies, though it may be an ascent of a different order. There is a similar discipleship reversal in vv 22-23 (par. Matt 5:11-12) which commends the toleration of hate and exclusion and rejection "on account of the Son of man," "for" (γάρ) this leads to a great reward in heaven.[66]

The cross saying of 9:23 combines with the aphorism in v 24 to portray a reversal course of discipleship (par. Mark 8:34-35 par. Matt 16:24-25).[67] Taking up the cross is likened in this way to losing one's life, a downturn which ultimately leads to salvation (σώσει).[68] The Lukan καθ' ἡμέραν emphasizes that following Jesus' passion trail is an ongoing aspect of discipleship, and it suggests that the saving of life is not inherent in but consequent upon the losing of life. As in 22:24-30, here too the descent is commended (note the trio of imperatives in 9:23), but the ascent is something to be hoped for.

[64]If "fall" should have moral connotations (i.e., a fall into sin, as probably in 20:18), "rise" could be symbolic of forgiveness (Luke shows a preference for ἄφεσις). On this understanding, however, "fall" and "rise" would still correspond to a single group. A moral sense for "fall," however, is unusual in Luke (the verb occurs 17x, but only in 20:18 is the moral sense a possibility [it occurs 9x in Acts without the sense of moral collapse]; the noun is in 2:34 only). It is more likely that the language pictorially represents the general shape of a life of discipleship (cf. ch. 8).

[65]Matthew's rendering of this saying is less overt about reward, speaking only about the loss of it (5:46). Conzelmann (*Theology*, 234) refers to Luke 6:35 in connection with the reward for endurance, but proceeds to empty it of promise by insisting that "... it is part of one's faith in this very message [of salvation] that one cannot count on a reward."

[66]Technically speaking, this reversal is restricted to 180 degrees.

[67]Contrast Luke 14:27, which mentions no reward for discipleship.

[68]Also note the eschatological perspective of vv 25-26.

In 9:46-48 Jesus demonstrates humility for the disciples who argue as to which of them is the greatest by associating himself with a child and commending the reception of such lowly ones,[69] for it is "the least" who is truly great. Here we see a reversal of definitions: to be least *is* what it now means to be "great"; there is no suggestion that the disciples receive a form of social or any other external elevation as a result of being the least. Similarities to 22:24-27 abound here, and an upward element akin to 22:28-30 is not entirely lacking.[70] The μέγας link between vv 46 and 48 suggests, in some sense, similar starting and ending points (22:24-27 alone has no such ending point), though the transformation of values changes the dimensions of reversal significantly.[71]

In 12:33 the Lukan Jesus instructs his disciples to sell their possessions and give alms, and (thus) secure for themselves treasure in heaven that does not fail or waste away. By contrast, Matthew's version of the saying includes no commended downturn parallel to Luke's "sell" and "give" (Matt 6:19-20). The idea of treasure in heaven suggests an eschatological end point for the transaction,[72] as does the imagery of goods that never deteriorate. The construction with the reflexive pronoun (ποιήσατε ἑαυτοῖς) does not conceal the probability that the acquisition of treasure in heaven is not a strictly human feat (cf. 12:32 on the generosity of the Father).

In 12:35-48 we find a collection of sayings and parables on discipleship (cf. secs. 2.5.2 and 8.3) which exhibit reversal motifs. The unparalleled section of 12:35-37 portrays "servants" (δοῦλοι) who are prompt to welcome their master home. As a result they will ascend to positions of honor at the master's table (cf. 22:30) and the master "will serve" them (διακονήσει; cf. 22:27). As in 22:24-30, here also we see a service-exaltation progression in an admonition-promise context, though an initial high regard for "greatness" or a similar fault is lacking in 12:35-37. And since there is no reference to an actual downward movement here (only existence on the lowly plane of service), it is fitting to classify 12:35-37 as a 180-degree reversal (cf. 22:28-30).

---

[69]See sec. 2.4.2 on the low view of children prevalent in antiquity.

[70]It may be admitted, however, that the 360/ 180 degree distinction pertains here somewhat roughly.

[71]Important also is the connection with Jesus' passion prediction (9:44), which draws another parallel between the disciples' course of condescension and Jesus' suffering.

[72]Cf. Fitzmyer, *Gospel*, 2:982-3; I. H. Marshall, *Gospel*, 532. Also see 16:9.

In 12:42-44 Jesus goes on to describe the faithful and wise servant (v 43) or "steward" (οἰκονόμος, v 42) who, as the one who is found responsibly carrying out his household duties, will be rewarded with additional powers upon the master's return.[73] This is not unlike the connection in 22:28-30 in which the apostles, having remained loyal to Jesus during his trials, are given kingship and promised thrones for judging the twelve tribes (cf. sec. 7.4).[74] Further, that 12:43-44 describes an eschatological scene seems to be implied by the focus throughout on the returning master together with the reference (v 40) to the coming of the Son of man.

There is a series of relevant reversal sayings in 14:7-14 which, like 22:24-30, have their setting at table. The first is a parable unique to Luke on choosing seats at a banquet (vv 8-10; cf. sec. 3.5.1). The principle commended is that of taking the "lowest" (ἔσχατον) place "so that" (ἵνα) the host may move the guest higher in the presence of everyone. Although this advice seems to be mere practical wisdom in the story world, with a παραβολή (v 7) one expects an application that transcends the specifics of the tale. The second reversal in the context (v 11) invites wider possibilities by generalizing the story: "For everyone who exalts himself will be humbled, and he who humbles himself will be exalted."[75] While this aphorism actually presents two opposite reversals, the preceding parable commends the pattern with the positive outcome. The active descent coupled with a passive[76] ascent may be likened to the reversal progression in 22:24-30.

In 14:12-14, a pericope without parallel in the other Gospels, Jesus admonishes his host to show hospitality to the destitute, thereby undercutting the social system[77] which obligated a person to reciprocate for beneficent deeds. There would be no social yield on such an "investment" since the poor cannot repay, but Jesus promises compensation "at the resurrection of the just" (v 14). Thus an eschatological return is held out to those who give up the rewards of reciprocity. Even if unstated, it is implied that the host had followed the custom of inviting the honorable

[73]Again, this is a 180-degree reversal since a downward movement to service is not specified.

[74]Cf. the reversals in 2 Tim 2:12 and Wis 3:8; also note Dan 7:22; Rev 3:21.

[75]For Barth (162) 22:28-30 is an exemplary demonstration of the reversal principle in 14:11 and 18:14. The notion that all of 22:24-30 exhibits such a pattern, however, is not mentioned.

[76]Most likely a divine passive (so Fitzmyer, *Gospel*, 2:1047; et al.).

[77]Cf. sec. 2.2.2.

(see v 7) and not the destitute, so Jesus' instruction (vv 12-14) would come as a rebuke (cf. the relation of 22:24 to vv 25-30).

The aphorism of 14:11 reappears in 18:14b-c in the Lukan Parable of the Pharisee and the Tax Collector (18:9-14) where the descent-ascent course clearly refers to a reversal in which humiliation is self-imposed, but exaltation is effected by God (note the cry to God in v 13). Thus we have a high-low-high pattern akin to that of 22:24-30. The fact that the tax collector turns from sin in his downward movement of confession also corresponds to 22:24-30, though he is not admonished to do so. In contrast to 22:24-30, however, it appears that the exaltation of the tax collector involves his being "justified" (v 14a), an event portrayed as accomplished in the present time of the narrative.

In 18:29-30 (par. Mark 10:29 par. Matt 19:29) we again see a down-then-up reversal in Jesus' words following the encounter with the rich ruler. No one who gives up the pleasures of family life for the kingdom of God will lack both present reward and eternal life in the age to come (this reversal echoes 18:22: renounce possessions and receive treasure in heaven [par. Mark 10:21 par. Matt 19:21]). Thus the path of discipleship is not only a way of self-sacrifice, but also a way *through* self-sacrifice to present and future reward.[78] Further, we again see the combination of a self-imposed downward course and a God-given elevation.[79] Also, that the way of discipleship corresponds to Jesus' own passion-resurrection reversal seems to be implied by the connection with vv 31-34.

4.5.2 Material in Acts

Although other potentially relevant reversals are present in Luke's Gospel,[80] the preceding survey prepares us now to turn to Acts. First we

[78]In the same way, Jesus anticipates not only his passion but his resurrection as well (vv 32-33).

[79]Reception rather than acquisition is the nuance of [ἀπο]λάβῃ here (v 30).

[80]E.g., the Parable of the Prodigal Son (15:11-32) is a story of reversal from riches to rags to riches (so Danker, *Luke*, 51-2; but note that the reversal aphorisms of vv 24 and 32 do not recall the initial elevation, but only narrate the latter half of reversal from "death" to "life"). In marked contrast to the 22:24-30 form, however, the "fall" of the prodigal is not along a commended course. The same can be said for Peter's denial as a fall into wrong behavior, though the agency of Satan complicates matters there (22:31-34). In 21:19 Jesus commends reversal discipleship by linking the endurance of persecution in the end-time with the reception of "life" (from ψυχή [cf. 9:24b on the link of preserving one's ψυχή and

note the three prison deliverances (5:19-21, 23; 12:1-11; 16:23-34) in which God miraculously releases the apostles or Paul and Silas. Each account is rich with irony accenting the power of God to overrule human rulers:[81] sentries guard empty cells (5:23); Peter walks by sleeping guards (12:6-11); worship induces an earthquake that unfastens Paul's and Silas's fetters and opens the prison doors (16:25-26).

The many downs and ups of Paul's life may be seen in this light as well. His humbling commission (9:1-18; cf. 22:6-16; 26:12-18) along with his rise to "power" as the one who spearheads the mission to diaspora Jews and Gentiles (9:15; 22:15, 21; 26:17-18) constitutes a central, overarching reversal in the Acts narrative. On a smaller scale, Paul's many escapes from danger amount to a recurring motif of threat and deliverance (e.g., 9:23-25, 29-30; 17:13-14; 22:17-21; 23:12-25; 27:42-43; 28:3-6). Along these lines, 14:19-20 seems clearly to reflect the passion and resurrection of Jesus in Paul's life of discipleship. Jews from Antioch and Iconium incite the citizens of Lystra against Paul, and the result is that they stone him and leave him for dead. But Paul "rises" (ἀναστάς) and carries on with his work (v 20).

Elsewhere in Acts adversities are transformed to yield positive outcomes. Persecution and scattering of Christians only advances the church into new fields (e.g., 8:1-8; 11:19-21; 13:44-48; 18:6, 9-11; 28:25-31).[82] Although often not named, it is apparent that God is a key character in the Acts narrative who overrules human rulers and brings gain out of what would seem to be loss (e.g., 16:30-34). God even brings about a reversal from death to life in the cases of Tabitha (9:36-43) and Eutychus (20:9-12).

The summary statement about Paul's first missionary journey provides a notable example of the descent-ascent form (14:22). There Luke describes how Paul and Barnabas exhorted the disciples saying that "through many tribulations we must enter the kingdom." The necessity of a downward turn through adversity is highlighted here by δεῖ. This echoes the divine necessity Luke so frequently attaches to the passion and resurrection of Jesus,[83] and again aligns Christian discipleship with the fall and rise of Jesus. The fact that a series of trials leads to a singular

being saved]).

[81]Tannehill, *Unity*, 30-1.

[82]Stanton, 94-5. Cf. Tyson ("Food," 71-4) on the recurring peace-threat-resolution-restoration progression in Acts.

[83]E.g., Luke 9:22; 24:26; Acts 26:23 (cf. Cosgrove, 174).

entry into the kingdom may imply that βασιλεία here has an eschatological sense (cf. Luke 22:28-30).

While the "shape" of reversals in Acts is often similar to that in Luke 22:24-30, it may be noted that the downturn is not usually self-imposed but brought on by the Christians' adversaries. Further, there is little development of the motif seen commonly in Luke's Gospel of a descent in the present age that leads to an eschatological ascent (though note Acts 14:22); in Acts reversals tend to turn full circle in the present-age world of the narrative. The frequent recurrence of 360-degree reversals together with the "many" of 14:22 (cf. "daily" in Luke 9:23) may suggest that a burden of Luke is to portray Christian discipleship as a series of reversals with positive ends, the whole of which takes place within an overarching, era-bridging reversal.

4.6 **Conclusion**

The preceding collection of reversals which bear some resemblance to Luke 22:24-30 may be thought of as contributing to a reader expectation grid: familiarity with such background reversals prepares readers in a certain way to encounter our text.[84] Before asking what the main features of that grid are and how it may shed a distinctive light on 22:24-30, it is useful to recall that the many reversals considered in this chapter are not precisely of one type. To be sure, we have repeatedly seen 360-degree, one-party reversals with positive ends involving some form of humiliation and exaltation. Nevertheless, few if any reversals agree with others in every aspect; the material is too complex for such a conception. Therefore, we will not be able to establish the contours of an expectation grid with great precision,[85] though useful conclusions can be drawn.

The following general observations concern the material from classical, Jewish and NT sources (excluding Luke-Acts). There is a widespread, multi-faceted group of reversals which share with Luke 22:24-30 the descent-ascent pattern. In many instances divine action is a key factor in effecting reversal, especially the upward movement.[86] In some

[84]York, 39; cf. sec. 1.3.

[85]I.e., it will not be possible in most cases to give great significance to a departure from the "norm" as signaling something new and distinctive. We may have more success here focusing on areas of broad agreement and their implications rather than emphasizing a text's uniqueness.

cases the downward element of a 360-degree reversal course is explicitly urged as a pattern for right living.[87] These ideas are prevalent enough in the literature to warrant the supposition that most of Luke's readers would have been aware of them and could have seen 22:24-30 in light of them. That is, the reader may have expected elevation to follow condescension, anticipated the involvement of the Father (and Jesus?) in effecting the upturn, and thought of 22:24-27 as the admonition half of a reversal whole. In short, the reader familiar with such backgrounds would have been better equipped to note these important features of the text than the reader unfamiliar with them.

Turning to Luke-Acts, though York's bi-polar reversal is a widespread Lukan form, also prominent is the 360-degree single-party pattern of 22:24-30. Numerous texts in the Gospel and Acts exhibit this form or one similar to it, and a familiarity with such texts would enhance the reader's consciousness of the following: the downturn element frequently commends unconventional conduct and/ or the endurance of adversity; the action of Jesus or God effects a consequent upturn;[88] the timing of events often spans into the future, even into the eschaton; the reversal pattern reflects Jesus' passion-resurrection;[89] humility/ suffering is often rewarded with honor/ deliverance. Taken together, the many relevant texts (several of which are unique to Luke-Acts) depict a course of experience for Jesus' followers, a pattern for a discipleship of reversal (cf. ch. 8). The reader who recognizes these various recurring Lukan reversal emphases may then be prepared to detect such features in 22:24-30, and to sense their importance to Luke.

It has been noted that a strand of reversal thought in Luke-Acts which resembles the form of 22:24-30 supports the argument for the unity of the text (cf. secs. 1.1 and 8.2). Since it is the case that repeatedly in Luke's writings a descent-ascent pattern forms a unified whole, the reader would be able to see 22:24-30 in a similar way: condescension is

[86]This is particularly evident in the reversal narratives (e.g., the Joseph story). In this regard, also note some of the classical examples.

[87]E.g., Sir 3:18; *T. Jos.* 10:1-3; 17:8-18:4; *T. Benj.* 5:4b; John 12:25-26; Phil 2:5-11; Jas 4:10; 1 Pet 5:6. These and other texts which envision a positive outcome for a reversal progression (e.g., Prov 18:12; Rom 8:17) could have functioned in their literary contexts as offering incentive for enduring necessary trials in the hope of future reward (cf. sec. 8.4).

[88]The reader who has the capricious reversals of *Tyche* in mind (cf. sec. 4.2) may take particular note of this feature.

[89]Léon-Dufour, "Testament," 273; cf. Stöger, 7.

not the end of the discipleship trail; honor follows humble service and endurance of trials. Further, this prevalent pattern also implies a unifying line for historiography as well as narrative.[90] That is, it serves to link eras such as those represented by 22:24-27 and 22:28-30, and to suggest a Lukan interest in the interrelation of present and future periods of salvation history (cf. secs. 3.5.1 and 9.3).

[90]We have seen that the joining of the ages is a common feature of the 360-degree reversal form in Luke and in non-Lukan backgrounds.

Chapter 5: Testamentary Genre

5.1 Introduction

The present chapter, like the previous one, develops background perspectives which center on the form rather than the content of Luke 22:24-30, though a strong secondary interest in the actual substance of Jesus' sayings is an inevitable concomitant. Specifically, claims that Luke 22:14-38 is fashioned on the model of the testamentary discourse will be probed, and the possible significance of such an understanding for an interpretation of vv 24-30 will be considered.

Accordingly, after addressing certain preliminary concerns (sec. 5.1) we will seek a description of testamentary literature in terms of content and function (5.2), and consider whether the Last Supper discourse of Luke 22:14-38 appears to be within the stream of this literary tradition (5.3). Only then will we be able to offer some proposals as to how the genre perspective may enhance our developing platform (i.e., Part One) for the analysis of 22:24-30 (5.4).

Discourses attributed to dying or departing prominent figures surface in a wide variety of ancient works (e.g., the Pentateuch and OT historical books,[1] the OT Apocrypha[2] and Pseudepigrapha,[3] Jewish writings of the NT era,[4] the NT,[5] and Greco-Roman works[6]). This

[1]E.g., Gen 49; Deut 31-34; Josh 23-24; 1 Kgs 2:1-10; 1 Sam 12:1-25; 1 Chr 28-29.

[2]E.g., 1 Macc 2:49-70; Tob 14:3-11. Munck includes 2 Macc 6:30 (to which v 31 may be added); 7:1-42; 4 Macc ("Discours," 157), but doing so seems to "stretch" the genre excessively.

[3]E.g., *T. 12 Patr.*; *T. 3 Patr.*; *As. Moses*; *T. Job*; *Jub.* 7; 20:1-23:7; 35; 36; 2 *Apoc. Bar.* 31:1-34:1; 44:1-46:7; 76:1-77:26; *1 Enoch* 91:1-19.

[4]See Jos. *Ant.* 4.309-31; 12.279-85; Philo *Vita Mosis* 2.288-92.

collection of literature spans many centuries and crosses cultural, religious and linguistic boundaries as well, so it is not difficult to imagine how certain variations on the form would have evolved within the larger generic sphere of influence (see further sec. 5.2).

Before examining the literature, some terminological clarification is needed. "Testament" has a variety of uses in the primary and secondary sources under consideration. Often it emphasizes the technical, legal sense of a "last will and testament" immediately associated with a death and having to do with the disposal of a testator's estate. Sometimes, however, the term corresponds more generally to the farewell address accompanying a death or departure, and technical understandings recede from view. In the present study "testament" is not restricted to any single sense, though literary rather than legal aspects dominate.[7]

The interest in genre and the emphasis on testaments as literature, however, does not eliminate from the present study an element of complexity arising from the possible historical roots of certain testaments, and the possible historical orientation of a given writing or writer.[8] In the case of 22:14-38 it is arguable that Luke, despite showing significant literary skill creatively to weave this discourse, reveals a keen interest in retaining much traditional material.[9] Therefore, in surveying testa-

[5]E.g., John 13-17; Acts 20:17-38; 1 Tim; 2 Tim; 2 Pet. It will be argued below that Luke 22:14-38 follows this genre as well.

[6]The most famous example is Socrates' farewell dialogue in Plato's *Phaedo* (see especially 115-118). See also Plutarch *Cato Min.* 66-70 and *Otho* 15-17. Kurz ("Luke 22:14-38," 262) and Stauffer ("Abschiedsreden," 29-30) cite additional testaments in Greco-Roman literature.

[7]Thus "farewell address/ discourse/ speech" or *Abschiedsrede* will typically be interchangeable with "testament."

[8]It is a plain fact, of course, that many testaments are fictitious accounts written centuries after their subjects had died (e.g., *T. 12 Patr.*). The fact that widespread use of posthumous discourses is seen in ancient literature, however, does not mean that the idea of delivering a farewell speech was restricted to the rhetorical arena and was absent from the arena of history. The literary form would, in fact, lack impact and a sense of reality if farewell speeches were unknown in human experience. Munck ("Discours," 163) notes that "la constatation de l'existence d'un genre ne diminue pas pour autant l'historicité de la scène et des paroles rapportées." Barrett cautions further that "real farewell speeches are apt to take the same form as fictitious ones" ("Address," 109; cf. Lövestam, 3). Eades seems to assume that testaments are necessarily fictitious (796-7; so too von Nordheim, *Die Lehre II*, 91-2 [arguing that no one takes notes at a dying man's bedside]).

[9]Only vv 15-17, 29-30a, 31-32,35-38 are completely without parallel in Synoptic traditions.

ments and examining Luke 22:14-38, it will not be possible wholly to bypass possible traditional or historical backgrounds; some movement between the various *Sitze im Leben* remains appropriate.

5.2 Description of the Testamentary Literature

The aim of section 5.2 is not to establish the existence of a testamentary genre. The broad and persuasive consensus of existing scholarship is that the genre did exist,[10] in spite of the fact that some of its expressions have led to various distinctive subforms (see further below). Neither is the present section put forward as ground-breaking research on the testamentary literature or genre; such a study would require a much more far-reaching analysis than it is possible to present here. Rather, the aim is to synthesize and at points critique existing scholarship, and to explore the nature of the genre so as to uncover a generic core in terms of content and function.[11]

Many writers provide lists of farewell speech components. Kurz, for example, presents a chart comparing 22 testamentary discourses from biblical and Greco-Roman sources on which he notes the presence, implied or indirect presence, or absence of twenty characteristics: 1) the testator summons successors; 2) speaks of his own mission; 3) declares his innocence, or that he did his job; 4) refers to his impending death; 5) exhorts hearers; 6) gives warnings/ final injunctions; 7) blesses hearers; 8) there are farewell gestures; 9) he gives tasks to successors; 10) there is a theological review of history; 11) he reveals the future; 12) makes promises; 13) appoints or refers to a successor; 14) the hearers bewail loss; 15)

[10]So the (sometimes implicit) assumptions of Becker, Berger, *Formgeschichte*, 75-80; Collins, "Literature" and "Testaments"; Gempf; Hollander and de Jonge; Kolenkow, "Genre" and "Testaments"; Kurz, *Farewell* and "Luke 22:14-38"; Léon-Dufour, "Jésus," "Letzte Mahl," "Testament," "Tradition"; Matera, *Passion*; Michel; Munck, "Discours"; Neyrey; von Nordheim; R. Schnackenburg, "Abschiedsreden"; Sellew; Stauffer, "Abschiedsreden" and "Farewell Speeches." M. de Jonge is in the clear minority when he questions in a review of von Nordheim, *Die Lehre I* (*JSJ* 12 [1981]: 112-17) whether there is enough evidence to speak of a genre. Sources that list examples of ancient testaments include R. Brown, *John*, 598; Dupont, *Discours*, 11-21; Eades, 796-7; Kurz, "Luke 22:14-38," 262; Léon-Dufour, "Jésus," 150-1, and "Tradition," 109; Michel, 48-54; Munck, "Discours," 155-170; Soards, 55, nn. 42-47; Stauffer, *Theology*, 344-7. See e.g., Michel (47-8) on the criteria for establishing the existence of a genre.

[11]A collection of 41 testaments from diverse sources have been surveyed for this study.

he refers to future degeneration; 16) renews covenant/ offers sacrifices; 17) speaks of the care of those left; 18) offers consolation to the inner circle; 19) there is didactic speech; 20) he refers to *ars moriendi.*[12] It must be noted that none of Kurz's 22 speeches contains all of these characteristics. The highest level of correspondence is seen in Deut 31 with fourteen of the characteristics (including two by implication); only six of the 22 speeches exhibit over half of the characteristics named above. Clearly, then, Kurz's list is not to be taken as a fixed paradigm but a reasonably comprehensive collection of features seen in a wide assortment of farewell speeches.[13]

Such a long list of speech components prompts one to ask which are most typical. A careful examination of Kurz's chart helps to address this matter (characteristics 1, 2, 4, 5, 6, 9, 12, 13 and 14 occur in nine or more of 22 speeches). Léon-Dufour's quest to establish the "points essentiels" is also instructive:[14]

> I. Un moribond (ou un homme qui va monter au ciel) prend congé des siens en les réunissant autour de lui pour leur faire ses «adieux», parfois à l'occasion d'un repas.... 2. Le moribond fait quelque exhortation à ses enfants, leur annonçant récompense ou châtiment, leur conseillant des œuvres de misércorde et de charité, leur rescrivant surtout l'union fraternelle. 3. Parfois il fait retour sur son passé, le

[12]Kurz, "Luke 22:14-38," 262-3. Stauffer (*Theology*, 344-7) offers a list of 27 elements from various farewell testaments. For lists of elements also see e.g., R. Brown, *John*, 598-600; J. Charlesworth, 1:773; Eades, 796; Gempf, 318-19; Léon-Dufour, "Tradition," 110, who follows Michel, 48-53; Matera, *Passion*, 161; Neyrey, 48; von Nordheim, *Die Lehre I*, 229-30; Roloff, *Apostelgeschichte*, 302; Sellew, 75-6. Regarding the several key components of Plato's *Phaedo*, Stauffer ("Abschiedsreden," 29) states, "Die verschiedenen Formelemente, die in diesem Abschiedsgespräch vereinigt sind, entwickeln sich aber auch mehr u. mehr zu selbständigen Formen der Abschiedsrede." Without disputing the important role *Phaedo* played in the development of a generic framework for farewell speeches, it would seem that Stauffer's perspective does not give due recognition to OT farewell discourses that may antedate Plato.

[13]In terms of the testament's structure, it seems that the most one can say is that the dying one gathers his group/ family and then exhorts them in some way (cf. Léon-Dufour, "Tradition," 110-11)—the literature is too varied to permit a more specific description. Apart from the death setting, one suspects that a wide variety of discourse types would share the basic gathering-exhorting structure. Therefore, an effort is not made in the present study to establish a typical testamentary structure.

[14]Léon-Dufour, "Jésus," 150-1 (for other characteristics see 151, n. 26). Radl (131) offers a similar list of basic components, as do Michel (54) and Munck ("Discours," 159).

proposant en modèle. 4. Il prophétise l'avenir de la communauté, ou la fin des temps.

For von Nordheim, the body of a testament commonly has three elements: review of the past, instructions for conduct and announcements of the future (only Léon-Dufour's first element [gathering] is left out).[15] In an attempt to get at the heart of the testament, however, von Nordheim contends,[16]

> Schließlich können der Rückblick auf die Vergangenheit und/ oder die Zukunftsansage auch ganz ausfallen, in kein Fall jedoch die Verhaltensanweisung. Ohne eine Anweisung zu einem bestimmten Verhalten ist also ein Testament kein Testament, nicht jedoch ohne die beiden anderen Elemente. Das Herz der Testamentsform schlägt also in der Verhaltensanweisung!

Further, even when present, recollections and prophecies are aimed at instruction for behavior.[17] This view, however, cannot be pressed to imply that mere behavior instructions from a dying person amount to a testament, but only that they are at the heart of the form.

Although instructions for behavior are typical (fifteen of Kurz's 22 speeches contain "exhortations"), it should be noted that they—and the drift of testaments in general—have a future orientation. Farewell instructions set out a standard for tomorrow, for the era of the dying leader's absence.[18] An aim is thus to minimize the prospect of future failings such as defections from the law.[19] Further, it is often on the basis of the past (i.e., the exemplary life of the testator) that statements about the future are formed—looking back is the way to find wisdom for life in the future.[20] Therefore, though von Nordheim elevates behavior instructions as the central and indispensable feature of the form, we will keep recollections and predictions in view as key features as well.

When one focuses on a certain subgroup of farewell discourses, however, other important elements appear. For instance, the OT testa-

---

[15]Von Nordheim, *Die Lehre I*, 229; cf. Berger, *Formgeschichte*, 76; Collins, "Testaments," 325-6.

[16]Von Nordheim, *Die Lehre I*, 233. Michel (49) makes the similar assertion that "Paränetische Wendungen ... sind ganz wesentlicher Bestandteil aller [Abschieds-] Reden."

[17]Von Nordheim, *Die Lehre I*, 234-5; cf. Kurz, "Luke 22:14-38," 264, n. 25.

[18]Radl, *Paulus*, 132; Roloff, *Apostelgeschichte*, 302. Berger (*Formgeschichte*, 78) thus points to testamentary aspects of the synoptic admonitions to watchfulness, for they center on the "Zwischenzeit" during which the master is away. The frequent prophecies and promises in testaments (in 11 of Kurz's 22 speeches) also reveal a keen interest in the future.

[19]Berger, "Hartherzigkeit," 22-3.

[20]E.g., von Nordheim, *Die Lehre II*, 145.

mentary tradition places a special emphasis on the action and blessing of God.[21] Recollections review the acts of God on behalf of his people, predictions anticipate divine action, and there are often exhortations to keep the law of God. Moses' farewell discourse in Deut 31-34, for example, is replete with the action of God: God has guided Moses, God tells Moses what to do, God will provide for Joshua, God's law must be kept, etc.[22]

This element is not absent in later writings,[23] but it receives less emphasis; instead an accent on the righteousness of a human figure comes to the fore.[24] Léon-Dufour states, "Die Testamente der Zwölf Patriarchen nehmen ihren Ausgangspunkt in der Gerechtigkeit eines Menschen, denn grundsätzlich schafft die Gerechtigkeit Segen, während die Ungerechtigkeit Unglück nach sich zieht."[25] This blessing is of course the blessing of God, but the accent comes to lie on the exemplary conduct of the one who is blessed. In 1 Macc 2:52-60 several OT figures are noted for their exemplary faith; it is "the acts of our fathers" and not the acts of God that receive primary attention (v 51).

J. Charlesworth maintains that, although the testamentary tradition was presaged in the OT, it "did not reach maturity until the time of the second temple."[26] Correspondingly, Munck observes that testaments "sont fréquents dans la littérature juive tardive," and lists several examples.[27] The *literary genre* (i.e., as opposed to the custom of farewell speeches or the existence of the earliest written testaments) probably stems from the Hellenistic period in which testaments flourished (so *T. 12 Patr.*, and other apocryphal or pseudepigraphical works), despite the

---

[21]So Léon-Dufour, "Jésus," 151; "Letzte Mahl," 41.

[22]Similar God-centered farewell speeches in the OT include Josh 23-24; 1 Sam 12:1-25; 1 Chr 28-29. Gen 49 is unusual in this regard, for only Jacob's words to Dan and Joseph mention God (but note the blessing of God in 48:3). 1 Kgs 2:1-10 is strange for its concern with vengeance, but reference is made to the importance of God's favor nonetheless.

[23]Baltzer notes (144-46) how God holds a prominent position in *T. 12 Patr.* (esp. in the testaments of Joseph, Simeon, Levi, Judah, Dan and Issachar [I add Zebulon]), and states, "It therefore does not suffice to say that the patriarchs recount their lives as examples of virtue and as warnings against their vices. They are also and above all exemplary in their relationship with God. On this point the Testaments stand completely in the tradition of 'Israel's wisdom,' that the 'fear of God' is the beginning of wisdom" (145).

[24]Ordinarily this human is the testator himself, but in the case of *T. Simeon* (5:1) and *T. Levi* (13:9) it is Joseph whose upright conduct is lauded.

[25]Léon-Dufour, "Letzte Mahl," 41.

[26]J. Charlesworth, 1:773.

[27]Munck, "Discours," 156. See also Kolenkow, "Testaments," 259.

presence of certain farewell discourses in OT historical books and classical sources.[28]

1 Enoch 91:1-19 may serve to illustrate certain common traits of testaments in the era of late Judaism. It has a heavily apocalyptic tone and contains a high proportion of prediction. Violence will increase, there will be plagues and oppression, the Lord will judge the heathen, the righteous will ultimately be blessed (vv 5-17). Apocalyptic does not appear to the exclusion of ethics, however, for Enoch offers repeated exhortations to moral behavior (vv 3-4, 18-19).[29] *1 Enoch* 91:1-19 also illustrates the shift away from the OT emphasis on God and divine action.

Other features found in some testaments in Hellenistic Judaism are a trip to heaven or a vision of the end-time. Kolenkow contends that such developments represent a borrowing of a type of material commonly used in the Gentile world.[30] Testaments of this kind frequently draw upon the insights gained from such a trip or vision to form a basis for an authoritative forecast at the time of death/ departure. Prediction is a common element in farewell speeches, but this apocalyptic twist shows how the testamentary literature has been adapted to fit various needs and interests.

Kurz points to yet another point of variation in the stream of testamentary writings:[31]

> [Biblical and Greco-Roman examples] differ significantly in tone, situation, vocabulary, and rhetoric. In Greco-Roman literature, the speakers of farewell addresses are generally statesmen or philosoph-

[28]So Berger (*Formgeschichte*, 76), who contends that the OT alone cannot account for the flourishing of testaments; there must also be an influence from Hellenism (cf. Becker, 1-5; Collins, "Testaments," 325).

[29]Kolenkow ("Testaments," 262-4) traces recent scholarship on testaments and notes two major viewpoints: Munck et al. emphasize how apocalyptically oriented the genre is, and von Nordheim et al. emphasize the primacy of ethics in testaments. Baltzer finds the juxtaposition of ethics and apocalyptic problematic ("... ethical instruction differs greatly from apocalyptic speculation. Other things being equal, one would trace each to a different *Sitz im Leben*" [153].), though an eschatological section with blessings and curses may be expected in testaments on the model of the covenant formulary (153-4). Kolenkow ("Testaments," 263-4) sees a greater coherence in the combination of apocalyptic and ethics since both are authoritative teaching. She further argues, "Apocalyptic teaching needs heavenly authority (a vision or trip to heaven); ethical teaching needs the authority of experience; and both assume reward and punishment" (264). Testaments that mingle ethical and apocalyptic elements include *T. Levi; 1 Enoch* 91:1-19; *2 Apoc. Bar.* 31-34; 44-46; Deut 33; 2 Pet.

[30]Kolenkow, "Genre," 61-4 (*1 Enoch* 91-94, *Life of Adam and Eve* 25-29, and *T. Levi* are cited as examples).

[31]Kurz, "Luke 22:14-38," 261.

ers. They show much concern with suicide, the meaning of death, questions about noble deaths, and life after death. Most of this is alien to deaths and farewells in the biblical traditions. Conversely, Greco-Roman death scenes lack the strong biblical emphasis on God's plan, people and covenant, or on theodicy and theological interpretations of history.

There is some debate as to the nature of the link between testaments and the inter-generational transfer of the OT covenant, for both are occasioned by a change of leadership,[32] and both set out standards of conduct for the future (see e.g., Josh 24:25-27). While it may be acknowledged that covenant and testament have natural points of intersection, a cogent argument for seeing them as independent forms can be mounted. Von Nordheim observes that the testamentary genre seeks to win a standard of conduct from hearers through logical argumentation which, among other things, points to the treasure of wisdom stored in the minds of the old and experienced, a treasure that ought not be lost. The covenant, however, belongs to a legal framework which enforces compliance through sanctions.[33] Nevertheless, the flexibility of the testamentary genre is seen in its association with covenant motifs.[34]

The divergent subforms of the farewell testament suggest that the literature is representative of an adaptable tradition. Its basic elements often fell within the areas of gathering at the time of death, exhortation, recollection and prediction, though the proportion and arrangement of such elements could vary greatly. Thus, although the perspective on Luke 22:24-30 provided by the testamentary genre has a measure of shape and substance to it, the differing subforms make us cautious as to what does and does not constitute a true farewell testament. The testamentary genre is a family of literature, and its children have traveled widely and developed uniquely. In the end each farewell discourse must be analyzed with careful attention not only to the general nature of the literary tradition which it reflects, but also to its unique content and function in its literary context.[35]

---

[32]Baltzer, 81; cf. Munck, 168. On the subject, see Baltzer, 137-63.

[33]Von Nordheim, *Die Lehre I*, 230, 234-6, 241; *Die Lehre II*, 89-91, 144. Similarly Collins, "Testaments," 339; Hollander, 3; Michel, 56-7.

[34]Von Nordheim (*Die Lehre I*, 231) maintains that the testamentary genre may be adapted to encompass other genres (e.g., the "Bundesformular," et al.).

[35]J. Charlesworth says in regard to the testaments in the OT pseudepigrapha that the unique features of the literature should incline one not to make much of the common title "Testament" (1:773). He also states, "It is clear the that testaments do not represent a well-defined genre ..." (ibid.), and, "No binding genre was employed by the authors of the testaments, but one can discern among

A few observations about the functions of ancient farewell speeches are also in order. Here we ask what effect a farewell address might have had on its readers? What would a testament accomplish that would have been left undone had an author chosen another type of speech or literary form? A simple and precise answer here is as hard to come by as is a simple answer to the above questions about content. Testaments would have had various functions to fit the literary works in which they appeared and the *Sitze im Leben* in which they had a role. One can, however, detect some common functions for testaments, and an acquaintance with these may provide a useful perspective when we turn to Luke 22.

An important distinction regarding function is made by Eades, namely that of *Sitz im Leben*.[36] A fictitious discourse naturally functions only in the *Sitz im Leben* of its writer (and later communities), but a discourse with a historical basis would also have had certain functions in the setting of its origin.[37] Therefore, although the following discussion of functions focuses on the testament in its literary setting, the possible existence of links with functions associated with historical roots is not simply overlooked.

A further perspective concerns the nature of the *Sitz im Leben* of a testament's author and readers. Harrelson maintains that in late Judaism the search for and retention of traditions from the past which testaments represented were owing to political, cultural and economic threats to Jewish society.[38] A farewell discourse embodies the mentality which seeks continuity in times of change and adversity.[39]

them a loose format ..." (ibid.). Soards (55 and n. 50) expresses a similar view. He rightly questions Léon-Dufour's attempt to match every element of Luke's testament (22:14-38) with some information in *T. Naphtali* as not allowing for sufficient variety in the literary genre (55, n. 50; cf. Léon-Dufour, "Letzte Mahl," 55, and elsewhere).

[36]Eades, 796. LaVerdiere notes that the farewell discourse is a way of having an important historical figure (i.e., Jesus) address the various issues which the community at the time of writing had to face. The farewell testament in Luke 22:14-38 "is Luke's most succinct answer to the question, 'What would Jesus say to us if he were among us as a historical figure today?'" ("Passion," 41).

[37]On the issue of historicity, see n. 8 above. Moreover, even if a given testament is thought to be fictitious, it still has functions on two levels (the story world and the setting of the readers/ hearers), both of which are important to the interpretation of a finished text.

[38]Harrelson, 209; cf. LaVerdiere, "Testament," 12; Michel, 54-5. This notion may shed some light on Luke 22:14-38, though it is difficult to establish such a reconstruction with certainty.

[39]Roloff, *Apostelgeschichte*, 302.

A function of a testament on the lips of an important historical figure is its capacity to lend authority to a writer's message, an authority enhanced by the setting of impending death.[40] By depicting one's writing as being in continuity with revered ancient figures and writings, an author can legitimize its content and/ or emphasize its importance, and thereby win acceptance of its message.

Another common function of the testament is dealing with the matter of "succession." Although it was more or less automatic for the eldest son to acquire the authority of the dying *paterfamilias* (cf. sec. 2.4.1), in other settings in which the heir to the "throne" had not already been chosen (e.g., Deut 31-34; 1 Macc 2:49-70) it would be crucial for testators to name their successors. A call for obedience to the successor, a feature that surfaces frequently, combines the functions of lending authority to a discourse and dealing with succession.[41]

The recollections and predictions common in testaments sometimes have historiographical functions. In a period of adversity a testament attributed to a respected ancient figure that promises the ongoing care of God for his people would offer encouragement, as would the recollections of God's provision in the testator's past. Thus a sweeping view of time, of life as we know it, may be encompassed in the farewell discourse, with the testator standing in the center confidently interpreting the course of history (cf. sec. 9.3).[42] Such portrayals may have consequent apologetic, legitimatory, pastoral or other functions in the testator's era.

Kurz claims that Luke 22:14-38 functions paraenetically on two levels: the story and the readers (and the two overlap greatly).[43] Although clearly not unique to farewell discourses, the paraenetic function finds a special nuance and emphasis: the testamentary setting gives paraenesis a heightened poignancy and urgency—last words focus on ultimate concerns.[44] While nearly all testaments involve some instructions for con-

---

[40]So Eades, 797; LaVerdiere, "Testament," 12. Kolenkow ("Testaments," 259) notes that the testament is authoritative because no one would be depicted as lying at the hour of death or judgment. The authoritative weight of a testament can also be employed to establish a point that may not be generally accepted (260).

[41]Reference to or appointment of successors is seen in Deut 31:7-8; 1 Kgs 2:1, 12; 1 Chr 28:5-7; 1 Macc 2:66; 3:1. On Luke's use of the farewell discourse to legitimize successors, see Kurz, "Luke 22:14-38," 265; Sellew, 77.

[42]So Léon-Dufour, "Tradition," 112-13; "Letzte Mahl," 42; Lohfink, *Sammlung*, 80. On historiographical functions see esp. Kurz, "Luke 22:14-38," 265-7. Cf. esp. Acts 20:17-38.

[43]Kurz, "Luke 22:14-38," 264-5. On paraenetic functions see also Matera, *Passion*, 164, 191; von Nordheim, *Die Lehre I*, 232-7.

duct, the Testaments of the Twelve Patriarchs offer an excellent model here with their frequent pinpointing of a central vice or virtue.[45]

It may also be noted that the above functions are not fully distinct from on another: the perceived authority of the speaker gives weight to paraenesis; succession is a way of interpreting and coping with changes history brings. Ultimately, therefore, as was the case in terms of content, one must study each testament on its own terms and in its literary setting in order to most adequately recover its functions.

Before turning to Luke 22:14-38 it may be reiterated that the variations between given testamentary discourses may often be great, but not so great as to cloud the presence of certain basic content elements (i.e., gathering, exhorting, reviewing, predicting)[46] and functions (i.e., to lend authority to a message, connect with the past, deal with succession, interpret history, set forth paraenesis). The variations on the form reveal a breadth of interest and a flexible quality of the testamentary genre.[47]

5.3 The Genre Classification of Luke 22:14-38

At this point we turn our attention to Luke's discourse in the Last Supper Narrative: Does Luke 22:14-38 appear to be within the stream of the testamentary genre?[48] While allowing for some unique aspects in this discourse, is it apparent that this text is sufficiently well aligned with the above description of the farewell testament to suggest that it was written/ compiled under a significant influence from that formal tradition? In order to address this question, two further questions will be posed: How do vv 14-38 correspond to the generic pattern, and how do they depart from it? First we consider the positive correspondences.

Before taking up the basic components of the testament, it may be established at the outset that Jesus' death is in view at five points in vv 14-38,[49] and three of them (1, 3 and 5) are without parallel in the Markan

[44]See Kurz, *Farewell*, 69.

[45]See n. 93 below.

[46]So Léon-Dufour, "Jésus," 150-1. Similarly Michel, 54; Munck, "Discours," 159; von Nordheim, *Die Lehre I*, 229; et al.

[47]Cf. n. 35 above.

[48]That Luke should be capable of adapting or writing within such a tradition seems apparent from the literary quality of his preface (Luke 1:1-4), his obvious acquaintance with the OT (LXX) in which many testaments appear, and his demonstrated capacity to impose a unity on disparate traditional materials (e.g., Luke 13:22-30 [according to Chilton, 184-5; Maddox, 124]; cf. Kurz, "Luke 22:14-38," 257; *Farewell*, 69).

[49]V 29 is not among them since it will be argued (sec. 7.4.2) that διατίθημι

Last Supper: 1) Jesus is the subject of παθεῖν in Luke 22:15. While παθεῖν can refer to suffering in general, the term in v 15 has the usual Lukan meaning of suffering unto death.[50] 2) Jesus gives the bread and wine as signs of his body and shed blood for the apostles (vv 19-20).[51] The separation of a body and its blood calls to mind an image of sacrifice and thus death.[52] 3) The apostles are to repeat the Lord's Supper "in remembrance" of Jesus (cf. 1 Cor 11:24), an injunction that clearly anticipates a period in which Jesus will be absent. 4) Jesus is about to be betrayed, and he must "go" (vv 21-22). In v 22 πορεύεται has the sense of a euphemism or technical term meaning "to die" (so ὑπάγει in Mark 14:21).[53] This is particularly clear in light of Luke 22:33 where Peter states that he is ready "to go" (πορεύεσθαι) with Jesus to prison and death. 5) Jesus' "service" (v 27c) includes his humiliation unto death (see the discussion in sec. 6.5.3).[54]

Jesus' plan to eat the Passover with the Twelve is described in Luke 22:8-14. In contrast to the description in Mark 14:12 (par. Matt 26:17), the Lukan Jesus takes the initiative to arrange for this shared meal (22:8). Since it is typical with testamentary discourses that the dying leader himself arranges for his group or family to be called together to hear his parting words,[55] Luke 22:8 may signal the writer's interest to recast the Last Supper in a testamentary form.[56]

Jesus gives three sets of exhortations to the assembled group, each of which is without parallel in Mark's Last Supper: 1) Vv 19-20 contain the injunction to continue to observe the cultic feast which is inaugurated then and there. 2) Jesus subsequently delivers a paraenetic injunction to turn away from worldly definitions of greatness and adopt the posture of humble service (vv 25-27). 3) Later he tells the Twelve to prepare them-

---

there means "to confer" and not "to will."

[50]Léon-Dufour, "Letzte Mahl," 44 and n. 45 (so Feldkämper, 208; Fitzmyer, *Gospel*, 2:1398; Guillaume, 145; F. Schütz, 20). Suffering in general may be seen in 17:25, but death is in view in 24:26, 46; Acts 1:3; 3:18; 17:3. Matera (*Passion*, 162) suggests that 22:15-18 constitutes a prediction of death by explaining that this is Jesus' last passover, but that view of vv 16, 18 is hard to prove.

[51]See sec. 6.5.3, n. 209, on the text-critical problem here.

[52]I. H. Marshall, *Gospel*, 802-3.

[53]Cf. BAGD, "πορεύομαι," 692, def. 2a; "ὑπάγω," 836-7, def. 3.

[54]The death predictions in vv 15, 19-20, 21-22 and 27 are given in direct speech, so the hearers in the story world are as aware as Luke's readers that the end has come for Jesus.

[55]See sec. 5.2 above; so e.g., Matera, *Passion*, 161.

[56]That Luke is dependent on Mark in Luke 22:7-14 is highly probable (so e.g., Schürmann, "Dienst," 99; *Paschamahlbericht*, 75-110; Soards, 116; Taylor, *Passion*, 46).

selves for a new era of conflict (v 36); adversities lie ahead in the period of his absence.[57]

Further, Jesus offers recollections of the past, though they are less prominent here than the other elements of the farewell genre. Recollections appear at three points, and again each is without parallel in the Markan Last Supper: 1) Although Jesus' reference to his service (v 27c) has symbolic dimensions, it probably encompasses actions from the whole of his ministry, including the passion, with and for the apostles (cf. sec. 6.5.3). 2) In v 28 Jesus briefly recalls the "trials" of his public ministry which the apostles have endured with him (cf. sec. 7.3.2). 3) Before exhorting the apostles to prepare themselves for coming conflict (v 36), he asks them, "When I sent you out with no purse or bag or sandals, did you lack anything?" (v 35), recalling the sending of the seventy (-two) (10:4).[58] The recollections may not constitute the lengthiest component of the speech (contrast e.g., many of *The Testaments of the Twelve Patriarchs*), but they do bring out important issues and imply that the past provides a crucial perspective as one looks to the future.

Five predictions of the future are also found in this discourse, three of which (3, 4 and 5) are without parallel in the Markan Last Supper. 1) Jesus forecasts a coming of the kingdom of God in which he will break his fast (vv 16, 18).[59] 2) The announcement of betrayal (vv 21-22) amounts to a prediction of an event in the immediate future. 3) The provision of seats at the anticipated banquet and thrones from which to rule the twelve tribes (vv 29-30) is also predictive.[60] 4) Peter's denial is prophesied (v 34), an event that for Mark occurs at the Mount of Olives (14:26-31).[61] 5) A time of adversity and conflict is implicitly predicted in the order to secure supplies and arms (v 36).[62]

Clearly, then, vv 14-38 present a discourse that exhibits the basic components of the testamentary genre: a man about to die gathers his

[57]At all three points Luke's imperative verbs signal instructions for behavior (ποιεῖτε in v 19; γινέσθω in v 26b; ἀράτω, πωλησάτω and ἀγορασάτω in v 36).

[58]Luke 22:35, however, recalls the past as a negative example; it will be contradicted in Jesus' subsequent instruction (v 36). Only vv 27c-28 highlight what is exemplary from the past.

[59]Cf. sec. 7.4.4 on the time frame for Jesus' anticipated feast.

[60]So Léon-Dufour, "Testament," 279-80. Neyrey (22) states regarding v 28, "that it is characteristic of farewell speeches to contain forecasts of difficult times coming upon one's followers." There is, however, nothing predictive in v 28 (see sec. 7.3.2 for a critique of Conzelmann's view on v 28).

[61]Reference to future degeneration is made in seven of Kurz's 22 speeches ("Luke 22:14-38," 262). Warnings against defection are common in testaments.

[62]The expression ἀλλὰ νῦν in v 36 shifts the perspective to this new era.

people to bid them farewell, and his words to them include exhortations, recollections and predictions.[63] Further, three of these four basic testamentary genre elements (gathering, recollection and exhortation) are wholly lacking in Mark's Last Supper Narrative.[64] To be sure, the death setting is plain in Mark 14:18-25, and the Markan Jesus does speak in such a way as to convey the importance of his death (v 24), but the key point here is that Mark's text nonetheless does not conform closely at all to the testamentary genre.

By way of clarification, the above breakdown of Luke 22:14-38 assumes a mixing of generic elements (i.e., we do not first have recollection, then exhortation, then prediction). Other attempts to outline the farewell form of vv 14-38 have sought to avoid such an interplay, but with limited success. For example, Matera breaks the speech down into three basic elements: in vv 14-23 Jesus announces his death; in vv 24-30 he recalls his past life; in vv 31-38 he looks to the future.[65] While Matera makes an important point in seeing recollection in both vv 24-27 and 28-30, there is much in vv 24-30 that does not fit under that heading (i.e., exhortation and prediction also surface). For Léon-Dufour, vv 24-30 teach the proper attitude for those whom Jesus leaves behind,[66] but this heading too, while pointing to a vital Lukan concern, seems too specific to embrace the whole unit (e.g., vv 29-30 seem to describe a reward *resulting from* a right "attitude").[67] Further, the precedent set by fare-

[63]Léon-Dufour ("Testament," 281) offers a similar summary of vv 14-38 as a farewell testament: "Confrontons encore une fois *le texte lucanien et la tradition testamentaire.* La plupart des motifs de cette forme apparaissent chez Luc: situation de mort imminente, convocation des disciples pour un repas au cours duquel la mort prochaine est annoncée, exhortation à un comportement qui réponde à celui du moribond dans le passé, encouragement dans la perspective d'un avenir merveilleux, avertissement du serieux de la situation des survivants, qui est celle d'une lutte incessante" (emphasis original). Also regarding the Lukan Last Supper, Schürmann (*Ursprung*, 148) summarizes, "Bei diesem Mahl gab Jesus aber nicht nur eine Stiftung und Gabe, er hielt auch eine Abschiedsrede, in welcher Rückblicke und Vorhersagen mit Verheißungen und Anweisungen eng verwoben sind."

[64]Only two predictions are present in the Markan account (those concerning Jesus' betrayal and his future drink in the kingdom of God). The conformity of Luke 22:14-38 to the testamentary genre is highlighted by a comparison with Jesus' Last Supper sayings in Mark and Matthew (so Michel, 63; et al.; cf. Léon-Dufour, "Tradition," 112). Correspondingly, some of the differences between Luke and Mark here may be explained by Luke's adoption of the testamentary model (so Sellew, 76).

[65]Matera, *Passion*, 162.

[66]Léon-Dufour, "Testament," 268. Vv 14-23 and 31-38 fall into categories roughly parallel to Matera's.

well speeches in general does not warrant the attempt to uncover a structure which neatly separates generic elements. Therefore, it seems appropriate to restrict our efforts here to noting the presence of testamentary components, regardless of their arrangement.

A more careful examination of the Lukan Jesus' farewell speech reveals additional features that have precedent in testamentary literature and/ or are particularly well suited to the farewell setting. The many predictions of vv 14-38 are highlighted by Jesus' striking success at prophesying. Talbert observes that vv 7-13 "... lend credibility to [these] predictions by showing a prophecy in another regard fulfilled to the letter."[68] Not only does Jesus the testator predict the future, but the apostles (in the story world) and the reader have good reason to believe that his predictions will come true (the same could be said of the Markan Jesus [14:12-17]).

Léon-Dufour offers a further testamentary perspective on Luke 22:19-20 in addition to its role in foreshadowing Jesus' death: "Précisément, ces deux versets (19-20) du récit cultuel assument une fonction dans le discours d'adieu: symboliser par un acte (double) le mode nouveau de la présence de Jésus aux siens, thème original par rapport à la littérature testamentaire."[69] The farewell setting naturally raises the problem of the testator's imminent absence, and the observance of the Lord's Supper then provides a unique means for continued communion with Jesus after his departure.[70]

Regarding succession, Jesus has prayed that Peter would withstand the "sifting" of Satan and ultimately turn and "strengthen" his brothers (vv 31-32). He is singled out for a unique responsibility (vv 31-32), and though Luke does not suggest that an equivalent replacement for Jesus can be found, Peter's role in Acts would suggest that he is the newly appointed leader of the apostolic band.[71] Neither Mark nor Matthew tell

[67]Perhaps the fact that Luke is working with some independent sayings in weaving this discourse (so e.g., Kurz, "Luke 22:14-38," 257) should prompt one not to press the speech into a structure with broad headings and readily distinguishable elements.

[68]Talbert, *Reading Luke*, 207-8.

[69]Léon-Dufour, "Testament," 271; cf. Roloff, *Apostolat*, 184-5. Luke's clause, "do this in remembrance of me," makes explicit the ongoing quality of communion with Jesus (contrast the Markan account).

[70]Seen from another angle, the Last Supper also involves the participation of Jesus' followers in his death (Feldkämper, 209). Also see ch. 8 on the concept of discipleship as a means of remaining in relationship with the risen Jesus.

[71]To see in vv 28-30 an interest in succession (so Bammel, "Das Ende," 47; J. McDonald, 86; Neyrey, 25-6; et al.) is to miss the implication of v 30a (cf. vv 16, 18)

of a prayer of Jesus for Peter or an implicit commission to strengthen the others, but then neither Mark nor Matthew have a developed farewell discourse at the Last Supper.

Perhaps it is also noteworthy that the testamentary genre's key components overlap one another in vv 24-30. Exhortations and recollections merge in the example of Jesus (v 27c). Léon-Dufour states, "Ce petit développement [22:24-27] correspond d'assez près à la rétrospective testamentaire sur le passé pieux du moribond et à l'exhortation qui en dérive."[72] Further, recollections and predictions are wedded closely in vv 28-30 (cf. sec. 7.4.1). Moreover, an interest in the apostles' future leadership roles is seen throughout vv 25-30 (cf. sec. 9.1). The overlap of important farewell speech features in vv 24-30 may imply a concentrated influence of genre on Luke's redaction/ composition of those verses.

Now we must review vv 14-38 again and ask how these verses depart from the testamentary genre. There seems to be an obvious problem here, namely that vv 14-38 do not contain a proper speech. That is, there are substantial narrative elements (vv 17a, 19a, 20a, 23-24) as well as direct speech, and the direct speech is in dialogue and not monologue form (speakers are Jesus [vv 15-22], apostles [vv 23-24, indirect speech], Jesus [vv 25-32], Peter [v 33], Jesus [vv 34-35a], apostles [v 35b], Jesus [vv 36-37], apostles [v 38a], Jesus [v 38b]). So perhaps it is not appropriate to describe 22:14-38 as any kind of speech.

A close examination of ancient farewell discourses, however, undercuts this objection. Joshua the testator engages in dialogue with the people of Israel (Josh 23-24), as does Samuel (1 Sam 12:1-25). Even the famous and influential farewell speech in Plato's *Phaedo* is a prolonged dialogue between Socrates and his friends, and it too is occasionally interrupted by the narrator. Other examples of NT, OT, apocryphal and Greco-Roman testaments that include significant elements of narrative and dialogue could also be named.[73] In short, then, the literary tradition simply does not "require" pure monologue of a farewell testament.[74]

---

that Jesus will again be present with the dining and ruling apostles (cf. secs. 7.4.3-4). Léon-Dufour ("Testament," 275-80) correctly observes that the matter of succession is addressed in vv 31-34 and not in vv 29-30.

[72]Léon-Dufour, "Testament," 273.

[73]E.g., John 13-17; Deut 31-34 (dialogue with God); *Jub.* 35; *2 Apoc. Bar.* 31-34; 44-46; Plutarch *Cato Min.* 66-70.

[74]LaVerdiere ("Discourse," 1544) calls attention to the positive contribution of narrative and dialogue in Luke 22:14-38 in giving direction to a discourse (cf. Sellew, 76; Kurz, "Luke 22:14-38," 251, 253). Von Nordheim (*Die Lehre I*, 231)

Another objection is that, unlike *The Testaments of the Twelve Patriarchs* and many OT and other testaments, Luke 22 does not record the actual death of Jesus nor mention anything about his burial.[75] On the contrary, there is a great deal of important action in the Lukan story before we come to the climactic moment of Jesus' death (23:46). Moreover, what would seem to be the testator's blessing is deferred to 24:50-51.[76] So if 22:14-38 presents a farewell speech, it is marred by its unfinished form.

This objection too ultimately amounts to little, though we do well to observe that Luke exercises some freedom in his attachment to the genre. Although this "death scene" lacks a death, it was noted above that Jesus' impending fate is clearly on the horizon in vv 14-38, so it is not wholly correct to say the death is omitted. Further, we face the same problem with Luke's other farewell address, Acts 20:17-38. Paul's speech to the Ephesian elders at Miletus is clearly is in the stream of testamentary genre,[77] but it also lacks the element of the testator's death.[78] Moreover, nowhere in Acts do we read of Paul's death; at the end of the narrative Paul is preaching the kingdom of God in Rome.

There is some debate as to whether Luke actually alludes to Paul's death here,[79] or merely adapts the farewell form to mark the end of an era.[80] It could be that Luke's focus is on Paul specifically in relation to the Ephesians, in which case the testamentary perspective connotes a death *to them*—they will see his face no more (20:25, 38).[81] In any case, one would expect that if the actual death of Paul was in view, we would learn something more about it before the end of Acts.[82]

similarly sees the presence of dialogue as posing no threat to the integrity of a testament (contrast Léon-Dufour, "Letzte Mahl," 47).

[75]Léon-Dufour, "Testament," 281.

[76]So Kurz, "Luke 22:14-38," 259; cf. Parsons, 55-8.

[77]So Michel (71), who calls the Miletus speech a "Musterbeispiel" of the genre. Others who agree that the Miletus speech is fashioned on the model of the farewell testament include Conzelmann, *Acts*, 176; Dibelius, *Studies*, 157; Gempf, 322; Kurz, "Luke 22:14-38," 252-3; Lambrecht, 326, 332-3; Lövestam, 2; Munck, "Discours," 159-61; von Nordheim, *Die Lehre I*, 238-9; Radl, *Paulus*, 127-32; Roloff, *Apostolat*, 227; against Haenchen (*Acts*, 596, who favors apology over testament). Lambrecht (332-3) lists the many features of the Miletus speech that are common in the testamentary tradition; the agreement is quite extensive.

[78]So too 1 Sam 12:1-25; 2 *Apoc. Bar.* 31-34 (cf. Michel, 48).

[79]So Conzelmann, *Acts*, 174; Gempf, 323; Munck, *Acts*, 205. Hemer ("Speeches," 81) cautions that one cannot be sure that Paul's death is in view.

[80]So Lambrecht (335-6), regarding the end of Paul's unhindered freedom that comes with his arrest. Hanson (203) has a similar view.

[81]Von Nordheim, *Die Lehre I*, 238-9.

The salient point, then, from this brief consideration of the farewell speech in Acts 20 is that if Luke is able to follow the testamentary genre there and yet adapt certain important elements of it, we may presume that he could do the same in Luke 22 when writing under the constraints of the resurrection event. This point, in fact, serves to illustrate the nature of the adherence to the testamentary genre we have seen in Luke 22:14-38, and in several other testaments from antiquity: both basic similarities and certain notable differences are observed when testaments are set side by side. J. Charlesworth's claim that "the testaments do not represent a well-defined genre" seems apt.[83]

Returning to the issue of the "farewell" elements of Luke 24 (and Acts 1), Kurz contends that Luke defers the "usual blessing" at the end of a farewell address to the end of the Gospel (24:50-51).[84] Further, there is significant teaching content in 24:44-49 including instructions for the time of Jesus' imminent absence (cf. Acts 1:4-8). Parsons argues that Luke returns in 24:50-53 to farewell elements omitted in 22:14-38, thus forming an *inclusio* encasing Jesus' passion-resurrection between a farewell address and its conclusion with his ascension in the pattern of the departing hero.[85]

The fact that the testamentary genre is somewhat "loose" and allows for a wide variety of speech types within its stream prompts one not to dismiss too quickly the idea that Luke 24 and Acts 1 present deferred conclusions to the Luke 22:14-38 Last Supper discourse.[86] And it cannot

[82]Dibelius' view (*Studies*, 158) that Luke wishes to end Acts on a triumphant note and thus leaves out the actual death of Paul hardly seems plausible. Can the marked turn of events in Acts beginning with Paul's arrest (21:27ff), after which he is repeatedly on the defensive, really be thought of as the portrayal of a triumphant end?

[83]J. Charlesworth, 1:773 (the comment is made in regard to *The Testaments of the Twelve Patriarchs*, but has some relevance for Luke-Acts as well) (cf. n. 35 above). There are other points at which Luke 22:14-38 are said to be at odds with the testamentary form (e.g., the paucity of references to the past [see Léon-Dufour, "Testament," 281]), but they are relatively minor points and may be overlooked for two reasons: 1) The Miletus speech demonstrates Luke's willingness to clearly follow the literary pattern and yet depart from it at certain points. 2) Luke 22:14-38 still exhibits significant agreement with the form, as is shown above.

[84]Kurz, "Luke 22:14-38," 259; cf. 1 Macc 2:69. Michel (52-4) classifies the blessing as a "ziemlich häufig" motif in testaments, though it is not as common as a setting of impending death, gathering of hearers, paraenetic expressions, and the death/ departure, which are present in "fast allen Reden."

[85]Parsons, 58. Regretably, Parsons does not spell out the purpose of this device, nor does he specify its focal point.

[86]Von Nordheim (*Die Lehre II*, 146) argues that NT testaments reveal ex-

be denied that the teaching material in Luke 24:44-49 and Acts 1:4-8 focuses on preparing the disciples to carry on without their leader, a common feature of farewell addresses. Further, the fact that Luke 24 and Acts 1 present what are portrayed as literally Jesus' last words after which he departs into heaven makes the departure setting explicit.

Two weaknesses of the effort to minimize the independent status of the speech in Luke 22 by linking it closely with sayings in Luke 24 and Acts 1, however, may be noted. 1) The speech in 22:14-38 does not provide the kind of instruction that would be relevant only until the final words of the departing Jesus are given. On the contrary, many teachings in 22:14-38 look ahead to the life of the church as narrated in Acts (e.g., those on the Lord's Supper, servant leadership, and the new era of conflict). 2) There is a profound change of tone from Jesus' testament to his parting words. The horizon of death is vividly present in Luke 22:14-38, as is the anticipation of betrayal, denial and new conflicts. Despite the hope of future celebration (v 30), the aura of vv 14-38 is ominous and sobering. By contrast, in Luke 24 and Acts 1, the dead testator has returned to life, the disciples rejoice and praise God (24:52-53), they turn their thoughts to the restoration of the kingdom (1:6), and are commissioned to bear witness to Jesus throughout the world (1:8; 24:47-48). Now the tone is one of hope and success and advance. This striking shift of mood favors a reading of the farewell testament in chapter 22 and Jesus' parting words in Luke 24 and Acts 1 as independent addresses.[87]

Having viewed Luke 22:14-38 against the backdrop of genre, we can now affirm that this text may fairly be classified as a discourse designed on the model of the testamentary genre.[88] This affirmation does not overlook the points at which vv 14-38 do not seem to "fit" the genre well. Rather, it is based on the recognition that an inexact fit was not

---

tensive broadening of the form.

[87]Munck (165) allows each of Matt 28:19-20; Luke 2:25-35; 22:21-38; 24:36-53; John 13-17; 20:19-23; 21:15-23; Acts 1:2ff to be called a "discours d'adieu," though it is arguable that this broadens the generic stream unduly. Michel distinguishes the "letzte Worte Jesu nach der Auferstehung" and the "Abschiedsworte Jesu vor Passion und Auferstehung" (57-63), though both fall under the broad heading "Abschiedsreden" (57).

[88]Others who have reached a similar conclusion include Ernst, *Evangelium*, 589; Kurz, "Luke 22:14-38," 251; LaVerdiere, "Discourse," 1543, and "Passion," 41, and "Testament," 8; Léon-Dufour, "Testament," 266, and "Jésus," 153; Lohfink, *Sammlung*, 66, n. 171; Roloff, *Apostolat*, 184; Schürmann, *Ursprung*, 148; Sellew, 75. Smith (620, n. 22) concedes that Luke 22:14-38 is Jesus' farewell address, but he prefers the model of the symposium as a literary framework for the text (cf. sec. 3.2).

unusual; the ancients who would have read or heard many variations on the farewell discourse theme would have found the unique discourse in Luke 22:14-38 well within the stream of the testamentary genre.

5.4 Genre and the Interpretation of Luke 22:24-30

Now we ask how an awareness that Luke 22:24-30 appears in a farewell testament can extend the platform built here (i.e., Part One) for the subsequent analysis of the text (Part Two). Here we are particularly eager to uncover connections between genre and meaning—lines from form which can lead to or influence the thought and expression of a text.[89] The death setting of testaments may be considered first. When death is at the door, people speak of ultimate concerns, issues that matter profoundly to them and to their hearers who must go on without them. Accordingly, a sense of urgency and earnestness characterizes farewell speeches, and it is present in Luke 22:24-30 as well. This is not to minimize the importance of other material in Luke's Gospel nor to overlook the focus on Jesus' death already present in pre-Lukan Last Supper traditions, but merely to highlight the poignant and emphatic tone of a farewell address.[90]

The testamentary genre may be linked to a text's meaning not only through urgency but also through focus.[91] The farewell address is an occasion for a clear summary of one's values or accomplishments,[92] or for conveying in no uncertain terms the key lesson(s) which a testator has to

[89]Unfortunately the literature on testaments has little to contribute here. Alter (179), however, rightly notes that an understanding of how a story is told helps bring one close to its meaning. Further, Munck's observations ("Discours," 163) are apt: "En précisant le genre des discours d'adieu, notre but n'est pas de constater l'existence d'une forme d'art qui peut prouver une dépendance littéraire, mais de découvrir une forme et de préciser son contenu pour arriver à une plus profonde compréhension des textes."

[90]Cf. Kurz, *Farewell*, 52, 69; Schlatter, *Lukas*, 423-4; Senior, 54. Von Nordheim (*Die Lehre I*, 237-9) maintains that the availability of a testator's treasure of wisdom "now or never" gives special weight to his words. It may be argued that the urgency of the testament is a property of its death setting and not of the genre itself—the words of the Markan Jesus at the Last Supper are no less urgent since they are in the shadow of impending death. However, it is the light *thrown upon a testator's discourse* (i.e., upon recollection, exhortation and prediction) by the death setting that yields a farewell discourse's distinctive poignancy.

[91]Kurz, *Farewell*, 53.

[92]Thus Bammel ("Testament," 76) points out that what Caesar Augustus achieved is recorded most plainly in his testament. Michel (51-2) and others observe a tendency toward self-exoneration in many testaments.

pass on and his most significant deeds which followers must take to heart. This perspective would prompt one to look for a summary of important deeds or values in Jesus' testament, or perhaps for teaching on a central virtue or vice (so *T. 12 Patr.*).[93] The fact that the only recollections in Jesus' farewell speech of his pious past are in vv 27-28, together with the observation that v 27 contains the most general and broadly applicable exhortation in the speech, may imply that vv 25-28 constitute the paraenetic core of the discourse.[94]

When a writer/ speaker follows the testamentary form, a decision is made to employ—in some recognizable way—its basic content and functions.[95] Major points of departure from the "pattern" may then clash with reader expectations and highlight striking features that would go unnoticed apart from an awareness of genre. For example, why does the Lukan Jesus speak so little of his exemplary life (only v 27c, and v 28 by implication)? Why might a forecast of the future not correspond to the time of the testator's absence (v 30)? How come the somber speech turns to language of victory and celebration (vv 29-30)?[96] And what is one to make of the obtuse (v 24), frail (v 34), betraying (vv 21-22) followers of Jesus? Testators sometimes rebuke their people for lamenting the leader's passing, but the apostles seem to be particularly at odds with Jesus. Could there be an emphasis on the tragedy of Jesus going to the grave utterly alone? Could this variation of the testamentary form be meant to highlight the fallibility of the apostles and other leaders in the church era (cf. sec. 8.4)?

An awareness of genre may also prompt the interpreter to analyze the interrelation of generic elements. For instance, the prediction of adversity and conflict (v 36) may be logically related to the recollections of the past; i.e., it may be implied that service and faithful perseverance (vv 27c-28) are to be continued when facing future trials (v 36).[97] More

[93]E.g., *T. Reuben* stresses the danger of sexual temptation, *T. Simeon* warns against envy, *T. Dan* speaks against anger, *T. Gad* proscribes hatred, *T. Jos.* commends piety and endurance in the face of temptation.

[94]Cf. Bossuyt and Radermakers, 475. Schürmann (*Ursprung*, 149) maintains that v 27 contains Jesus' "zentrale letzte Anweisung über die Ordnung in der Jüngergemeinde."

[95]A related point could be made in terms of reader expectations: when a reader recognizes the testamentary form, the expectation of its conventional features is aroused (cf. York, 39).

[96]Léon-Dufour ("Testament," 276) observes that Jesus is no gloomy testator; he speaks as if he is already in glory.

[97]Cf. the OT motif of God's past faithfulness as a ground for hope for the future when the testator is absent (e.g., Deut 31-34; Josh 23-24; 1 Sam 12:1-25).

broadly, the testamentary interest in recollection as well as prediction reveals an awareness of the passage of time: how can the future be shaped in light of what can be learned from the past? We have already seen that the Passover (sec. 3.3) and the Lord's Supper (3.5.1) call attention to the sweep of salvation history. Perhaps the testamentary framework of Luke's discourse would intimate an accentuated interest in the linkage of past and future in the person of Jesus the testator.

The farewell genre allows a text to be impacted by some poignant paradoxes.[98] While the whole orientation of the form assumes the imminent absence of the testator, Jesus anticipates a future reunion with the apostles at his kingdom table (v 30; cf. vv 16, 18). The looming reality of the resurrection and an accompanying hope of future reunion shows through in Jesus' testament, and it gives the speech a distinctive quality.[99] The genre has taught the reader to think in terms of absence, but in this respect the Lukan Jesus defies expectation to speak of presence (also see vv 19-20).[100]

---

[98]Cf. Käsemann, *Testament*, 4-5.

[99]LaVerdiere, *Testament*, 13. Also see secs. 7.4.2 and 9.2 on the non-testamentary sense of διατίθημι (v 29)—surely a striking feature in a testamentary discourse. Luke 22:14-38 is not the only testament to anticipate life after death (cf. Plato *Phaedo* 63B-C), but the image of a dying man describing a future reunion with his disciples is unusual in a testament, and it is striking.

[100]The broader perspective gained by examining the functions of speeches in historical writings generally seems to give little aid in the quest to interpret Luke 22:24-30. Much has been written on the speeches in Acts (e.g., Bruce, *Greek Text*; Glasson; Hemer, *Acts*; Schweizer, "Speeches"; Wilckens) and the conventions of ancient historiography (e.g., Barrett, *Luke*; Debelius, *Studies*; Hemer, *Acts* and "Luke"; Kurz, "Luke 22:14-38"; LaVerdiere, "Discourse"; I. H. Marshall, *Historian* [esp. 21-76]; Mosley; van Unnik, "Historiography"), but the question of historical authenticity has to a great degree suffocated these discussions, and the role of discourses in historical writings has been largely overlooked. Further, likening Lukan and historical writings is complicated by the fact that Luke's Gospel contains a far higher percentage of direct speech than did the writings of earlier or contemporary historians (in Luke's Gospel 68% of the verses contain direct speech [so Hemer, *Acts*, 417]; this is in marked contrast to Josephus where only 59 of 673 short sections of *Jewish War* contain direct speech, and the first book of Polibius which has hardly any oration in direct speech [ibid.]). When much of a work consists of direct speech, one is hard pressed to demonstrate that discourses deliver key information. A speech in a distinctive style (i.e., a testament), however, may signal certain emphases.

5.5 Conclusion

In the present chapter we have explored the family likeness of ancient Greco-Roman, Jewish and Christian farewell speeches in terms of content and function. There is value for the purposes of interpreting individual testaments in recognizing the existence of this literary tradition and its influence upon given discourses within its (relatively wide) stream. Regarding the correspondence of Luke 22:14-38 to the genre, there is enough agreement to warrant the conclusion that the text has been deliberately cast in this generic form, a conclusion highlighted by comparisons with the Markan and Matthean Last Supper accounts. Finally, the question of the relationship between the testamentary genre and the interpretation of Luke 22:24-30 has been raised: how might genre have an impact on meaning? It has been proposed that an awareness of a text's testamentary genre gives aid for its interpretation by calling attention to or accentuating the atmosphere of urgency, the presence of a focus, departures from the testamentary form, and the interrelation of farewell components.

PART TWO:

ANALYSIS OF LUKE 22:24-30

Chapter 6:
Luke 22:24-27: Greatness in Service

6.1 Introduction

While Part One of this study has centered on background perspectives, Part Two presents a direct analysis of Luke 22:24-30. The preceding findings constitute a multi-faceted platform upon which we may now stand to examine the Lukan text in detail. An interest in backgrounds, however, remains; Part Two will not only build on the findings of Part One, at points certain new background contexts will also be explored. Thus there is an ongoing interplay of looking closely and stepping back which will allow Luke 22:24-30 to be seen in the light of relevant background material. Nonetheless, the basic progression from Part One to Part Two is that of general to specific, context to text.

The aim of the present chapter is to discern facets of the meaning of Luke 22:24-27 through a close analysis of the text. To achieve this aim we will probe 22:24-27 from various angles: the use of sources will be considered (6.2) and the general flow of thought in vv 24-27 will be traced (6.3). This will set the stage for an in-depth examination of the event narrated in v 24 (6.4) and Jesus' response given in vv 25-27 (6.5). The concrete and vivid quality of Luke's language will be kept in view throughout, for an adequate understanding of vv 24-27 depends on an ability to "feel" the sometimes sharp social, political and religious edges of the text.

6.2 Sources for Luke 22:24-27

Although determining Luke's use of sources is only one step in the larger process of discerning the meaning of a finished Lukan text, it can provide valuable guidance in the search for that meaning and for the task of estimating the degree to which such meaning is Luke's own. What then is the relationship between Luke 22:24-27 and Mark 10:41-45?

	Mark 10:41-45		**Luke 22:24-27**
1	**41)** καὶ ἀκούσαντες οἱ δέκα		
2	ἤρξαντο ἀγανακτεῖν	—	**24a)** ἐγένετο δὲ καὶ φιλονεικία
3			ἐν αὐτοῖς,
4	περὶ Ἰακώβου καὶ Ἰωάννου.		
5			**b)** τὸ τίς αὐτῶν δοκεῖ εἶναι
6			μείζων.
7	**42a)** καὶ προσκαλεσάμενος αὐτοὺς		
8	ὁ Ἰησοῦς λέγει αὐτοῖς·	—	**25a)** ὁ δὲ εἶπεν αὐτοῖς·
9	**b)** οἴδατε ὅτι		
10	οἱ δοκοῦντες ἄρχειν τῶν ἐθνῶν	—	**b)** οἱ βασιλεῖς τῶν ἐθνῶν
11	κατακυριεύουσιν αὐτῶν	—	κυριεύουσιν αὐτῶν
12	**c)** καὶ οἱ μεγάλοι αὐτῶν	—	**c)** καὶ οἱ ἐξουσιάζοντες αὐτῶν
13	κατεξουσιάζουσιν αὐτῶν.		
14			εὐεργέται καλοῦνται.
15	**43a)** οὐχ οὕτως δέ ἐστιν ἐν ὑμῖν,	—	**26a)** ὑμεῖς δὲ οὐχ οὕτως,
16	**b)** ἀλλ'	—	**b)** ἀλλ'
17	ὃς ἂν θέλῃ		
18	μέγας γενέσθαι ἐν ὑμῖν	—	ὁ μείζων ἐν ὑμῖν
19	ἔσται ὑμῶν διάκονος,	—	γινέσθω ὡς ὁ νεώτερος
20	**44)** καὶ	—	**c)** καὶ
21	ὃς ἂν θέλῃ ἐν ὑμῖν εἶναι		
22	πρῶτος	—	ὁ ἡγούμενος
23	ἔσται πάντων δοῦλος·	—	ὡς ὁ διακονῶν.
24			**27a)** τίς γὰρ μείζων,
25			ὁ ἀνακείμενος ἢ ὁ διακονῶν;
26			**b)** οὐχὶ ὁ ἀνακείμενος;
27	**45a)** καὶ γὰρ ὁ υἱὸς τοῦ ἀνθρώπου	—	**c)** ἐγὼ δὲ
28			ἐν μέσῳ ὑμῶν εἰμι
29	οὐκ ἦλθεν διακονηθῆναι ἀλλὰ		
30	διακονῆσαι	—	ὡς ὁ διακονῶν.
31	**b)** καὶ δοῦναι τὴν ψυχὴν αὐτοῦ		
32	λύτρον ἀντὶ πολλῶν.		

6.2.1 The Case for Dependence on Mark

The matter of verbal agreement requires close attention here, for verbal factors have been used to defend both Markan and non-Markan source claims.[1] Ernst observes that twenty-one of Luke's sixty-seven words in vv 24-27 are found in Mark 10:42-45 (31%).[2] Soards, however, clarifies the issue by isolating a Lukan core which is dependent on Mark: while vv 24 and 27 are unparalleled, vv 25-26 are related to Mark 10:42-44.[3] Twenty of Luke's thirty-five words in vv 25-26 are matched by words in Mark (57%).[4]

Soards also describes the "remarkably similar" structure of Mark 10:41-45 and Luke 22:24-27; it consists of three parts:[5]

Mark		**Luke**
10:41	Introduction	22:24
10:42-44	Example and Teaching	22:25-26
10:45	Christological Conclusion	22:27

Page also detects "substantial resemblances" of structure shared by these pericopae which are "noteworthy," and summarizes,[6]

> In both, the issue which gives rise to Jesus' teaching is the disciples' concern with greatness, and, in both, His teaching includes three elements—(a) He contrasts the way greatness is expressed among Gentiles with that which ought to appertain among His followers, (b) He advocates a reversal of the pattern normally encountered in the

---

[1]E.g., Soards, 42 (Markan); Taylor, *Passion*, 62-3 (non-Markan).

[2]Ernst, *Evangelium*, 592 (and yet "... redaktionstechnische Argumente [sprechen] für eine unabhängige lk Sondertradition."); cf. Taylor, *Passion*, 61; Schürmann, *Abschiedsrede*, 64.

[3]Soards, 42. V 24 and Mark 10:41 share only καί (a conjunction for Mark, an adverb for Luke), and Luke 22:27 and Mark 10:45 have only forms of διακονέω in common. Cf. Bossuyt and Radermakers, 474; Taylor, *Passion*, 62-3.

[4]Soards, 42. We may note in addition here the conceptual similarity between Luke's φιλονεικία (v 24) and Mark's ἀγανακτέω (v 41) (so Taylor [*Jesus*, 186-7, n. 2], in spite of the fact that he favors a non-Markan source for Luke here).

[5]Soards, 31.

[6]Page, 148. Others who call attention to the structural similarities of these texts are Arens, 125; Crossan, *Fragments*, 289; Green *Death*, 46; Howard, *Das Ego*, 231; Jeremias, *Theology*, 293; Kertelge, "Menschensohn," 229; I. H. Marshall, *Gospel*, 811; Tödt, *Son of Man*, 207; Vööbus, *Prelude*, 31. A. Schulz (*Nachfolge*, 255) and Taylor (*Mark* 443) claim that the similarity of structure suggests a single historical basis (against Geldenhuys, 563; Hill, 77; Page, 150-2). Schürmann (*Abschiedsrede*, 84) rightly observes that Luke 22:27 differs in structure from Mark 10:45.

world, and (c) He appeals to His own example of service to illustrate His teaching.

The structural center of each pericope forms a hinge upon which the two contrasted principles of power and service turn. In Luke 22:26 and Mark 10:43 this hinge consists of an οὐ ... ἀλλά construction: with οὐ Jesus negates the option of power-based greatness (to which he likens the disciples' behavior), and with ἀλλά he commends to the disciples service-based greatness (with which he associates his own example). Structure thus merges with sense, for the two accounts share the same general line of thought.[7]

In sum, Luke 22:25-26 and Mark 10:42-44 have a relatively high level of verbal agreement (57%), and Luke 22:24-27 and Mark 10:41-45 have a common structure and a similar basic sense. Such claims have been taken as supporting the view that differences between the two accounts may simply be owing to Lukan redaction of a Markan *Vorlage*.[8]

6.2.2 The Case against Dependence on Mark

In spite of the above arguments, however, a case against dependence on Mark may be mounted. This will require us to weigh differences between the Lukan and Markan pericopae to determine whether they are substantial and whether they are typical of Lukan redaction; after all, the mere presence of discrepancies does not eliminate the possibility that Luke adapted a Markan original.

Although the level of verbal agreement noted above is significant, its *quality* must be assessed. Page notes the following:[9]

[Word statistics for vv 24-27] give an exaggerated impression of the

[7]So Schmid (327), who claims that vv 24-27 and Mark 10:35-45 are harmonious "im Grundgedanken." Cf. Ernst, *Evangelium*, 592.

[8]Regarding vv 25-26, Feuillet (378) and Schlosser (59-60, 65) are among those who claim that Luke rewrote Mark in Lukan style. Those who assert that Luke redacts Mark in at least part of vv 24-27 include J. Bailey, 35; Beare, *Records*, 227; Büchele, 169; Chance, 77; Danker *Jesus*, 348; L'Eplattenier, 252; Esler, 208; Fitzmyer, *Gospel*, 2:1412; George, *Études*, 193, 276-7; Gillman, 145; Gormley, 89; Goulder, *Luke*, 2:731; Kiddle, 277-9; Knox, 122; Kodell, "Death," 222; Lagrange, 548-9; Lampe, 840; Loisy, 515-16; R. Pesch, "Last Supper," 64; Perry, "Passion-Source," 260; Rese, 163; Rienecker, 503; Schlosser, 60-5; Schmid, 327-8; Schmithals, *Lukas*, 210; Schweizer, *Luke*, 333; Sellew, 79-80; Smith, 630; Soards, 39; Vööbus, *Prelude*, 31; Walasky, 36; Wilson, 50.

[9]Page, 149. Others who minimize the importance of verbal agreement here include Creed, 267; Schürmann, *Abschiedsrede*, 64-5; Taylor, *Passion*, 61-3.

extent of the verbal agreement, since only 16 words appear in the same form in both, and that includes 4 definite articles, 4 conjunctions, 3 third person plural pronouns, and the phrases οὐχ οὕτως and ἐν ὑμῖν. No verbs appear in exactly the same form in both passages, and the only noun they have in common is ἐθνῶν.

Also regarding quality of verbal agreement, one notes that κυριεύουσιν and ἐξουσιάζοντες (v 25) are paralleled in Mark only by forms prefixed with κατά.[10] Luke is ordinarily quite fond of compound verbs,[11] but here he would have omitted the κατά prefixes of Mark 10:42. Further, Luke uses comparative μείζων (v 26) while Mark has positive μέγας. Luke has the present imperative γινέσθω (v 26), but Mark has the aorist infinitive γενέσθαι.[12] And Luke has the articular substantive participle ὁ διακονῶν (v 27), but Mark has the anarthrous infinitive διακονῆσαι.

Moreover, Soards concedes that there is precious little to link vv 24 and 27 with the Markan text.[13] In addition, in vv 25-26 Luke "adds" the non-Markan reference to "kings" and the idea of "being called" or "calling oneself" a "benefactor." Further, Luke includes the double question form (v 27a), he does not use μέγας to describe political rulers (cf. Mark 10:42), he omits the copula in his cryptic v 26a (cf. Mark 10:43a), he refers to actual instead of potential greatness (cf. Mark 10:43b-44),[14] and he includes ὁ νεώτερος, ὁ ἡγούμενος and ὁ διακονῶν (cf. διάκονος, πρῶτος and δοῦλος in Mark 10:43b-44). Can we maintain that Luke was dependent upon Mark when he would have departed from the Markan text to such a great extent?[15]

---

[10]Additionally, Luke's οἱ ἐξουσιάζοντες functions as a substantive, but Mark's κατεξουσιάζουσιν "parallel" is a finite verb. The differences in usage between Luke's δοκεῖ and Mark's οἱ δοκοῦντες are even greater, though the presence of the root in both pericopae may be suggestive of some type of relationship.

[11]So Green, *Death*, 46; Schürmann, *Abschiedsrede*, 70, n. 234; Sellew, 79; cf. sec. 7.3.2 on Luke's preference for δια- compounds. The claim that the removal of Mark's κατά prefixes would soften the negative portrayal of political authorities is questioned by K. Clark (207-12), who argues that neither κυριεύω nor κατακυριεύω is inherently negative (cf. sec. 6.5.1 below).

[12]Moreover, γίνομαι serves opposite purposes in the two accounts (becoming great in Mark, becoming like the youngest in Luke).

[13]Soards, 30-1.

[14]Percy, 244; Thériault, 218; Wiefel, 370; et al.

[15]Scholars who claim that Luke draws from a non-Markan tradition throughout vv 24-27 include Arens, 126; Bammel, "Testament," 75; Best, *Disciples*, 148; Borsch, *Son of Man*, 23, n. 82; Creed, 267; Crossan, *Fragments*, 288; Dodd, 50-2, 61; Easton, 324; Ernst, *Evangelium*, 592; Feuillet, 378-9; Green, *Death*, 46; Grundmann, 400; Higgins, *Jesus*, 39; Howard, *Das Ego*, 231; Jeremias, "Löse-

The matter of literary context is a key concern here. T. W. Manson observes that, at the point where we would expect to find a parallel to Mark 10:35-45 (after Luke 18:34), Luke retains material immediately preceding and following the Markan unit (Luke 18:31-34 par. Mark 10:32-34; Luke 18:35-43 par. Mark 10:46-52).[16] The Lukan pericope, however, is in the Passion Narrative, following the Last Supper and during Jesus' farewell discourse (vv 14-38), but Mark includes the dispute and teaching in Jesus' Judean and Perean ministry (10:1), before his entry into Jerusalem (11:1ff). Thus, if Luke 22:24-27 is dependent on Mark 10:41-45, we are dealing with a transposition.

It may be noted, however, that Luke tends not to transpose Markan pericopae.[17] Jeremias argues, "Up to the passion narrative there are only two insignificant deviations: Luke 6.17-19; 8.19-21.... Deviations in the order of material must therefore be regarded as indications that Luke is not following Mark."[18] While this assertion may be a bit strong, the precedent set by Lukan redactional activity would still heavily weigh against the theory that 22:24-27 is transposed from Mark 10:41-45.

geld," 225; "Umstellungen," 117-19; *Words*, 97-9; Leonard, 239; Liefeld, 1027; Lohse, *Märtyrer*, 118; Luce, 332-3; Mann, 414; T. W. Manson, *Sayings*, 337; I. H. Marshall, *Gospel*, 811; Page, 149-52; Roloff, "Anfänge," 55; A. Schulz, *Nachfolge*, 253; Schürmann, *Abschiedsrede*, 64-5, 92; Streeter, 210; Sweetland, "Lord's Supper," 24; Taylor, *Jesus*, 187; *Passion*, 62-3; Tödt, 207; Wellhausen, 123; J. Wenham, 259-60; P. Winter, 159. Cf. Schürmann (*Abschiedsrede*, 63, n. 213), who lists others favoring either a Markan or non-Markan source.

[16]T. W. Manson, *Sayings*, 337. "This suggests that Lk. already has another version of the dispute and the saying of Jesus, probably already connected with the Passion story, and that he drops the Marcan account in favor of his own,..." (ibid.). Jeremias notes that Luke 18:15-43 (par. Mark 10:13-52) constitutes the third of four major blocks of material taken over from Mark ("Umstellungen," 116; similarly Neirynck, "Argument," 805-6; cf. Goulder, *Luke*, 1:44, on Luke's "block policy").

[17]So e.g., Jeremias, *Words*, 69; Grundmann, 400 and n. 1; Howard, *Das Ego*, 231-2; Léon-Dufour, "Récits," 1447; Lohse, *Märtyrer*, 118; Schürmann, "Dubletten," 339, n. 9; against Schmid, 328; Sparks, 219-22.

[18]Jeremias, *Words*, 98. Sparks (220-23) contests Jeremias's claim that Luke transposes Markan material so infrequently. In his rebuttal, Jeremias states that he is "completely united" with Sparks's claims that Luke does transpose words, phrases or subject-matter within or between sentences and sections, but he finally states, "... daß Lukas ganze Perikopen des Markus umgestellt hat, das allerdings bezweifle ich" ("Umstellungen," 115-16). Things are entirely different, however, in Luke 22 where there are six deviations from the Markan pericope sequence (117-18). Jeremias concludes that from 22:14 to the end of his Gospel, Luke follows his "special tradition" (118-19).

The two accounts also differ regarding the immediate occasion for Jesus' teaching (despite conceptual similarities between φιλονεικία and ἀγανακτέω). In Mark it is an appeal from James and John for positions of honor in Jesus' glory that leads to the indignation of the other ten disciples (10:35-41). Luke, however, omits the account of the ambition of James and John. No basis for the dispute in 22:24 is explicitly given (see further sec. 6.4), nor does Luke suggest that it centered around any subgroup of the disciples. It simply arose "among them" (ἐν αὐτοῖς), and thus corresponds to the Markan occasion only in the most general terms.

It is also noteworthy that gospel traditions preserve more than one account of a dispute among the disciples regarding greatness or rank, together with Jesus' corrective response. Perhaps Luke 22:24-27 is more closely related to 9:46-48 (cf. Mark 9:33-37) than it is to Mark 10:41-45.[19] Maybe there is even a link with other material (e.g., ὁ μείζων in Matt 23:11,[20] or a footwashing tradition similar to that in John 13).[21]

Furthermore, the view that Luke is dependent on Mark but omits the cause of the disciples' indignation (i.e., the request of James and John) out of respect for the disciples[22] may be misguided. In Mark's account it is chiefly James and John who are cast in a bad light, but according to Luke there is no reason not to blame all the apostles (we are only told that the quarrel arose "among them"). Moreover, Luke's Last Supper setting is very significant: What could be more damaging than depicting the Twelve so negatively at such a holy moment?[23] Perhaps it is more likely that Luke has retained a Last Supper quarrel from a non-Markan source than transposed the Markan incident to the Last Supper.

If Luke is following a non-Markan tradition in 22:24-27, there would be an explanation for the low quality of verbal agreement with Mark 10:41-45 and for the differing literary contexts. And if that non-Markan tradition was also related to Mark's source, or was perhaps

[19]Cf. secs. 6.4 and 6.5.3 below on 9:46-48 (also see sec. 4.5.1).

[20]So Schürmann, *Abschiedsrede*, 75, 79; against Schlosser, 56-9.

[21]See further section 6.5.3.

[22]So A. Schulz, *Nachfolge*, 252; Schmithals, *Lukas*, 210. A positive portrayal of the disciples is typical of Luke according to S. Brown, 66-74; Dupont, "Ministères," 142; Feuillet, 378; Ford, 117; Grundmann, 401; Schlosser, 55 (see further sec. 7.3.2).

[23]So J. Bailey, 43; Roloff, *Apostolat*, 185; cf. Glöckner, 180; Goulder, *Luke*, 2:731; Tannehill, *Unity*, 262-3; even S. Brown (72) makes a concession along these lines. Moreover, note that, despite the omission of the James and John incident, twice in Luke the disciples dispute over greatness (9:46; 22:24) (so Loisy, 515; Tiede, *Luke*, 384).

even known to Mark, we would have an explanation for the similar structure and sense of Luke and Mark's texts, despite the improbability of direct literary dependence.

Page suggests that Luke and Mark not only reflect independent traditions, but may "actually refer to separate incidents, and that Mark 10:45 and Luke 22:27 contain distinct logia."[24] The traditions do recount more than one dispute over greatness among the disciples, and it would be surprising if the itinerant Jesus did not often repeat key teachings such as that in vv 25-27. The fact that both the Markan and Lukan pericopae are credible in their respective contexts may also favor the possibility of distinct incidents and/ or logia.[25] But Page's claim does not account for the strong similarity of structure and sense of Luke 22:24-27 and Mark 10:41-45, a similarity which he himself highlights.[26] Why should these two pericopae have such similar "shapes" if they do not, *in some manner*, stem from related sources or a single trunk of tradition?

A point related to the source discussion is that, even if Luke is not dependent on Mark here, there is evidence that, at least at certain points, Luke is following a source. It is most likely that the double question of v 27a reflects a Semitic tradition or milieu,[27] and the fact that Luke was inclined to avoid that form[28] suggests that v 27a probably is not merely the

---

[24]Page, 150; so Geldenhuys, 563; Hill, 77.

[25]Page, 151. Feuillet claims that the Lukan and Markan pericopae fit in their respective contexts, but does not argue from this for two distinct incidents and/ or logia (379). To be sure, the incident of Luke 22:24 clashes with its setting in that it shows the apostles to be out of touch with Jesus (see above), but it is credible as an escalation of events from v 23 (see sec. 6.4 below) and in light of the interest in leadership and authority which is so prominent in the Lukan discourse (cf. ch. 5). In the case of Mark's context, the ambition of James and John makes the indignation of the Ten quite believable.

[26]Page, 148.

[27]Cf. rabbinic texts cited in Str-B (2:257) with double questions: "Which is greater, the protector or the one protected?" (*Gen. Rab.* 78 [50a]). "Which is greater, the one who loves or the one who causes others to love?" (*Sipre Deut.* 11.21 § 47 [83a]). "Which is greater, the one who loves the king or the one whom the king loves?" (*Mek. Exod.* 22:20 [101a]; cf. 22:3 [96a]). These examples probably reflect a standard Semitic figure of speech that was current in the NT era. Cf. Arens, 128; Grundmann, 401; I. H. Marshall, *Gospel*, 814; Schürmann, *Abschiedsrede*, 80; Schlosser, 67.

[28]Jeremias (*Sprache*, 101-2) notes that, although Luke retains double questions from Mark six times (Luke 5:21, 22-23; 6:3-4, 9; 20:2; 21:7), on eight occasions he avoids the Markan form (Luke 8:11, 16, 25; 9:25, 41; 20:22; 22:46, 71). For this reason Jeremias claims that double questions in the non-Markan sections of Luke

product of Luke's own creativity. Similarly, the apostles' drastic lack of perception seen in v 24 may suggest that Luke, who sometimes softens the traditional portrayal of the apostles,[29] found the quarrel and associated sayings already in the Last Supper setting in his source(s).[30]

In summary, there appears to be insufficient evidence to conclude that Luke follows Mark in all or part of 22:24-27. Rather, the evidence of similar structure and sense along with dissimilar language and context suggests that Luke here follows a non-Markan source, but one that is related to or perhaps even identical to Mark's own source.[31] Accordingly, though Mark 10:41-45 will be used with considerable caution, it still provides a ray of indirect light for the interpretation of Luke 22:24-27 and will need to be consulted periodically in the quest to discern the meaning of Luke's text.[32]

6.3 The Flow of Thought in Luke 22:24-27

Before beginning an in-depth analysis of vv 24-27, it will be helpful briefly to clarify the general flow of thought—the logical progression—of this event-response sequence. To be sure, this is no substitute for a detailed and nuanced analysis of the text.[33] Nevertheless, as an exploration of the basic structure of thought undergirding vv 24-27, section 6.3 both opens up and counts against certain key possibilities for the meaning of the text before us.

There are two factors that prompt one to look closely at the flow of thought. First, φιλονεικία (v 24) is not intrinsically negative.[34] Can we be sure that Luke portrays the apostles unfavorably and that vv 25-27 con-

(e.g., 2:49; 6:39, 41-2; 7:31; 10:26; 11:11-12; 18-19; 13:15-16, 18; 16:11-12; 22:27) should be assigned to a non-Lukan tradition. Cf. Cadbury, *Style*, 81; Schlosser, 67.

[29]Cf. n. 22 above, and sec. 7.3.2.

[30]Cf. Page, 151; Plummer, 500 (why would Luke put it *there* if he did not know the occasion for the event?).

[31]Cf. Green, *Death*, 46; Kollmann, *Mahl*, 176, 222-3; Loisy, 515; Patsch, 174-5; A. Schulz, *Nachfolge*, 255; Taylor, *Mark*, 443. Mann's view that the two accounts represent different translations of a single Aramaic original (414) allows for a remarkably free style of translation.

[32]Keeping an eye on the Markan passage may give clues as to the logion's pre-Lukan sense as well as facilitate the effort to separate traditional and redactional elements.

[33]For an analysis of this kind see especially secs. 6.4 and 6.5.

[34]See LSJ, "φιλονικία," 1937-8.

stitute a rebuke? Second, Lull's innovative interpretation of vv 24-30 has challenged many of the standing assumptions about the sense of vv 24-27. Fortunately there is *within* this text a key to the flow of thought that will enable us to address these problems.

First, however, it is in order to spell out the problems further. Since NT usage of φιλονεικία is restricted to Luke 22:24 (though note the adjectival form in 1 Cor 11:16), background for Luke's use of the term must be sought elsewhere.[35] Liddell and Scott uncover two senses in the classical literature, either "*love of victory, rivalry, contentiousness,* mostly in a bad sense," or "in a good sense, *competition, emulation, emulous eagerness.*"[36] Field suggested some time ago that the good sense is probably in view in Luke 22:24, and though Bauer lists only negative meanings, he cites Field regarding the usage of φιλονεικία in v 24.[37] Are the Lukan apostles truly quarreling, or are they merely having a friendly round of social competition? Perhaps v 24 presents no obstacle to the common view that Luke tends to portray the apostles favorably.[38]

The problem presented by Lull has implications for an analysis of the flow of thought in vv 24-27 that are more far-reaching than those surrounding the φιλονεικία question. He argues for a significantly different line of thought than that of the scholarly consensus, namely that the usual negative view of rulers in v 25 is not justified upon careful analysis of vv 24-30.[39] That rulers are called benefactors implies that they are supposed to benefit their subjects.[40] V 26 then turns to the situation at hand; the application of the principle in v 25 is first stated negatively (v 26a) and then positively (v 26b).[41] Regarding Luke 22:26a Lull claims,[42]

> If we did not have Matt 20:26a before us, it might have occurred to someone to supply καλεῖσθε ("you are called") as the elided finite verb. For v 26a is bound closely to v 25: "they are called benefactors, but you are not [called] thus [namely, benefactors]". In v 26a, therefore, the contrast between the apostles (ὑμεῖς) and those who are called

---

[35]On φιλονεικία see further below in secs. 6.3 and 6.4.

[36]LSJ, "φιλονικία," 1937-8. Moulton and Milligan offer the very late papyrus, POxy 16.1860.7 (VI/VII CE), in support of a positive understanding (MM, "φιλον(ε)ικία," 670-1).

[37]Field, 75-6; BAGD, "φιλον(ε)ικία," 860.

[38]See above, n. 22.

[39]Lull, 290. He suggests that the double promise of vv 28-30 makes the argument begun in v 24 look like a single positive thesis about greatness (294).

[40]Lull, 295-6.

[41]Lull, 296.

[42]Lull, 296.

"benefactors" is not prescriptive but descriptive.

The positive application of the principle in v 25 begins in v 26b. "The ἀλλ' ('rather') introduces a contrast with v 26a, not with the thesis in v 25."[43] Thus the response to the dispute is not "Here are the rulers, you are acting like them, but you ought not" (the consensus view), but "Here are the rulers, you are not acting like them, but you ought to." Ultimately the problem Lull raises can be reduced to the question of the implied verb in v 26a. A future indicative[44] with imperatival force (cf. Matt 20:26a) would support the "consensus" view,[45] but a present indicative would favor Lull's view.[46]

To address this issue and the question about φιλονεικία, we must step back and see the series of contrasts in vv 26b-27.[47] By working backwards we will be able to understand the basic thrust of Luke's reference to kings and rulers (v 25). This in turn will shed light on the two difficulties before us.

The contrast pairs of vv 26b-27 may be depicted as follows:

Position A	**Position B**
the greatest	the youngest (v 26b)
the leader	the servant (v 26c)
the diner	the table servant (v 27a)
the diner	Jesus the table servant (v 27b-c)

The Lukan Jesus uses this progression to contrast roles of high power or status (Position A) with roles of low power or status (Position B). In this way he illustrates his point with three vivid and concrete images.[48] In the fourth case he associates himself with one side in this flow of contrasted roles. The fact that Jesus identifies with the youngest/ servant/ table servant will prove to be *the decisive factor* in solving the problems raised by Lull's thesis and the ambiguity of φιλονεικία.

The reference to the service of Jesus in v 27c functions in vv 26b-27 to affirm Position B. Because Jesus is associated with the youngest/ servant/ table servant, we may presume that Luke affirms these low power,

[43]Lull, 296.

[44]An imperative is impossible with οὐ, as Arndt (442) correctly observes.

[45]E.g., perhaps ἔσεσθε or ποιήσετε.

[46]E.g., perhaps ἐστέ or Lull's καλεῖσθε.

[47]Wiefel (369) notes the importance of the text's "Kontrastschema."

[48]See further sec. 6.5 on the social, religious and other dimensions of these contrasted positions.

low status roles in some way. In brief, the message to the apostles is this: follow Jesus and adopt Position B.

Careful attention to the words and actions of Jesus in the context of vv 24-27, however, reveals that vv 26b-27 do not present simple, one-dimensional contrasts: Jesus the servant remains a leader,[49] and he does not commend to the apostles the abdication of leadership duties.[50] However, *for the purposes of the teaching in vv 25-27,* Jesus emphasizes his standing among the apostles as servant.

Accordingly, it is logical to conclude that Position B in each contrast pair of vv 26b-27b is favored in the Lukan framework. Jesus' example is the linchpin of the argument, and it filters back to weigh against the behavior or attitudes of the greatest/ leader/ diner. Indeed, this assertion receives explicit support from imperative γινέσθω (v 26b) which directs the apostles to become "like the youngest" (and note that the same verb is implied in v 26c). In fact, even if Jesus' example had not been referred to, v 26b would still drive us to the same understanding of vv 26b-27: the contrast pairs force one to make a choice, and Jesus commends Position B.

Next we may ask how the reference to kings and rulers (v 25) relates to the contrast pairs of vv 26b-27. Lull contends that the kings and rulers function positively, for as benefactors they "... are supposed to 'benefit' their subjects."[51] He then likens the concept of benefitting others to the sense of διακονῶν, thus aligning the kings and rulers with the injunction in vv 26b-27 to become like a servant.[52] In this way Lull is able to bypass the lowly and self-denying dimension of servanthood (cf. sec. 2.4.3) and yet draw attention to the dimension of the concept involving acting with others' interests in view. So it is that "... those who use their power *to benefit and serve others* are 'the greatest.'"[53]

[49]See sec. 6.5 below on the servant Jesus as leader.

[50]See further the discussion in sec. 6.5.3.

[51]Lull, 295-6.

[52]Lull, 297, 299. By likening Jesus to the "benefactors" of v 25, Lull makes the same mistake that Danker makes (*Benefactor*, 404; *Jesus*, 346), though Lull (289-94) is anxious to distance his interpretation of vv 24-27 from that of Danker: both writers link Jesus with a position and function that is opposite Jesus' side of the contrast pairs. To be sure, Jesus is portrayed by Luke as one who performs beneficent deeds (so εὐεργετῶν in Acts 10:38), but the fact that the title "benefactor" is so closely tied with the high power, high status Position A in Luke 22:25-27 suggests that Luke's point there is not to portray Jesus as "servant-benefactor." (Cf. Danker's surprisingly positive comments about Lull's thesis ["Paul's Debt," 267, n. 2]).

[53]Lull, 297, emphasis original.

This interpretation, however, comes to grief upon careful examination of v 25 in relation to the contrast pairs of vv 26b-27. Lull concedes that the "monarchs" and "those who have authority" (v 25) correspond to "the greater" and "the one who rules" (v 26b-c),[54] but he does not observe that this correspondence necessarily pits the kings and ruling benefactors along with those who represent Position A against the servant Jesus and against the force of the imperative in v 26b. Indeed, the social and political similarities of the kings/ rulers (v 25) and the greatest/ leader/ diner (vv 26b-27) are very strong. Alternatively, no such similarities exist between the kings/ rulers and the youngest/ servant/ table servant.[55] So it appears that the kings and rulers must take their place in the logical flow of vv 25-27 as figures contrasted with the servant Jesus, and, accordingly, as negative examples.[56]

This finding puts us in a position to understand Luke's cryptic expression, ὑμεῖς δὲ οὐχ οὕτως (v 26a). Since the kings and rulers function as negative examples whom Luke contrasts with the positive example of Jesus, v 26a should be recognized as having the sense of a prohibition. Against Lull, v 26a is prescriptive (or proscriptive), not descriptive. The apostles are being rebuked by the Lukan Jesus for somehow acting like the kings and rulers of v 25, not for failing to do so. A future indicative with imperatival force (e.g., ἔσεσθε [cf. Matt 20:26a]) may be understood in Luke 22:26a.[57]

---

[54]Lull, 297.

[55]Although it would not have been impossible for rulers in antiquity to adopt serving roles, in general such a notion is historically inaccurate (cf. ch. 2). Further, the association of the kings and rulers of v 25 with the duties of servants betrays insensitivity to the social elevation routinely attached to the role of the benefactor, and it is not supported by the force of κυριεύουσιν (v 25a; cf. secs. 2.2.2 and 6.5.1).

[56]As to whether they are portrayed negatively for harsh or ostentatious rule rather than normal rule, see further sec. 6.5.1 below.

[57]While Luke does not generally hesitate to use the present indicative copula (cf. e.g., vv 27, 28), a possible Lukan inclination to avoid the Semitic future indicative copula with the force of an imperative is observed by Schlosser (63) in Luke 6:36 par. Matt 5:48. While it has been argued above that Luke 22:24-27 is not dependent on Mark 10:41-45 but related to it only through some type of common tradition, the fact that Mark's two usages of ἔσται (10:43b-44) are absent in Luke 22:26b-c and Mark's ἐστιν (10:43a) is lacking in Luke 22:26a may lend some limited support to the view that Luke may be inclined to omit but still imply ἔσται with imperatival force. These observations would also weigh against the view that Luke implies a present indicative in v 26a.

We may now return to the ambiguity of φιλονεικία, for the above discussion of Lull's thesis and the alternative understanding of Luke 22:25-27 sheds the necessary light on that problem. The apostles are preoccupied in v 24 with a concern over which of them is "greatest" (μείζων), and by viewing that verse from the vantage point of vv 25-27 we quickly see that "the greatest" is aligned with Position A. This quality which the disciples prize is overturned by Jesus: "let the greatest (μείζων) among you become like the youngest,..." (v 26b). While conventional values readily recognize that the diner is "greater" (μείζων) than the table servant, Jesus commends the role opposite this conventional expression of superiority (v 27). Attention to the flow of contrasts in vv 26b-27 thus reveals that the prizing of greatness is precisely what Jesus opposes, and he does so by command and reference to his own example of service.[58] It seems clear, then, at least at this stage in the analysis of vv 24-27, that Jesus' response in vv 25-27 constitutes a stern correction of the apostles' misguided high regard for greatness.

The flow of thought in vv 24-27 may be summarized as follows: The example of Jesus (v 27c) and imperative γινέσθω (v 26b) serve to affirm Position B in the contrast pairs (vv 26b-27). Verbal and thematic features in the contrast of Positions A and B then pit the kings and ruling benefactors against Jesus, suggest v 26a be taken as a prohibition, and imply a very serious problem among the apostles (v 24).

In the remainder of this chapter the claims of section 6.3 will not be assumed as final conclusions, for they provide only a general framework within which to conduct more in-depth study of vv 24-27. Nevertheless, as the flow of thought in this text as set out in section 6.3 is confirmed and elaborated in the following, it will become apparent that the preceding analysis focusing on the structure of 22:24-27 has significant, far-reaching implications for our larger objective to discern the text's meaning.

6.4 The Apostles' Quarrel (22:24)

Here in section 6.4, and in 6.5 to follow, the event and response of vv 24-27 will be examined in detail. V 24 has a two-part structure: 1) a reference to a form of discussion among the Twelve, and 2) a very brief description of the subject matter of that discussion. The stitch that ties the two parts together is the neuter article τό, which Luke utilizes fre-

[58]See sec. 6.4 below for additional negative aspects of the event in v 24.

quently to introduce indirect questions (1:62; 9:46; 19:48; 22:2, 4, 23, 24; Acts 4:21; 22:30).[59]

An important question raised by v 24 regards the occasion of the quarrel. Luke states briefly and without explanation that it simply "happened" (ἐγένετο). It may be noted that the question of occasion, while often asked by those concerned chiefly with historical events behind the Gospel writings,[60] is of importance as well when focusing on the Lukan narrative. In story as well as history, one expects to be able to uncover causes for events and motives for actions.[61] The successful unfolding of a plot depends on such connections, even if they are subtle. To be sure, the gospel "genre" has a way of sometimes providing mere *Stichwort* ties, or (rarely) undiscernible links between events and their occasions. Ordinarily, however, the evangelists give some clues as to the logical threads that unite their narratives. So we ask, What may occasion the quarrel over greatness at the Lukan Last Supper?[62]

Among the possible answers are the following: 1) competition for seats of honor at the banquet table;[63] 2) a discussion as to who would perform the duties of table servant;[64] 3) recollections of Jesus' messianic identity (9:20; 19:38) and the apostles' ambitions to gain power by vying for position in Jesus' "cabinet";[65] 4) a reaction to Jesus' comments on his betrayer (vv 21-23).[66] Each suggestion will be considered in turn.[67]

---

[59]Fitzmyer, *Gospel*, 1:108, 2:1412; cf. Sabourin, *Luc*, 345.

[60]So Green, *Death*, 45, and many others.

[61]Against Loisy (515), who argues that there is no point in asking what the occasion of the quarrel in v 24 is since it has only literary value. Arguing as G. Schneider does, that "Die Szene steht bei Lukas kaum an ihrem geschichtlichen Platz" (*Evangelium*, 2:450), does not eliminate the need to search for an occasion in the Lukan story line.

[62]To be sure, there is something surprising and puzzling about a quarrel over greatness at the Last Supper, but Otto goes too far in claiming that it is without motive (271; cf. Wiefel, 369). Cf. sec. 6.2.2 above on the credibility of v 24 in its context.

[63]So e.g., Dalman, 115; Hauck, 265; Hendricksen, 970; Hooker, *Son of Man*, 145; Plummer, 500 (the footwashing is Jesus' enacted rebuke); cf. sec. 3.3; see also Schürmann (*Ursprung*, 138) and Ernst (593) on table position in Judaism.

[64]While this view is without support in the literature, it seems to be a sensible speculation in light of Jesus' statement in v 27c. Also, Jesus' allusion to the status of table servants (v 27a-b) may imply that "the greatest" would expect to avoid service duties.

[65]So e.g., Rasmussen, 74; Rengstorf, 246 (such ambitions are typical in the company of kings); Rienecker, 503.

[66]So e.g., Danker, *Jesus*, 347-8; Fitzmyer, *Gospel*, 2:1414-5; Fransen, 25;

The social significance of seating arrangements at ancient banquets has been discussed (ch. 3). Here we may simply recall that a status-based "seating chart" would govern the (perhaps unspoken) allocation of ranked positions at table. That Luke opposes a high regard for table position is apparent from 14:7-11 and 20:46. A related possibility is that an overemphasis on the apostles' status as free men (cf. the Passover background, sec. 3.3) and their expression of this status through reclining (v 14) may be seen in combination with a concern for prestige exhibited in table positions, with the result that the narrative atmosphere is charged for a conflict concerning status. Given the Passover setting and Luke's opposition to seeking seats of honor, such a reconstruction seems possible. The fact that Luke gives us no explicit clues to this effect, nor even strong implicit ones, however, weighs against such an understanding.

Moreover, if the quarrel had to do with table positions, we would expect the conflict to arise at the time seating arrangements were dealt with, i.e., before the meal. By v 24, however, the meal is over (cf. v 20, μετὰ τὸ δειπνῆσαι). Although the language of v 24 actually leaves the time of the quarrel indefinite,[68] Luke's story gives us no reason to suppose that it takes place at any time other than precisely after the comment on the betrayer (vv 21-23) and before the teaching on service (vv 25-27). The second suggestion above runs into the same problem: Why would the matter of who was to serve tables be addressed after the meal?

The third suggestion is not so easily dismissed, for there is no reason why efforts to curry the favor of the king (cf. 19:38) could not take place at table after dinner. Another contextual factor, however, arises to oppose this view, namely that Jesus has just spoken of his imminent betrayal and death (vv 15, 19-20, 21-22; cf. sec. 5.3). Surely this claim would dash the hopes and ambitions of followers who wanted to come into power at the side of Jesus Messiah.[69] Further, the immediate con-

Godet, 296-7; Grundmann, 401; Liefeld, 1027; Loisy, 515; Lull, 294; I. H. Marshall, *Gospel*, 810-11; Neyrey, 21; Otto, 272; Tannehill, *Unity*, 263; Tiede, *Luke*, 384; cf. Finegan, 13; Zahn, 680. Lagrange (549) claims that the connection between vv 24 and 23 is not logical but merely sequential; this makes the dispute less offensive.

[67]The selection of Peter and John to prepare for the meal (22:8) has also been associated with the quarrel over greatness, as Green observes (*Death*, 45). Knight (815) suggests that the quarrel results from a discussion as to who would wash the others' feet, but this takes us outside the Lukan story. For Horn (212, 214) the quarrel corresponds to conflicts based on "Standesunterschiede" which are presumed to exist in the Lukan community.

[68]So Arndt, 442.

text of v 24 (i.e., v 23) may reveal that this time the apostles begin to comprehend Jesus' passion prediction (cf. 9:44-46; 18:31-34). Their thoughts are on betrayal and setback, not victory. Thus the Lukan story line does not support the view that visions of messianic conquest prompt the apostles to quarrel over greatness.

This brings us to the fourth option, and it is by far the most defensible in terms of the Lukan narrative sequence. V 24 is linked to vv 21-23 by grammatical, structural and thematic ties. The grammatical ties consist of δέ and καί (v 24).[70] Either of these particles alone may be overlooked as a mere connecting device that lacks importance for the meaning of the text, but the combination of the two implies that καί is adverbial: "And a quarrel *also/even* arose among them,..."[71]

A synopsis makes the structural and thematic links visible:

	v 23	**v 24**
1	καὶ αὐτοὶ ἤρξαντο συζητεῖν	ἐγένετο δὲ καὶ φιλονκεκία
2	πρὸς ἑαυτοὺς	ἐν αὐτοῖς
3	τὸ τίς	τὸ τίς
4	ἄρα εἴη ἐξ αὐτῶν	αὐτῶν
5	ὁ τοῦτο μέλλων πράσσειν	δοκεῖ εἶναι μείζων

There are structural counterparts on each line: 1) form of interaction; 2) sphere of interaction; 3) Lukan device to introduce an indirect question which turns attention to one person; 4) sphere in which that person is to be found; 5) action or quality of that person. It seems unlikely that this arrangement would be without significance for an interpretation of v 24.

By turning to the thematic or conceptual links between vv 23 and 24, the sense of the parallel becomes clearer. We may first consider the connection between the apostles' "discussion" (συζητεῖν, v 23) and their sub-

[69]Vv 29-30 reveal that Jesus can speak of his future reign in the face of impending death, but they do not constitute or affect the occasion for the event narrated in v 24.

[70]For Evans (795) and Zahn (679), καί produces a poor connection here. I. H. Marshall (*Gospel*, 811) and Schürmann (*Abschiedsrede*, 66, 69), however, rightly see a positive contribution of καί to the thought connection between vv 23 and 24.

[71]Since καί precedes φιλονεικία, we would ordinarily expect it to influence that word (i.e., "And there was also/ even a quarrel among them,..."). That reading is surely possible, and it fits well with the escalation of intensity from the "dispute" (συζητεῖν) of v 23 (see further below). More likely still, however, is the idea that adverbial καί influences not a single word but the thrust of the clause itself (cf. Smyth, §§ 2881, 2883). The translation, "And a quarrel also/ even arose among them," is intended in this way.

sequent "quarrel" (φιλονεικία, v 24). Bauer claims that the ten NT usages of συζητέω fall into two categories, "discuss" or "dispute, debate, argue."[72] Of Luke's three usages elsewhere, only in 24:15 does it seem to have the neutral sense, "discuss." In Acts 6:9 and 9:29 there is an element of competition or conflict implied (i.e., "dispute").[73] In no case, however, does the act of discussing or disputing appear to be negative in and of itself.[74] In Luke 22:23 "dispute" may be favored over "discuss" because of the nature of the subject at hand; surely the reference to a betrayer would lead to more than a dispassionate conversation. We must note, however, that Luke tells of no rebuke or correction for this "dispute"—that only comes with the φιλονεικία of v 24.[75] This observation along with the fact that Luke does not see συζητέω as intrinsically negative suggests that the connection between vv 23 and 24 is one of escalation, not mere addition. The translation "even" for adverbial καί in v 24 seems to bring the escalation aspect out more clearly than "also" would.

The thematic parallels between vv 23 and 24 extend beyond the dispute-quarrel link. In both verses there is a turning inward toward and focusing upon the community of twelve, and in both cases this introspection is to identify an individual (τίς ... ἐξ αὐτῶν and τίς αὐτῶν), namely the betrayer and the greatest. And in both cases the individuals isolated are opposed by the Lukan Jesus (vv 22, 25-27). Indeed, it would seem that there is a sense in which betrayal and prizing greatness are somehow akin to each other.[76]

How then might the dispute of v 23 constitute an occasion for the quarrel of v 24?[77] A possible reconstruction is as follows: Being named

[72]BAGD, "συζητέω," 775.

[73]Mark uses the term six times ("discuss" in 1:27; 9:10; "dispute" in 8:11; 9:14, 16; 12:28), and in each case Luke has a parallel pericope which lacks συζητέω. An examination of these Lukan contexts, however, does not reveal a tendency to avoid the term.

[74]It may, however, lead to negative actions (Acts 6:9-11; 9:29).

[75]The μειζῶν *Stichwort* connection between v 24 and vv 25-27 clarifies that Jesus' response is tied directly to the event of v 24, not the combined events of vv 23 and 24.

[76]So Beck, "Imitatio Christi," 33; LaVerdiere, "Passion," 43; cf. Meynet, *Initiation*, 166.

[77]Some interpreters who see the occasion for the v 24 quarrel in the sayings and event of vv 21-23 fail carefully to address this question, and merely say that one discussion gives rise to (so Lull, 294; Zahn, 680) or degenerates into (so Tiede, *Luke*, 384) another.

the betrayer would be a terrible prospect in Luke's story (so the verdict of v 22). Accordingly, Luke may be depicting the dispute of v 23 as one filled with alarm and anxiety, and with defensive reactions; though Luke omits Mark's "Is it I?" (Mark 14:19), a similar anxious attitude may be implied in v 23. In the context of defensive reactions against the accusation of disloyalty,[78] an impulse to name the greatest—particularly to put *oneself* forth as the greatest[79]—may then involve a quest to prove one's loyalty to Jesus. Further, it would be a contest to name the *one* (singular τίς) most trusted by Jesus (and perhaps most important to Jesus). It is not enough to say, "I'm loyal to Jesus, I wouldn't do it." Rather, it may be that individual apostles are portrayed as trying to prove themselves *most loyal* of all.

Since the content of vv 25-27 shows that Jesus responds to more than claims of superior loyalty (images of social, political and religious greatness fill his rebuke), however, it may be implied that the Lukan logical connection between vv 23 and 24 is somewhat loose, or (more likely) that the reader is to presuppose an evolution in the quarrel from claims of superior loyalty to claims of superiority in other respects. It is not difficult to imagine this progression, for the one who is most loyal to a leader would be recognized as an excellent candidate for positions of great responsibility—it is easy to see how "most loyal" could slide into "most important."[80]

In summary, it appears that, in terms of the Lukan story line, the immediate occasion of the v 24 quarrel is the v 23 dispute, though it is not impossible that other factors (e.g., table position and posture) may have had a role in shaping the sequence of events. Vv 23 and 24 are linked by grammatical, structural and thematic ties, and a logical progression (albeit one that is implicit) between the two events may be uncovered. These connections imply that for the apostles to prize greatness is not unlike betrayal. The connection between vv 23 and 24 thus accents the

[78]Cf. Kurz, *Farewell*, 62; Otto, 272-3; Tannehill, *Unity*, 263.

[79]Alternatively, there is a discussion in which certain of the Rabbis seek to ascribe greatness to other Rabbis rather than claim it for themselves (*m. ʾAbot* 2.8).

[80]While with this analysis the connection between vv 23 and 24 is not explicit, links between vv 23 and 24 on the one hand and links between vv 24 and 25-27 (see further sec. 6.5) on the other require some such reconstruction. *For Luke* v 24 looks backward and forward. This bi-directional character of v 24 allows one to see the event of v 23 as the occasion of the Lukan quarrel, and the rebuke of vv 25-27 as containing its remedy, though this requires a progression from defending one's loyalty to exclaiming one's importance.

seriousness of the apostles' error in their high regard for greatness (this supports an emphasis of sec. 6.3).

Having discussed the occasion for the quarrel of v 24, we may now turn our attention to a few of the finer details of v 24 before examining Jesus' response in vv 25-27. In particular, an attempt will be made to gain a fuller and more nuanced understanding by examining φιλονεικία in greater detail, by considering the importance of the expression δοκεῖ εἶναι, and by probing further the sense of μείζων.

It was noted above (sec. 6.3) that φιλονεικία is not intrinsically negative. Liddell and Scott cite a number of positive classical usages related to athletic contests where φιλονεικία might be translated "competition, rivalry."[81] Field calls attention to a later usage (Aelian. *VH* 1.24) which is said to imply no "unfriendly feeling."[82] There, however, though Heracles had "dissolved" (διαλύεται) his previous enmity toward Lepreus, their subsequent φιλονεικία is modified by νεανική (φιλονεικία δ' οὖν αὐτοῖς ἐμπίπτει νεανικὴ καὶ ἐρίζουσιν ...), an adjective that can have a good *or* bad sense (i.e., "vigorous; high-spirited" or "vehement").[83] Thus it seems that Field's case may be overstated.

More importantly, however, the above positive usages are not as close to Luke's Gospel as are the negative usages of φιλονεικία or its cognates in the NT, LXX, Philo and Josephus. 1 Cor 11:16 contains the only other NT occurrence of the word group. There "contentious" (so RSV) is an apt translation for φιλόνεικος describing those who contest Paul's view on head coverings. Something of the nature of the opposition is reflected in Paul's firm resistance to it ("... we recognize no other practice, nor do the churches of God."); a neutral competitive disposition is not in view.

All five occurrences of the word group in the LXX have a negative sense. In Ezek 3:7 the Lord informs the prophet that the house of Israel will not listen to him because they would not listen to the Lord; the whole house of Israel is "defiant and obstinate" (JB, from φιλόνεικοί εἰσι καὶ σκληροκάρδιοι).[84] In Prov 10:12 the parallelism with νεῖκος[85] implies a

---

[81]E.g., Xen. *Ages.* 2.8; *An.* 4.8.27; *Cyr.* 7.1.18; *Hiero* 9.6; *Oec.* 21.10; Dit., Syll. 685.15. But even here the negative side of the term is not far off; Plato cautions that the "conflict and rivalry" (ἅμιλλά τε καὶ φιλονικία) of the games must be κατὰ νόμον (*Lg.* 834c.).

[82]Field, 76; Aelianus is dated in II/III CE.

[83]LSJ, "νεανικός," 1163. Additionally, δέ is probably adversative here.

[84]The parallel with σκληροκάρδιος and the designation of those who refuse

negative sense for φιλονεικοῦντας.[86] 2 Macc 4:4 refers to a distinctly unfriendly feeling of Simon toward Onias, a "contentiousness" that even led to murder. In 4 Macc 1:26 φιλονεικία is listed along with other negative attitudes[87] which, taken together, constitute a "malicious" (κακοήθης) disposition. 4 Macc 8:26 paints a negative picture by likening a φιλονεικία to a θανατηφόρος ("fatal poison," or here, "fatal obstinacy"; cf. Jas 3:8).

In the works of Philo and Josephus, forms of the word occur thirty-three and thirty-four times respectively.[88] In both writers a positive meaning can be uncovered,[89] but it is by far the exception to the usual sense:[90] over ninety-five percent of usages in Philo and Josephus are negative. Although the presence of a few occurrences with a positive sense reveals that such an understanding was still known in the first century, the heavily predominant negative understanding of the word group in these writers correlates with NT and LXX usages and weighs in favor of a negative sense at Luke 22:24.

This claim combines with the above arguments as to the flow of thought in vv 24-27 (sec. 6.3) and the juxtaposition with v 23, both of which supported a negative understanding of the event of v 24.[91] Additionally, the sequence of negative event and corrective response in 9:46-48 provides an important background for discerning the negative quality of φιλονεικία in 22:24.[92] Schürmann calls attention to the parallel to 9:46

to listen to God and his prophet support the negative interpretation for the term (φιλόνεικοι here translates חִזְקֵי־מֵצַח, "stubborn" [cf. Isa 48:4]).

85"Quarrel, strife, feud" (so LSJ, "νεῖκος," 1165).

86The puzzling negative (τοὺς μή φιλονεικοῦντας) may be inserted to highlight the contrast of v 12b with 12a (Toy, 207). The sense of v 12 is noticeably clearer in the MT.

87They are ἀλαζονεία ("arrogance"), φιλαργυρία ("love of money"), φιλοδοξία ("love of vain glory") and βασκανία ("envy").

88So Ibycus Scholarly Computer; Rengstorf, *Concordance*, 302.

89There are only three such instances: Philo *Det.* 45 ("contest"); *Spec. Leg.* 4.111 ("striving vigorously"); Jos. *Ant.* 15.290 ("striving intently").

90Negative meanings include "contentiousness" (Jos. *Ag. Ap.* 1.160; Philo *Leg. ad Gaium* 218), a "quarrel" that leads to blows (Jos. *Ag. Ap.* 2.243) or murder (*Ant.* 7.182), and "aggressiveness" that leads to death (15.166, 168).

91Among those who see the event of v 24 as distinctly negative are Fitzmyer, *Gospel*, 2:1416; Zahn, 679; against Evans, 795; Field, 76; et al. Horn claims that φιλονεικία is "einem ... rein negativ besetzten Topos" in both Hellenistic Greek and Jewish literature (212-13). This may be an overstatement, but it is not far from the truth.

92The remarkably similar structure of 9:46 and 22:24 beckons for such comparisons. See further below (this section, and secs. 6.5 and 4.5.1) on 9:46-48.

in 5:22, and rightly maintains, "Jesus kennt die 'Gedanken der Herzen' ..., die als solche immer negativ sind."[93]

To obtain a fuller understanding of the event in 22:24, we turn to the expression δοκεῖ εἶναι. The issue is not who wants to be greatest (diff. Mark) or is greatest, but who *seems to be* the greatest. It is a question of appearances, of reputation.[94] Bauer maintains that intransitive δοκέω has the basic sense, "to seem,"[95] and though this can be broken down into submeanings, all involve the matter of relative perception. The same verb in Mark 10:42b (though in a different form and context) also has to do with appearances of greatness, and it is probably a remnant of Luke and Mark's shared source or related traditions.[96]

The expression δοκεῖ εἶναι μείζων in Luke 22:24 reflects a social setting with a strong consciousness of honor and shame. Malina claims that shame was a positive value in the first century Mediterranean world, and he explains,[97]

> Conscience is sensitivity to what others think about and expect of the individual; it is another word for shame in the positive sense.... [One] is ever aware of the expectations of others, especially significant others, and strives to match those expectations. This is the dyadic personality, one who needs another simply to know who he or she is.

Although for many modern people it is a virtue to be unaffected by the opinions of others, in the ancient Near East the same trait would commonly have been thought of as a vice. It is noteworthy that Daube detects in Luke a distinctive consciousness of "shame culture."[98]

The high premium placed on one's standing in the eyes of others could combine in ancient peasant societies with a perception of "limited

---

[93]Schürmann, *Lukasevangelium*, 576.

[94]Fitzmyer, *Gospel*, 2:1416.

[95]BAGD, "δοκέω," 201-2, def. 2. Cf. Kittel ("δοκέω," 233), who sees the sense "to count for something, to be of repute" in Mark 10:42 and Gal 2:6-9.

[96]Luke's rendering is probably the less primitive since the Markan saying is somewhat unfavorable toward political rulers (Luke is interested in a peaceful coexistence with political powers [cf. nn. 124 and 217 below]).

[97]Malina, *World*, 67, cf. 44. Hoffmann and Eid (195) similarly claim that religious prestige was very important in law-oriented societies. See Knoche (422) and B. Winter ("Benefactors," 90-2) on the importance of public expressions of honor (and see also the discussion below in sec. 6.5.1). The work of Pitt-Rivers (*People*, esp. 112-15) on shame consciousness is helpful.

[98]Daube, 356 (though not all of his examples are persuasive). A keen concern for honor and shame is at the root of the patron-client system of social relations (sec. 2.2.2).

good"[99] to produce great tensions and difficulties. Foster surmises, "It is as if the obvious fact of land shortage in a densely populated area applied to all other desired things: not enough to go around."[100] A corollary is that a person only improves his position (financial, social, etc.) at the expense of others.[101] In a peasant society, an effort to get ahead would be perceived by others as a hostile action (cf. Mark 10:41).[102] Given this social framework, it is plausible that an atmosphere of fierce anger would underlie the quarrel of Luke 22:24, the whole affair then taking on a yet more intensified negative quality.

The presence of δοκέω makes the indirect question of v 24 quite difficult to answer (i.e., it is a matter of appearances and perceptions, so who can give a "right" answer?). Further, it may be noted that Jesus' response in vv 25-27 does not actually constitute an answer.[103] The question itself, however, reveals an attitude which the Lukan Jesus opposes, so it is not surprising that it is left unanswered: it is the wrong question to ask.

[99]This expression is usually traced to the important study of peasant societies by George M. Foster: "By 'Image of the Limited Good' I mean that broad areas of peasant behavior are patterned in such fashion as to suggest that peasants view their social, economic, and natural universes—their total environment—as one in which all of the desired things in life such as land, wealth, health, friendship and love, manliness and honor, respect and status, power and influence, security and safety, *exist in finite quantity* and *are always in short supply,...*" (296, emphasis original). De Ste. Croix ("Attitudes," 1-9) contends that Luke, like the other synoptic evangelists, seeks to portray Jesus' ministry as taking place in the countryside, i.e., within the peasant framework.

[100]Foster, 296. Kaplan and Saler question some aspects of Foster's case (e.g., that one peasant's good health must be at the expense of another's [203]), though they recognize the value of his study. Note especially Foster's clarifying comments on 311 (e.g., the mentality of limited good is not exclusive to peasant societies). Gregory (77-83) also challenges Foster's thesis, and proposes an alternative explanation for the peasant mentality regarding economic matters. The "expectation of circumstantially balanced reciprocity" is said to account for the generosity of the wealthy and for pressure on them to share with the poor. It is debatable, however, whether this model, which describes the peasant mind-set as one assuming that the wealthy simply *should* share (77), uncovers an adequately powerful motivating force to fuel the ancient custom of benefaction/ gift giving (contrast the image of limited good with its notion, "Your gain is my loss").

[101]Foster, 297; cf. F. Bailey, 314; S. Johnson, "Message," 18; Malina, *World*, 75-6; Moxnes, *Economy*, 76-9.

[102]Such fears were, of course, often justified in light of the harsh realities of peasant life in the Roman world (e.g., high taxes and rents which lined the pockets of wealthy urbanites, rigorous farming conditions, short life expectancy, exposure of children; see MacMullen, *Social Relations*, 32-4, 52-3; "Peasants," 260).

[103]So Sabourin, *Luc*, 345; Schürmann, *Abschiedsrede*, 68.

The subject matter of the apostles' quarrel centers on μείζων.[104] Implications from both the context and language trends favor taking this comparative form as superlative, "greatest."[105] While Luke uses μέγας frequently,[106] in only eight contexts does it correspond to persons,[107] and in only three is *relative* personal greatness at issue (7:28 [2x]; 9:46, 48; 22:24, 26, 27).[108]

In 7:28 and 9:48 the possession of greatness is portrayed positively (cf. 22:26b), but in 9:46 the preoccupation with greatness leads to correction (cf. 22:24). This calls for some elaboration. In 7:28 "the least" (ὁ μικρότερος) in the kingdom of God is greater than John, and in 9:48 it is again "the least," the one who receives Jesus by valuing and identifying with the lowly child (cf. sec. 2.4.2), who is finally great. Thus, in both cases there is a positive, reformed greatness which involves or consists of lowliness. This finding may support the view that the problem in 22:24 lies not so much in being great as in prizing relative greatness or viewing true greatness as a course of social ascent (see further sec. 6.5.3 below). The conventional assumption that possessing greatness involves the rejection of lowliness is thus challenged.

We can enhance our understanding of the concern for greatness by turning from usages of μέγας in Luke-Acts to see 22:24 in the light of its immediate literary context. Although it has been argued that the dispute in v 23 occasions the quarrel of v 24, the vivid contrasts of vv 25-27 offer even more color and concreteness for an analysis of greatness in v 24, so we turn to a study of those verses.

In summary of v 24, it has been argued that usages of φιλονεικία close to Luke support the finding (cf. sec. 6.3) that Luke portrays the apostles negatively in v 24. The juxtaposition of a dispute over the identity of

[104]The term reappears in vv 25 and 27 and thus unifies vv 24-27.

[105]Since it is likely that more than two apostles are involved in the Lukan dispute (there is no clue that all twelve are not involved), "greater" is not preferred (so also 9:46). Fitzmyer (*Gospel*, 2:1416) notes that μείζων was normally used for superlative μέγιστος in Hellenistic Greek since the superlative had begun to disappear from the language. Cf. BDF, § 60; Zerwick, §§ 148-50. μείζων is a true comparative in 7:28 (2x); 12:18; 22:27a.

[106]μέγας appears 33x in Luke, 31x in Acts.

[107]Luke 1:15, 32; 7:16, 28 (2x); 9:46, 48; 22:24, 26, 27; Acts 8:9; 19:27, 28, 34, 35.

[108]Acts 8:9 may also have a special importance here in that Simon was claiming greatness for himself, and his quest brought about the downfall from his great standing.

the betrayer (v 23) with the quarrel over greatness further highlights the negative quality of the latter event.[109] The link with v 23 may also suggest that Luke depicts the defense of one's loyalty to Jesus as the central factor which occasions the quarrel over greatness. The fact that Jesus' response in vv 25-27 reveals other concerns, however, implies that the quarrel of v 24 evolves from defense of one's loyalty into defense (or assertion) of one's greatness. V 24 may be translated, "A quarrel even arose among them as to which of them seemed to be the greatest."

6.5 Jesus' Response (22:25-27)

While the antithetical structure of 22:25-27 provides perhaps the single most useful key for interpreting vv 24-27,[110] to think of vv 25-27 as a series of contrasts is a slight oversimplification. To be sure, the verb γινέσθω in v 26b and the logical antithesis between terms like ἀνακείμενος and διακονῶν function to build a contrast structure that, in short, says, "Adopt Position B, not Position A." However, when Jesus is described in v 27c as ὁ διακονῶν, he does not cease to be leader. This is apparent from his adaptation of the role of Passover president who interprets the meal (vv 19-20), and from his standing as the patriarch/ testator (see ch. 5). Also, delivering exhortations (vv 19, 25-27, 36) and prophecies (vv 15, 16, 18, 21-22, 30, 31-34) is in the domain of leadership, not to mention the conferring of kingship (vv 29-30). Moreover, it will be demonstrated below (sec. 6.5.3) that Jesus' rebuke is not directed toward the elimination of the apostles' greatness, but its transformation (v 26b-c). Thus one must examine these contrasts carefully, making note of what is and is not being overturned.

Extensive attention to vv 25-27 (and parallel passages) in scholarship and in the church has, in some cases, dulled the senses of modern interpreters to the vivid, sharp and concrete imagery Luke employs.[111] While our observations on patterns of authority and subordination in the ancient world (ch. 2) may help begin to peal back layers of overfamiliarity

[109]Luke shows great candor by including this scandalous event in his narrative (so Arndt, 442).

[110]Understanding one contrast aids in the interpretation of the next (so Horn, 213).

[111]See Hoffmann and Eid, 195-7. Regarding Mark 9:30-37, Achtemeier states that these "mind-bending paradoxes" have "craggy outlines" which have been "worn smooth by centuries of meditation and comment,..." (183, cf. 181).

with vv 25-27, the following analysis is intended to extend and clarify that process.

6.5.1 **Illustration (v 25)**

After an introductory formula (v 25a), Luke presents Jesus' comment on kings and rulers (v 25b-c). The grammar of v 25b-c requires attention at two points: How does αὐτῶν function in each of its two occurrences? Is καλοῦνται passive or reflexive? The discussion of "benefactors" below will take up the latter question.

Regarding the former question, one notes that both κυριεύω ("be lord, rule") and ἐξουσιάζω ("have authority") take a genitive for the person over whom rule or authority is exercised.[112] While αὐτῶν in v 25c could be possessive (i.e., "their authorities," with ἐθνῶν as its antecedent), the precedent of v 25b and the ordinary use of the genitive with κυριεύω (cf. Mark 10:42 [2x]) would favor similar usages in both instances (i.e., "rule over them,... exercise authority over them").

In order to establish which kings are in view in v 25, it is useful to probe the sense of τῶν ἐθνῶν. Does the expression speak in general terms of "the nations" (i.e., all peoples), or is it more outwardly focused on "the Gentiles"? A problem with the former understanding is that the expression would be so broad that it would specify very little: why not just say "kings" with no further description? Also noteworthy is the fact that, apart from the peculiar case of the Herodian client kings, there were no Jewish monarchs in either the era of Luke or the time of Jesus; kingship in the NT world had fallen into the hands of the Gentiles. Further, v 25b and c are linked by the repetition of αὐτῶν, and even though the custom of bearing the title "benefactor" was known in Jewish circles,[113] it derives from Hellenism.[114] An outward focus on "the Gentiles" may also be supported by the use of αὐτῶν rather than ἡμῶν (considering the reality of the long arm of Roman rule, one might expect the latter).[115]

[112]So BAGD, "κυριεύω," 458 (cf. Gen 37:8); "ἐξουσιάζω," 279 (cf. 1 Cor 7:4).

[113]The high priest Onias III held the title (2 Macc 4:2). Kötting (856) sees the εὐεργέτης word group as a Greek infiltration into the LXX (e.g., 2 Macc 5:20; 10:38).

[114]So Bertram, 654; Danker, *Jesus*, 348; Deissmann, 249; Evans, 796; Feuillet, 375; Fitzmyer, *Gospel*, 2:1417; Geldenhuys, 564; Klostermann, 211; Knox, 121; Rengstorf, 246; Sabourin, *Luc*, 345-7; Schlosser, 54; Schmid, 328; Sherwin-White, 137; Walasky, 37, n. 125.

[115]It is not impossible that a hint of denial of foreign occupation accounts

Although Bousset claims that the mere mention of "king" would have had a negative ring in the ancient Orient,[116] a survey of βασιλεύς usages in Luke-Acts suggests that Luke thought otherwise. The term occurs eleven times in Luke and twenty times in Acts, usually in a neutral sense (i.e., a king is merely named without reference to his good or bad conduct or qualities).[117] To be sure, Luke maintains that Herod's kingship goes to his head, and his opinion of such conduct is most critical (Acts 12:20-23); other negative portrayals are seen as well (e.g., 4:26). But there is no indication in Luke-Acts that Luke is critical of all kings, or of kingship itself.

A careful analysis of κυριεύω and ἐξουσιάζω points in the same direction: the actions of kings and rulers in v 25 are not described as unusually harsh or oppressive. That kings govern and rulers exercise authority is, for Luke, a simple, more or less neutral statement of fact.[118] K. Clark even argues from an "inclusive sweep" of the NT, LXX, papyri of the Hellenistic-Roman era, the Apostolic Fathers and early Christian apologists that neither κυριεύω nor κατακυριεύω (cf. Mark 10:42) ever carry negative connotations.[119] While this assertion seems a bit extravagant regarding κατακυριεύω,[120] Clark's arguments regarding κυριεύω are persuasive; it is best understood simply to mean "to rule over."[121] Similar

---

for the language. It may also be noted that Lukan usage of ἔθνος would favor "the Gentiles" (only in 24:47 does the plural form with the article encompass Israel), though this is not a weighty factor.

[116]Bousset, *Religion*, 376.

[117]Luke 1:5; 14:31 [2x]; 23:2, 3; Acts 7:10; 9:15; 13:21, 22. A negative portrayal of kings is apparent in Luke 21:12.

[118]So Easton, 324; Ernst, *Evangelium*, 594 (Luke is not critical here, yet there simply is no analogy for Christian leadership in the political sphere); Evans, 795; Foerster, "κύριος," 1097; Lagrange, 549; Rasmussen, 74; Schmithals, *Lukas*, 210; Walasky, 36-7. This is in contrast to the views of many interpreters who take κυριεύω here negatively (i.e., as excessive domination or oppression): e.g., Bossuyt and Radermakers, 474; Cassidy, 39, 60; Danker, *Jesus*, 348 (tyranny is in view); *Benefactor*, 324; L'Eplattenier, 251 (v 25 is a polemic against political authorities); Fitzmyer, *Gospel*, 2:1415-16; George, *Études*, 276; Gooding, 333; Liefeld, 1028; Reiling and Swellengrebel, 691; Schillebeeckx, 71; Schmid, 328; G. Schneider, *Evangelium*, 2:450; Senior, 67; Tiede, *Luke*, 385.

[119]K. Clark, 207-212.

[120]Cf. 1 Pet 5:2-3 where the three-part parallel structure implies a negative sense for κατακυριεύω in v 3. Foerster ("κύριος," 1098) and Mann (414) allow for an intensified and potentially negative form of rule with the addition of the κατά prefix to κυριεύω. The fact that κατακυριεύω in Mark 10:42 extends the action of ἄρχειν would suggest some sort of intensification of rule (contrast Luke 22:25 where κυριεύω extends no other action).

claims can be made for the neutral sense of ἐξουσιάζω.[122] To be sure, this is not to imply that kings in the ancient Near East did not rule their subjects in an overbearing or oppressive manner.[123] The point is simply that, in terms of conventional standards for the rule of monarchs in the first century, Luke's description of kings and benefactors in v 25 does not call attention to the misuse of power.[124]

Before turning to the problem that arises with a neutral description of kings and rulers (i.e., the apparent conflict with the role of the kings and rulers as negative examples in the flow of thought in vv 24-27 [sec. 6.3]), we must turn our attention to the reference to "benefactors" and the use of καλοῦνται (passive or reflexive?). Does Luke envision rulers claiming the title "benefactor" for themselves, or receiving it from others? Here we must step back from Luke to get a historical perspective (also cf. sec. 2.2.2).

Although the custom of conferring the honorific title εὐεργέτης on rulers and public figures can be traced back to the fifth century BCE,[125] it

---

[121]K. Clark, 212. He points out (210) that the only lexicon to include the negative idiom "lord it over" for κυριεύω is the Arndt-Gingrich revision of the fourth edition of Bauer's *Wörterbuch*, despite the fact that "lord it over" was not found in that edition, nor was it added in the fifth. It remains in the 1979 BAGD edition ("κυριεύω," 458). Clark suspects that English translations went awry when "lord it over," introduced in 1719 by Cornelius Nary for whom the idiom had no negative connotation, was retained in English Bible translations of the twentieth century, in spite of the fact that the idiom had taken on a distinctly negative connotation (211-12). A negative rendering of κυριεύω in 2 Cor 1:24 as "lord it over" (so RSV) is not required in that context. Verses 23-24 make good sense when translated, "Not that we rule over your faith, but we work with you for your joy,..." The contrast is between ruling over and working together, not ruling oppressively and working together.

[122]Cf. BAGD, "ἐξουσιάζω," 279, with the definition, "*have the right* or *power for someth.* or *over someone.*" In Luke 22:25 the substantive means "*one who is in authority.*" Foerster ("ἔξεστιν," 574) claims that the term usually means simply "to have and to exercise ἐξουσία," though it can have reference to the misuse of power (e.g., Eccl 8:9).

[123]On the contrary, consider Nero's vanity, thirst for power and revenge, and his theft from the rich. Also recall Caligula's reckless cruelty and megalomania. Cf. sec. 2.2.

[124]The view of Esler (207-9, in critique of Cassidy and Walasky), that Luke is more interested in portraying Christianity as an unthreatening and positive element in Roman society than in challenging Roman rule (so Thériault, 218-21), has some merit. A long period of church-state co-existence had become conceivable. For this reason it is probable that Mark 10:42, with its potentially more harsh κατα-forms, represents a less developed version of the tradition than does Luke 22:25.

became widespread in the Hellenistic and Roman periods.[126] Bertram observes, "The manifold use of benefactor and benefit is linked with the civilised outlook of Hellenism. Gods and heroes, kings and statesmen, philosophers, inventors and physicians are hailed as benefactors because of their contributions to the development of the race."[127] Nock claims, "In classical times and thereafter it [εὐεργέτης] was a regular term in civic degrees to denote a man whose name was thus to be set on stone and recorded as one of the city's benefactors (comparable to the lists of benefactors kept by the Universities of Cambridge and Oxford)."[128] Sometimes εὐεργέτης is paired with other titles of praise, especially σωτήρ.[129] Trajan, for example, is described as ὁ παντὸς κόσμου σωτὴρ καὶ εὐεργέτης.[130] Many other kings have held the title "benefactor" as well (e.g., Augustus, Tiberius, Nero, Vespasian, Ptolemy II and Ptolemy VIII, and the Syrian King Antiochus VII).[131]

It should be noted that the title was not always held by rulers or public figures who genuinely provided benefits to the people. Josephus recalls the occasion in CE 64 when the Jews hailed the wicked Albinus "as a benefactor" (ὡς εὐεργέτην) only because the governor over the Jews, Gessius Florus, was more wicked still.[132] Danker notes that certain security officials in Hierapolis around CE 100 "... were guilty of oppressive exactions and at the same time had the nerve to pressure villagers in reckoning them among their benefactors."[133] Certain ruthless Egyptian

[125]So Skard (6), citing Herodotus 8.136 and Thuc. 1.136. In the fouth century BCE the term is used to describe King Antigonus (*Inscr. Prien.* 2.6; cf. MM, "εὐεργέτης," 261).

[126]Bertram, 654.

[127]Bertram, 654. Deissmann (248) points to an inscription from Cos around CE 53 in which the people of the island designated Gaius Stertinius Xenophon, physician of Claudius, as εὐεργέτης for his valuable services to the people of Cos.

[128]Nock, 725.

[129]Note the examples cited in Nock, 720-35.

[130]*IG* 12.1.978 (cited in MM, "εὐεργέτης," 261; cf. Jos. *J. W.* 3.459). Although both titles were applied to gods and heroes, Nock claims that εὐερηέτης "has its roots in the human area," and it is less dramatic than σωτήρ (725).

[131]Regarding figures who held the title, also see Fitzmyer, *Gospel*, 2:1417; Kötting, 851-6; T. W. Manson, *Sayings*, 338; Luce, 333.

[132]Jos. *Ant.* 20.253 (although Albinus concealed his villany, Florus was openly wicked).

[133]Danker, *Benefactor*, 294. Danker ("Paul's Debt," 267, n. 2) also cites Aischines *Against Ktesiphon* 247-8 on the need to guard against those who claim title to being public benefactors. So it was with Ptolemy VII, ὁ αὑτὸν μὲν Εὐεργέτην ἀνακηρύττων (Athen. *Deip.* 12.549d). Cf. Plut. *Alex.* 5C = *Mor.* 338C: οἱ δ'

kings who held the title "benefactor" (e.g., Ptolemy II) were nicknamed κακεργέτης by their disgruntled subjects.[134] Thus, despite the fact that being given the title "benefactor" was typically the result of having performed a concrete act of beneficence,[135] holding the title was no guarantee that one was or remained a true benefactor.

The discovery of unauthentic benefaction supports another observation, namely that the title "benefactor" was highly prized and sought after. B. Winter clarifies that a benefactor was typically recognized *publicly*, a gesture of praise in compensation for a good deed.[136] Public praise of benefactors could include a formal commendation hailing the goodness of the benefactor, the awarding of a gold crown, and the gift of a permanent seat of honor in the theater.[137] Dio Chrysostom claims that a public proclamation included "three words" to acclaim the benefactor's goodness, and though it is not known just what those words were,[138] Dio maintains that for some the reception of them was "more precious than life itself."[139] In societies which were keenly conscious of honor and shame,[140] and in which honor was acquired not through possession of things but acts of beneficence,[141] to be named a "benefactor" would be near to achieving the pinnacle of prestige.[142]

Εὐεργέτας οἱ δὲ Καλλινίκους οἱ δὲ Σωτῆρας οἱ δὲ Μεγάλους ἀνηγόρευσαν ἑαυτούς. Elsewhere Plutarch alludes to the thirst for titles in classical times (*Arist.* 6). See H. Betz ("De Laude," 374) on Plutarch's critical assessment of the adoption of honorific titles.

[134]See Luce, 333; Danker, *Jesus*, 348.

[135]So Kötting, 851, 855.

[136]B. Winter, "Benefactors," 90-1. Benefactions could even be "loans" to be repaid with gratitude.

[137]B. Winter, "Benefactors," 91-2. On crowning see *IE* 1390; *BMI* 452; Dio Chrys. *Or.* 66.2; on the granting of seats of honor in the theater see Dio Chrys. *Or.* 75.7. The motion made by a member of a city's council and endorsed by the council to recognize a benefactor constituted the wording of an inscription as that benefactor's formal commendation.

[138]B. Winter ("Benefactors," 91) cites H. Crosby's conjecture (*Dio Chrysostom* [LCL 5], 247, n. 2) that they may have been ἀνὴρ ἀγαθός ἐστι.

[139]Dio Chrys. *Or.* 75.7-8; 66.2; cited in B. Winter, "Benefactors," 91. Nock observes that the title εὐεργέτης is often given to the gods, and that possessing it could inspire great envy (724-5).

[140]Cf. sec. 6.4. The great thirst for honorific titles witnessed in Greco-Roman societies (so Danker, "Accomodation," 396; cf. Kötting, 857) reflects this mentality.

[141]So Malina, *World*, 34; cf. Veyne, 101-2. Such acts were sometimes performed at great risk to the benefactor (Danker, "Endangered Benefactor," 40-3; "Paul's Debt," 265-6).

[142]The fact that Greco-Roman societies were highly stratified (so Meeks,

It is this background that gives a dimension of realism to the option of καλοῦνται as reflexive rather than passive. One can understand why rulers or wealthy and influential public figures would on occasion pressure people into granting the honor,[143] or even find means to simply assign the title to themselves. Many favor the middle voice in v 25c, for that way an otherwise apparently positive reference to benefactors appears tainted by pride, and the following prohibition (v 26a) follows more naturally. Plummer was an early exponent of this view, and he suggests that claiming a great title for themselves is in fact what the disciples are doing in v 24.[144]

A survey of Lukan usages of καλέω may also shed some light on the sense of καλοῦνται in v 25c. A middle-passive form of καλέω appears thirty-three times (19x in Luke, 14x in Acts). If we eliminate instances in which the reflexive is impossible (i.e., when the subject is impersonal, personal subjects that could not or would not "call" themselves in the sense described, and the technical senses "to invite" and "to summon"), eleven texts remain (omitting 22:25).[145] Upon careful examination, however, in each instance the passive is almost certainly the voice intended. Reference is made either to a person's name presumably given at birth, or a person's second name noted to distinguish one Judas or Mary or Simon from another. Thus, there is no precedent in Luke-Acts for a reflexive meaning of καλοῦνται in 22:25, but rather a precedent for the passive sense.[146]

Urban Christians, 53-5; et al.) would have accentuated the status distinctions accompanying the reception of an honorific title like "benefactor."

[143]The fear of suffering harm at the hands of tyrannical rulers prompted citizens to grant malefactors honorific titles (Plato *Rep*. 344B-C). Cf. Danker, *Benefactor*, 294.

[144]Plummer, 501. For Kötting (857) "die Titelsucht" is the problem in v 25c. Others favoring reflexive καλοῦνται in v 25c are Creed, 268; Danker, *Benefactor*, 324; "Endangered Benefactor," 44; *Jesus*, 348; "Paul's Debt," 267, n. 2; L'Eplattenier, 251; Fitzmyer, *Gospel*, 2:1416; Geldenhuys, 564; Klostermann, 211; Luce, 332; Morris, 308; Reiling and Swellengrebel, 691; Rickards, 446; cf. NIV and TEV. Correspondingly, many see irony in "benefactors": Bertram, 655; Cassidy, 39; Deissmann, 249; Loisy, 516; Luce, 333; Nock, 726; Schmid, 328; G. Schneider, *Evangelium*, 2:450.

[145]They are Luke 1:60; 6:15; 8:2; 10:39; 19:2; 22:3; Acts 1:23; 7:58; 13:1; 15:22, 37.

[146]Favoring passive καλοῦνται in v 25c are Bertram, 655; Easton, 324; Evans, 795-6; Hauck, 265 (though there is still an element of irony); Lull, 295-6; cf. NAB, NEB, RSV, NRSV. It may be noted that Lukan omissions of καλέω from Mark or Q do not provide any significant new information here.

This is not a decisive finding for the voice of καλοῦνται in v 25c, however, since none of the other καλέω texts in Luke-Acts are associated with the naming of a "benefactor" or the reception of an honorific title. Indeed, εὐεργέτης occurs only in Luke 22:25 in the NT, and its cognate forms in Acts 4:9 and 10:38 have nothing to do with the idea of being called or calling oneself a benefactor. Still, despite the fact that the practice of claiming honorific titles for oneself was known, the routine and predominant procedure in antiquity was for public officials and prominent figures to be given the title. Further, the probable neutral sense of κυριεύω (v 25b) would support a neutral description in the parallel clause (v 25c). Taken together, these factors weigh in favor of passive καλοῦνται in v 25c.

The description in v 25 of kings and leaders, then, is probably neutral (i.e., it reflects the status quo). To say that kings rule and authorities are called benefactors is not *in and of itself* a negative portrayal. It is only in light of the progression of thought in context (i.e., vv 23-24, 26-27) that the picture of kings and rulers takes on a negative hue. It is probable, then, that Luke wishes to pinpoint something negative about *ordinary* patterns of ruling (not just oppressive rule) and *usual* concerns for public honor (not just the improper acquisition of titles).[147] Correspondingly, there is something *extraordinary* to which the Lukan Jesus summons the apostles.

What, then, might v 25 implicitly oppose? The nature of Jesus' sayings in vv 26b-27 suggests that the social dimensions of the actions described in v 25 are of interest to Luke. Being hailed as a benefactor belongs to a status system in which the acceptance of that title involves the unspoken reception of a superior position over those who grant it.[148] It is an expression of the prevalent social network of patronage and clientism in which a client is confirmed in his inferior position to that of a beneficent patron.[149] The acceptance of the social implications which accompany conventional rule and the standard forms of public recogni-

[147]So Rasmussen, 74-5. Ernst contends that the world's power holders illustrate a false greatness (593).

[148]Mott, 195; cf. Clarke, 137; P. Marshall, 2, 10; Rasmussen, 74-5; Veyne, 70, 103 (acceptance of a benefaction signifies the recipient's subordinate standing and his promise of obedience to the superior benefactor).

[149]Moxnes (*Economy*, 137) rightly observes that in 14:1-14 Luke undercuts certain fundamental bases of the patron-client system (cf. 158-9). On patronage and clientism, see sec. 2.2.2.

tion for good deeds is an important negative, albeit implicit, dimension of Luke 22:25.

More particularly, however, it appears that it is not merely the acceptance of the social status which attends positions of leadership, but the preoccupation with such status which the Lukan Jesus counters. This is the attitude of the apostles in v 24, one which prizes honor and values prestige. Such an attitude reflects a misunderstanding of the nature of authority in the economy of Jesus, and it is to be replaced by a new and unconventional model of leadership. Beginning in v 26 the alternative way is set forth, so we turn to vv 26-27.

6.5.2 Prohibition (v 26a)

This clause functions as a hinge in Jesus' response to the apostles' quarrel: v 25 presents a negative example, v 26a a prohibition, and vv 26b-27c a corrective commendation. It is only in v 26a that Jesus turns to the apostles and applies the illustration of v 25 directly to them: "But not so with you!"[150] As argued above (sec. 6.3), even though οὐ requires an indicative verb, this phrase probably has imperatival force: the apostles must not—in some still unspecified respect—conduct themselves as the kings and ruling benefactors of v 25.[151] In view of the extended discussion of v 26a in section 6.3, we turn to vv 26b-27.

6.5.3 Commendation (vv 26b-27)

In v 26b we meet the alternative (ἀλλά) course Jesus lays out for the Twelve. With ὁ μείζων v 26b recalls the original issue over which the apostles quarreled (and cf. v 27a), and with μείζων and νεώτερος Luke sets the text on a course of contrasts leading to an encounter with the definitive example in whom the apostles are to see the remedy for their error: that of Jesus himself.

It is important to note that vv 26b-27c do *not* suggest that none of the apostles is to be ὁ μείζων. On the contrary, v 26b assumes the existence of such a one "among you" (ἐν ὑμῖν),[152] and comparative ὡς in each

[150]The ellipsis here suggests that ὑμεῖς is probably not emphatic.

[151]The "parallel" in Mark 10:43 par. Matt 20:26 is of some (albeit limited) value here in confirming the general structure or flow of thought in Luke 22:24-27 and supporting the claim that v 26a is prohibition, not description.

[152]Dupont, "Ministères," 148; Klostermann, 211; Soards, 31, n. 16; Tannehill,

contrast of v 26b-c serves to distinguish the directive from one that would abolish all distinctions among the Twelve. That is, the greatest is now to become somehow *like* the youngest, and the leader *like* the servant. The combination with γινέσθω would seem to prohibit a predicative usage of ὡς here (i.e., why include "as" if the aim is for "the greatest" literally to become or take on the duties of "the servant/ youngest"?). Therefore, though the Lukan Jesus may envision a profound reformation of the idea of greatness and leadership, he does not call for its elimination.[153]

It is very likely that Jesus' injunction in v 26b-c is not directed to just one person (despite the singular substantives), for the quarrel of v 24 necessarily implies that more than one apostle was overly concerned with greatness. Although Luke does not specify how many of the Twelve were at fault, it is natural that Jesus' sayings would apply to all that were. Further, it seems unlikely that the model of Jesus as the servant-leader (v 27c) would be put forward by Luke as an example for only one of the Twelve.

There is a certain sense of surprise that νεώτερος[154] brings to the text. In contrast to "greatest" one expects something like "least" (cf. 9:48), not "youngest."[155] In the ancient Near East, however, the aged

"Study," 201; Wiefel, 370.

[153]Hoffmann and Eid, 227. Luke does not wish to eliminate all forms of rank and rule (Fitzmyer, *Gospel*, 2:1417); cf. Luke 7:28. Hierarchy is not inherently bad (Lagrange, 550). The Lukan Jesus does not commend anarchy (Schmithals, *Lukas*, 210). Power must be exercised to protect and serve the poor, but it is the power *of God* when rulers serve (Hamel, 78). The servant can be a leader (Léon-Dufour, "Letzte Mahl," 48); authority is a way of service (Feuillet, 377). It is only "self-important" leadership that Jesus opposes here (Neyrey, 23). On the Lukan interest in legitimate authority for the good of the community, see also Lull, 297; Meynet, *Initiation*, 167; Mott, 196; against; Moxnes, "Meals," 166; R. Pesch, "Kleine Herde," 116; Roloff, "Amt," 512.

Minear (*Heal*, 20-1) claims that at the heart of 22:25-27 is the demand for a reversal of the "directional flow of authority." The contrast is between authority which operates downward and that which emanates upward. This view, however, overlooks the fact that it is primarily the nature of the exercise of authority, not the direction of its flow that is challenged in vv 25-27. Comparative ὡς (v 26) and v 32 imply that there are still leaders in the community. Reversing the direction of rule merely paves the way for the oppressed to become oppressors (cf. Hamel, 81; Meynet, *Initiation*, 167). Mott's view is preferred: "It is not the fact of rule that is proscribed, but the personal misuse of authority. The function of authority is an acceptable inequality insofar as it is of service to everyone, but it does not carry any implication of superior dignity or worth" (196).

[154]As with μείζων in v 24, comparative νεώτερος has a superlative sense.

were granted great respect and even veneration;[156] theirs was a privileged status—not unlike that associated with benefactors. Conversely, children and youth were generally held in very low esteem (cf. secs. 2.4.1-2).[157] Thus, the directive to become "like the youngest" (v 26b) would probably, by implication, involve a call to renounce high estimations of one's importance. This is akin to the thrust of 9:47-48 (cf. 18:15-17) where Jesus summons the quarreling disciples to identify with lowly children and thereby "receive" him.

Additionally, many have observed that the terminology of v 26 corresponds to that used occasionally in Acts and elsewhere in the NT to describe roles or offices in the early church.[158] In Acts 5:6 (cf. v 10) οἱ νεώτεροι appear on the scene without any introduction, thus giving the impression that they may constitute a specific established group in the church.[159] The term ἡγούμενους has a possible reference to a standing group of church leaders in Acts 15:22, and in Hebrews (13:7, 17, 24) it is a technical term for church leaders in general.[160] It may also be noted that διακονῶν (along with its nominal cognate διακονία) could be a technical term for a church office or responsibility (cf. Acts 6:1-4).[161]

The case for seeing in Luke 22:26b-c a focus on set roles in the early church is not overwhelming, however, for Luke makes only minimal use

---

[155]This is so despite the fact that μέγας can imply a great (i.e., old) age.

[156]Liefeld, 1028; Tiede, *Luke*, 385.

[157]On νεώτερος in Luke 22:26, see Hendricksen, 971; Morris, 308; Rienecker, 503 (the young are to do serving tasks).

[158]E.g., Arens, 126; Best, *Temptation*, 140-1; Dupont, "Ministères," 147-8; Fitzmyer, *Gospel*, 2:1417; Goulder, *Luke*, 2:731; Higgins, *Jesus*, 38; Kremer, 215; Lampe, 840; Loisy, 516; Matera, *Passion*, 164; Reiling and Swellengrebel, 692; Roloff, "Apostel," 442; Schmid, 328; Schürmann, *Abschiedsrede*, 76-8, 94; Sweetland, "Lord's Supper," 25; Vööbus, *Prelude*, 32, n. 14.

[159]So Behm, "νέος," 898; Ernst, *Evangelium*, 594; I. H. Marshall, *Gospel*, 813; G. Schneider, *Evangelium*, 2:450. Note the "lowly" nature of their task. For Klostermann (211) the contrast with νεώτερος suggests that μείζων here is a substitute for πρεσβύτερος.

[160]Some see church leaders and perhaps a specific "office" in ἡγούμενος in Luke 22:26c (e.g., Evans, 796; Goulder, *Luke*, 2:733; Hoffmann and Eid, 189-90; Karris, *Gospel*, 716; Laub, "Autorität," 185 and n. 67; Sabourin, *Luc*, 346; against George, *Études*, 390, n. 2, who does not see the technical sense of ἡγέομαι from Hebrews in the Acts usages). The testamentary genre of vv 14-38 invites the reader to expect a focus on future leaders (so Karris, *Gospel*, 716). This, however, does not require church offices or set leadership roles in vv 26-27.

[161]So Ernst, *Evangelium*, 593; Horn, 213; et al. This is not to imply that there is no recollection of the vivid social imagery of διακονέω, which has its roots in the idea of table service (cf. sec. 2.4.3 and ch. 3).

of the terms of vv 26-27 in contexts referring to church duties or positions. The juxtaposition of several terms here "under one roof" may be significant, but other explanations seem more plausible.[162] To be sure, the Lukan Jesus contrasts not just abstract ideas of worldly greatness with Christian greatness, but styles of governance in the world with those for the church. The implications of vv 25-27 for church leadership, then, are sufficiently apparent, but this is so without having recourse to the less-than-persuasive claim that specific "offices" are in view.[163]

Some see behind vv 25-27 a problem involving the misuse of authority in the Lukan community.[164] A comparison with Mark 10:43-44 may imply that Luke has followed or formed a line of tradition that is readily applied to a setting of church leadership, and accordingly one can at least agree with Tiede, "... that Luke is hoping the leaders in his own community are overhearing."[165] The fact that different reconstructions may be equally plausible, however, prompts us to leave open the question of a problem in the Lukan *Sitz im Leben*.[166]

The form of Jesus' response to the apostles' quarrel changes significantly in v 27, though without interrupting the progression of contrasts between Positions A and B. Picking up on ὁ διακονῶν in v 26c, v 27a presents a double question: "For which is greater, the diner or the table servant?"[167] This sets the stage for a challenge to the conventional and thus expected affirmative answer.

In v 26c, where διακονῶν is contrasted with ἡγούμενος, the simple translation "servant" is fitting. But in v 27a, where διακονῶν is con-

[162]I.e., perhaps νεώτερος recalls the low esteem of children and youth, ἡγούμενος recalls the imagery of v 25, and διακονῶν anticipates the example of Jesus in v 27c. It may also be noted that comparative ὡς in 22:26b weighs against the idea that there νεώτερος is a technical term for a church "office."

[163]L'Eplattenier (254) correctly sees an ecclesiological interest in vv 25-27 (cf. Wiefel, 370).

[164]E.g., Horn, 212, 214; Sabourin, *Luc*, 345; Schweizer, *Luke*, 336 (Luke opposes an understanding of the episcopate as power); Talbert, *Reading Luke*, 210.

[165]Tiede, *Luke*, 384.

[166]Esler (e.g., 183-5, 198-200) is less cautious in this regard, basing certain Lukan emphases in a postulated social setting of his community. Tuckett (144-5), however, cautions against minimizing the varied ways in which language can function (e.g., reflecting social structures, challenging them, or disregarding a text's social setting).

[167]Here (diff. vv 24 and 26) the *Stichwort* μείζων has the comparative sense. On the double question as a Semitic wisdom device, cf. n. 27 above.

trasted with ἀνακείμενος, table imagery is clearly in view, so there the translation "table servant" seems apt. That the table servant did not hold a position of dignity is evident not only from our survey of backgrounds,[168] but is also implied by emphatic οὐχί in the rhetorical question of v 27b: "Surely it is the one who reclines, is it not?"[169]

In v 27c the rebuke for the quarreling apostles comes to a climactic and decisive conclusion when Jesus identifies himself as "the servant."[170] The reference to his own conduct is the trump card of the argument, and it provides the definitive corrective illustration for the Twelve. Here the Lukan Jesus defies the conventional assumptions upon which v 27b rests, and he affirms a contrary stance.

Before examining v 27c in detail, however, it may be useful to glance back at Luke's account of the Passover preparations (vv 7-13) and reflect briefly on the duties which Peter and John (v 8) are asked to perform. Peculiar to Luke's account is the naming of Peter and John to make the meal preparations. Schürmann draws attention to two key points here: 1) for Luke, Peter and John are the recognized leaders of the apostolic band; 2) they are sent to carry out service duties.[171] V 8 may then illustrate in advance Jesus' words in our text: "Jesus selbst fungierte als Tischdiener (22,27; vgl. 12,37; Jo 13,1ff), und auch die angesehensten Apostel hatten Dienstaufgaben bekommen (Lk 22,8ff.)."[172] The backdrop for v 27 which vv 8-13 constitute could also arouse reader expectations and enhance readers' comprehension of the radical reversal of values which Jesus exemplifies.[173]

With the pronoun ἐγώ, v 27c constitutes a response which matches the emphasis of the rhetorical question in v 27b.[174] By using this climactic "I," then, the Lukan Jesus claims the right to command the apostles by the model of his life.[175] So v 27 presents an example of the Lukan *imitatio*

[168]See sec. 2.4.3 and ch. 3; cf. Hoffmann and Eid, 198; Cranfield, *Mark*, 341.

[169]οὐ anticipates the positive answer.

[170]On the reasons for translating "servant" and not "table servant," see below (also see below, this sec., on the use of ὡς in v 27c). ἦλθον in ms. D is probably an assimilation to Mark 10:45a (cf. Beyer, 84).

[171]Schürmann, "Dienst," 100-1.

[172]Schürmann, "Dienst," 101.

[173]Recall ch. 2 on the magnitude of a move from master to servant.

[174]The contrast with v 27b means that δέ in v 27c is adversitive (Klostermann, 211).

[175]Schmid, 328-9; Tiede, *Luke*, 384. The fact that ἐγώ is aligned with Position B and the imperative of v 26b confirms that Jesus' self-reference is exemplary

Christi motif (cf. 6:40), one that reverses the "Wertordnung" of socio-cultural norms.[176]

The phrase ἐν μέσῳ ὑμῶν εἰμι has been taken by some as a later liturgical expression to highlight the personal presence of Jesus in the Lord's Supper.[177] While it is possible that v 27c was repeated in early church liturgy, it should not be overlooked that ἐν μέσῳ ὑμῶν εἰμι also makes good sense in the context of vv 24-27 as wording which stems from the Lukan Jesus in confronting the quarreling apostles. Present tense εἰμι is fitting (see below), and ἐν μέσῳ ὑμῶν pinpoints the sphere in which Jesus both sees a problem and requires a solution (i.e., among the apostles and, by implication, other leaders in the Christian community).[178]

The expression ἐν μέσῳ ὑμῶν may also recall the close connection for Luke between Jesus' presence and the coming of the kingdom of God (cf. 17:21; see further the discussion in sec. 7.4.3), thereby implying a striking new concept of authority which is operative in the kingdom. Further, the phrase seems to call attention to the union of Jesus and the apostles (cf. sec. 7.3.2), despite their departure from his service orientation.

The last phrase in v 27c, ὡς ὁ διακονῶν, requires careful attention, for the meaning of v 27, and indeed vv 25-27, is heavily dependent on this description of Jesus.[179] Is ὡς comparative as in v 26b-c, or might it be predicative?[180] An initial exegetical reflex gives us pause at the idea of a different sense for ὡς in v 27c in such close proximity to the comparative usages. Further, comparative ὡς in v 27c could help alleviate the difficulty in having Jesus both recline (v 14) and serve (v 27). In favor of the predicative usage, however, according to Schlosser, is the narrower (literal) meaning of διακονῶν in v 27 compared to v 26.[181] Nevertheless, even though v 27a envisions literal table service (so the contrast with ἀνακείμενος), the usage in v 27c could enlarge the understanding of service which is in view (cf. v 26c).

---

for Luke. Also see Feuillet, 371; Roloff, "Apostel," 442; Thysman, 148. Meynet (*Initiation*, 176) sees in 22:27 a likeness to the OT motif, "Be holy, for I am holy" (Lev 11:44; 19:2; 20:7-8, 26).

[176]Horn, 213; cf. A. Schulz, *Nachfolge*, 255.

[177]See Howard, *Das Ego*, 235; Minear, *Heal*, 21; Vööbus, *Prelude*, 32-3.

[178]So Schmithals, *Lukas*, 210. See further sec. 6.6 below.

[179]Note that this is the third usage of διακονῶν in the space of two verses; "service" evidently comes to the fore in Jesus' correction of the apostles.

[180]Schlosser (67-8) favors the latter (cf. BAGD, "ὡς," 898; Sellew, 32-3).

[181]Schlosser, 68.

The decision on ὡς is complicated by the ambiguity of the copula: Is εἰμι descriptive, customary or perhaps durative?[182] The latter two uses of the present tense open up possibilities for v 27c which encompass the service of Jesus performed before or "beyond" the actual Last Supper setting. Further, the verb "to be" can have a literal or figurative sense. Thus to ask in what sense Jesus is, or is likened to, the servant is to pose a difficult question, as the number of different interpretations in the literature indicates. We will consider the following possibilities: 1) Jesus' service at the Last Supper is that of footwashing (cf. John 13:1-20). 2) Jesus adopts the actual role of table servant at the Last Supper. 3) Jesus' administration of the Passover and his distribution of its elements constitutes his service. 4) Jesus is the servant in that his life has included repeated acts of service (table service perhaps among them) for the apostles. 5) Jesus is the servant in that his coming (i.e., his life, suffering, and anticipated death and resurrection) constitutes a complex act of profound service to his disciples. The first three possibilities envision a concrete act of service in the upper room (i.e., descriptive εἰμι), while the last two involve a broader view of Jesus' life as involving (customary εἰμι) or amounting to (durative εἰμι) service. In the following, each possibility will be considered, though not in such a way as to suggest that they do not overlap.

Commentators offer an array of views proposing some type of link between v 27c and John 13.[183] Reasons for considering this possibility include the following: a) The setting for both the Lukan word and the

---

[182]The term "customary" corresponds to Brooks and Winbery's "iterative" present (85-6).

[183]Those who note a "parallel" or call for comparison include Bossuyt and Radermakers, 474; Green, *Death*, 45; Fitzmyer, *Gospel*, 2:1415; T. W. Manson, *Sayings*, 339; Sabourin, *Luc*, 345-6; Streeter, 423. Cf. also J. Bailey, 33-7; Ernst, *Evangelium*, 592; Feuillet, 400-1; Fransen, 25; H. Klein, 172 (Luke and John had "eine parallele Vorlage"); Kollmann, *Mahl*, 161, 223; Lagrange, 550; Léon-Dufour, "Testament," 274; Liefeld, 1028; Osty, "Points," 147; Plummer, 500; Tresmontant, 620; Wellhausen, 123; Zahn, 681 (footwashing was the waiter's duty). See esp. the list of studies in Soards, 32, n. 19. Richter (e.g., 205, 214-15, 220-1, 240-1) traces the Luke 22:27c - John 13 connection in the history of interpretation. Among the interpreters who see no true link between John's footwashing and Luke 22:27 are Easton, 324 (the idea is "very hazardous"); Evans, 798; Harrington, 251; Muhlack, 89; Rengstorf, 247; J. Robinson, 146, n. 1; Roloff, "Anfänge," 58; Schmid, 329 (the idea is "unhaltbar"). On the broader issue of the relationship between Luke and John, and the many striking convergences of Lukan and Johannine traditions, see e.g., J. Bailey; Boismard (Luke was active in the redaction of John); Cribbs, "St. Luke" and "Study"; de Dinechin; Guillet; H. Klein; Maddox, 158-79; Osty, "Points"; Richter; Sabbe; Segovia.

Johannine incident is the Last Supper where a farewell discourse is delivered; b) in both accounts Jesus is described or portrayed as both servant and master;[184] c) an act like Jesus' footwashing would find a logical basis in a quarrel over greatness; d) in both texts Jesus refers to his own exemplary service; e) in both cases this reference is to stimulate a behavior change among the disciples.[185]

We may pursue the possibility of a Luke-John link here and perhaps bring an increased measure of clarity to the debate by approaching the issue from two angles: First, is there adequate evidence to suggest that in 22:27 Luke intends to call the footwashing event or tradition to the minds of his readers? Second, is there adequate evidence to suggest that a common root of tradition lies beneath the Lukan description and the Johannine event?

J. Bailey answers the first question in the affirmative; he claims that Luke, being aware of an oral tradition of the footwashing incident, alludes to that act in v 27c.[186] This view is put forward as an alternative to the notion of Creed and others[187] that John was familiar with the Lukan Last Supper discourse and spun his footwashing story from Luke 22:27c. The chief difficulty with Bailey's view is that one must credit Luke with tremendous restraint in reducing such a rich narrative to the conceptual kernel of διακονῶν, despite the absence of this term in John's narrative[188] (by contrast, according to Creed's view John must be credited with extraordinary imagination). Can we suppose that, even if Luke's readers had been aware of a footwashing tradition, they would have recognized a reference to it here on the basis of διακονῶν alone, a term that already has an established role in the contrast structure of the Lukan pericope (vv 26c,

---

[184]J. Bailey (34) concedes that διακονέω does not appear in the Johannine account (so too Sabbe, 296, n. 39; Sellew, 81). But note the use of δοῦλος in John 13:16.

[185]Also of possible relevance are the mediating position of Jesus between the Father and the disciples (Luke 22:29; John 13:20 [cf. Guillet, 113-22]), the initiative of Satan with Judas (Luke 22:3; John 13:2 [cf. Osty, "Points," 146]), and the occasional overlap of sequence of the Lukan and Johannine Passion Narratives (see Cribbs, "Study," 50).

[186]J. Bailey, 33-7.

[187]Creed, 370; Barrett, *John*, 436; Goulder, *Luke*, 2:733; Sabbe, 287, 296, n. 39; also see J. Bailey, 36, n. 7, for others who share Creed's view. Besides J. Bailey, those who oppose this understanding include Dodd, 62; J. Robinson, 146, n. 1; H. Weiss, 302.

[188]J. Bailey contends that Luke was reticent to use the full form of the footwashing tradition "because it might appear to compete with, and so detract from, the institution of the eucharist" (37).

27a)? In short, if Luke intended to refer to the footwashing in 22:27, one would expect some sort of stronger and more obvious connection with that event.[189]

Nevertheless, the case for a common root of tradition may still be plausible. To explore this issue, we will weigh the above points of similarity between Luke 22:27 and John 13:1-20. Regarding item c), the footwashing may seem like a fitting response to a quarrel over greatness, but John gives no indication that a problem among the Twelve which occasioned the action was associated with the tradition.[190] Also, items b), d) and e) are paralleled in Mark 10:41-45 as well as in John 13, and in Mark at least there is one point of verbal agreement with Luke 22:27c (i.e., διακονέω). Moreover, because both Mark and Luke have Jesus correct the Twelve for a known error, it is more explicit in those Gospels than in John's footwashing that a behavior change is needed.[191]

The Last Supper/ farewell setting (item a), however, is shared by Luke and John only, a factor that casts both accounts in a particular light (cf. ch. 5): both involve an interpretation of Jesus' death as service (see further below) in the shadow of his impending passion, and both turn attention to the period of Jesus' absence. When this common ground is taken together with points b), d) and e), the significant conceptual similarities of Luke 22:27 and John 13 seem to be more than coincidental. This

[189]By way of clarification, this conclusion leaves open the question of whether Luke or his readers were aware of the footwashing event or tradition. The point is simply that 22:27c gives too little information to suggest that in that verse Luke *intends* to call attention to the footwashing. Soards (36) correctly observes that we have no reason to doubt that both Luke and John were content with their narratives the way we read them, an observation that weighs against an alleged Lukan deliberate reference to the footwashing. Although T. W. Manson (*Sayings*, 339) suggests that Luke 22:27 would have tremendous force if it followed a footwashing story (so too Sabourin, *Luc*, 345-6), this assertion overlooks the possibility that v 27 might seem to be a statement of the obvious in such a setting (Rienecker's claim [504] that v 27 makes an ideal signature under the footwashing story faces a similar difficulty).

[190]The only event in the John 13 narrative that could be worthy of rebuke is the anticipated betrayal of Judas. The footwashing, however, cannot be intended as a correction of that act because the betrayal has not yet happened when Jesus dons the towel (v 4).

[191]Cribbs ("Study," see esp. the chart on 50) has argued that the sequence of pericopae in Luke's Passion Narrative is closer to the Johannine order than the Markan order. Cribbs's argument, however, is flawed at many points, and ultimately it adds little to the case for a Luke-John connection.

enhances the plausibility of the argument that there is some common core of tradition beneath to two accounts.[192]

The case for a link here between Luke and John both gains and possibly loses strength when the texts are set against the backdrop of the custom of footwashing in antiquity. The gain comes from the fact that footwashing was ordinarily done when a guest entered a house, not at a later time and especially not during a meal.[193] Both John and Luke, however, portray Jesus as a servant at the meal. In John this is indicated by the present tense genitive absolute in 13:2, implying that the rising and washing (v 4) were "during" the meal. If one takes the copula in Luke 22:27c as a descriptive present (see the discussion below), we have a similar scenario. Thus, since both possibly reflect a departure from custom, a measure of support may be given to the case for a common basis underlying Luke 22:27c and John 13:1-20.

A possible loss comes from the fact that footwashing typically was not among the duties of the table servant (διάκονος/ διακονῶν), but those of the household slave (δοῦλος).[194] Washing the feet of one's master was a very lowly duty, one which a Jewish slave could supposedly refuse to perform,[195] but the table servant was to be a step above the household slave who performed the most menial duties.[196] To be sure, it is not always possible to make a neat distinction between "servant" and "slave"; some slaves had important duties, some servants did very menial tasks (cf. sec. 2.4.3), and the relevant terms sometimes overlap (e.g., Luke 17:7-10, where δοῦλος is the subject of διακονέω). Especially in a small household, a slave or servant might have been given a very wide variety of tasks. However, there may still be significance, even if limited, in the fact that Luke 22:27 uses servant language while John 13 has slave imagery.

[192]Klappert ("Arbeit," 101) maintains that Luke and John *independently* report a tradition of Jesus' service at the Last Supper.

[193]See esp. Luke 7:44. Cf. R. Brown, *John*, 2:565; Knight, 815; Mau, 1207. The Rabbis do set out certain regulations for the washing of hands during banquets (a practice facilitated by table servants) (cf. *b. Ber.* 46b, 47a), but footwashing is another matter.

[194]So Evans, 797-8; Hooker, *Jesus*, 74; Rengstorf, 247; against Zahn, 681. Note that in 1 Kgdms 25:41 Abigail says to David, ἰδοὺ ἡ δούλη σου εἰς παιδίσκην νίψαι πόδας τῶν παίδων σου.

[195]See *Mek. Exod.* 21.3.82a; Gentile slaves and women and children, however, were obliged to perform this duty. On the menial nature of footwashing, cf. Mark 1:7 and par.; *Jos. As.* 20.1-5.

[196]Hoffmann and Eid, 196-8; on possible distinctions between δοῦλος and διάκονος, see also Boulton, 417; Roloff, *Apostolat*, 121-3.

Ultimately, the information gained from reflection on the ancient custom of footwashing adds a certain amount of weight to each side of the argument, perhaps more to the case for than the case against a common root of tradition beneath Luke 22:27c and John 13:1-20. Considering the points of similarity noted above as well, then, it is perhaps more likely than not that a shared root of tradition lies beneath these Johannine and Lukan texts.

This conclusion, however, is of little help in our quest to recover the Lukan sense of Jesus' service in 22:27c. Even on the assumption that Luke and John do reflect a common tradition, it remains uncertain whether the footwashing gesture itself was in the tradition or is John's interpretation of a story which spoke of Jesus' act of Last Supper service yet did not spell out its specific form. Further, even if the actual footwashing was present in the tradition, it is still quite unlikely that Luke consciously refers to that gesture here. Accordingly, it would seem inappropriate to suppose that the nature of Jesus' service *in the Lukan narrative* should be thought of narrowly as a footwashing.[197]

An interpretation which also sees in v 27c a reference to a concrete act of service at the Last Supper is alternative 2) above: Jesus adopts the actual role of table servant and performs the concrete act of waiting on the apostles at the Last Supper.[198] This view has the advantage of being perhaps the most straightforward understanding of v 27c as a simple claim, though it does not rule out an abstract or religious form of service symbolized by the concrete act.[199]

---

[197]To be sure, the action of the Johannine Jesus and the self-description of the Lukan Jesus ultimately are close in sense, but this is fully understandable on the basis of a shared root of tradition. It would seem that there are four possibilities for Luke's knowledge of the footwashing event or tradition: 1) he did not know of it; 2) he knew of it but it had no influence on his composition/ redaction of the saying in 22:27c; 3) he knew of it, he did not aim to call it to his readers' attention, but it shaded his thinking as to what Jesus' service involved; 4) he knew of it and in v 27c deliberately referred to it. We have argued against option 4) (see above), but options 1), 2) and 3) remain as possibilities.

[198]So Glöckner, 178; Green, *Death*, 45 (by implication); Grundmann, 402 (citing 12:37 in support; but Schlatter [*Lukas*, 424] rightly sees in 12:37 a reference to the "Festmahl Gottes" and not to the Last Supper); Jeremias, *Words*, 205; Prast, 259 (though the reference also includes the service of Jesus' life); Rengstorf, 247; Wellhausen, 123.

[199]If *only* the concrete act of serving tables were in view, one would wonder what basis the apostles would have had in Acts 6:2 to refuse "to serve" (διακονεῖν) at table.

An obstacle for this view, however, is that, according to the context of v 27, Jesus is *not* the actual table servant at the Last Supper. As the subject of ἀνέπεσεν (v 14),[200] Jesus adopts the posture of diner, not servant. Furthermore, Jesus' role at table as interpreter of the meal is clearly that of the one who presides at the Passover.[201] In this way Luke portrays Jesus not as waiter but as *Hausvater.*[202]

This, however, does not settle the matter, for it is not impossible that Luke portrays Jesus as both servant and host/ master at the Last Supper.[203] Weighing against this notion is the fact that a great gulf stood between the status of lowly table servants and that of privileged diners (cf. sec. 2.4.3 and ch. 3).[204] This view also implies the strange situation in which one man in a group of thirteen has to perform the duties of both servant and administrator—not a particularly even distribution of labor. Nevertheless, by sending the apostolic leaders to do service duties (v 8) and by functioning as Passover president while describing himself as ὁ διακονῶν, the Lukan Jesus shows that he is a very unconventional leader. This lays a foundation for the possibility that Jesus might be understood to perform a concrete act of service. The very notion that the domains of the lofty and lowly are separated by a vast and unbridgable chasm (cf. ch. 2) may in fact be precisely what Jesus is here challenging. The vivid clash with custom illustrated by a leader's service gesture would then be crucial to the text's thrust. If Jesus is portrayed as literally performing some service duty, however, it is most unlikely that such an action would exhaust the sense of the service in view in v 27c (see further below).[205]

Alternative 3), that Jesus' Passover administration and distribution of the elements at the Last Supper constitute his service, also takes at

[200]ἀναπίπτω is essentially an equivalent of ἀνάκειμαι.

[201]Cf. Exod 12:26-27; *m. Pesaḥ.* 10.4-5.

[202]So Beare, *Records*, 227; Creed, 267; Evans, 798; Howard, *Das Ego*, 236-7; Schlosser, 68; Schmid, 329; Schürmann, *Abschiedsrede*, 83 (v 27c is a "Bildwort"); *Ursprung*, 137 (though Jesus would yet be table servant in the kingdom of God); Sellew, 81; Vööbus, *Prelude*, 31; Wiefel, 370; cf. Loisy, 516; Otto, 272.

[203]E.g., Grundmann,401; Karris, "Food,"68; Smith,631-2; Tiede, *Luke*,384-5.

[204]See Roloff ("Anfänge," 57-8), who argues that the *Hausvater* distributes the bread and wine, "... und kann als solche noch nicht als διακονεῖν gelten" (58, citing Str-B [4:621] in support [cf. *b. Ber.* 46a; *y. Ber.* 6.10a.61; 6.10d.4]; also see Schmid, 329).

[205]If v 27c had only a literal sense, it would be an unmotivated statement of the obvious. To be sure, the Lukan Jesus' service is not obvious to the reader until it is mentioned, but once mentioned v 27c does not "work" well in the story world because it only discloses to the apostles what they already know.

face value the Lukan implications that Jesus both presides and serves. It differs, however, in not being obliged to explain Jesus' changing of hats. Here only one action is in view, namely the distribution of bread and wine, and that act *is* Jesus' service.[206] This view, however, severs a key aspect of what it means to be a servant, namely self-giving lowliness. As implied earlier (sec. 6.3), the basic concept of service involves both benefitting others and a humble posture, but when it is maintained that presiding is service, a vital aspect of the concept is lost. Further, alternative 3) does not do justice to the flow of thought in vv 26b-27b in which ὁ διακονῶν is a role which is very low in status.

Alternative 4), that Jesus is the servant in that his life has included repeated acts of service for the apostles (table service perhaps among them), opens the door to wider possibilities. Here διακονῶν recalls Jesus' humble lifestyle oriented toward the benefit of his disciples (e.g., perhaps his instructing, guiding, correcting and caring for them). This is close to alternative 5), that Jesus is the servant in that his entire "coming" (i.e., his life, suffering, and anticipated death and resurrection) constitutes an act of profound service to his disciples. The difference is that in the former case the use of εἰμί is customary, but in the latter it is durative.[207] Neither 4) nor 5), however, excludes the possibility that Jesus actually performs a service action at the Last Supper; such a gesture may still be in view representing a larger form of service.

To explore options 4) and 5), we may first consider whether a broader form of Jesus' service in v 27c would have significance chiefly for the apostles' community life or their religious/ spiritual experience.[208] Is the primary focus on the interrelations of the apostles or on the relationship of the Twelve to God? The Last Supper setting includes a rich statement that centers on Jesus' religious "service": Jesus declares that his

[206]So H. Klein, 170 (who speaks of Jesus' "Hausvaterdienst"); Minear, "Glimpses," 326; Plummer, 501; Schmithals, *Lukas*, 210; against Roloff, "Anfänge," 57-8; cf. Lull, 298.

[207]Many argue for an understanding of v 27c as a reference to the whole "coming" or life or typical lifestyle of Jesus: e.g., Schmid, 329 ("Aber V. 27b kann sehr wohl als bloßes Bildwort verstanden und auf Jesu ganzes Lebenswerk gedeutet werden,..."); similarly Arndt, 442; Evans, 798; Fitzmyer, *Gospel*, 2:1418; Godet, 297; Horn, 213; Klostermann, 211; Lagrange, 550; Léon-Dufour, "Jésus," 153, 164; "Letzte Mahl," 48; Plummer, 501-2; Prast, 259; Radl, *Lukas*, 106; Roloff, "Anfänge," 57-8; *Apostolat*, 187; G. Schneider, *Evangelium*, 2:450-1; Schürmann, "Jüngerkreis," 25; Schweizer, *Luke*, 339; Wiefel, 370.

[208]This is not to imply that Luke sees a sharp division between these aspects.

body is "given for you" (τὸ ὑπὲρ ὑμῶν διδόμενον) and the new covenant in his blood is "poured out for you" (τὸ ὑπὲρ ὑμῶν ἐκχυννόμενον) (22:19b-20). Although scholarship has debated the integrity of the text of vv 19b-20, a growing consensus accepts the persuasiveness of the evidence adduced to support the originality of these verses.[209] There the Lukan Jesus points to the soteriological value of his life-giving (i.e., suffering and anticipated death) for the disciples. For some, then, v 27c recalls this redemptive "service" of Jesus (cf. Mark 10:45b).[210]

The appeal to vv 19b-20, however, works two ways. One might also suggest that, because the earlier reference is to Jesus' death as a religious form of service, Luke would not be repetitive and point to the same idea again so soon after vv 19b-20. In v 27c, then, the death of Jesus, or at least its religious significance, would not be in view (see further below). Indeed, for many the proximity of v 27c to vv 19b-20 is seen as a possible reason for Luke's omission of the saying in Mark 10:45b.[211]

Also important for determining the nature of Jesus' service in v 27c is the presence in the immediate literary context of the event in v 24. That is, v 27c together with vv 25-27b constitute a corrective response to the

[209]To be sure, the text-critical problem of vv 19b-20 is a difficult one (see Fitzmyer, *Gospel*, 2:1387). One can, nevertheless, be reasonably confident that the longer text-tradition is original because of the overwhelming number of mss. from all ancient text-types (proto-Alexandrian, Alexandrian, proto-Caesarean, Caesarean, Syrian, Antiochian) that include vv 19b-20 (Metzger, *Commentary*, 174, 176). On the principle of *lectio difficilor* one may also favor the longer reading with its perplexing two cups. It may be noted that the latest editions of the Nestle-Aland and UBS Greek NT texts have removed the brackets which had once surrounded these verses. In favor of the longer text are Aland and Aland, 306; Arens, 146; Fitzmyer, *Gospel*, 2:1387-8; Fuller, 215; Kollmann, *Mahl*, 162; Lull, 298; Petzer, 127; Schweizer, *Luke*, 333; et al. For Kurz (*Farewell*, 58-9), the testamentary genre of 22:14-38 weighs in favor of vv 19b-20 as genuine (the Eucharist greatly enriches the farewell dimensions of Jesus' speech).

In favor of the shorter reading is the difficulty of explaining the origin of the shorter text if the longer were original. Metzger's suggestion (ibid., 174), however, that the Bezan editor, puzzled with the cup-bread-cup sequence, eliminated with second mention of the cup despite the inverted order thus produced, seems plausible. Additionally, the similarities of the longer text and 1 Cor 11:24b-25 are probably due to Luke's familiarity with the liturgy in Pauline churches rather than a later interpolation from 1 Cor (so Metzger, ibid., 176-7). See Vööbus ("Text") for a recent defense of the shorter text (cf. Maccoby, 263).

[210]So Roloff, "Anfänge," 58.

[211]E.g., Arens, 145-6; Fitzmyer, *Gospel*, 2:1414; Fuller, 216; Otto, 272; Schlosser, 70 (this is a possibility); G. Schmid, 329-30; Schürmann, *Abschiedsrede*, 91; Wilson, 50.

apostles' quarrel over greatness in v 24. Accordingly, v 27c comes as part of a reply to the social/ communal problem of prizing power and status, and it points the way to a solution in that sphere.

Although the application of v 27c to a social problem does not require the service of the Lukan Jesus to be restricted to the social sphere, alternatively it is quite possible that an act of "service" with wider dimensions could still find a proper application in the realm of community interrelations (so Mark 10:41-45; 1 Pet 2:21-24; cf. Rom 15:1-3; Phil 2:6-8).[212] Correspondingly, it may be that v 27c does recall Jesus' self-giving death from vv 19b-20, but does so to emphasize its significance for the sphere of human relationships.

In favor of the idea that the death of Jesus is in view in v 27c is the lack of an otherwise sufficiently "lowly" facet of Jesus' experience in the context that would correspond to the humble social standing of "servant" (cf. above, and sec. 2.4.3). Jesus' acts of teaching, guiding and caring for the Twelve constitute "service" in that they are performed for the good of others, but it is not obvious that they involve the kind of lowliness and self-denial one expects a servant to endure. The death of Jesus as portrayed in vv 19b-20, however, involves both humble self-giving and benefit for others.[213] While the horizon for v 27c of interrelations among the apostles (i.e., vv 24-27) would favor a Lukan emphasis on the lowliness of servanthood, the proximity to our text of the reference in vv 19b-20 to Jesus' benefit-giving death and the necessity of the provision of benefit for servant imagery to be complete may suggest that, for Luke, religious aspects of Jesus' service remain in view in v 27c.

Jesus' serving death may be viewed from certain other angles as well. In section 3.5.1 it was noted that, in Luke, Jesus' table fellowship with sinners is representative of his saving acceptance of meal compan-

---

[212]So Thysman, 170; against Dehandschutter, 546.

[213]Among those who see Jesus' death in view in v 27c are Büchele, 169; Dodd, 61; Gillman, 145; Glöckner, 178; Goulder, *Luke*, 2:731 (though the Pauline idea of substitution in vv 19-20 is wholly absent); Hengel, *Atonement*, 73; Rasmussen, 75; Schweizer, *Luke*, 339; Tannehill, "Study," 199-200; *Unity*, 257; against Taylor, *Jesus*, 187. Schmithals's (*Lukas*, 211) view of v 27c as alluding to Jesus' exemplary martyrdom fails to explain how such a death "serves." For a critique of the martyr interpretation see Matera, *Passion*, 151. In favor of an ethical interpretation of v 27c are Arens, 126, n. 30; Beck, "Imitatio Christi," 33; Hoffmann and Eid, 196. Others see the ethical implications of v 27c, but allow for theological dimensions of Jesus' service here, e.g., Ernst, 595; Fitzmyer, *Gospel*, 2:1418; Karris, *Gospel*, 716; cf. also Feuillet, 401; Gillman, 145; Glöckner, 178.

ions who are receptive to his message. The apostles at the Last Supper may well be thought of as sinners (they quarrel with each other [v 24], and betray [vv 21-22] and deny [v 34] Jesus), yet Jesus is among them as servant (v 27c). An implication here may be that Jesus' service involves a saving solidarity with his wayward apostles.[214]

The Passover context (vv 1, 7, 8, 11, 13; cf. sec. 3.3) brings the covenant to mind, and v 20 connects Jesus' self-giving with the establishment of the new covenant (cf. Jer 31:31-34 with its emphasis not on liberation from foreign captivity but on release from sin). With the forgiveness of sin and the writing of the Law on one's heart (31:33-34), the apostles will be enabled to exercise their new passover freedom to follow Jesus' way of service.

Two factors, however, make it appropriate to include Jesus' life-style among the apostles as well as his anticipated death in his "service" of v 27c. First, the following clause (v 28), though shifting the orientation of Jesus' words somewhat, looks to Jesus' past (note the perfect participle διαμεμενηκότες [cf. sec. 7.3]). Second, as noted in chapter 5, it is in keeping with the testamentary genre for a testator to recall his exemplary past.[215] Nonetheless, the weight of emphasis still falls on Jesus' passion service—his impending death and (probably) a corresponding practical gesture of table service at the Last Supper.

When we return to εἰμί and the question of a descriptive, customary or durative present, it is difficult to reach a decision. The customary use is least probable since it would not include Jesus' death in his service. The descriptive present, however, is a strong possibility since, though calling attention to a concrete action at the Last Supper, it would not rule out a larger sense for Jesus' service. Also possible is the durative present which focuses on the big picture of Jesus' serving life, including his passion, yet without excluding the possibility of a concrete Last Supper service deed. To be sure, it is only probable and not certain that Luke would have us believe there was a concrete act of service at the Last Supper, though if Jesus did wait on tables in the upper room it would have been a striking and appropriate illustration of the self-giving, benefit-oriented way of servant-leadership. Ultimately either the descriptive or durative present may be favored since both allow for a Last Supper gesture as well as Jesus' larger serving and saving action. Concerning comparative or pre-

[214]V 22 would seem to count Judas out of this group.

[215]E.g., Gillman, 145; Léon-Dufour, "Letzte Mahl," 47; Matera, *Passion*, 164.

dicative ὡς, the likelihood that the Lukan Jesus does perform a deed of table service would favor the latter, though again the focus on the concrete action would not conceal an allusion to the ultimate act of condescending service in Jesus' impending death.

In summary of 22:25-27, the Lukan Jesus orders a transformation of the idea of "greatness." He calls the apostles to turn away from the high power, high status ways of rule which prevail in the world, and to lead as lowly, humble servants committed to the care of others. By pointing to his humiliation in being a servant to them (i.e., his exemplary action and lowly death), Jesus clinches the argument and delivers the definitive model for servant-discipleship. Vv 25-27 may be translated, "He said to them, 'The kings of the Gentiles rule over them, and those in authority over them are called "benefactors." But not so with you! Rather, let the greatest among you become like the youngest, and the leader like the servant. For which is greater, the diner or the table servant? Surely it is the diner, is it not? Yet I am among you as the servant.'"

6.6 Conclusion

Two terms are used three times in Luke 22:24-27: μείζων (vv 24, 26, 27) and διακονῶν (vv 26, 27 [2x]). "Greatest" is where the apostles begin, "service" is where Jesus directs them. In terms of the broad strokes of Luke's pen, then, there is an injunction to turn from the prizing of greatness and the corresponding preoccupation with one's own status, and to adopt the lowly posture of a servant and attend to the needs of others. The finer details of the text all support this broader reversal from high to low, from self to others.

The contrasts in vv 25-27 enable one to return to v 24 with a fuller and clearer idea of the type of greatness at issue there, for the response provides clues as to the nature of the problem itself. The contrasts are packed with images of authority, so we may suppose that the quarrel of v 24 includes assertions of superior power or position. The negative portrayal in the illustrations of v 25 drawn from models of ordinary secular rule imply that the apostles seek to replicate patterns from the authority systems of the world. Thus there is a "worldly" quality about the apostles' concern for greatness that Jesus rebukes. Also, the social dimensions of each contrast in vv 25-27 show that the problem of v 24 is one that poses a threat to healthy community life and not merely personal life. There must be a new idea of greatness and authority in the church, namely that it is given for the purpose of humbly working to support the welfare of the community, enhancing rather than undermining its esprit de corps.

Some have suggested that in vv 24-27 Luke attacks political rulers and structures of his day.[216] This approach, however, overlooks Luke's broader concern to guide the church to a peaceful co-existence with civil authorities.[217] Although a negative illustration from public life is given (v 25), the primary point is to learn to do otherwise *within Christian circles*.[218] Ultimately the text is about the true nature of Christian authority,[219] and as such it constitutes an element of Luke's ecclesiological paraenesis.[220] In the Christian community there will be leadership, but it is to involve the subjection of the leader to even the "lowliest" members.

We may also observe that the contours of 22:24-27 are sharp and its contrasts are severe. The peaks of power and status range from kings to the lofty, honorific positions of public benefactors to the luxury of dining with servants ready and waiting. In sharp contrast we find the role of self-denying and often despised servants. The gulf between the great and the lowly is deep and wide, and one must "feel" that expanse in its social, political and religious dimensions for the teaching of Jesus in vv 25-27 to take on its true emphasis (cf. ch. 2). Correspondingly, there can be no doubt that the Lukan Jesus calls the Twelve to a radical and drastic departure from the status quo.

Stepping back from a close analysis of our text, the Last Supper setting for the admonition of the Lukan Jesus in vv 25-27 suggests a possible connection, namely that the observance of the Lord's Supper clashes with the prizing of greatness; this symbolic meal should instead be characterized by a spirit of unity and a pattern of community service.[221]

---

[216]E.g., Cassidy, 39; cf. Hoffmann and Eid, 196, 200.

[217]Thériault, 218-21; cf. Esler, 207-9; Stöger, 7-8.

[218]To be sure, Luke's negative portrayal of kings and benefactors and the social elite (vv 25-27; cf. sec. 6.3) does constitute an implicit critique of conventional expressions of power and greatness, and it does have implications for political rule itself. Nonetheless, challenging the political status quo is not Luke's aim here.

[219]So e.g., Dupont, "Ministères," 145; Tiede, *Luke*, 384.

[220]So Roloff, "Anfänge," 55-7 (cf. "Apostel," 442-3).

[221]As Schürmann maintains, "Die Eucharistie verbietet Rangstreitigkeiten und verpflichtet zum Bruderdienst" (*Ursprung*, 138; cf. Léon-Dufour, "Letzte Mahl," 48; Matera, *Passion*, 164; Wiefel, 370).

Chapter 7:
Luke 22:28-30: Perseverance and Reward

7.1 Introduction

The aim of the present chapter is to discern facets of the meaning of Luke 22:28-30 through a close analysis of the text. As with chapter 6, however, here also we will frequently be able to draw upon the background perspectives of Part One, as well as other backgrounds, and thus carry on the interplay of looking closely and stepping back. In the following, the question of sources for 22:28-30 will be considered (sec. 7.2), and several issues will be examined concerning the apostles' perseverance in trials with Jesus (7.3) and the conferral of kingship upon the apostles (7.4).

7.2 Sources for Luke 22:28-30

As argued in section 6.2, determining Luke's use of sources is but one step in the larger process of discerning the meaning of a finished text, but it can provide valuable clues for the task of isolating Lukan interests and emphases. What then is the nature of the parallel between Luke 22:28-30 and Matt 19:28?

	Matthew 19:28		**Luke 22:28-30**
1	**28a)** ὁ δὲ Ἰησοῦς εἶπεν αὐτοῖς		
2	ἀμὴν λέγω ὑμῖν ὅτι		
3	ὑμεῖς	—	**28)** ὑμεῖς
4			δέ ἐστε
5	οἱ ἀκολουθήσαντές	—	οἱ διαμεμενηκότες
6			μετ᾽
7	μοι	—	ἐμοῦ
8			ἐν τοῖς πειρασμοῖς μου
9			**29)** κἀγὼ διατίθεμαι ὑμῖν
10			καθὼς διέθετό μοι ὁ πατήρ μου
11			βασιλείαν
12			**30a)** ἵνα ἔσθητε καὶ πίνητε
13			ἐπί τῆς τραπέζης μου
14	ἐν τῇ παλιγγενεσίᾳ	—	ἐν τῇ βασιλείᾳ
15			μου
16	**b)** ὅταν καθίσῃ		
17	ὁ υἱὸς τοῦ ἀνθρώπου		
18	ἐπὶ θρόνου δόξης αὐτοῦ		
19			**b)** καὶ
20	**c)** καθήσεσθε	—	καθήσεσθε
21	καὶ ὑμεῖς		
22	ἐπὶ	—	ἐπὶ
23	δώδεκα		
24	θρόνους	—	θρόνων
25	κρίνοντες	—	[[κρίνοντες]][1]
26	τὰς δώδεκα φυλὰς	—	τὰς δώδεκα φυλὰς
27	[[κρίνοντες]]	—	κρίνοντες
28	τοῦ Ἰσραήλ	—	τοῦ Ἰσραήλ

These texts have similarities at lines 3-7, 14 and 20-28. There are three points of correspondence in lines 3-7: 1) One notes the presence and placement in both texts of ὑμεῖς, though second person pronouns are natural in direct speech.[2] 2) The common form of the substantive articular participles (masculine nominative plural) to describe the apostles is noteworthy, and διαμένω and ἀκολουθέω here may be close in sense.[3] 3) In both texts Jesus speaks of the apostles' attachment to him (μοι and ἐμοῦ).

[1]Double brackets indicate a word out of sequence.

[2]Even the nominative is natural for emphasis or contrast (cf. sec. 7.3.1).

[3]Beasley-Murray, 274; Howard, *Das Ego*, 178.

Five points of dissimilarity may also be isolated here, but it should be pointed out that each of these can be understood on the basis of the evangelists' redactional patterns or contextual factors: 1) Only Matthew's saying has the ἀμήν introduction, but Luke is inclined to omit this construction.[4] 2) Luke's ἐστε forms an independent clause, but Matthew's construction exhibits *casus pendens.*[5] Matthew's context permits the omission of a finite verb here, however, since the next verb not in a subordinate clause is second person plural (line 20). Conversely, the use in Luke 22:29 of an independent clause (and that with a first person singular verb) makes Luke's inclusion of a finite verb in v 28 natural. 3) Luke's participle is perfect but Matthew's is aorist, and διαμένω and ἀκολουθέω do have some different nuances of meaning. A preference for δια- compounds (see sec. 7.3.2), however, may account for Luke's word choice, and the reference to "trials" in the plural may invite the perfect tense with its element of continuation. 4) Luke's μετά is without parallel in Matthew, but one supposes that this is due to the fact that διαμένω is intransitive while ἀκολουθέω is transitive. 5) Although Matthew has no parallel to Luke's ἐν τοῖς πειρασμοῖς μου (line 8), Matt 19:27 does refer to the high cost of following Jesus. Further, Luke seems to have a special interest in πειρασμός (see sec. 7.3.3).

Thus the similarities of Luke and Matthew at lines 3-7, though not extensive, are not outweighed by apparent points of dissimilarity. There appears, then, to be a kernel of agreement in these two texts in which Jesus directly addresses his loyal disciples describing positively their allegiance to him, and in each case using a substantival participle form.[6]

Turning to line 14, a possible link may be seen in the common preposition ἐν with dative articular substantives to specify the realm in which the apostles' reward is to be realized. Luke's τῇ βασιλείᾳ, however, is modified by possessive μου while Matthew's τῇ παλιγγενεσίᾳ is absolute. Also, the Lukan expression gives the setting for eating and

[4]Boring, 176-7; Fitzmyer, *Gospel*, 2:1418. Luke omits Mark's ἀμήν at Luke 9:27; 21:3; 22:34, and perhaps at 7:47; 11:29; 12:10; 22:18. Only three times does Luke add ἀμήν to the gospel traditions (4:24; 12:37; 23:43 [Fitzmyer, *Gospel*, 1:113]). ἀμήν appears 31x in Matt but only 6x in Luke (others claim that the phrase is probably a Matthean addition at 19:28 [so Beasley-Murray, 273; Howard, *Das Ego*, 178]).

[5]The fact that *casus pendens* is "a sign of unadorned speech" (BDF, § 466) may favor Matthew's text as being closer to Q than Luke's (see further below).

[6]This shared form implies a common source for Matthew and Luke (Bammel, "Testament," 80; Theisohn, 163).

drinking (v 30a), but Matt 19:28 lacks meal imagery. Although both παλιγγενεσία and βασιλεία have an overlapping shade of meaning pointing to the eschaton[7] and both appear with ἐν, those facts do not provide a persuasive basis for the claim of a close relationship here.

A stronger correspondence is seen at lines 20-28. Precise verbal agreement is found on four lines (20, 22, 26 and 28), lines 25 and 27 represent a single point of verbal agreement with slightly different sequencing, and line 24 shows agreement that is marred only by a difference of case. In this section only lines 21 and 23 are lacking in verbal agreement, yet these two points of dissimilarity are easily explained,[8] as are the differences of case and sequence.[9] Such minor discrepancies need not prevent one from inferring that Matthew and Luke here stand in a close relationship. When this finding and the significant parallels on lines 3-7 are taken together,[10] there is substantial support for the view that Matt 19:28 and Luke 22:28-30 are rooted in a common source, i.e., Q.[11]

[7]So BAGD, "παλιγγενεσίᾳ," 606, def. 1.b; cf. "βασιλεία," 134-5, def. 3. Schürmann claims that Matthew envisions "das Weltende" while Luke has the prior rise of messianic rule in view (*Abschiedsrede*, 50).

[8]Matthew's καὶ ὑμεῖς ("you also," line 21—not parallel to the Lukan καί on line 19) is necessary in its context because of the reference to the Son of man sitting on the throne of his glory. Luke has omitted δώδεκα (line 23) on account of the placement of the saying; he does not wish to imply that a throne is reserved for the betrayer referred to in vv 21-23 (so Schürmann, *Abschiedsrede*, 51-2; cf. sec. 7.4.3).

[9]Dupont argues that ἐπι with genitive θρόνων is a correction of the original accusative form as reproduced in Matthew ("Trônes," 369; but the distinction is not crucial to the meaning of the phrase [Theisohn, 165]). The Lukan separation of the object (line 26) from its dependent genitive (line 28) is rhetorically stylized speech (BDF, § 473); this secondary construction puts emphasis on Ἰσραήλ (Schürmann, *Abschiedsrede*, 53). Dupont ("Trones," 370) and Theisohn (166) similarly claim that the Lukan word order here (lines 26-28) constitutes a stylistic improvement over Matthew's more original version.

[10]Another possible point of contact may be reflected in both evangelists' modification of παλιγγενεσίᾳ with sayings about the rule/ authority of Jesus (Matt on lines 16-18, Luke on 9-11 [v 29]). This general conceptual similarity may suggest a traditional basis for these "unparalleled" sections. The complete dissimilarity of language and style here, however, and the fact that in both cases the interests of the evangelists are apparent (cf. Matt 25:31; see n. 18 below on Lukan features of v 29) weigh against a Luke-Matthew relationship at this point.

[11]Boring, 176; Kollmann, *Mahl*, 161, 223; Schmahl, 29, n. 43 (listing several who agree with this claim); Trautmann, 191. Bammel ("Das Ende," 45-8; "Testament," 81) regards Luke 22:29, 30b as the original end of Q (Matthew omits the equivalent of Luke 22:29 because διατίθεμαι is not suitable in Matthew's context ["Das Ende," 46; against Broer, 123]) (for Wiefel [371] vv 28, 30b stem from Q). Alternatively, T. W. Manson (*Sayings*, pp 216-7), Streeter (288) and Leonard (240)

Before examining the content of Luke 22:28-30, it is in order to ask whether Luke or Matthew has the more primitive form of the saying at hand. Although arguments have been mounted for the primitive character of both the Lukan[12] and Matthean[13] versions, it would seem that Matthew preserves the nearer likeness to Q. Support for this conclusion comes from Matthew's unusual παλιγγενεσία.[14] It is easier to imagine that the Matthean temporal qualifying phrase (lines 16-18)[15] and the Lukan reference to "the kingdom" (line 14) were included to interpret Q's παλιγγενεσία,[16] than that Matthew himself inserted this synoptic hapax only to go on and clarify the expression.[17] To this we add Matthew's more primitive form (*casus pendens* [lines 5-14], repetition of "twelve" [lines 23 and 26]) and Luke's stylistic superiority (copula [line 4], rhetorically styled word order [lines 26-28]), and a conclusion is suggested: even

assign Matt 19:28 to an M source and Luke 22:28-30 to L. Higgins claims that the differences between Luke 22:28-30 and Matt 19:28 along with "only two tolerably close resemblances [our lines 3-7 and 20-28] ... tell strongly against their derivation from a common source" (*Jesus*, 107), yet he concedes that the sayings probably stem ultimately from a common tradition (*Son of Man*, 115). For J. Wenham (259-60), Luke is here independent of Matthew (against Goulder, *Luke*, 2:733).

[12]E.g., Schürmann, *Abschiedsrede*, 37-8 (note Matthew's expansion to "all" [v 29] and Luke's restriction to the Twelve), 54; Theisohn, 167-8; D. Wenham, *Rediscovery*, 132.

[13]E.g., Higgins, *Son of Man*, 115; Howard, *Das Ego*, 180, n. 4 (noting the two senses of βασιλεία in Luke 22:29-30a and the mixed metaphors of table and throne in v 30); Kollmann, *Mahl*, 223; W. Pesch, 73-4; similarly S. Schulz, 331-2. Luke is said to show signs one would expect from a writing leaning in the direction of synoptic development (so Bultmann, *History*, 159; Howard, *Das Ego*, 181; S. Schulz, 331; against Jeremias, *Theology*, 275). The comparative brevity of the Matthean version may also argue for its relative antiquity.

[14]Elsewhere in the NT only in Titus 3:5.

[15]Perhaps this phrase stood in Q already. If so, the primitive nature of Matthew's version is yet more apparent.

[16]As such, Luke's ἐν clause may reflect the form of Q.

[17]Although Gundry (392) and others maintain that Aramaic and Hebrew reveal no equivalent to the term παλιγγενεσία, Derrett ("Palingenesia," 52-3) contends that Hebrew supplies the key: the term is equivalent to πάλιν γενέσθαι, has the sense of "resurrection" (not "new world" or "restoration") and renders לְהֵחָיוֹת, "to be caused to live again" (so *m.* *ʾAbot* 4.22). Efforts to harmonize with Titus 3:5 have obscured Matthew's sense (51). By contrast, Beasley-Murray (274-5) argues that the term was borrowed by the Q tradition from Greek culture to represent the concept of restoration with its many facets in the Jewish tradition. Matthew's readiness to use ἀνάστασις (22:23, 28, 30, 31) may weigh against Derrett's view, as would the precedent of usage outside the NT (BAGD, "παλιγγενεσία," 606-7). Thus in Matt 19:28 "the restoration" or "the new world" is preferred.

though both versions show signs of redaction,[18] Matthew's seems to be more primitive and Luke's more developed.[19] Since departures from sources may offer particularly telling signs of an evangelist's interests, in

[18]So e.g., Beasley-Murray, 273; Howard, *Das Ego*, 177. The phrase "truly I say to you" (line 2) is typical for Matthew (so Howard, ibid., 178; S. Schulz, 330-1); ἀκολουθέω (line 5) echoes Peter's question in v 27 and may be redactional (Goulder, *Luke*, 2:732-3 [though arguing for Luke's use of Matthew, Goulder does not build a case for Matthean priority here]); the ὅταν clause (lines 16-18) is probably a Matthean insertion to clarify the unusual παλιγγενεσία (so Schürmann, *Abschiedsrede*, 50); and "you also" (line 21) is made necessary by the addition of the ὅταν phrase; the similarities of 19:28 and 25:31 also arouse suspicions of Matthean redaction (Dupont, "Trônes," 366) (perhaps 25:31-46 represents a further attempt to illustrate and interpret παλιγγενεσία [Howard, *Das Ego*, 179]).

Lukan redaction may also be seen: δέ (line 4) is added to connect with v 27 (see sec 7.3.1); ἐστε (line 4) constitutes a stylistic improvement over Matthew's (i.e., Q's) *casus pendens* (Theisohn, 164-5); ἐν τοῖς πειρασμοῖς μου (line 8) is of special interest to Luke (cf. sec. 7.3.3); κἀγώ (line 9) is often used by Luke to introduce Jesus' sayings (so Howard, *Das Ego*, 180, citing 11:9; 20:3; 24:49); διαμένω (line 5) and the two uses of διατίθημι (lines 9 and 10) may reflect Luke's preference for δια- compounds (see sec. 7.3.2); the action of the Father in giving βασιλεία (lines 10 and 11) has precedent in Luke (12:32); the table imagery (lines 12 and 13) connects with the Lukan setting (Schürmann, *Abschiedsrede*, 61-2); "eat and drink" (line 12) is a favored Lukan formula (cf. Luke 5:30, 33; 10:7; 12:19; 17:8 [2x], 28; Acts 9:9; 23:12, 21) and often signals Lukan redaction (so Kollmann, *Mahl*, 224; S. Schulz, 332, n. 67, against Schürmann, *Abschiedsrede*, 45-6); βασιλεία (line 14) is probably a clarifying interpretation of the original παλιγγενεσία, and it echoes the Lukan kingdom theme in vv 16, 18 and 29; the omission of "twelve" with "thrones" (line 23), the change of case (line 24) and the change of word order (lines 25 and 27) have already been attributed to Lukan redaction (see nn. 8 and 9 above).

[19]E.g., Dunn, *Jesus*, 36; Schweizer, *Church Order*, 29, n. 73. Conversely, S. Schulz favors the priority of Matthew (330-1; so also Beare, *Matthew*, 400; Horbury, 524; Howard, *Das Ego*, 180-1; Schmahl, 32-3; see Trautmann [192] for various views). Theisohn suggests that Luke's unusual διαμεμενηκότες is more original than Matthew's ἀκολουθησαντές, yet he claims that Matthew's *casus pendens* suggests originality because it is the more difficult reading (Theisohn, 164-5; cf. BDF, § 466). Schmithals' claim (*Lukas*, 211) that Luke's lack of "twelve" with "thrones" (v 30b, cf. Matt 19:28b) is more original because it reflects the absence of such a concept in Q disregards the more probable explanation that Luke omits the term to avoid the suggestion of a throne for Judas (cf. sec. 7.4.3). Ott's suggestion that the Matthean aorist participle is more original than Luke's perfect participle because Luke's switch to perfect eliminates the idea of past trials and conforms to the framework of a Satan-free ministry in Luke (89) puts the cart before the horse. Assuming a Satan-free framework (so Conzelmann [*Theology*, 16, 28, 124, n. 1; cf. Wiefel, 372], based on Luke 4:13 and 22:3) and the absence of a reference to the past in Luke's perfect participle, this is a plausible argument. But we may not be certain that Luke portrays the pre-passion ministry of Jesus as Satan-free (Fitzmyer [*Theologian*, 161-2] argues persuasively against the idea [cf. Garrett, 42-3]), nor that οἱ διαμεμενηκότες makes no reference to the past (cf. secs. 7.3.2 and 7.3.3).

the following analysis of vv 28-30 we will be especially alert for Lukan signals as to the meaning of the text.[20]

To sum up, Luke 22:28-30 appears to be the less primitive version of a Q saying paralleled in Matt 19:28, though both versions show signs of modification. The significant points of agreement on lines 3-7 and 20-28 imply that Luke is closely related to the Q sayings in Luke 22:28, 30b. Luke 22:29-30a, however, has only remote "parallels" in Matt 19:28.[21] Since vv 29-30a also present concepts and language which are of special interest to Luke,[22] there is support for the idea that vv 29-30a are included as a result of redactional interests.[23] To be sure, this is not to minimize the importance of vv 28, 30b to the author of Luke, but only to underscore something of the distinctiveness of vv 29-30a.

7.3 Persevering with Jesus through Trials (22:28)

With the above discussion of sources for vv 28-30 in mind, we turn now to an analysis of Luke 22:28. First the possible significance of the juxtaposition of v 28 with v 27 is considered (7.3.1). Then v 28 itself is examined in detail: section 7.3.2 considers the persevering solidarity of the apostles with Jesus, and 7.3.3 focuses on the trials they share.

7.3.1 The Juxtaposition of v 28 with v 27

A brief analysis of v 28 in its relation to v 27 may shed light on the interpretation of both verses, and indeed of 22:24-30 as a whole. Rele-

[20]It is quite difficult to determine whose placement of the saying is more original. D. Wenham argues that the sayings of 22:28-30 were originally part of the eschatological discourse (Luke 12, 17, 21) and became attached to the Last Supper because of its similar eschatological ideas (*Rediscovery*, 132; Neyrey [23] and Otto [273] also claim that Luke's placement is secondary; for Schürmann [*Abschiedsrede*, 54-63] vv 28-30 originally followed v 20). The relocation of the prediction of Peter's denial from the Mount of Olives (so Mark 14:26-31) to the Last Supper (Luke 22:33-34) shows Luke's willingness to rearrange material in this context (Feldkämper, 207). Alternatively, Matt 19:27, 29 flows very well without v 28, so one can imagine that Matthew's placement of the thrones saying may be secondary as well (against W. Pesch, 74). In short, it is difficult to demonstrate that either Matthew's or Luke's placement reflects the original context in Q (Trilling, 217).

[21]See the above discussion about line 14; cf. also n. 10.

[22]Cf. n. 18 above and the discussions in secs. 7.3 and 7.4 below.

[23]The likelihood that vv 29 and 30a have traditional bases (probably distinct ones) is discussed in sec. 7.4.3.

vant questions include these: Why is ὑμεῖς included? What is the sense of δέ? How is the evident structural echo of v 27 (ἐγὼ δὲ ... εἰμι) to be understood?[24] Does this linking device suggest that emphatically placed "you" in v 28 is being directly contrasted with "I" in v 27?[25]

Nominative ὑμεῖς would ordinarily signal either contrast or some other emphasis.[26] Since the immediate literary context is replete with other personal pronouns ("I" [v 27], "me" [v 28], "I" and "me" [v 29]), we might suppose that ὑμεῖς here draws a contrast. "You" in v 28, however, does not naturally contrast with "I" in v 27[27] (nor with "me" in v 28), for the action of "you" in v 28 is "with" Jesus; his solidarity with the apostles and not his distinction from them is emphasized. Neither does the pronoun contrast with κἀγώ in v 29, for "I" there begins a staircase of persons ("I" and "you," "me" and "my Father") with its own specific contrasts or comparisons.[28]

Emphasis, not contrast, would seem to be the main purpose of ὑμεῖς here.[29] Fitzmyer translates v 28, "You are *indeed* the ones who have

[24]Lull points this out (299-300) (cf. sec. 1.1 above). Since there is a shift of theme and emphasis from vv 27 to 28, the presence of this common construction in both verses may signal an intention of the writer to narrow the gap and make a connection. Indeed, the writer/ editor of D makes a rather ambitious attempt to smooth the gap even more with a lengthy replacement for ὑμεῖς δέ ἐστε, but it is almost certainly secondary. We are cautious when D stands alone (so K. and B. Aland, "Introduction" to NA26, 49), and here the reading of D is longer and easier (αὐξάνω points to the disciples' development in serving [cf. v 27] and would give grounds for the word of praise in v 28), and thus highly suspect.

[25]Lull (300) sees not contrast but comparison: both Jesus and the disciples serve/ suffer (vv 27-28).

[26]BDF, § 277; Turner, *Syntax*, 37. Turner (37-8) notes that the nominative personal pronoun is sometimes without emphasis or antithesis, but he does not comment on v 28.

[27]Against Rienecker, 504.

[28]Schürmann (*Abschiedsrede*, 57) contends that ὑμεῖς in v 28 originally contrasted with κἀγώ in v 29, though he does not develop the role of κἀγώ in contrast with the persons in v 29. Zahn's claim (681) that ὑμεῖς contrasts with abstract "anderen" takes one well beyond the horizons of the text. Gormley's claim (93) that ὑμεῖς draws a contrast with the betrayer may seem attractive at first, but it fails for two reasons: 1) The nearest reference to the betrayer is in v 23, so one must leap back not only over "I" (v 27) but also over the negative members of the contrast pairs (vv 26b-27b) and the rulers (v 25—and they are explicitly contrasted with the disciples) to find the unnamed party contrasted with ὑμεῖς; 2) Luke has not indicated that Judas is not still in the upper room at v 28 and is not among those addressed as ὑμεῖς (although see sec. 7.4.3 on the basis for Luke's omission of "twelve" with "thrones" [line 23]).

stood by me in my trials."[30] It is not a contrast of the Twelve with some other party, but a stress on the fact that the Twelve themselves have actually stood by Jesus. To be sure, this emphasis draws a contrast, but it is a contrast not between different groups but between the actions of a single group at different times. The apostles required a rebuke for their quarrel (vv 24-27), but they nonetheless had previously been loyal to Jesus. The tension (or contrast) between these negative and positive behaviors thus warrants the use of the emphatic pronoun.

This idea is clarified by the particle δέ. Although it is often fitting not to translate this preferred Lukan term,[31] the flow of thought makes best sense when we take it as adversative: "*But* you are ..." This understanding helps to clarify the otherwise uncomfortable juxtaposition of the proud quarreling apostles with the apostles who stood by Jesus in his trials; it does not remove the tension, but it allows one to begin to reconcile the apostles' divergent forms of conduct.

The emphasis of ὑμεῖς, however, may best be rendered not "indeed" but "in fact." This idiom fits well with adversative δέ, and it builds a bridge between the disloyal behavior of the apostles here in the upper room and their noble conduct during Jesus' trials. Together with adversative δέ, then, the expression takes the negative character of the apostles' pursuit in v 24 (cf. sec. 6.4) seriously, yet it turns attention to previous positive behavior. In this way v 28 signals a turn in the narrative reversal structure of 22:24-30 (cf. sec. 4.1): the apostles have not yet been set on the upward course (see vv 29-30), but the basis for that ascent is seen in v 28 (cf. sec. 7.4.1) with the shift away from their failings and Jesus' correction (vv 24-27).[32]

The contrast of the apostles' past and present behaviors, however, is descriptive. In terms of prescribed or commended action, a close comparison which follows the lines of the structural tie noted above (ἐγὼ δὲ ... εἰμι and ὑμεῖς δέ ἐστε) joins vv 27 and 28: what Jesus is aligns with

---

[29]Although ὑμεῖς is present in his source (see line 3 above), Luke's retention of it along with ἐστε (which he probably has added) allows for an emphatic use in this case. (The elipsis in v 26 implies that ὑμεῖς there is probably not emphatic [cf. sec. 6.3].)

[30]Fitzmyer, *Gospel*, 2:1411, emphasis added; so also Reiling and Swellengrebel, 693.

[31]So Fitzmyer, *Gospel*, 2:1411; Neirynck highlights a preference for δέ by noting that Luke changes Mark's καί to δέ 54 times, but changes Mark's δέ to καί only four times (205).

[32]See further secs. 1.1, 4.1, 4.6 and 8.2 on the unity of 22:24-30.

what the apostles have been. Further, there is a conceptual linkage of "serving" (this time δουλεύων) and "trials" in the other Lukan farewell address in which Paul recalls "serving the Lord with all humility and with tears and with trials ..." (Acts 20:19).[33] Moreover, adversative δέ and emphatic ὑμεῖς in v 28 ("But you are in fact...") turn to trials with serving still in view; the failure to serve appears to trigger the recollection of the apostles' successful perseverance in Jesus' trials. Thus the serving and trials come close together, and this strengthens the link between the elements making up the 360-degree reversal form of 22:24-30 (cf. sec. 4.1).

7.3.2 **Persevering with Jesus**

Several questions surface regarding διαμεμενηκότες: Why does Luke choose this unusual verb (he uses it only once elsewhere [1:22])? What were the possibilities for the meaning of διαμένω? What temporal definition does the perfect tense suggest? Does v 28 coincide with a wider Lukan emphasis on the apostles remaining true to Jesus?

διαμένω may be uncommon in Luke-Acts, but compounds with δια- are characteristic.[34] Regarding the breadth of Lukan usage, 96 of the 118 NT δια- compounds appear in Luke-Acts (81%), and 48 (41%) in Luke-Acts only.[35] As for volume of usage, 275 of the 589 NT δια- compound occurrences (47%) are found in Luke-Acts, yet the Lukan writings constitute only about 25% of the volume of the NT. It is thus apparent that Luke's δια- compound vocabulary is very broad and his usages are frequent,[36]

[33]The close connection of πειρασμῶν with ταπεινοφροσύνης and δακρύων supports the idea that for Luke the endurance of trials is a lowly experience. This in turn enhances the link between service and trials in Luke 22:27 and 28. One also notes that the πειρασμός usages in 22:28 and Acts 20:19 are close in sense (cf. secs. 5.3 and 7.3.3).

[34]Jeremias, *Sprache*, 290; Moulton and Howard, 300. Jeremias also claims that the substantive participle *form* in v 28 is a sign of Lukan redaction (ibid., 290), but Theisohn's assertion that the form probably antedates Luke because it is shared by Matthew (οἱ ἀκολουθησαντές) and is presumed to stem from Q is more convincing (163).

[35]A further 9% appear more frequently in Luke-Acts than in all the other NT writings together.

[36]Some statistics regarding δια- compounds are as follows: Of the 118 δια- compounds utilized in NT writings, Matt has 29, Mark 24, Luke 53, Acts 63, and Luke-Acts 89. The number of δια- compounds unique in the NT to given writings are Matt (7); Mark (0); Luke (16); Acts (27); Luke-Acts (46). The number of actual usages in given writings out of the 589 in the NT are Matt (54); Mark (43); Luke

an observation that may arouse the suspicion of Lukan special interests in 22:28.

It may be useful at this point to step back from Luke's writings and note certain basic features of compound forms generally[37] and δια- compounds in particular. Blass and Debrunner observe that *koine* Greek has a certain fondness for composite verbs where the classical language was content with simple forms.[38] This fact prompts the interpreter to be cautious in assessing the significance of compounds for a NT writer like Luke: when so many compounds appear so often, it becomes quite difficult to be sure of corresponding special emphases.[39]

With this in mind, it remains useful to note typical nuances of δια-forms. This is best accomplished by comparing compound and simplex forms, though it is not implied that δια- constructions were chosen by Luke or other writers in a process involving the initial selection of a verbal root and the conscious addition of a prepositional prefix.[40] Moulton and Howard observe that a "perfectivising force" is conspicuous in δια-compounds; the sense of "through and through" is present, and this comes to mean "thoroughly."[41] The perfective action of δια- verbs may operate on a temporal or spatial plane; when such verbs have less concrete dimensions, they may yet carry the idea of "thoroughness."[42]

A glance at Lukan usages of δια- compounds leads to two general observations: 1) When a simplex verb typically emphasizes concrete action, the δια- form may well have a broader, figurative idea (e.g., as with διατηρέω, διανοίγω and διασπείρω). 2) If the root tends to refer to an

(113); Acts (162); Luke-Acts (275).

[37]Robertson (562-3) discusses the effect of a prepositional prefix on the meaning of a verb: it may have no effect on a verb's sense (e.g., ἐξέρχομαι is the same as ἔρχομαι ἐκ), it may perfect or intensify the verb's action (e.g., κατεσθίω, "to eat up"), or it may change the meaning of the root and blend with it (e.g., intransitive πορεύομαι becomes transitive as διαπορεύομαι in Acts 16:41; cf. Heb 11:29). Perfecting or intensifying a verb's action is perhaps the most common effect.

[38]BDF, § 116; cf. Moulton and Howard, 268-9; Robertson, 160-1, 558.

[39]Cf. Robertson, 563.

[40]It would of course be possible for a NT writer to coin compounds in this way (Moulton and Howard [268-9] maintain that Paul does so), but ordinarily compounds would have had a history of their own and a certain measure of independence from root forms.

[41]Moulton and Howard, 300-2 (a given action is carried *through* to a definite result).

[42]Moulton and Howard, 301-2 (e.g., διαμαρτύρομα, which means "to solemnly declare").

action in simple terms, the δια- form may well stress the duration of the action, or highlight its difficult or thorough-going nature (e.g., διασῴζω and διασπείρω).[43]

Approaching the matter from another angle, μένω itself appears twenty times in Luke-Acts (Luke 7x, Acts 13x). Every usage in Luke and seven of thirteen in Acts have the technical sense, "to dwell, lodge." Three times in Acts it means "to wait, await," and three times it means "to continue (in an existing state)." In no case is there a developed figurative nuance for Luke (contrast the Johannine μένω); the ideas of loyal endurance and spiritual allegiance are absent. When the term means "wait" or "continue," it does not accent the action's duration. Luke's use of μένω thus leaves room for an intensive sense for διαμένω in 22:28.

By surveying occurrences of διαμένω elsewhere, we may be able to shed more light on Luke 22:28.[44] In 1:22, the term connotes mere temporal continuation of a condition ("he [Zechariah] made signs to them and 'remained' dumb"). Two of the three non-Lukan NT usages of διαμένω point to action of very long or eternal duration. In Heb 1:11, it is said of God, in contrast to creation which will perish, that he "endures." In 2 Pet 3:4, critics of the gospel are characterized as saying that all things "continue" as they have from the beginning. The third non-Lukan NT usage (Gal 2:5) lays emphasis not on temporal duration, but on Paul's action to "preserve" the gospel truth from corruption by those who placed too great a stress on keeping the law. The sense of διαμένω here is colored by the context in which the gospel is under threat; endurance in the face of opposition is implied.

Of the 22 LXX διαμένω usages,[45] seven involve action continuing forever. Ben Sirach contains a heavy proportion of LXX διαμένω usages (8 of 22); the emphasis there is on practical and ethical matters (e.g., Sir 12:15; 22:23; 27:4; 40:17; 44:11). Sir 22:23 is particularly noteworthy in connection with Luke 22:28. The injunction ἐν καιρῷ θλίψεως διάμενε

[43]Bösen claims that the δια- prefix in 22:28, quite apart from the subsequent reference to πειρασμοί, implies that there are "Schwierigkeiten" in view which make endurance difficult (138). Hendricksen sees an accent on enduring action: "to remain continually (with someone), to stand by (him)" (979).

[44]Perfect tense and participle forms of διαμένω appear in the NT at Luke 22:28 only.

[45]The present, future and aorist tenses of διαμένω are well represented in the LXX. No perfect forms are seen, and the one present participle (Ps 18:9) is not used as a substantive, so its correspondence to the usage in Luke 22:28 is not close.

αὐτῷ is set in synonymous parallelism with πίστιν κτῆσαι ἐν πτωχείᾳ μετὰ τοῦ πλησίον. Three useful points may be made here: 1) διαμένω is parallel in thought to πίστιν κτῆσαι; διάμενε αὐτῷ *alone* may be translated "remain *faithful* to him!"[46] 2) διαμένω is directly associated with adverse circumstances: "in (the) time of tribulation" and "in (his) poverty." 3) The faithful endurance of trials with a friend results in the reception of a reward[47] ("... that you may rejoice in his prosperity; ... that you may be heir with him to his inheritance").[48]

More generally, in summary of numerous occurrences of διαμένω in the NT, LXX, and non-biblical Jewish, Hellenistic, classical and non-literary sources, the following observations may be made: 1) Many references to eternal or very long periods of continuance are found;[49] 2) Several references to continuance in the face of difficulties also appear;[50] 3) Usages in contexts centering on personal loyalty or faithfulness surface;[51] 4) A few texts associate διαμένω with important related terms and thereby clarify its usage;[52] 5) There are several references to simple continuance that do not allude to difficulties, an action's duration, or intensified dimensions.[53]

To further explore the sense of v 28, we turn our attention to Luke's choice of tense. The probable departure from Q's aorist ἀκολουθήσαντές to include perfect διαμεμενηκότες may suggest a special Lukan interest.

[46]Skehan and Di Lella (315) translate, "remain true." By contrast, in Diodor. 14.48.4, διαμένω requires ἐν τῇ φιλίᾳ to complete the idea (on διαμένω for remaining in a relationship of personal loyalty, cf. Ign. *Trall.* 12.2).

[47]Cf. the ἵνα connection between Luke 22:28 and 29-30 (see sec. 7.4.1).

[48]Two perfect participles in non-biblical Greek (Dit., Syll. 194.31 [cf. Larfeld, 356]; Polyb. 3.55.1) clearly refer to past actions from which present states result.

[49]E.g., Heb 1:11; 2 Pet 3:4; Alex. 34; *Ep. Arist.* 258; Hp. *Aph.* 3.28; Xen. *Cyr.* 8.2.7; *Herm. Sim.* 9.29.2; Thphr. *Hist. Pl.* 7.5.5; BGU II 362.4.12 (with substantive διαμονή); POxy II 237.8.40; Irenaeus *Adv. Haer.* 2.1.

[50]E.g., Gal 2:5; Sir 22:23; Diodor. 4.16.3; *Herm. Sim.* 9.29.1; 9.24.4; Plato *Protag.* 344 B; *Ep. Arist.* 259.

[51]E.g., Sir 22:23; Diodor. 14.48.4; Ign. *Trall.* 12.2.

[52]E.g., Isocr. 8.51 refers to "our democracy" which "flourishes" (αὐξανομένην) and "endures" (διαμένουσαν) in times of peace and security; Pol. *Phil.* 1.2 speaks of the Philippians' faith which still "flourishes" (διαμένει) and bears fruit for the Lord Jesus Christ who "endured" (from ὑπομένω) death "for our sins"; see also Acts 10:48 ms. D; *Ep. Arist.* 226; Thphr. *H.P.* 7.5.5; D. S. 14.48.4; Irenaeus *Adv. Haer.* 2.1.

[53]E.g., PTebt. I 27.40; Xen. *Ap.* 30; Isocr. 8.51; Jos. *Ant.* 14.266; *Ep. Arist.* 226; 204; *Herm. Sim.* 9.28.5; 9.30.2; Pol. *Phil.* 1.2; Epict. 2.16.4; see also a number of LXX usages.

Since the perfect tense typically focuses on a present state resulting from a past action,[54] it may be that a Lukan purpose in v 28 is to draw attention to the connection of past and present, to the span of time which separates the two points or periods (cf. sec. 9.3). Further, διαμένω by nature involves some kind of *continuing* action, regardless of its tense. While it has not yet been established that in v 28 διαμεμενηκότες involves continuing loyalty (see further below), such a concept does find a special emphasis in the unparalleled "daily" of 9:23 (cf. Acts 14:22) and in the addition to the Markan tradition of ἐν ὑπομονῇ at Luke 8:15.

Our perspective on οἱ διαμεμενηκότες in 22:28 may be further clarified by examining Luke's use of substantive perfect participles elsewhere. Even when a past action receives a certain emphasis, it is still associated with or implies its present resultant state (e.g., 1:45;[55] 14:10; 16:18 [diff. Mark]; Acts 18:27; 19:28; 21:20, 25; 25:7).[56] Alternatively, Luke also uses substantive perfect participles to focus on a present state or action, although this is coupled with an implied past action (e.g., Luke 4:18; 5:24 [diff. Mark]; 6:25 [note νῦν]; 7:12). Thus it appears that Luke's substantive perfect participles do not depart from the general parameters of the perfect tense with its basic interest in a present state which results from a past action.

Regarding the temporal reference of οἱ διαμεμενηκότες, Conzelmann contends that Luke 22:28 points to the endurance of trials "now" and excludes the time before the reinvigorated activity of Satan (22:3).[57]

---

[54]Brooks and Winbery, 104. Blass and Debrunner describe the perfect tense as denoting "the *continuance* of *completed* action" (BDF, § 340, emphasis original—but can a completed action be continued?). The aorist, however, usually describes an action without reference to its continuance (see BDF, § 318).

[55]Since "the Lord" is the speaker here, one might argue that τοῖς λελαλημένοις should be understood on the analogy of γέγραπται ("it is written" [e.g., 2:23; 4:4, 8, 10; 19:46; etc.]) functioning more or less like the present tense. The presence in the immediate literary context of 1:45, however, of a now-completed speech act (1:28-37) weighs in favor of a reference to past action. Yet it is improbable that this explicit reference to Gabriel's speech should give the perfect tense here an exclusive focus on the past action; there are resulting effects of that action that profoundly influence the unfolding narrative.

[56]S. Brown observes that πεπιστευκότες in Acts 18:27; 19:18; 21:20, 25 "expresses the present state of being a Christian which results from the past act of becoming a Christian" (9, n. 11). Similarly, a present state resulting from past fidelity to Jesus is said to be in view with διαμεμενηκότες in Luke 22:28 (ibid.). The matter of how far back into the past the action originated, however, is not discussed (see further below).

[57]Conzelmann, *Theology*, 80-1, 83; so also Ott, 85-9; S. Schulz, 330; cf.

It is important to note, however, that Conzelmann does not eliminate *all* reference to the past in this interpretation of the perfect form; though the emphasis is said to rest heavily on the present faithfulness of the apostles, they nonetheless have had to face temptation with Jesus since the beginning of the Passion and Satan's reinvigorated activity.[58] Thus, despite a heavy emphasis on present endurance, Conzelmann's understanding of v 28 in its narrative setting allows for (at most) a few days of *past* time in which apostolic endurance of temptations with Jesus could have taken place.[59]

Accordingly, S. Brown's opposition to Conzelmann's interpretation of 22:28 regarding the temporal reference of the perfect tense is flawed. Brown states that διαμεμενηκότες here "denotes the *continuance* of completed action,"[60] yet he does not reckon with the possibility of a past action that had begun only since the start of the Passion, though that is what Conzelmann argues for.[61] In reality it is the amount of past time denoted by διαμεμενηκότες about which Brown and Conzelmann disagree, not the presence or lack of it: Brown argues, "It is true that the apostles, according to Luke's presentation, *remain* with Jesus during his Passion. But this is simply the continuation of their fidelity to him during his public ministry."[62] But Conzelmann claims that, though the emphasis is on "the temptations" that hold sway now, the conflict they bring upon Christians goes back only to the beginning of the Passion.[63]

Wiefel, 372. Roloff (*Apostolat*, 185-6) argues similarly that the perfect participle here is "im resultativischen Sinne zu verstehen.... So ist das Wort nicht Verheißung einer Belohnung für bisheriges Ausharren, sondern Ankündigung der jetzt beginnenden neuen Lage. Was nun kommt, ist die Zeit der Anfechtung und Versuchung,..."

[58]Conzelmann, *Theology*, 83

[59]Note the break in time between 22:6 and 7.

[60]S. Brown, 9, emphasis original (citing the awkward definition in BDF, § 340); Brown rightly notes that διαμένω is not "one of those few Greek verbs whose perfect has wholly the sense of a present" (9; so Turner, *Syntax*, 82; cf. BDF, § 341).

[61]Lohfink (*Sammlung*, 66, n. 171) and I. H. Marshall (*Historian*, 87, n. 4) similarly overstate Conzelmann's view by denying that it contains any reference to the past, even the past since 22:3.

[62]S. Brown, 9.

[63]Conzelmann, *Theology*, 80-1. We may add here that a *strictly* present understanding of διαμεμενηκότες in v 28 would be highly improbable for two reasons: 1) Verb tense aside, the root διαμένω does not logically fit with an action that is strictly in the present. "Continue" or "endure" or "remain" (etc.) are by nature actions with a history. 2) The most immediately present action of the apostles in the Lukan context (the quarrel in v 24) can hardly be construed as a "continuing"

Conzelmann's understanding of v 28, however, has a serious defect. Leonard's alternative thesis moves in the right direction when he asserts that Luke does not point out any temptations endured by Jesus between the event of 22:3 and the saying in 22:28.[64] It could be argued, however, that Satan's entry into Judas (v 3), the prospect of death (vv 15-22), the anticipation of betrayal (v 21) and the endurance of quarreling apostles (v 24) reveal a Lukan depiction of Jesus as facing trials (if not temptations) at the Last Supper, and it is because of this that Leonard's argument is inadequate to topple Conzelmann's analysis.

Going beyond Leonard, however, it is essential to note that the Lukan Passion Narrative contains no reference to an adverse experience endured by Jesus *with the apostles* (22:28) between the time of Satan's new initiative (22:3) and the time Jesus is portrayed as delivering the saying at hand. None of the incidents described in 22:3-27 which could be construed as "trials" for Jesus are experienced by Jesus with the apostles: there is no reference to the Eleven being aware of the events in vv 3-6,[65] not to mention suffering over them with Jesus; Luke makes no reference to the apostles anticipating or sharing any suffering of Jesus over the announcement of betrayal (vv 21-3);[66] and clearly, if Jesus found the apostles' quarrel a "trial," he bore that burden alone. Thus there is no experience between vv 3 and 27 to which the description of v 28 could apply (see further sec. 7.3.3 on the trials which are in view).

In addition to our observations regarding δια- compounds and the perfect tense, some attention to the role of διαμεμενηκότες in its context may prove useful. While it is left to section 7.3.3 to explore the sense of πειρασμοῖς, at present it may be noted that the connection with "trials" implies that the apostles have undergone some sort of challenge or threatening experience. A simple temporal or local sense for "remain" is not adequate to describe the apostles' endurance of adversity. This factor, then, together with the usual intensive/ perfective force of δια- com-

with Jesus. It does not seem that present ἐστε in v 28 plays a significant role in settling this question of timing, for either a past, present or combined sense for διαμεμενηκότες could fit logically with ἐστε.

[64]Leonard, 242-3.

[65]Indeed, their ignorance may be inferred from v 23

[66]Against Harrington, 251. Rather, the Twelve respond to Jesus' announcement by debating *among themselves* (πρὸς ἑαυτούς) as to the identity of the betrayer (v 23).

pounds, the dimensions of διαμένω in the NT and other sources, and the role of the perfect tense, count in favor of a sense for διαμεμενηκότες in v 28 which connotes standing firm, being loyal, persevering.

If, then, διαμεμενηκότες means more than just being in Jesus' presence, it follows that v 28 is not a neutral statement of fact but an affirmation, a word of praise.[67] To be sure, this understanding seems to widen the gap between vv 24-27 and 28 (rebuke is followed by praise). The reference of the perfect tense to past action, however, as well as the fact that Luke's Passion Narrative up to v 28 reveals no trial endured by Jesus with the apostles, allow v 28 to look back to a previous period, thus lessening the tension between vv 24-27 and 28.

A wider view of Luke-Acts reveals a tendency to portray the apostles positively, so a word of praise in v 28 may not be so surprising. S. Brown and others argue that the positive portrayal is typical.[68] Luke's omission of the apostles' abandonment of Jesus (Mark 14:50) is often noted in this connection, as is Satan's demand with the prediction of Peter's return after his denial (22:31-2) and the omission of the reference to Peter as "Satan" (Mark 8:33). Brown's view as to why this is important for Luke is this: "The *fides apostolica,* whose perseverance in the moment of stress is the object of Luke's concern in his Passion account, will constitute in the Age of the Church the source of strength for the perseverance of the Christian."[69] A positive portrayal of the apostles is

[67]So Gormley, 91, n. 11 (διαμένω involves remaining behind when others have left); cf. Lull, 300, n. 72 (διαμένω here has the sense of παραμένω, a term used to compliment faithful slaves). Many describe the disciples' action connoted by διαμεμενηκότες favorably as "fidelity" (S. Brown, 63, cf. 66; Fitzmyer, *Gospel,* 2:1415) or "faithfulness" (Tannehill, *Unity,* 268-9) or "persistent loyalty" (Plummer, 502, arguing on the basis of the verbal compound with δια-, the perfect tense and the prepositional phrase) or "Treue" (Bösen, 138; Hauck, 265; Rengstorf, 247; Schürmann, *Ursprung,* 128; Wellhausen, 124). Hauck states, "Rückblickend lobt er ihre **Treue**, die sich in ihrem Ausharren bei ihm erwiesen hat" (265, emphasis original; T. W. Manson, *Sayings,* 339, and Lagrange, 551, also see here a word of praise). For Schürmann (*Abschiedsrede,* 40), however, vv 21-23 and 33-34 imply that Luke did not create the "Jüngerlob" of v 28.

[68]S. Brown, 66-74; similarly Dupont, "Ministères," 142 and n. 29; Feuillet, 378; Ford, 117; Grundmann, 401; Schlosser, 55; against Bailey (43; a motive of "pious reconstruction" would not include 22:24 [cf. Goulder, *Luke,* 2:731; Tannehill, *Unity,* 262-3]).

[69]S. Brown, 74; similarly Dupont, "Ministères," 141-2. Laying the narrative and theological footings for an "Acts of the Apostles" was a constraint felt by neither Mark nor Matthew, so a Lukan tendency to occasionally omit or soften critical portrayals of the disciples may be understood. A general ethic of faithful

a common Lukan feature, yet we may temper Brown's claims by noting that 9:46 and 22:24 constitute important exceptions to this tendency (cf. secs. 6.3 and 6.4).

A brief discussion of the prepositional phrase μετ' ἐμοῦ may shed more light on the sense of v 28. We note first that this phrase appears to be rooted in the Q tradition: ἐμοῦ corresponds to Matthew's μοι (line 7), and though μετά is made necessary by Luke's choice of intransitive διαμένω, Matt 19:28 also refers to the disciples' association with Jesus (lines 5-7). Without overlooking the traditional basis here for μετ' ἐμοῦ, however, unparalleled usages of the phrase or similar expressions elsewhere in Luke-Acts imply that μετ' ἐμοῦ in 22:28 has significance for Luke. As will be seen, it coincides with an emphasis on the strong solidarity of Jesus and the apostles, and its placement at the Last Supper (diff. Matt 19:28) is rich with significance for this union.[70]

To track down a possible Lukan interest in solidarity with Jesus, we may consider the importance of μετ' ἐμοῦ on the lips of Jesus in 23:43. In addition to the vivid portrayal of the penitent criminal's present sharing of suffering at the height of Jesus' Passion, future union with Jesus is also in view: "Truly, I say to you, today you will be *with me* in paradise." Thus Luke shows an interest in an ongoing union with Jesus in his Passion and into the next world.[71] In Acts 4:13 the boldness of Peter and John before the Sanhedrin is attributed to their having "been *with* Jesus."[72] Here the point seems to be that having been in Jesus' presence enables his disciples to remain loyal and testify faithfully in the face of adversity.[73]

---

endurance of ongoing trials and temptations is also a frequent theme in Luke-Acts (see Luke 8:15 and the addition of ὑπομονή to Mark, the addition of "daily" at 9:23, and teaching on persistent prayer in 11:5-13 and 18:1-8).

[70]See Kümmel, *Promise*, 121; Ellis, "La fonction," 149; Ernst, *Evangelium*, 596. Monsarrat (41) contends that v 28 coincides with the whole Last Supper scene in which Luke accents attachment to Jesus (see vv 14-15, 19-20, 24-27, 28, 29-30).

[71]The connection between suffering with Jesus and resulting reward is also seen in Rom 8:17 and 2 Tim 2:11-12 (cf. Acts 14:22; Rom 6:3-4; 2 Tim 4:7-8; Jas 1:12). Cf. ch. 8.

[72]Here σύν is used (σὺν τῷ 'Ιησοῦ ἦσαν), but the preference of σύν over μετά is typical of Luke in narration (so Luke 8:38; 22:14; esp. 24:29; an exception to this tendency is Acts 11:21). Schürmann contends that σύν is Luke's preferred preposition (total NT σύν usages are Matt 4x, Mark 6x, Luke 23x and Acts 51x [disregarding compounds]), and that the presence of μετά in 22:28 argues for a pre-Lukan source (*Abschiedsrede*, 40). Luke's use of μετά elsewhere (e.g., 23:43), however, may conflict with this claim.

It is noteworthy that the "with Jesus" motif seems to surface elsewhere in the immediate literary context of Luke 22:28. Could there be a solidarity echo in "among you" (v 27)? The Lukan Jesus could have simply said, "I am the one who serves," and the apostles would have seen that the attitude of service was being commended to them (vv 25-27b). The phrase ἐν μέσῳ ὑμῶν may thus underscore the importance of Jesus' union with the apostles (cf. sec. 6.5.3, and see sec. 7.4.3 on 17:21), a tie that was threatened by the prizing of greatness (v 24). Additionally, eschatologial union with Jesus appears to be at the heart of the reward in vv 29-30. The banquet described will take place at Jesus' table in Jesus' kingdom—the apostles will dine *with* him (cf. sec. 7.4.3).[74] Thus the motif of being with Jesus is implied in verses preceding and succeeding v 28.

---

[73]Additional yet related facets of Luke's concept of union with Jesus appear when we consider texts in which Jesus is with his followers (contrast Luke 22:28 where it is the apostles who are with Jesus). The motif is seen in 22:15 where Jesus says to the apostles, "I have earnestly desired to eat this Passover with you before I suffer." The solidarity of the risen Jesus with the Emmaus disciples is described in 24:30, and the strong echo of the institution of the Last Supper (22:19a; cf. 9:16) is not to be missed.

In Acts the "Jesus with" theme is developed to emphasize the effect of Jesus' presence in the church and with its leaders. Acts 11:21 recounts how "the hand of the Lord" ("Lord Jesus," v 20) was "with" (μετά) the evangelists of Cyprus and Cyrene so that a great number believed and turned to the Lord (and this amidst times of "persecution" [11:19; cf. 4:3, 21]). A dramatic account of the effective presence of Jesus with Paul at Corinth is seen in 18:9-11: "And the Lord said to Paul one night in a vision, 'Do not be afraid, but speak and do not be silent; for "I am with you" (ἐγώ εἰμι μετὰ σοῦ), and no one shall attack you to harm you; for I have many people in this city.'" Union with Jesus provides Paul with needed support in a time of trial (note the possibility of fear and the threat of harm), enabling him to carry out an extended ministry in this hostile environment (see vv 12-18).

Looking more broadly at the motif of union with Jesus, one notes that the apostles required a replacement for Judas who had been with Jesus while he came and went among them (1:21-2). Luke 10:16 (par. Matt 10:40) also points to the solidarity of Jesus and his disciples: "He who hears you hears me, and he who rejects you rejects me, and he who rejects me rejects him who sent me" (cf. Acts 9:4-5). Note also Luke 9:48 where receiving a child amounts to receiving Jesus (thus one obtains fellowship with Jesus).

[74]And because the one who confers kingship on the apostles has kingship himself (v 29), the apostles will rule under and thus *with* Jesus when they sit on thrones (v 30b).

7.3.3 The Trials of Jesus

Matt 19:28 has no counterpart to τοῖς πειρασμοῖς in Luke 22:28. To be sure, the idea of following Jesus (Matt 19:27, 29) is not without cost, but this is a self-imposed loss, whereas Luke's trials are imposed from without. This distinctive wording probably signals a departure from Q, so we may suspect that Lukan concerns are clearly reflected.

What observations can be made about ἐν τοῖς πειρασμοῖς μου? We may first clarify its sense by noting that a temporal aspect is in view. Plural πειρασμοῖς implies repeated or continuing experiences, and the perfect tense and root meaning of διαμένω also allow for ongoing activity. Thus a period of time during which the apostles have stood by Jesus is in view.

But does ἐν correspond to Jesus or to Jesus and the apostles together? That is, do the apostles remain at Jesus' side while he endures trials, or do they actually share the trials with him? The following discussion of πειρασμός will shed some light on this matter, but at present we may note that neither option fits well with the text. Possessive μου means that it is Jesus' trials that are in view. Nevertheless, it has been argued above that διαμένω here connotes more than merely remaining in the proximity of Jesus; it points to the apostles' persevering loyalty to Jesus, and implies that, at least to a degree, they have suffered with him.

A key question here is, What trials are meant? That question may be clarified by adding others: When did the trials begin? How long did (do) they go on? Do they center on passion suffering? Are they diabolical, or are they of divine or human origin ("temptations" or "trials")?[75]

The question of when the trials began is closely connected to the above discussion about the temporal reference of διαμεμενηκότες, for the time of the apostles' perseverance with Jesus *is* the time of these trials. That suggests a pre-passion time frame for the trials of v 28. This claim, however, needs to be sharpened.

What can we learn from the Lukan usages of πειρασμός and πειράζω in the quest to further pinpoint the antecedent event(s) to which v 28 refers? Luke prefers the noun form while Matthew and Mark prefer the

[75]The πειρασμός/ πειράζω word group has a broad enough semantic field to encompass both possibilities (cf., BAGD, 640-1), and all three Synoptics employ the term in both ways. Garrett (43, n. 30) and Monsarrat (41) are among those who highlight the work of Satan in Jesus' "trials."

verb.[76] πειράζω is not used in the synoptic Passion Narratives, but each evangelist uses the noun for Jesus' admonition to the apostles at Gethsemane (Matt 26:41; Mark 14:38; Luke 22:40, 46). In the Synoptics it is always Jesus who is "tested" or "tempted" when the verb form is used; the noun, however, can apply to Jesus, the disciples or others. The only usage of πειρασμός in Acts (20:19, also plural) is in Paul's farewell speech to the Ephesian elders where it refers to troubles instigated by the Jews, not diabolical temptations. This may be a helpful sidelight for understanding the usage in Jesus' farewell speech.

We may limit our attention at present to the fourteen πειρασμός/ πειράζω usages in Matthew, Mark and Luke where Jesus is the one experiencing testing/ temptation. Eight of these refer to trials of human origin where skeptics wish to "test" Jesus,[77] and all eight use the verb. Seven of the eight are in Matthew or Mark, but only one is in Luke. Luke has a parallel pericope for each Markan or Matthean usage, but he does not retain πειράζω in his pericopae.[78] Evidently he does not wish regularly to depict Jesus as one who is the object of human examination. Thus it would seem unlikely for Luke to have purely human testing of Jesus in view at 22:28 since he reveals a tendency to omit that usage of πειράζω from his sources.

Five synoptic usages speak of temptations of diabolical origin.[79] All of these come from a single pericope, namely Jesus' temptation in the wilderness. In no other case (setting Luke 22:28 aside) does πειρασμός/ πειράζω clearly originate with Satan.[80]

---

[76]πειρασμός occurs in Matt 2x, Mark 1x, Luke 6x and Acts 1x (NT 21x); πειράζω occurs in Matt 6x, Mark 4x, Luke 2x and Acts 5x (NT 38x).

[77]Mark 8:11 par. Matt 16:1 par. (?) Luke 11:16; Mark 10:2 par. Matt 19:3; Mark 12:15 par. Matt 22:18; Matt 22:35

[78]It is possible that Luke 11:16 is transposed from Mark 8:11, and the occurrence of ἐκπειράζω in Luke 10:25 similarly means "to test." The idea of people "testing" God is found 2x in Acts (5:9; 15:10), but these cannot be taken as referring to Jesus.

[79]Noun form: Luke 4:13; verb form: Mark 1:13 par. Matt 4:1 par. Luke 4:2; Matt 4:3.

[80]Diabolical involvement may well be in view in Luke 22:40, 46 (especially considering how Luke calls attention to Satan's activity in the Passion [22:3, 31]), but there it is temptations for the apostles, not Jesus, that are in view. The fact that Jesus' prayer is sandwiched between these references may, however, imply that he too endures satanic temptation. τοῦ πονηροῦ in Matt 6:13 is probably masculine, "the evil One." Here again it is the experience of Jesus' disciples, not Jesus himself, that is in view (though Jesus' own prayer life may be reflected).

All five of the diabolical and the eight human origin πειρασμός/ πειράζω instances point to testing/ tempting of limited duration; none are depicted as life-long experiences of Jesus. So if it is the entire public ministry of Jesus that Luke has in mind at 22:28, that usage of πειρασμός would be without precedent in the Synoptics. The fact that 22:28 contains plural πειρασμοῖς while every other synoptic occurrence of the noun is singular, however, may leave the door open for a long-term series of trials (cf. Acts 20:19).

S. Brown contends that, because "trials" in v 28 is plural, "dangers" and not diabolical temptations are in view.[81] But this explanation is not satisfactory for two reasons: 1) Although πειρασμόν in Luke 4:13 is singular, the qualifying πάντα points to a plurality of temptations of diabolical origin.[82] 2) The sense of anarthrous singular πειρασμός is sometimes close to that of the plural form. For instance, "Lead us not into temptation" (Luke 11:4 par. Matt 6:13) speaks in general terms of ongoing temptation, of many temptations.[83]

The pseudo-plural usage of Luke 4:13, however, could hardly have been in Luke's mind at 22:28, for the apostles had not even been called at that point in the narrative, so they could not yet have endured trials with Jesus.[84] Also, the anarthrous singular usages of the noun do not refer directly to Jesus' experience. So we cannot expand the possibilities for seeing diabolical temptation at 22:28 by countering Brown's argument. How, then, can the origin and nature of the trials of v 28 be determined? Since the occurrences of the πειρασμός/ πειράζω word group have not provided an answer, we must look beyond them to continue the quest.

It was argued above (sec. 7.3.2) that Jesus' trials shared with the apostles (22:28) cannot have begun after the event described in 22:3. It is also apparent that they must have begun after the calling of the first disciples (Luke 5:1-11) for Jesus to have endured them together with the apostles. What sort of experiences does Jesus have with his disciples in Luke 5-21 that may be construed as "trials"? What can we learn from references to "Satan" or "the Devil" or "the Enemy," and instances of "persecution" or "suffering"?

[81]S. Brown, 9 (citing a parallel of πειρασμοί and κίνδυνοι in Cyranides); so also Gillman, 146.

[82]So Fitzmyer, *Theologian*, 163.

[83]Cf. the reference to *daily* bread.

[84]Evans, 799.

In no case in Luke (or Matthew or Mark) is it stated that ὁ σατανᾶς presents Jesus with an adversity experienced *with the apostles* that we may correlate with the "trials" of 22:28. The same is true of definite διάβολος and ἐχθρός.[85] In the Synoptics and Acts, the disciples are frequently warned of θλῖψις, but Jesus is never said to experience it himself. When Jesus is the subject of ἀνέχω, it refers to his "bearing with" the disciples themselves, not their solidarity with him. ὑπομονή in the Synoptics and Acts is never presented as the experience of Jesus, and the one time that Jesus is the subject of ὑπομένω, it means merely "to remain," not "to endure" (Luke 2:43). Jesus is the object of διώκω only in the post-Pentecost era (Acts 9:4, 5; 22:7, 8; 26:14, 15). So again we find no clearly pertinent information in the quest for Jesus' experience with the apostles which Luke 22:28 recalls.[86]

By taking another approach, however, we can find a more satisfactory solution to this problem. An overview of the content of Luke 5-21—apart from more narrow word study—reveals an array of adversities in the public ministry of Jesus experienced in the company of the apostles. One notes repeated clashes with Pharisees and scribes and other Jewish groups or officials who oppose and plot against Jesus.[87] Woes against (11:39-52) and warnings about (12:1; 20:46-47) such Jewish parties also suggest conflicts with them.[88] It appears that the Lukan Jesus also finds the disbelief of his "generation" to be troubling (7:31-5; 9:41; 11:29; 17:25; cf., 8:53). Jesus was refused entry by a particular Samaritan village (9:51-56), and he had nowhere to lay his head (9:58). The many clashes with demons constitute another major form of conflict in his ministry, and they suggest that Satan is not absent from the narrative scene between 4:13 and 22:3.[89] Finally, his affection for Jerusalem coupled with its rejection of him (13:34; 19:41) would have brought anguish to the Lukan Jesus.[90]

[85]The depiction of Satan in Luke 10:18-19, however, would seem to contradict Conzelmann's conception of a Satan-free era in the Lukan framework.

[86]Although the focus of 9:22 (cf. 17:25) is on passion suffering ("The Son of man must suffer many things" [πολλά παθεῖν]), "many things" could encompass Jesus' pre-passion trials. Still, πολλά may function adverbially here, and Luke 24:46, Acts 1:3 and 17:3 use πάσχω as a technical term for the death of Jesus, so it is likely that Luke 9:22 refers to passion trials.

[87]5:30; 6:2 (note reference to disciples with Jesus); 7-11; 7:39; 10:25; 11:38, 53-54; 13:14-17; 14:1-6; 15:2; 16:14-15; 20:1, 19-20, 27ff; note also the fact that Jesus has "adversaries," 13:17.

[88]The cleansing of the temple (19:45-46) may also be associated with the general conflict with the Jewish establishment.

[89]See n. 19 above.

In summary, it is probable that Jesus' "trials" in 22:28 are the adversities experienced with the apostles before the reinvigorated activity of Satan (22:3) and after the first calling of disciples (5:1-11). To be sure, the heightened activity of Satan during the Passion and the nature of Jesus' experience as portrayed in Luke 22-23 (including literal trials as well as profound suffering) imply that Jesus' trials do not end at the time of his farewell discourse. That the final week of the Lukan Jesus' earthly life is a time of accelerated stress and suffering is not in doubt.[91] What is highly doubtful, however, is that 22:28 refers to passion trials. The perfect tense and μετ' ἐμοῦ in v 28 combine to rule that possibility out. The trials described in 22:28 are not chiefly diabolical, though the Lukan Jesus' many encounters with demons prompt us to recognize a diabolical element.[92] τοῖς πειρασμοῖς μου in v 28 is a collective plural hearkening back to an array of troubles Jesus faced with the Twelve in his day-to-day ministry experience: rejection by his beloved Jerusalem, hostility and opposition from Jewish sects and leaders, dullness and disbelief of his generation, and clashes with demonic powers.

Finally, it may be asked whether the perseverance of the apostles described in v 28 is chiefly ethical ("you have fulfilled your discipleship and carried out my teaching ...") or christological ("you have continued to confess me ..."). Although there is probably an important ethical aspect of the apostles' perseverance in trials, and although it is hard to imagine how one might practice christological confession amidst trials without also persevering in an ethical discipleship, for two reasons it is arguable

[90]A number of interpreters conclude that "trials" of Jesus entire public ministry are in view in 22:28: Bösen, 138-9; S. Brown, 9; Danker, *Jesus*, 350; Ernst, *Evangelium*, 595; Evans, 799; Fitzmyer, *Gospel*, 2:1418; Gillman, 146; Goulder, *Luke*, 2:733; Jeremias, *Theology*, 74; Karris, *Gospel*, 716; Kremer, 215; K. Kuhn, "New Light," 112, n. 51; Lagrange, 551; Leivestad, 59; Matera, *Passion*, 165; Rienecker, 504; G. Schneider, *Evangelium*, 2:451; Schürmann, *Ursprung*, 128; Senior, 28-31, 71; Tannehill, *Unity*, 268-9; Taylor, *Jesus*, 188. Those who favor temptations only of the Passion for v 28 include: Baumbach, 191-2; Conzelmann, *Theology*, 80-1, 83; Ott, 85-9; S. Schulz, 330; Wiefel, 372.

[91]Perhaps Luke's choice of πειρασμός in v 28 subtly foreshadows the Gethsemane story (cf. vv 40, 46), though again one quickly notes that the apostles fall asleep rather than stand firm at Jesus' side in that crucial hour.

[92]Schürmann claims that satanic and human trials are mingled in v 28; Jesus' "Schwierigkeiten" are associated with persecution from the Jews, but "der Gegner" is nonetheless behind them (*Abschiedsrede*, 39; similarly I. H. Marshall, *Gospel*, 816).

that v 28 has a christological emphasis: 1) πειρασμός is probably Luke's addition to the Q saying,[93] and much of what we have seen to constitute the "trials" here in view involves the pointed rejection of Jesus and his message. The apostles' loyalty thus includes their recognition of Jesus' superiority over his rivals (e.g., the Jewish establishment and demonic powers). 2) A key Lukan "with Jesus" text (Acts 4:13; cf. sec. 7.3.2) stresses the connection between being in Jesus' presence and bearing witness to him boldly (and note the sharp christological thrust in 4:12). Therefore, it is probable that in 22:28 Jesus especially commends the apostles for their persevering witness to him and to his distinctive mission and message.

In summary of v 28, it is probable that Matthew's form of the logion is closer than Luke's to the original Q form. Emphatically placed ὑμεῖς and adversative δέ develop a contrast between the apostles' quarreling and their previous faithful behavior, yet the shared structure of vv 27c and 28 likens Jesus as he is to the apostles as the have been (service and perseverance in trials thus dovetail). V 28 recalls approvingly the perseverance of the apostles with Jesus, and διαμεμενηκότες alludes to the associated difficulties and perhaps long duration of their allegiance to him in the face of trouble. V 28 needs to be seen against the backdrop of a strand of thought in Luke-Acts highlighting the importance of solidarity with Jesus. The reference to Jesus' trials hearkens back to pre-Passion experiences of Jesus with the apostles in which he endured resistance, disbelief, opposition and demonic activity. V 28 may be translated: "But you are in fact those who have been persevering with me through my trials."

7.4 The Conferral of Kingship (22:29-30)

We now turn to a direct analysis of 22:29-30 which approaches that text from four angles: the basis upon which Jesus confers kingship on the apostles (sec. 7.4.1); the nature of the act of conferral (7.4.2); the content or substance of conferral (7.4.3); and the timing of conferral (7.4.4).

---

[93]Kollmann, *Mahl*, 223.

7.4.1 The Basis of Conferral (v 28)

In section 7.3.2 it was argued that v 28 constitutes a word of praise from Jesus to the Twelve for their perseverance with him in his trials; διαμεμενηκότες does not refer merely to the apostles having been around Jesus, but to their continuing loyalty in the face of adversity. Despite certain failings (e.g., 9:46; 22:24), Jesus views the companionship of the Twelve over the course of his public ministry positively.

With vv 29-30 following immediately upon this commendatory word, it seems logical that Jesus confers kingship as a consequence of the apostles' behavior affirmed in v 28. The Lukan καί (in κἀγώ, v 29) would then be taken as consecutive ("and so").[94] Without consecutive καί here the logical connection between vv 28 and 29 breaks down; commendable behavior would be followed by but not related to a great reward.[95]

7.4.2 The Act of Conferral (v 29)

We now turn to the act of conferral in vv 29-30, its basis having been seen in v 28. We will first identify the persons involved, and then consider the nature of the act of conferral. Jesus is the subject of διατίθεμαι, the principal verb of vv 29-30, so the chief burden of vv 29-30 is to elaborate upon his deed. But Jesus does not act alone; ὁ πατήρ is the subject of διέθετο, the second occurrence of the same verb in v 29. This

[94]See BAGD, "καί," 392, def. I. 2. f.; cf. BDF, § 442.2. Lull's ecbatic καί makes the same connection between vv 28 and 29 (301, n. 80). It is also possible to describe the καί in v 29 as inferential; this highlights the ground in v 28 while the consecutive understanding emphasizes the result in v 29. Lull claims that "... the promise in vv 29-30 is offered in return for the apostles' loyalty (v 28)" (301; similarly e.g., Bösen, 135-6; Eltester, 134; Ernst, *Evangelium*, 596; Fitzmyer, *Gospel*, 2:1418; Gormley, 93; LaVerdiere, *Luke*, 261; Léon-Dufour, "Testament," 276; Lohfink, *Sammlung*, 80-1; Rienecker, 504; Schlatter, *Lukas*, 424; Schmid, 330; A. Schulz, *Nachfolge*, 124; Schürmann, *Ursprung*, 149; Wellhausen, 124; Zahn, 681-2; cf. Godet, 298; Kollmann, *Mahl*, 161, 224).

[95]The performance-reward connection in Lukan thought (cf. secs. 2.5.2, 4.5, 8.3-4) may thus be reflected here. Adverbial καί related to καθώς would similarly damage the link between vv 28 and 29. Otto (273) recognizes that v 28 makes a transition between vv 24-27 and 29-30, and thus implicitly concedes the role of v 28 in unifying 22:24-30 as a finished text. His claim that the "temptations" of Jesus had not yet taken place by the time of the Last Supper, however, is not persuasive (cf. sec. 7.3.3 above).

aorist indicative places the Father's action in past time,[96] but Jesus acts in the present (i.e., at the time of his discourse).[97]

The actions of Jesus and the Father are connected by καθώς. G. Schneider takes καθώς as comparative; it points to the correspondence between Jesus' and the Father's actions.[98] Lagrange, however, favors a causal understanding of καθώς and makes the Father's action the ground for Jesus' action.[99] The former view would accent the manner of Jesus' conduct, the latter the reason for it. Bauer notes that causal καθώς occurs especially as a conjunction at the beginning of a sentence,[100] but here the placement is mid-sentence. Moreover, a survey of Luke's καθώς usages[101] elsewhere does not reveal a single causal καθώς, while the comparative sense is dominant. Further, the causal interpretation overlooks and thus distorts the logical, consecutive connection between vv 28 and 29.[102] In light of these observations, the comparative sense is preferred.[103]

The third party involved here is the inner circle of twelve, the apostles (v 14). The series of givers and receivers in v 29 is now complete: the Father conferred something on Jesus, and Jesus similarly (καθώς) is now conferring something on the Twelve.[104] The apostles, then, are passive

---

[96]Luke does not specify the point in past time at which the Father acted (10:22 ["all things have been delivered to me by my Father"] may correlate with 22:29, suggesting Jesus' pre-passion reception of kingship; 1:33 offers little help in this instance).

[97]διατίθεμαι here is best understood as an aoristic present because 1) comparative καθώς likens it to aorist διέθετο, and 2) the nature of the act (whether to assign, covenant or will [see below, this sec.]) is momentary and not continuing or repeated (this rules out the customary or durative present). Cf. Acts 16:18; 26:1; see BDF, § 320; Turner, *Syntax*, 64; Brooks and Winbery, 89. The descriptive present would be a secondary possibility here.

[98]G. Schneider, *Evangelium*, 2:451; so I. H. Marshall, *Gospel*, 816; et al.

[99]Lagrange (551), translating καθώς "selon que"; Roloff (*Apostolat*, 188) translates "weil" (similarly Broer, 150).

[100]BAGD, "καθώς," 391, def. 3 ("since"); similarly BDF, § 453.

[101]Total occurrences: 17x in the Gospel, 11x in Acts.

[102]To be sure, causal καθώς would not necessarily imply that the connection between vv 28 and 29 is undermined because Jesus was *bound* to confer kingship upon the Twelve as a result of the Father's past action. But even if the Father's action were to be thought of as an enabling rather than a binding ground for Jesus' action, the importance of the link between vv 28 and 29 would be significantly diminished.

[103]This claim may be refined by noting that comparative καθώς is not without an underlying causal, or grounding, element. That is, even though Luke's point here seems to be to compare the actions of the Father and Jesus, the action of the Father is a necessary prerequisite for the action of Jesus.

recipients in vv 29-30; though Jesus earlier urged them to humble themselves (vv 25-27), here he is the agent of their elevation.[105]

Next we consider the nature of the action: What is the sense of διατίθημι in this context? Is it used in basically the same way on both occasions in v 29? διατίθημι occurs seven times in the NT (3x in Luke-Acts, 4x in Hebrews). The other Lukan occurrence is in Acts 3:25 where Peter is speaking to Jews: "You are the sons of the prophets and of the covenant which God *made* with your fathers ..." Here, as happens frequently in the LXX, διατίθημι occurs in connection with διαθήκη and means "to make (a covenant)," or simply "to covenant." Usages of διατίθημι in Hebrews offer partial support for this understanding; twice it means "to covenant" (8:10; 10:16), but twice (though in one context) it is associated with a death and means "to will, bequeath" (9:16, 17).

Bauer distills three meanings for διατίθημι from primary sources: 1) to decree, ordain; 2) to assign, confer something; 3) to dispose of property by a will.[106] The first meaning is seen in Acts 3:25, and it is the typical understanding of διατίθημι when it is used in connection with διαθήκη. Out of 87 occurrences of διατίθημι in the LXX, 76 (87%) are in connection with διαθήκη (for כָּרַת בְּרִית) and have this meaning. When διαθήκη is lacking, διατίθημι sometimes still carries the idea of establishing a covenant (1 Chr 19:19; 2 Chr 5:10; 7:18; Ezek 16:30), but it can also mean "to assign, confer" (Jdt 5:18; 2 Macc 9:28). The meaning "to will," however, is entirely lacking in the LXX.

Behm notes, however, that in other Greek literature the technical meaning "to will" does occur frequently.[107] The substantive articular participle ὁ διαθέμενος ("the testator") in Heb 9:16, 17 has this sense.[108]

[104]Guillet notes John's usages of καθώς similitudes which have to do with Jesus' relation to the Father and his consequent relation to the disciples (113-15; e.g., John 15:9; 20:21). Luke 22:29 resembles the Johannine pattern in setting the Father's action in the aorist tense, and in making the relation of the Father to Jesus primary and that of Jesus to the disciples secondary (115-16). Guillet maintains that multiple attestation (occurrences in Luke and John, along with Rev 3:20-21) suggests an origin for the three-part formula with Jesus himself (121) (it is unlikely that John was familiar with Luke's writing [117]).

[105]So the common reversal pattern seen in Luke-Acts (see sec. 4.5 [cf. Luke 14:11; 18:14]).

[106]BAGD, "διατίθημι," 189-90.

[107]Behm, "διατίθημι," 104-5; so BAGD, "διατίθημι," 189-90, def. 3.

[108]Also see e.g., Isaeus 1.26, 34; BGU 448.24; Dit., Or. 509.6, 16; POxy. 99.9, 15. In Jos. *Ant.* 13.407 we read similarly that Alexander bequeathed the kingdom (or

Even if Luke intended the typical LXX meaning "to make (a covenant)" or the related meaning "to assign, confer" at 22:29, he surely would have been aware that the testamentary nuance existed, and it has been argued (sec. 5.3) that 22:14-38 is cast in the form of a testamentary discourse. Luke's usage at Acts 3:25 along with findings from the LXX may incline one to shy away from the meaning "to will" at Luke 22:29,[109] but the possibility is by no means excluded. To clarify the meaning of διατίθημι here, then, we will need to approach the matter from another direction.

Recalling the above findings for καθώς will prove useful at this point. If καθώς in v 29 were causal, then there would be no necessary implication that the Father and Jesus were acting in a similar manner;[110] καθώς would point to the ground for Jesus' act, not its pattern. But having argued for comparative καθώς, our options for the sense of διατίθημι are consequently lessened. J. Behm maintains that "the διατίθεσθαι of Jesus corresponds to that of the Father, who is certainly not making His will,..."[111] Comparative καθώς makes it is necessary for the two usages of διατίθημι to have essentially the same sense,[112] and if Jesus' action is that of a man making his will, the Father's divinity is placed in question.[113]

"royal power," LCL) to Alexandra (τὴν βασιλείαν εἰς τὴν Ἀλεξάνδραν διέθετο). Here the meaning "to will" is required by the context.

[109]One recalls here Luke's heavy dependence upon the LXX, both stylistically and for direct or implied citations (so Goulder, *Luke*, 1:212-13, 218, 251; et al.).

[110]Occasionally the NT presents a causal καθώς that retains something of its comparative dimension (perhaps Eph 4:32, and similarly Matt 6:12 par. Luke 11:4 with ὡς), but more commonly the causal use does not involve comparison (so John 17:2; Rom 1:28; and perhaps 1 Cor 5:7).

[111]Behm, "διατίθημι," 105. Similarly Ernst, *Evangelium*, 596; Klostermann, 212; Lagrange, 551; Lohfink, *Sammlung*, 80; I. H. Marshall, *Gospel*, 816; W. Pesch, 75; Schürmann, *Abschiedsrede*, 41, n. 145. Also see Danker, *Jesus*, 350; Fitzmyer, *Gospel*, 2:1419; Grundmann, 404; Hauck, *Evangelium*, 265; Hooker, *Son of Man*, 145-6; Reiling and Swellengrebel, 694; Schlatter, *Lukas*, 424.

[112]Against Tannehill, "Study," 202, n. 26; Kurz, *Farewell*, 64.

[113]A large and complex issue raised here has to do with the proper limits of metaphorical language. Although it is true that whenever people speak of God they do so by some analogy from human experience, vivid symbolic language such as "to will" increases the possibilities as well as potential hazards for making a point of comparison. Caird notes that when a metaphor is used to compare two things, they are not to be considered alike in all respects; there is a point of comparison to be seen, to the exclusion of irrelevant facts. Communication breaks down if that point is wrongly identified (*Language*, 145).

In a text with a metaphor similar to that in Luke 22:29 (Rom 8:15-17), it is clearly acceptable for Roman believers to be described as "joint heirs" with Christ without suggesting that Jesus' Father is dead or dying. The value of being related

It must not be overlooked, however, that the death of Jesus *is* on the horizon at v 29 (cf. sec. 5.3). It was alluded to in the reference to his coming suffering (v 15), foreshadowed in the words of institution (vv 19-20), implied in Jesus' prediction of his betrayal (vv 21-22) and his self-description as a servant (v 27), and it is in view again at v 33. So a proper setting for Jesus to execute his last will and testament is present, and many argue that in v 29 Luke portrays the dying Jesus bequeathing his kingship to the apostles.[114]

But how do those who take this perspective handle comparative καθώς and its connotation of like actions by the Father and Jesus? Can they avoid envisioning the death of God? Fitzmyer responds to I. H. Marshall's opposition to the testamentary understanding by asserting, "The 'idea of a will or testament' is scarcely excluded, because God is the subject,... it [διατίθημι] is used figuratively, 'I bequeath to you.'"[115] In Fitzmyer's view, then, it is not a problem for Jesus and the Father to similarly will or bequeath something, for, at least in the case of the Father, that action is figurative.

Comparative καθώς, however, makes this view problematic. The comparison it draws breaks down if, while both usages of διατίθημι reflect the root concept "to will," one is figurative and the other literal. And Jesus' action, from Fitzmyer's perspective, is that of a man whose literal death is in view and who accordingly makes his actual testamen-

---

to God and united with one's brother Jesus Christ is the point of the metaphor, not the suggestion that God is on his deathbed. A relevant Lukan text is Acts 13:19 where God is the subject of κατακληρονόμησεν. The fact that God continues to act in subsequent generations (vv 20-23) clearly shows that the point of comparison is not to portray God in the place of a human father who leaves an inheritance at the time of death. (See also BAGD, "διαθήκη," 183, def. 2, on the testamentary metaphor in relation to God.)

[114]E.g., Fitzmyer, *Gospel*, 2:1419; Fransen, 25; Jervell, *Luke*, 79; Klostermann, 212; K. Kuhn, "New Light," 112; Kurz, *Farewell*, 64; Lull, 301; Rienecker, 504; G. Schneider, *Evangelium*, 2:451; Tannehill, "Study," 202; Wellhausen, 124; Zahn, 682, n. 58. In a testament, the natural sense for διατίθημι is that of making a disposition at death (e.g., *T. Levi* 1:1; *T. Zeb.* 1:1; *T. Naph.* 1:1; *T. Benj.* 1:1).

[115]Fitzmyer, *Gospel*, 2:1419, referring to I. H. Marshall, *Gospel*, 816. Fitzmyer cites Jos. *Ant.* 13.407, but there Alexander's act of bequeathing the kingdom to his wife Alexandra is literal, and it gives no support to the idea of a figurative interpretation of διατίθημι. Fitzmyer also seems to confuse matters here by stating the God is the subject of διατίθημι in the phrase "I bequeath to you." In fact, Jesus is the subject of "I bequeath" while God ("the Father") is subject in the clause "as he bequeathed to me."

tary disposition. It is of course conceivable that elsewhere Luke could associate a literal act with a figurative version of the same act, but here καθώς weighs against this possibility. Much more probable for v 29 is the suggestion that we have a true comparison, and both usages of διατίθημι have the meaning "to make (a covenant)" or the close idea "to assign, confer," and not "to will, bequeath."

Moreover, the presence in the literary context of v 29 of allusions to Jesus' coming death ought not overshadow clear allusions to his future life. Vv 16 and 18 anticipate a post-passion feast in the kingdom, and the promise of v 30a envisions the apostles at Jesus' table in his post-passion kingdom—they will again eat with him. Jesus' death may be on the horizon, but the burden of vv 29-30 is not to draw attention to this fact. Rather, a dominant concern here is to assure the apostles of their reunion with Jesus in his future life. This constitutes a striking departure from the testamentary genre (cf. ch. 5), and as such it reveals a sense in which Jesus stands apart from other testators. The Lukan Jesus makes a journey through death and on to the Father (9:31, 51; 19:12);[116] death is but a stop along this testator's path.

Returning then to the possibility of a covenantal understanding of διατίθημι in v 29, two observations must be made: 1) there is an occurrence of διαθήκη in the literary context of v 29, namely in v 20; 2) there is manuscript evidence for a tradition that inserted διαθήκη in v 29. These points require some elaboration.

In v 20 Jesus says, "This cup which is poured out for you is 'the new covenant' (ἡ καινὴ διαθήκη) in my blood."[117] Could it be that Luke wishes to bring the concept of the new covenant back to center stage in v 29?[118] The strong connection between διατίθημι and διαθήκη in the LXX (as echoed in Acts 3:25) may prompt us to think so. In the vast majority of the LXX usages, however, the noun and the verb occur in the same immed-

[116]See e.g., LaVerdiere, "Passion," 39; Fitzmyer, *Gospel*, 164-71.

[117]See sec. 6.5.3, n. 209 on the text-critical problem of vv 19b-20.

[118]Scholars who see a link in Lukan thought between the new covenant of v 20 and the action described in v 29 include Beasley-Murray, 276; Flew, 40; Gormley, 94; Jeremias, *Words*, 195, n. 3; Liefeld, 1028; Roloff, *Apostolat*, 186; R. Schnackenburg, *Herrschaft*, 121, 175; Schürmann, *Abschiedsrede*, 42, 58. Wiefel (372) maintains that διατίθημι in v 29 has connotations of "Bundesgedanken Israels," though he does not require a link with v 20 (cf. Tresmontant, 621-2). Among those who deny the likelihood of such a connection are Catchpole, "Matthew xxv. 31-46," 376-7; Plummer, 502; Schmahl, 31. Lagrange (551), Lohfink (*Sammlung*, 83) and I. H. Marshall (*Gospel*, 816) see the matter as uncertain.

iate literary context, but here a number of sayings and events separate vv 20 and 29. Thus it is not obvious that there should be a connection between the two verses which gives v 29 a covenantal sense.

It may be recalled that the verb denotes the making of a covenant in certain LXX texts even when the noun is not present (e.g., 1 Chr 19:19; 2 Chr 5:10; 7:18; Ezek 16:30). This observation suggests that διατίθημι became so saturated with covenant thought through its typical association with διαθήκη that it did not require the noun's presence to signal the making of a covenant. Still, in Luke 22:29 we cannot assume διαθήκην to be the implied object of either occurrence of διατίθημι because another object is named in the immediate context (see sec. 7.4.3). Further, even if the idea of the new covenant referred to in v 20 were in Luke's mind at v 29, we would hesitate to translate "I covenant to you a kingship," for to do so is to mix metaphors. To covenant involves the establishing of an oath or agreement, but for a "kingship" to be given we expect a different type of action.[119] "Assign" or "confer" are more appropriate; they fit with an object like "kingship" in a way that "to covenant" would not.

Two manuscript traditions sought to alleviate the lack of a strong link with v 20 by inserting διαθήκην into v 29 as the object of διατίθημι.[120] We can be fairly sure, however, that they do not preserve the original Lukan text because the reading without them is more difficult, and because external evidence for the text as it stands is substantial.

To further assess the possible covenantal understanding of v 29, we must again consider the role of comparative καθώς and its implication of similar actions for both usages of διατίθημι in v 29. We would thus have a covenant that is mediated by Jesus: God covenants with Jesus and Jesus then covenants with the apostles. This is problematic because the idea of a covenant between the Father and Jesus is foreign to Luke-Acts. Moreover, the new covenant described in Jer 31:31-34 does not involve a

[119]To be sure, the establishing and intergenerational transfer of the covenant in Israel is at points loosely connected to the giving of authority (e.g., Gen 17:6, and the role of Moses at Sinai as a ruler), but it would still be odd for βασιλείαν to be the direct object of διατίθημι when it means "to covenant."

[120]Mss. A Q 579 *pc* and sy[h] represent a text tradition that inserts διαθήκην in v 29 after καθώς as the object of διατίθεμαι. Ms. 579 also replaces βασιλείαν with another διαθήκην as the object of the second verb, διέθετο. For v 29 ms. 579 would then read, "I am making a covenant with you as the Father made a covenant with me." This simplifies the grammar of the sentence and makes an explicit connection with v 20, but by so doing implies that it is not original.

mediating action; instead God deals directly with the houses of Judah and Israel.[121]

Thus we conclude the discussion of the action described in v 29 by claiming that Jesus' action is best understood simply as a *conferral,* a bestowing upon or giving to the apostles.[122] The action of the Father in conferring on Jesus is the pattern upon which Jesus' deed is based, and this comparison weighs against testamentary and covenantal understandings of v 29.

7.4.3 The Content of Conferral (vv 29-30)

We may now turn to the matter of the conferral's content or substance: What is it that the Father conferred on Jesus? And what does Jesus confer on the Twelve? Answering the first of these questions is not difficult: βασιλείαν is the object of διέθετο. What is meant by βασιλείαν will require further thought, but in terms of grammar it is clear enough that the Father conferred βασιλείαν on Jesus.

Answering the second question, however, is quite difficult. The two basic possibilities for the direct object of διατίθεμαι are 1) βασιλείαν also, in which case a single noun functions as object of two finite verbs in the same sentence (and διατίθεμαι is separated from its object by a subordinate clause);[123] and 2) the ἵνα clause of v 30a, in which case there are no shared direct objects, but διατίθεμαι is separated from its object clause by yet another word.[124] Neither answer eliminates the rough edges of the text here.[125]

---

[121]Heb 9:15 describes Christ as the "mediator" (μεσίτης) of a new covenant, but this is in the sense that he has brought the new covenant into effect, not that God first covenanted with him, and he in turn covenanted with God's people.

[122]Evans, 800. Kurz ("Luke 22:14-38," 253) sees in v 29 an authority transfer to the apostles (cf. Schürmann's "Vollmachtsübertragung" [*Abschiedsrede*, 42, 47]), but the constraints of comparative καθώς point to a different understanding. A transfer, unlike a conferral, suggests the loss of authority by Jesus (but v 30a) and (so καθώς) the Father.

[123]So Bösen, 137-9; S. Brown, 64; L'Eplattenier, 253; Godet, 298; Gormley, 94; Hauck, *Evangelium*, 265; Hendricksen, 972; Leaney, 270; Lohfink, *Sammlung*, 81; Lull, 301-2; I. H. Marshall, *Gospel*, 816-17; Plummer, 502; Reiling and Swellengrebel, 693; A. Schulz, *Nachfolge*, 123; Schürmann, *Abschiedsrede*, 44; Tannehill, "Study," 201, n. 21; Wellhausen, 124; Wiefel, 372.

[124]So Arndt, 442; Creed, 269 (a shared direct object is awkward); Dawsey, *Voice*, 51; Flew; 40; Geldenhuys, 565; Klostermann, 212; Lagrange, 551; W. Manson, 243-4; W. Pesch, 75; Taylor, *Jesus*, 188; Zahn, 682, n. 58.

[125]I. H. Marshall comments, "Both constructions give the same basic mean-

Regarding the first alternative, though it is unusual for Luke to have two finite verbs share a single direct object, the phenomenon does occur in Luke 14:4, Acts 7:6 and 17:27.[126] There, however, a single pattern (verb- object- καί- verb) is used each time, whereas Luke 22:29 follows a much different pattern (verb- indirect object- comparative clause [with verb- indirect object- subject]- object). Thus the distance from the first verb to its object here is unusually great.

The second alternative with v 30a as an object clause similarly suspends the object of the first verb. It is also difficult because transitive διατίθημι does not seem to fit well with such an object clause. That is, it seems strained to say, "I confer on you, that you may eat and drink ..." without naming some more concrete object that is being conferred. With the object clause διατίθημι takes on an almost intransitive sense, yet elsewhere in the NT and in the LXX it is almost always transitive.[127] The object clause alternative may seem a bit less strained if we were to take ἵνα in v 30a as a substitute for an infinitive[128] and translate, "I confer on you to eat and drink ..." This way the conferring and the thing conferred are brought a little closer together. Nevertheless, this alternative still seems strained in comparison with "I confer kingship on you."

A look at the wider context (i.e., v 30b), however, sheds some light on the grammar of v 29. To be sitting on thrones executing judgment over Israel is to exercise authority.[129] For the apostles to be elevated to this lofty position, they must be authorized by Jesus and assigned by him to their royal thrones. Thus the saying in v 30b fits well with the idea of the apostles being given a share of Jesus' royal authority (βασιλείαν) in v 29. If, however, it is only Jesus who receives βασιλείαν, the sudden elevation of the apostles is surprising and unfounded; he has royal authority but they have only been granted seats at Jesus' banquet table, and dining

ing, since the content of 'rule' is detailed in v. 30, ..." (*Gospel*, 817). While recognizing the closeness of the two options, a key difference is that one makes the apostles possessors of βασιλείαν while the other does not. The possession and use of authority is a central theme in 22:24-30, so it remains important to seek an answer to the direct object question for v 29.

[126]I have attempted here to include all occurrences of this construction in Luke-Acts.

[127]Only 3x in the LXX (87x total) is διατίθημι intransitive (1 Chr 19:19; 2 Chr 7:18; Ezek 16:30), and elsewhere in the NT it is always transitive.

[128]See BAGD, "ἵνα," 377-8.

[129]This is true whether one favors an eschatological or church age interpretation of vv 29-30 (on the question of timing, see sec. 7.4.4 below).

does not carry with it the right to sit on royal thrones. Thus, βασιλείαν is probably the shared direct object of the two verbs in v 29.

It has been suggested that the stylistic unevenness resulting from the direct object problem in v 29 implies multiple sources.[130] That is, if Luke wrote 22:28-30 on his own, or if he passed it on from tradition (assuming a single author for the unit), we might expect a clearer grammatical flow. But if Luke sought to pass on the sacred traditional sayings of Jesus along with his clarifying redactional adaptations and additions, a measure of unevenness at points in the finished product would be natural. The synopsis above shows that v 29 (lines 9-11) is without parallel in Matthew, and it would be hard to imagine Matthew omitting such material if it were original in Q.[131] Thus it seems likely that v 29 has been added or adapted by Luke from an L source, and if that is so, it is possible that v 29 clearly reflects Lukan interests.

Before turning to a discussion of the kingship idea (v 29) along with the other usage of βασιλεία in v 30, we must look more closely at the hinge between vv 29 and 30. Is ἵνα here final (either the stronger "in order that" or the weaker infinitive substitute "to"), epexegetical or consecutive? The consecutive understanding is least probable since it would imply that future eating and drinking were not thought of as intentionally related to the conferral.[132] The final sense is, of course, most common in the NT and in Luke-Acts.[133] Lohfink, however, favors epexegetical ἵνα here and translates v 30a, "*und zwar in dem Sinne, daß* ihr in meiner βασιλεία an meinem Tische eßt und trinkt ..." [134] The term introduces a clause that amplifies and explains the content of the conferral made in v 29.

Since it would perhaps be a bit cryptic to say "I confer kingship" without explanation, and since it is probable that Luke is joining material from different sources at this point and thus creating a need for clarification of the relationship between Jesus' sayings, it is arguable that ἵνα is epexegetical. A final ἵνα would clarify the sense of v 30a—it is the aim of

[130]So Schürmann, *Abschiedsrede*, 45.

[131]So Broer, 150.

[132]The term ἵνα occurs 61x in Luke-Acts, but its use is consecutive only 2x.

[133]Dawsey (*Voice*, 51) argues for final ἵνα in v 30 (so Lull, 301-2; et al.).

[134]Lohfink, *Sammlung*, 81 (cf. n. 214), emphasis original. Similarly A. Schulz, *Nachfolge*, 124. Jeremias (*Sprache*, 291) cites Luke 1:43 in support of ἵνα in 22:30a as non-final. Zerwick (§ 410) claims that in 1:43 ἵνα is epexegetical (so BDF, § 394).

the action in v 29. Epexegetical ἵνα, however, allows light to be shed on both parts—v 30a amplifies and explains v 29.

A final ἵνα would in fact bring added ambiguity to the context. Having assumed the final sense, Lull asks which verb in v 29 it refers back to.[135] That is, does the Father confer kingship on Jesus in order that the apostles may eat and drink, or does Jesus confer kingship on the apostles in order that the apostles may eat and drink? But with epexegetical ἵνα this unclarity disappears; it is naturally the conferral by Jesus on the apostles that is expanded on in v 30a. After all, the apostles are not involved in the Father's conferral upon Jesus, and since the ἵνα clause elaborates on the future experience of the apostles, we may presume that it is spelling out some facet of that which Jesus confers on them. Although final ἵνα of course remains a possibility for v 30a, an appreciation of Luke's editorial needs and skills would tilt the balance in favor of epexegetical ἵνα.

We now turn to βασιλεία. It is βασιλείαν which, ultimately, constitutes the content of conferral, for it is the direct object of both verbs in v 29. The epexegetical ἵνα further implies that the explanatory comments in v 30 aim to flesh out the conferral of βασιλεία. In addition, v 30a describes events that take place ἐν τῇ βασιλείᾳ of Jesus, and v 30b is rich with royal imagery. Thus we must ask some searching questions about βασιλεία, its Lukan usages and its meaning in the present context.[136]

The fact that forty-six of Luke's fifty-four usages of βασιλεία are in the Gospel gives the impression that the term has a strong traditional base (it appears 55x in Matthew and 20x in Mark).[137] There are, however, some unique Lukan redactional tendencies and emphases to be noted.[138] Only Luke connects "the kingdom of God" with verbs of proc-

---

[135]Lull, 301-2.

[136]Citing Luke 6:20 and 12:32, Zahn contends, "Daß die Jünger Jesu in das zukünftige Gottesreich nicht nur als Bürger aufgenommen werden, sondern auch an der königlichen Herrschaft Christi über die Welt als seine Mitherrscher teilnehmen sollen, hat Jesus nicht erst hier gesagt, hier aber doch deutlicher als anderwärts" (682). However, though the disciples are given ἡ βασιλεία in 6:20 and 12:32, there is no mention of their sharing Jesus' authority as co-rulers (contrast 22:29-30).

[137]I. H. Marshall (*Historian*, 89-90, 136) stresses Luke's faithful transmission of traditions concerning the kingdom, though some distinctives are conceded (90, 129). In general, Luke retains Mark's concept of the kingdom as both present and future (136).

lamation, and he does so thirteen times.[139] Luke 12:32 adds to a tradition (see 6:20; 18:16-17) in which the kingdom is something given or possessed (cf. 22:29).[140] Luke also employs spatial metaphors in connection with βασιλεία.[141] Carroll detects a Lukan interest in the composition of the kingdom; specifically, it is the reversal of its composition—the elevation of the lowly and the humiliation of the powerful—which is noted.[142] Winton argues that the "many-sided" Lukan use of kingdom language is itself unique among the Gospels.[143]

The complexity of Luke's portrayal of "the kingdom (of God)" makes it difficult to pinpoint a basic sense for the expression, but it seems appropriate, in general, to emphasize God's rule rather than God's realm.[144] To be sure, both ideas are present in Luke-Acts, but Luke's emphasis on preaching the kingdom seems to make best sense when the kingdom involves the saving action of God and not merely the realm over which he rules (so too with possessing the kingdom). Also in favor of the centrality for Luke of the dynamic rule of God is an emphasis on the kingdom/ kingship of Jesus (see further below)—it is easier to imagine Jesus having a rule subordinate to God's than having a realm within or other than God's realm.

To sharpen this discussion, however, we must zero in on Luke 22:29-30 and examine βασιλεία in its context. Are there significant differ-

---

138Since 21 of Luke's 46 Gospel usages are unparalleled, this may be expected.

139Merk, 204 (texts and verbs are listed); cf. Carroll, 81; Fitzmyer, *Gospel*, 1:154-5; Maddox, 132-3; I. H. Marshall, *Historian*, 129; Völkel, 61; Winton, 153.

140So Carroll, 83 (see also Acts 2:30-36); cf. Nolland, *Luke*, 283; Winton, 153.

141Traditional at 13:28; 14:15; 16:16; 18:24-25; unparalleled at 13:29; 22:16; 23:43 (cf. 22:30) (see Fitzmyer, *Gospel*, 1:156; Winton, 153-4). For Polag (49), being *in* the kingdom is not a spatial or temporal idea, but a reference to a sphere, the "Heilsbereich." This understanding, however, does not seem to fully do justice to contexts which emphasize spatial or temporal features (e.g., 10:9, 11; 13:29; 22:16, 30).

142Carroll, 84-87. Since he does not restrict Luke's concept of "the kingdom" to βασιλεία occurrences (81-2; so Merk, 211), Carroll is able to see a reversal of the kingdom's composition in texts such as Luke 1:51-54 (84-5). An interest in the composition of the kingdom is hardly unique to Luke, but the use of reversal as a way of rearranging its composition does appear to be a distinctive emphasis (cf. sec. 3.5.1 on Luke's reversal of conventional standards for table fellowship).

143Winton, 154. Additional aspects of Luke's complex concept surface in 18:29 (the idea of acting "for the sake of" [ἕνεκεν] the kingdom) and 17:20 (on the "coming" of the kingdom; cf. traditional usages at 11:2; 22:18).

144So I. H. Marshall, *Historian*, 129; cf. Schürmann, *Lukasevangelium*, 330-1; Winton, 154. By contrast, Fitzmyer (*Gospel*, 1:156) sees the balance of emphasis in Luke on spatial "kingdom" rather than on dynamic "kingship."

ences between the term's occurrences in vv 29 and 30a? First, in v 30 the term has the article, but in v 29 it does not. Second, in v 30 one also notes the presence of possessive μου, but in v 29 βασιλείαν is absolute.[145] Third, in v 29 βασιλείαν is that which the apostles are presently given, but in v 30 it is that realm in which the apostles will feast with Jesus.

Regarding the first difference, the effect of making βασιλεία indefinite is said to accent its dynamic quality and thus connote ruling power ("kingship") rather than a realm of rule ("kingdom").[146] Alternatively, however, anarthrous βασιλεία could naturally be translated "a kingdom"; the absence of the article allows for either possibility.[147] Thus we will need to approach the issue from other angles.

Regarding the second difference mentioned above, it may be noted that, despite the fact that the term is absolute, βασιλείαν in v 29 is the possession of Jesus—in past time the Father conferred it on him. Thus this "difference" has no real substance.

Before considering the third difference, it may be noted here that Luke puts some stress on the concept of the kingship of Jesus[148] by introducing it in three contexts without parallel in the Synoptics (1:33; 22:29-30; 23:42).[149] Further, he is the only evangelist to make Jesus the subject of βασιλεύω (1:33),[150] and in his version of the Parable of the Pounds

[145]L'Eplattenier claims that Luke in vv 28-30 echoes 12:32 where βασιλεία is also absolute, and that everywhere else he writes "Royaume *de Dieu*" (253, emphasis original). But this confuses the matter in two ways: 1) only one of the two βασιλεία occurrences in vv 28-30 is absolute; 2) Luke's three unparalleled references to Jesus' kingdom (1:33; 22:29-30; 23:42) are overlooked.

[146]So Bösen, 136, n. 6; Geldenhuys, 565; L. Johnson, *Possessions*, 120; Wellhausen, 124. Bauer (BAGD, "βασιλεία," 134-5, def. 1) sees dynamic rule in v 29.

[147]Though a shift from an indefinite to a definite noun (as in vv 29-30a) is at times merely due to the fact that indefinite nouns become definite when referred to a second time, the language of vv 29-30a requires another explanation (see further below).

[148]Howard, *Das Ego*, 180. Cf. also L'Eplattenier, 253; Fitzmyer, *Gospel*, 2:1419; George, "Royauté," 62, 68-9; Navone, *Themes*, 90; "Banquet," 160-1; Thompson, 260; Tyson, *Death of Jesus*, 131-2; against Dupont, "Trônes," 389; I. H. Marshall, *Historian*, 89-90. To be sure, the motif is not wholly unique to Luke (cf. Matt 2:2; 21:5; Mark 15:2ff).

[149]Bauer (BAGD, "βασιλεία," 134-5, def. 1) and Ellis ("Present," 36) both take βασιλεία in Luke 23:42 as "kingship" rather than "kingdom." This seems odd in light of the spatial nuance of εἰς.

[150]The widely attested tradition of Jesus being called "king of the Jews" is used by Luke as it is by the other evangelists, but no distinctive findings (positive or negative) about a possible Lukan interest in "the kingdom of Jesus" have sur-

(19:11-27), unlike Matthew's, Jesus is allegorically portrayed as a nobleman who journeys to receive "a kingship."[151] In Acts Luke portrays Jesus as the Davidic king (2:30-36), and he expresses the theme of Jesus' messianic identity by using the title "Jesus Christ" ten times, a title not found in Luke's Gospel. Jesus is the one who represented the "consolation of Israel" (Luke 2:25; cf. v 39) and who would "redeem Israel" (24:21). The Lukan "kingdom of Jesus" references may be seen in this light, for they reflect the Jewish hope for a restored Israel in the messianic era.[152] It would be best, however, not to infer that Luke depicts Jesus' kingdom as something separate from "the kingdom of God." Rather, the prevalence in Luke of the phrase "the kingdom of God" (32x in the Gospel) probably forms the appropriate interpretative backdrop for the few references to Jesus' kingdom.[153] Luke thus highlights the closeness of God and Jesus in the the kingdom's operation.[154]

The third apparent difference between the βασιλεία usages in vv 29 and 30 is less tangible than articles and pronouns, but perhaps more important. Jesus confers kingship upon the apostles in the present, but their eating and drinking in his kingdom will come in the future. To time we add place, for while there are no spatial connotations with the usage in v 29, in v 30 Jesus' βασιλεία is where the apostles will eat and drink at Jesus' table. Schürmann states,[155]

> V. 29 und V. 30a ist der Basileia-Begriff unterschiedlich verwendet: V. 29 ist an eine königliche Vollmacht, die als solche Gegenstand einer juridischen Übertragung sein kann, gedacht. V. 30a dagegen ist

faced in this area.

[151]Fitzmyer, *Gospel*, 2:1233.

[152]See further below, this sec. Cf. Klausner, 237-42 (here drawing on biblical texts only); also see G. Moore, 2:323-76 (drawing on biblical and rabbinic sources) on Jewish future hopes and messianic expectations in the NT era (cf. de Lange, 125-36). We may note further that the eschatological expectations present in Lukan kingdom of Jesus contexts (Luke 1:33; 22:30; 23:42) do not conflict with Jewish hopes for national deliverance in the messianic age, for in the first century CE Judaism made no sharp distinction between these expectations (so e.g., G. Moore, 2:323).

[153]The fact that Jesus both anticipates the breaking of his fast in the "kingdom of God" (22:16, 18), and promises a banquet in his own kingdom (v 30) within the boundaries of his Last Supper discourse supports this claim.

[154]So Bösen, 137; Leivestad, 60; K. Schmidt, " βασιλεία," 581 (v 29 highlights this link between Jesus and God); Untergassmair, *Kreuzweg*, 78-9.

[155]Schürmann, *Abschiedsrede*, 46. Similarly S. Brown, 64; Fitzmyer, *Gospel*, 2:1418-19; Geldenhuys, 565; Grundmann, 403; Joüon, 355; I. H. Marshall, *Gospel*, 816; R. Schnackenburg, *Herrschaft*, 51; S. Schulz, 332, n. 66; Wellhausen, 124.

wohl als ein zuständlicher Bereich verstanden, in dem das messianische Mahl lokalisiert vorgestellt ist.

Further, if both usages referred to a realm, the apostles would have a kingdom within Jesus' kingdom, an arrangement that would splinter Jesus' and God's domain and which would seem contrived. Also, it is not defensible that such a division would correspond to twelve domains for the twelve tribes in eschatological Israel, for the βασιλεία given to the apostles in v 29 is singular. More likely is the idea that the apostles are given a responsibility in Jesus' realm. In v 29 βασιλεία would then refer to royal rule, but in v 30a to the realm of king Jesus.

A possible rationale for the emphasis in vv 29-30 on the kingship of Jesus may surface as we glance back to v 27c where Jesus speaks of his presence "in the midst" of the apostles (cf. sec. 6.5.3). In contrast to kings and benefactors (22:25), Jesus rules from the position of servant. The unparalleled expression ἐν μέσῳ ὑμῶν in v 27c may recall 17:21 (ἡ βασιλεία τοῦ θεοῦ ἐντὸς ὑμῶν ἐστιν—also without parallel), where the presence of Jesus and the kingship of God are closely aligned.[156] Indeed, Merk contends that "Die Gegenwart Jesu ist ... konstitutiv für das lukanische Verständnis der βασιλεία τοῦ θεοῦ."[157] If 22:27c connects the presence of Jesus with the kingship of God in this way, and if Jesus presents himself in v 27 as an alternative to ordinary kings, then it is not wholly surprising that sayings on the kingship of Jesus—a rule carried out under the Father's sovereignty (v 29)—should follow.

To better understand the content of conferral we may look into the two images used in v 30 to illustrate or explain βασιλεία. In v 30a Luke uses table imagery to flesh out βασιλεία, and in 30b we have the image of thrones. Both are rich with significance for the meaning of 22:28-30 and 22:24-30 as a whole, and they will be discussed in turn.

First, however, we must briefly consider this mixing of metaphors. Schürmann argues that the linking of v 30a and 30b is not original; a pre-Lukan redactor made the connection.[158] For Beare this unevenness im-

---

[156]That ἐντός is best translated "among, in the midst" rather than "within" is suggested by the fact that Jesus' audience is the Pharisees (Fitzmyer, *Gospel*, 2:1161; against I. H. Marshall, *Gospel*, 655 [Marshall does favor "among," but does so because Luke nowhere else describes the kingdom, unlike the Spirit, as something internal]).

[157]Merk, 216; see also 211-12, 220.

[158]Schürmann, *Abschiedsrede*, 50; cf. Bösen, 135. See further below (and cf.

plies that the Lukan version of Q is secondary to Matthew's,[159] a view that is in line with the above arguments for the more primitive nature of Matt 19:28. If, however, the mixing of table and throne metaphors in Rev 3:20-21 represents a pre-Lukan tradition, there would be a precedent for Luke's joining of table and throne imagery.[160] In any case, it would be appropriate not to overstate the importance of a possible tradition-historical rift in Jesus' sayings when Luke joins them closely in his finished text,[161] nor should it be supposed that table and throne images are without points of similarity.[162]

Turning to the *table* image,[163] the nature of the banquet of v 30a is clarified by the fact that it is in Jesus' kingdom and at Jesus' table; the apostles will dine *with Jesus* in his kingdom in reward for their faithful

n. 18) on Luke's redaction at v 30a.

159Beare, *Matthew*, 400. George (*Études*, 277) claims that the image of the feast fits badly with that of thrones and judgment. Further, there is a tension between the presence (v 29) and future coming (v 30a) of βασιλεία. Both the messianic feast and the kingship of Jesus, however, are Lukan preferences, so the insertion of v 30a is probably Luke's doing (ibid.; Kollmann, *Mahl*, 223-4; against Broer, 150).

160Establishing a Luke-John link here is very difficult: What "direction" would the traditions have traveled? How important would such a link be for an interpretation of Luke or Revelation? The connection of table and thrones in Rev 3:20-21 may not be a close one since the promise of thrones (v 21) is part of the standard closing section of the seven letters (2:1-3:22) spoken regarding ὁ νικῶν (2:7, 11, 17, 26; 3:5, 12, 21), but the offer to enter and eat with the one who opens the door to Jesus (3:20) concludes the body of the letter to Laodicea. While it is true that certain of the "he who conquers" sections of the seven letters seem to be crafted to fit their respective letter bodies (e.g., esp. 3:4-5; see also 2:11, 17), one notes that there is nothing about ruling or thrones in the letter to Laodicea (3:14-22). Although this latter point may reinforce the idea that thrones and the meal image are linked for the author of Revelation, it is noteworthy that another of the "he who conquers" sections includes the promise of authority (2:26-27), though again the idea is not anticipated in the body of the letter. This may imply that the promise of authority functioned as a general form of reward, and that the table-throne connection of 3:20-21 is not representative of a thematic unity.

161For Bösen (135-7), both table and thrones illustrate the rule given in v 29 (the apostles will rule while they dine). Although this merging of the images gives a plausible explanation of Luke's finished text, it may not adequately account for the tension of logic the mixed metaphors present.

162Table and throne, when seen against the backdrop of ancient patterns of authority and subordination as well as banquet customs, are as close to each other as are honor and power (cf. sec. 2.2 and ch. 3). Indeed, Luke 22:25-27 reveals close connections between positions of power and the privileged status of diners (both are aligned with Position A [cf. sec. 6.3]).

163Cf. ch. 3 on table motifs as a background for Luke 22:24-30.

perseverance *with Jesus* during his trials. Guillaume maintains, "Le repas dans le royaume est ... comme la prolongation et le renouvellement éternel du dernier repas de Jésus avec les siens; comme pour ce dernier repas, les Douze se retrouveront *autour de Jésus* «à sa table en son royaume», à une place de choix."[164] So union with Jesus continues to be a feature of the text at hand (cf. v 28, and v 27), though vv 29-30 bring a crucial change of venue and atmosphere.[165]

The nature of the feast anticipated in v 30a is clarified somewhat by the repetition from v 21 of the phrase ἐπὶ τῆς τραπέζης. With reference to this phrase Leaney argues, "For Luke the present table has a great significance as the forerunner or type of the table at the Messianic Banquet which is to inaugurate the kingdom."[166] Indeed, for Luke, as in the Passover context (cf. secs. 3.3 and 3.5.1), the table is an image of the outworking of salvation in the successive stages of history (see also sec. 9.3).

Since it is not ordinarily thought that the coming banquet in the kingdom is reserved for the Twelve alone, questions have arisen about v 30a and its role in vv 28-30. Schürmann suggests that an effect of its inclusion (by a pre-Lukan editor) may have been to give the surrounding context the impression of a wider field of application and thus eliminate the restriction of the promise in v 30b to the apostles alone.[167] We have seen that openness and not exclusiveness characterizes the Lukan Jesus' table relations (sec. 3.5.1). Nonetheless, the fact that the Lukan Jesus

[164]Guillaume, 149, emphasis added.

[165]Much as Jesus' call to service and his commendation of perseverance in trials (vv 25-28) lead into an elevation to seats of honor in Jesus' company at his coming royal banquet (vv 29-30), so also a form of fellowship with Jesus follows the condescension of welcoming children (cf. sec. 2.4.2) and constitutes the upward reversal movement in 9:48 ("receiving" the child involves "receiving" Jesus) (cf. sec. 4.5.1).

[166]Leaney, *Gospel*, 270; cf. Bösen, 76, 134; Guillaume, 146-9. The banquet of v 30a represents the fulfillment of the feast anticipated by Jesus at the Last Supper (vv 16, 18).

[167]Schürmann, *Abschiedsrede*, 59. The impulse to widen the application of vv 28-30 may also account for the Lukan omission of δώδεκα in v 30b (52), though a desire to avoid depicting a throne for the betrayer (vv 21-23) is more likely (51-2). Schmid observes (330) that elsewhere in Luke (and the Synoptics) the heavenly banquet is promised to all the elect and not just to the Twelve (e.g., Luke 13:29; 14:15-24). Also favoring a wider application for v 30a than the Twelve alone are Beasley-Murray, 277; Godet, 298-9; Horbury, 524 (the Lukan text [diff. Matt] shows generalizing of the Phylarchs and patristic generalizing of the apostles); I. H. Marshall, *Gospel*, 814; Senior, 73.

elsewhere offers table fellowship to disciples in general and not only to the Twelve does not make it necessary to have the wider group in view at every mention of a future banquet (see further below on the scope of the promise in v 30b).[168]

There is a problem of logic with the (probably secondary) connection between the conferral of kingship (v 29) and the banquet at Jesus' table (v 30a). Creed objects that "to dine at a king's table is not a sign of sharing his authority."[169] This problem is more acute with a final ἵνα in v 30a, but it remains with epexegetical ἵνα nonetheless. Why does one need kingship to feast with Jesus? To be sure, dining imagery is combined with kingdom language elsewhere in Luke (13:29; 14:15; 22:16, 18), and dining at the king's table is an OT motif (e.g., 2 Sam 9:7-13; 1 Kgs 2:7; 2 Kgs 25:29; Jer 52:32-33) (cf. sec. 3.3). But even if it is necessary to have royal authorization to share in a king's banquet, that is far from being granted royal ruling power as the apostles are in Luke 22:29.

It seems likely that this tension is owing to Luke's joining of v 30a to v 29, sayings probably drawn from separate contexts or distinct sources (other than Q).[170] While sitting on thrones to rule Israel is an act that would fit well with the conferral of kingly authority, it is hard to imagine that Luke would break up such a unity if vv 29, 30b stood together in the tradition(s) he received. Thus it appears that v 29 is brought to the context by Luke. And since v 30a is without parallel in Matthew and includes typical Lukan motifs of table imagery[171] and the kingship of Jesus, we may be inclined to attribute its inclusion to Luke as well.[172] This editorial activity would then account for the various signs of unevenness around and between vv 29 and 30a.

---

[168]Guillaume's view (149) that the apostles will have choice seats at a banquet nonetheless attended by many other guests seems to be a reasonable way of interpreting the broader Lukan motif of the eschatological supper.

[169]Creed, *Luke*, 269; cf. Loisy, 517-8; R. Schnackenburg, *Herrschaft*, 121.

[170]That vv 29-30a are to some extent rooted in source material seems to be implied by the grammatical difficulties they present (see above on the direct object difficulty, the sense of ἵνα, and here on difficulty of authority as a basis for dining; and see below on the difficulty of the change of verb mood in v 30b). That vv 29 and 30a each come from different sources or contexts seems to be implied by the unevenness of the seam between them (W. Pesch [74-5] argues that 22:29-30a was originally a single, independent logion, yet he still observes that the construction of the text is unclear).

[171]Perhaps 22:16 and 18 prompt Luke's inclusion of the banquet promise (v 30a) in the Last Supper discourse.

[172]Cf. n. 159 above.

One may still wonder why Luke did not place the banquet promise after the thrones saying. Although this is a very puzzling feature of the text, it may be that Luke's placement of the banquet saying is to prevent the reader from supposing that the apostles will possess *all* authority in the coming kingdom. V 30a reminds one that Jesus is the king,[173] and it suggests that the conferral of kingly power in v 29 amounts not so much to a transfer of authority as to a sharing of authority. Placing v 30a after the thrones saying would correct an inflated idea of the apostles' authority, but placing it before the saying prevents the misunderstanding in the first place. In addition, we have seen in vv 24-30 an emphasis on the union of Jesus and the apostles, and the existing placement of the banquet promise may give emphasis to such relational aspects.

We now turn to an examination of the *throne* image in v 30b.[174] Although Matthew's δώδεκα before "thrones" is without parallel in Luke, there is a text tradition that inserts the term there.[175] This reading, however, is quite probably a later interpolation from Matthew (or Q). If the omission were original in Luke, there could be more than one reason for it. Luke may have omitted the second "twelve" in v 30b for stylistic reasons. Cadbury observes that Luke often replaces a repeated noun with a pronoun,[176] or merely eliminates the doubling.[177] The motivation that "twelve" is omitted to widen the application of the text (cf. above) has more difficulties, for the idea of judging/ ruling becomes distorted when access to thrones is not significantly limited. It is most likely that Luke has dropped δώδεκα because he seeks to avoid designating a throne for Judas whose act of betrayal was just predicted (vv 21-22).[178] Since Matt

173Thus an instance of Luke's christological table revelation (cf. sec. 3.5.1).

174Elsewhere Luke also portrays the granting of authority as a reward (12:43-44; 19:17, 19). A. Schulz (*Nachfolge*, 124) notes that ruling over God's people is sometimes seen as a reward in Jewish theology. Enthronement imagery is common in apocalyptic texts (e.g., Dan 7:9-10; Matt 25:31; Rev 3:21; 20:4-5; *T. Job* 33), an observation that may favor an eschatological interpretation of Luke 22:29-30 (see sec. 7.4.4).

175Mss. include $\aleph^2$ D (f^{13}) 892^{mg} *al* it $sy^{s.c.h^{**}}$ bo^{ms}.

176This happens 12x diff. Mark and 1x diff Matt (Cadbury, *Style*, 83-5). Ernst (*Evangelium*, 597-8) sees stylistic improvement as the simplest explanation for Luke's omission of "twelve" here.

177Cadbury (*Style*, 83ff) cites 23x diff. Mark and 6x diff. Matt.

178So Fitzmyer, *Gospel*, 2:1419; Hauck, 265; Klostermann, 212; Lagrange, 552; Loisy, 518; Schmahl, 32; Schmid, 331; S. Schulz, 332; Schürmann, *Abschiedsrede*, 51-2; Theisohn, 166; Trautmann, 196; Wiefel, 372; et al.

19:28 is in a different context, Matthew faces no corresponding tension. It may be presumed, however, that Luke's text still implies twelve thrones to match the "twelve tribes of Israel."[179]

Luke's grammar has again come under fire at v 30b for the sudden shift of tense and mood. The verbs of v 30a which fill out the ἵνα clause are present subjunctive, but in v 30b we have future indicative καθήσεσθε. It seems probable that this shift of mood and tense signals the close of the v 30a insertion[180] just as the difficult notion of receiving authority to dine drew attention to that insertion initially. It is possible that this mood and tense shift is merely Luke's way of freeing himself from ἵνα so as to avoid writing an overly long sentence,[181] but considering the mixed metaphors (v 30a-b) and the shift from a present (v 29) to future (v 30a) sense for βασιλεία, the more probable explanation is that Lukan conflation of distinct traditions accounts for a certain unevenness in the text.

Next we focus on the nature of the thrones in v 30b. In light of the context (vv 29-30 and beyond), and considering the possibilities for κρίνοντες, what type of actions are the apostles expected to perform upon their thrones? Are they thrones upon which judges sit to pass sentence, or upon which rulers sit to govern their subjects?[182] Further, is it appropriate to try to separate judging and ruling in this way?

The quest to understand the apostles' responsibility on their thrones will be approached first from the perspective of the text's wider literary backdrop. Here Daniel 7 may be taken into account.[183] The similarities of this passage to the present text include the following: Daniel also speaks of a plurality of thrones (7:9); the giving of the βασιλεία to the Son of man

[179]So the necessity to replace Judas (Acts 1:12-26).

[180]Dupont ("Trônes," 360), I. H. Marshall (*Gospel*, 817-8) and Sellew (86) contend that the mood change signals a seam of traditions. Zerwick observes, however, that ἵνα with the future indicative has precedent in Hellenistic Greek (§ 340; so too BAGD, "ἵνα," 377, def. I. 2; see Acts 21:24).

[181]Similarly Lagrange, 552; Reiling and Swellengrebel, 694. Lull (302) sees v 30b as syntactically unrelated to the ἵνα clause of v 30a, but rather to v 29a (Jesus' conferral on the apostles). V 29b then is the basis for the promise of v 30a. The two verses thus exhibit a chiastic structure.

[182]The fact that Luke uses θρόνων rather than βῆματων is not a deciding factor since a forensic image is possible for θρόνος (so Dan 7:9-10; Matt 25:31-46; Rev 20:11-15 [though vv 4-5]) (cf. BAGD, "θρόνος," 364; Schmitz, 162).

[183]The possible relation of Luke 22:30b to Daniel 7 is discussed by Dupont, "Trônes," 382-6; Gerhardsson, 128; Jeremias, *Theology*, 265; Lindars, *Son of Man*, 126; Quesnell, 65; Schweizer, *Matthew*, 389. Evans (800) assumes the imagery of v 30b is from Daniel 7.

by the Ancient of Days (v 14) bears some resemblance to the Father's conferral of βασιλεία on Jesus; there is also a giving of βασιλεία to the saints (vv 18, 27).

The strength of this parallel with Luke 22:30b depends on the interpretation of Daniel's "Son of man" (7:13). If this expression is taken to refer to an individual,[184] then οἱ θρόνοι in 7:9 probably stands for two thrones only, one each for the Ancient of Days and the Son of man.[185] Although the giving of βασιλεία to the saints (vv 18, 27) could imply additional thrones, this act is removed from the tribunal scene, so it is natural to suppose that only two thrones are in view. Thus, given an individual Son of man, the parallel in Dan 7 does not offer a close precedent for the twelve thrones implied in Luke 22:30.

If, however, one reconciles the giving of βασιλεία to the "Son of man" (v 14) as well as to the "saints" (v 18) by suggesting that the former may be a representative of or even identical to the latter, other possibilities surface.[186] It is beyond the scope of the present work fully to address this interpretative crux in Daniel, but a few comments may nonetheless be useful. The idea that "Son of man" in Dan 7 is a title for a corporate or representative figure has the merit of making sense of giving "kingship" to two parties—in some sense the two are one. Further, the fact that both the Son of man and the saints receive everlasting βασιλεία (vv 14, 18, 27) brings the two parties yet closer together. Perhaps the greatest obstacle to a significant parallel between a corporate Son of man in Dan 7 and our text would be the lack of an intermediate figure in Daniel's vision corresponding to Jesus in Luke 22:29. A difficulty with either a corporate or representative Son of man in Daniel 7 as a background for our text is that Dan 7:14 associates the giving of βασιλεία to the Son of man with the tribunal itself,[187] whereas in Luke the intermediate figure had received βασιλεία in past time and presently confers on the apostles.

[184]Although there were various interpretations of Daniel's Son of man in the NT era, the drift of messianic hope was then in favor of an individual figure (Caragounis, 143-4; cf. Ferch, 9; Klausner, 520-5), so the idea of a corporate Son of man would have been in decline (cf. Montgomery, 323).

[185]Dan 7:9d refers explicitly the throne of the Ancient of Days, and the close connection of the conferral of authority on the Son of man in v 14 with the court scene described in vv 9-10 suggests a second throne for him.

[186]Claiming that "Son of man" is a corporate title for Israel are Klausner, 229; Montgomery, 323-4; Porteous, 111; against Caragounis, 74, 248-50; Ferch, 176-9.

[187]ἐδόθη corresponds to past time from the narrator's perspective, but its action is contemporaneous with the end-time scenario (so ἤρχετο in v 13).

In short, then, whether the Son of man of Dan 7 may have been seen by Luke as an individual, corporate or representative figure, the parallel with 22:29-30 is not particularly strong. To be sure, it is quite possible that Luke is influenced in some manner by the imagery and language of Dan 7, but a close connection is unlikely.[188] If Luke does depend on the Dan 7 background, this would support an eschatological time frame and an ongoing form of judging/ ruling (as opposed to a momentary passing of sentence) for 22:30b.[189]

By focusing on the Lukan context again, we may be able more clearly to define the purpose of the thrones in v 30b. The banquet of v 30a is said to take place in Jesus' "kingdom," and that description explicates in some sense the conferring of "kingship" in v 29. Vv 29-30a thus set the scene with images of royal rule and privileges in the royal realm. When we come to "thrones" in v 30b, then, it is more natural to envision thrones of kingly rule than judgment seats in a "court of law." This is not to imply that kings did not fulfill judicial functions (see further below) or that judging and ruling are not closely related activities (cf. sec. 2.3), but only to make the basic observation that v 30b is likely to lay more emphasis on the responsibility of the apostles to rule over the twelve tribes than to pass sentence upon them.

We may now focus our attention more closely on the participle κρίνοντες. Occurrences of κρίνω in the Synoptics (Matt 6x, Mark 0x, Luke 6x) describe the actions of the apostles only at Matt 19:28 par. Luke 22:30. In Acts the term is used three times for the action of the apostles and elders at the Jerusalem Council (15:19; 16:4; 21:25) where it refers to the delivering of a verdict. Apart from Matt 19:28 par. Luke 22:30, the verb is used in the Synoptics and Acts for a future action only when God is the subject. Most importantly, in the Synoptics and Acts the verb usually

[188]Casey (202) is doubtful of any Lukan use of Dan 7. We may add that "Son of man" in Matt 19:28 (line 17) perhaps makes a stronger link to Dan 7, though the probability that this is Matthew's addition means that little can be made of its absence in Luke.

[189]So the implications of an "everlasting" possession of βασιλεία (Dan 7:14, 18, 27). Fitzmyer (*Gospel*, 2:1419) points to Ps 121(122):4-5 as another possible LXX text echoed by Luke (cf. Schmahl, 34-5). There again we have plural "thrones," the thrones are for judgment (θρόνοι εἰς κρίσιν), and there is a reference to the "tribes of the Lord." But there is no mention of those who sit on these thrones, nor of the one(s) judged. And there is no conferral of authority to judge. As with Daniel 7, it is possible that shadows of this passage lie behind our text, but the links do not suggest a definite or direct influence.

involves delivering a judgment or has the technical sense "to decide," but it never means "to rule, govern."[190]

So NT usage supports the meaning "to pass sentence," but the Lukan context (i.e., vv 29-30) favors the broader idea "to rule, govern." A look at uses of κρίνω outside the NT may help us get beyond this impasse. In the LXX κρίνω frequently translates שָׁפַט emphasizing the governing action of the judges (cf. sec. 2.3.1).[191] Although this nuance is absent in the NT, its prominence in the OT would surely have been known to one as well acquainted with the LXX as Luke was. Such a finding opens up the possibility that v 30b depends upon the model of OT judges, a possibility that correlates with Luke's OT echo in "the twelve tribes of Israel."[192]

It is conceivable, however, that Luke's κρίνω reflects not so much the governing function of OT judges as the judicial function of OT kings (e.g., see 2 Kgdms 15:1-6; 3 Kgdms 3:16-28). If this were so, it would be primarily the delivering of a judgment which the Lukan text implies. But it is preferred not to exclude the broader idea of ruling for two reasons: 1) Although Jewish kings are seen performing judicial duties on occasion, the ruling king is the dominant OT model of royalty (legal proceedings would be one of many aspects of the larger responsibility to rule). 2) In Judges it is stressed that God raises up the governing judges (e.g., 3:9, 15; 6:11-18; cf. sec. 2.3.1), a pattern that resembles the conferral of kingship from the Father and Jesus to the apostles (Luke 22:29).[193]

---

[190]Dupont ("Trônes," 371-2) makes the same claim for all 115 usages of κρίνω in the NT.

[191]E.g., Judg 3:10; 10:1-2; 12:7; 15:20; 16:31. κρίνω can also translate שָׁפַט with the meaning "pass sentence" (e.g., Gen 16:5; 31:53; Exod 5:21; Judg 11:27; 2 Kgdms 18:19; Ps 7:8). Note also Wis 3:8 where synonymous parallelism likens future κρινοῦσιν and κρατήσουσι: "they shall judge" is explained by "they shall have dominion." Further, the fact that the Lord "shall reign" (βασιλεύσει, also v 8) favors "rule" over "judge" for κρίνω.

[192]Many interpreters favor the view that governing judges are in view in Luke 22:30b: Arndt, 443; Bammel, "Das Ende," 46; Caird, 240; Danker, *Jesus*, 351; W. D. Davies, 363; Fitzmyer, *Gospel*, 2:1419; Geldenhuys, 565; Gundry, 393; Joüon, 355; Leaney, *Gospel*, 270; Léon-Dufour, "Testament," 276; Navone, *Themes*, 25; Schmahl, 35; Schmid, 330; G. Schneider, *Evangelium*, 2:451; Tannehill, "Study," 201, and *Unity*, 270, n. 120; W. Pesch, 74. Seeing a passing of sentence are Boring, 178; Dupont, "Trônes," 371-2; A. Schulz, *Nachfolge*, 122. See further Jervell (*Luke*, 79, n. 26) for additional perspectives.

[193]To be sure, OT monarchy is not wholly outside of divine approval and involvement (e.g., 2 Sam 2:1-4), but the motif in Judges of divine initiative is noteworthy.

To clarify the sense of the action in view in v 30b, it is useful also to note whom the apostles will be "judging/ ruling." In light of Luke's understanding of and hopes for "the twelve tribes of Israel" (see below, this sec.), v 30b cannot be thought of as involving some sort of punitive passing of sentence. Still, Lukan and NT usages of κρίνω may prompt us to retain a forensic element here. Ultimately, however, it does not seem necessary to choose ruling or judging to the exclusion of the other,[194] even though the prevalence of βασιλεία in the context of v 30b (vv 29, 30a; cf. vv 16, 18) may tilt the balance toward the kingly model with its predominant broad idea of ruling.

We may now step back from vv 29-30 and note the "distance" the apostles have come. In vv 25-27 Jesus called them to adopt the lowly and despised role of domestic servants (cf. secs. 2.4.3 and 6.5), and in v 28 they were commended for their loyalty to Jesus in adversity. Now, however, the narrative describes their dramatic elevation to seats of privilege and power. The magnitude of the reversal is not to be overlooked.[195]

Having discussed the nature of the action the apostles are to perform on their thrones, we now focus on that group they are to rule. What is Luke's understanding of "the twelve tribes of Israel"? Is there any reason to suspect that it denotes something other than the Jewish people, Israel of the OT? Some see in "the twelve tribes of Israel" a symbol for the Christian community,[196] but can this non-Jewish interpretation find support in Luke-Acts? We will approach this question by considering verbal evidence and the wider Lukan view of Israel.

There is no usage of Ἰσραήλ or Ἰσραηλίτης in the Synoptics or Acts which does not refer to the Jewish people/ nation, the Israel of the OT.[197]

---

[194]For Wiefel (372) v 30b speaks of "herrschendes und richtendes Thronen."

[195]Recall from ch. 2 both the distance between top and bottom of the prevailing patterns of authority and subordination, and the sense in which social and/ or political forces kept a person in his/ her place.

[196]E.g., S. Brown, 64; Danker, *Jesus*, 350-1; Ellis, *Gospel*, 255; I. H. Marshall, *Gospel*, 818; Navone, *Themes*, 25; Sweetland, "Lord's Supper," 25; Tannehill, "Study," 201. Others see in "the twelve tribes of Israel" a reference to a renewed, ideal, or true Israel (an Israel related to yet in some way different from the OT Jewish people), but define its makeup less precisely (e.g., Caird, *Luke*, 240; George, "Royauté," 62; Guillaume, 149; Lohfink, *Sammlung*, 79).

[197]In Luke-Acts 26 out of 26 Ἰσραήλ usages (omitting 22:30) and 5 out of 5 Ἰσραηλίτης usages in Luke-Acts point to literal Israel, the Jewish people (cf. A. Wainwright, 76).

Acts contains one reference to the "twelve tribes" (26:7) and another to the "twelve patriarchs" (7:8), and both have literal Israel in view. The use of the word "Jew" in Luke-Acts is "a conundrum" according to Tiede because of its various positive or negative uses on the lips of speakers, in narration, etc.,[198] but there is no doubt that this term also has the literal Jewish people (or some sub-section of them) in view. Thus it does not appear that Luke attaches a new Christian meaning to the various terms and phrases that have traditionally been used to describe Israel of old (contrast Gal 6:16).

By looking at Luke's view of Israel more broadly (i.e., within the wider scope of the salvation-historical framework of Luke-Acts), it appears again that Luke does not envision a new Christian Israel separate from Israel of old. The infancy narrative sets the stage with hopes concerning Jesus that are expressed in the language of scriptural promises to Israel:[199] Simeon was "looking for the consolation of Israel" (2:25) and Anna the prophetess spoke of the child Jesus to "all who were looking for the redemption of Jerusalem" (v 38). At the end of the Gospel, Cleopas and his companion declare that they had hoped Jesus was "the one to redeem Israel" (24:21; cf. vv 27, 44). The disciples ask the risen Jesus if he will then "restore the kingdom to Israel" (Acts 1:6).[200] Zacchaeus, in the hour of his salvation, is described as a "son of Abraham" (Luke 19:9; cf. 13:16).[201] The need to describe at length the replacing of Judas (Acts 1:15-26) reveals Luke's concern to show the reconstituted circle of twelve apostles as corresponding to the twelve tribes of Israel.[202] Paul's defense before Agrippa is framed in terms of his Jewish background (26:4-5), and he claims to be on trial because of his "hope in the promise made by God to our fathers" (vv 6-7).

Further, it is arguable that the Gentile mission in Acts is not presented so as to indicate that God has given up on the Jews.[203] Despite a

---

[198]Tiede, "Glory," 148, n. 18; cf. Fitzmyer, *Theologian*, 188-9.

[199]Tiede, "Glory," 146.

[200]Jervell (*Luke*, 82) claims that Acts 15:16ff makes reference to such a restoration. Also see Tiede, "Glory," 146. Acts 1:7 corrects the apostles' misunderstandings regarding the timing, not the sphere of the restoration (i.e., Israel).

[201]Fitzmyer (*Gospel*, 1:188) observes that Luke presents Abraham not as a prototype of Christian believers but as the Father of the Jews (Luke 1:73; 16:24-31; Acts 7:2) (so Dahl, "Abraham," 140, 147).

[202]Fitzmyer, *Theologian*, 188; cf. A. Clark, 67. Horbury (503-4, 522) discusses the possibility that the twelve princes of Num 1:4-16, being alive in the first century mind as a group of rulers comparable with the patriarchs, may have influenced the development of the concept of the Twelve as a governing body.

significant measure of Jewish rejection, there remain large islands of Jewish acceptance which jut out amidst the opposition.[204] Paul's act of turning to the Gentiles does not imply the abandonment of the Jews, nor does 28:28 describe the final failure of Paul's mission to Israel.[205] The Gentile mission is in fact rooted in ancient promises made to Israel:[206]

> Gentile Christians are associated with Jewish Christians and find with them the same salvation "through the grace of our Lord Jesus" (15:11), but they find it not because "the law and the prophets" have been abrogated and are no longer normative, but because the law and the prophets themselves have provided for their share in the very promises made to the fathers of old.... Thus, the very law and the prophets that remain normative for the repentant Israel provide for the association of Gentile converts to it as the one reconstituted people of God.

Thus, in light of Luke's literal sense for Ἰσραήλ and related terms, and the Lukan salvation-historical framework which sees the movement spearheaded by Jesus and the apostles as a single development within Judaism, it is best to take "the twelve tribes of Israel" in Luke 22:30b as referring to the Israel of the OT, the people of God. Luke does not envision a new Israel which becomes marked off from Israel of old, but an Israel which has returned to its roots and whose Messiah has come welcoming all who would repent and believe.[207]

---

[203]Against Haenchen ("History," 278), who states, "Luke has written the Jews off" (similarly J. Sanders, 63). Tannehill ("Israel," 80-1) similarly sees in the Lukan portrayal a negative end for Israel, but (against Sanders) this grieves Luke—it is a tragedy. For George ("Israël," 523-5), Luke the Gentile is uninterested in the fate of Israel (now one more pagan nation among others); the mission to the Gentiles is his dominant concern. By contrast, Chance maintains that Luke still has hope for Israel (141).

[204]Brawley, 156 (see e.g., Acts 2:41; 4:4; 5:14; 6:1, 7; 9:42; 12:24; 13:43; 14:1; 17:12; 21:20). Cf. Jervell, *Luke*, 44-9.

[205]Nolland claims that Acts 13:46; 18:6 and 28:28 do not imply that Jewish rejection opens the way for the Gentile mission (*Luke's Readers*, 90-128; so Dahl, "Abraham," 151). He persuasively argues that the often overlooked καί in 28:28 is adverbial: "[the Gentiles] also will hear" (107; against J. Sanders, 81; Tannehill, "Rejection," 98 [καί is left untranslated]). Nolland summarizes, "As a matter of timing it is the rise of Jewish opposition which precipitates concerted Gentile mission in each city.... However, the plan of God is that in each place Jews first and also Gentiles should be brought to faith in Christ, so that he might be 'revelation to the Gentiles' and 'glory ... to Israel'" (128; see also 106-18 on Luke's pattern of a twin concern that both Jews and Gentiles be reached with the gospel).

[206]Fitzmyer, *Theologian*, 194-5; cf. George, "Israël," 523; Jervell, *Luke*, 43; L. Johnson, *Possessions*, 123; Weatherly, 117.

7.4.4 The Timing of Conferral (vv 29-30)

In discussing the timing of conferral we must first distinguish the time of the initial act from the time when that conferral is completely fulfilled, its privileges and responsibilities being fully realized by the apostles. To determine the timing of the initial act, we need only return to present tense διατίθεμαι in v 29. It is now, at the Last Supper and during Jesus' speech, that Jesus confers kingship upon the apostles.[208] That conclusion is obvious, but it does little to specify the time of the conferral's full realization.

Subjunctive ἔσθητε and πίνητε clearly anticipate a *future* meal at Jesus' table in his kingdom. After all, it would be senseless for Jesus to confer upon the apostles the right to do at present what they were already doing, namely dining with him. Moreover, καθήσεσθε necessarily anticipates a future realization, and the timing for the present participle κρίνοντες is contemporaneous with καθήσεσθε. So the present conferral must await a future fulfillment.[209] What must still be determined, however, is *how far in the future* the conferral's fulfillment was to be. Does Luke 22:30 describe the privileges and responsibilities of the apostles as leaders in the church age, in the eschaton,[210] or in both eras?[211] The line

---

[207]Dahl, "Abraham," 151. Salmon (79-81) insightfully points to a number of features of Luke-Acts which imply a Jewish orientation for the author (e.g., many distinctions among Jews, much attention to Torah observance, an idea of Gentile mission as outward looking, references to the Christian movement as a sect within Judaism), but it is doubtful that she is able to establish the point that "Luke perceives himself to be a Jew" (79).

[208]S. Brown makes much of present tense διατίθεμαι as favoring a non-eschatological interpretation of vv 29-30 (64; similarly Neyrey, 27; Tannehill, "Study," 201; against G. Schneider, *Evangelium*, 2:451; Voss, 108), but overlooks the important implications of verb moods and tenses in v 30. V 29 is made to stand alone as though it had no important links with v 30.

[209]So Schürmann, *Ursprung*, 125, and *Abschiedsrede*, 41, 46-7, 51; George, *Études*, 277; against S. Brown, 64, n. 247.

[210]In the present study, "eschaton" and "eschatological" are taken to correspond to the future age of the consummation, the time of the return of the Son of man (12:40; 21:27), an era in which there is a radically new world order.

[211]This question is placed by Kaestli (59), Matera (*Passion*, 165), and many others. Those favoring a church age focus in vv 29-30 include Bossuyt and Radermakers, 476-7; S. Brown, 64; L. Johnson, *Possessions*, 120, and "Kingship," 152; Karris, *Gospel*, 716; Neyrey, 27-8; G. Schneider, *Theologe*, 84; Sweetland, "Lord's Supper," 25; Wanke, 65. Arguing for an eschatological focus are Bösen, 134-9;

of thought one discerns in vv 24-30 is deeply affected by one's decision here on the timing of the conferral's fulfillment.

To address this matter it may be noted first that the timing in Luke's version is less explicit than it is in Matt 19:28. Not only does Matthew's ἐν τῇ παλιγγενεσίᾳ ("in the restoration") more explicitly look to the age to come than Luke's ἐν τῇ βασιλείᾳ, but Matthew's unparalleled clause "when the Son of man sits on the throne of his glory" definitely has an eschatological sense (cf. Matt 25:31). The timing of the apostles' sitting and judging is then connected to the eschatological enthronement of the Son of man by "you also" and the repetition of the verb "sit."

The lack of these features in Luke 22:29-30 has led some interpreters to suppose that Luke is here signaling a deliberate departure from the eschatological sense of the original logion to shift its focus to the church age.[212] Having argued above in favor of the generally more primitive nature of Matthew, the absence of these eschatological elements in Luke does give us pause. What may have motivated this type of redaction? A careful reexamination of Matt 19:28 and Luke 22:28-30 may help address this problem.

Luke's lack of the previously mentioned eschatological features in Q (so Matt 19:28) may be explained as follows. The saying about the coming of the Son of man (lines 16-18) was, in all likelihood, introduced by Matthew to explain the difficult traditional expression ἐν τῇ παλιγγενεσίᾳ, and thus was not available to Luke. With the words "you also" (line 21) Matthew then connected the saying about the Son of man to the

---

Degenhardt, 214; Esler, 192-3; Finegan, 14; Ernst, *Evangelium*, 596; Evans, 801; George, *Études*, 277; Godet, 298-9; Gormley, 94; Grundmann, 403; Guillaume, 149; Jeremias, *Theology*, 234, 249, 251, 274; Jervell, *Luke*, 79; Kaestli, 59; Kollmann, *Mahl*, 161, 224; Kremer, 215; K. Kuhn, "Lord's Supper," 70, n. 19; Léon-Dufour, "Testament," 276, and "Récits," 1476; Lohfink, *Sammlung*, 81-2; Lull, 301-3; Mánek, "Umwandlung," 64; Mearns, 195; Muhlack, 111; Navone, *Themes*, 26-7; W. Pesch, 75; Schmid, 330; R. Schnackenburg, *Herrschaft*, 61, 188, and "Abschiedsreden," 68; A. Schulz, *Nachfolge*, 124; Schürmann, *Abschiedsrede*, 62, and "Jüngerkreis," 22; Talbert, *Reading Luke*, 210; Taylor, *Jesus*, 189; Tiede, *Luke*, 385; Trautmann, 195; Wiefel, 371-2. Among those who see both church age and eschaton are Chance, 78-9; Kurz, *Farewell*, 64-7; Loisy, 518; Matera, *Passion*, 165; Senior, 74-6.

[212]So e.g., S. Brown, 64; Howard, *Das Ego*, 181; S. Schulz, 331. Dupont bases the timing of the thrones saying on Matthew's explicitly eschatological version (and the eschatological sense of the text's supposed root in Daniel 7), and does not ask the question whether Lukan redaction reveals a departure from that meaning ("Trônes," 364-8).

thrones logion. The omission by Luke of ἐν τῇ παλιγγενεσίᾳ (i.e., its replacement with ἐν τῇ βασιλείᾳ) is probably due to its difficulty rather than an interest in weakening the saying's eschatological reference.[213]

Various findings concerning Luke's patterns of word usage noted above favor an eschatological rather than church-age understanding. Regarding occurrences of "throne" (5x in Luke-Acts, 62x in the NT), one notes that in no case (setting Luke 22:30 aside) is a governing role of the apostles over Israel (or the church) in view.[214] Regarding usages of βασιλεία in the Synoptics and Acts, we may observe that when the term has the post-Easter period in view it is almost always eschatological.[215] "Table" language is not prominent in Acts, and the typical Gospel formula "eat and drink" (14x in Luke, only 3x in Acts) is largely replaced by "breaking of bread" in Acts (e.g., 2:42, 46; 20:7, 11; 27:35).

It is true that the apostles in Acts deliver a "judgment" (from κρίνω) for the church in Syrian Antioch (15:1-35), and that Paul then applies this ruling in other cities as well (16:4). But there are two problems with seeing in the Jerusalem Council a fulfillment of Luke 22:30b: 1) The decision was not made by the apostles alone, but together with "the elders" (15:6, 22); 2) Strictly speaking, though Peter's testimony in vv 7-11 would have been influential, it was James who delivered the decision (v 19, διὸ ἐγὼ κρίνω ...), and he was not an apostle (cf. 12:2). It is acknowledged that Luke describes the apostles as recognized leaders in the Jerusalem church (4:35), respected teachers (2:42), and as having unusual power for their ministry (v 43). Nevertheless, it is only on this general level that a correspondence between Luke 22:29-30 and the church-age role of the apostles as described in Acts is seen. If Luke had intended vv 29-30 to correlate with the church age, a far stronger correspondence with the content of Acts could be expected.

Neyrey argues, however, that because vv 24-27 and 31-32 have present-age actions of the apostles in view, it is in keeping with the Lukan line of thought to interpret vv 28-30 as having reference to the apostles' church-age leadership.[216] To be sure, if all other things were equal, this factor could perhaps shift the balance to a present-era sense

[213]It may also be noted that βασιλεία in Luke often describes a future rule or realm in the age to come (e.g., 1:33; 13:28, 29; 21:31; 22:16, 18; 23:42).

[214]Further, throne imagery is common in apocalyptic texts (cf. n. 174 above).

[215]11x in Matt, 3x in Mark, 10x in Luke, 1x in Acts. The church era is in view 0x in Matt, 1x in Mark, 1x in Luke (following Mark), and 0x in Acts.

[216]Neyrey, 26-7; against Léon-Dufour, "Passion," 501.

for vv 29-30. Although context gives important clues for the exegesis of a text, however, it cannot be made determinative for meaning—it is not a barrier that can prevent Luke from shifting his focus from the present era to the eschaton, or vice versa, should he wish to do so.

A more significant objection is that, because Jesus breaks his fast (vv 16, 18) and eats with the disciples after the resurrection (24:30, 41-43; Acts 1:4; 10:41), he is said to be announcing the arrival of the kingdom. This is then the feasting in view in Luke 22:16, 18 and 30.[217] Two problems with this view are 1) it is hard to envision these post-resurrection meals as a reward, yet that is what the connection between vv 28 and 29-30 points to; 2) if Luke saw the fulfillment of vv 29-30 in these post-Easter meals, we would expect the dining to be paired, in some way, with ruling, but a fulfillment for v 30b is lacking.[218]

A similar objection to the eschatological interpretation of the meal in v 30a is that the eucharistic practice of the Christian community as portrayed in Acts (e.g., 2:42, 46; 20:7, 11; 27:35; cf. Luke 24:30) involves the very table fellowship with Jesus in his kingdom predicted in Luke 22:30a.[219] This view, however, fails to reckon adequately with the instruction in 22:19 (τοῦτο ποιεῖτε). That is, Jesus commands the observance of the Lord's Supper, but he promises a banquet at his table in his kingdom. Thus we encounter an obstacle of logic: does it make sense for Jesus in v 30a to promise a future meal which in v 19 he commands the apostles to observe? This tension, however, is eliminated if v 30a is seen to correspond to the eschatological age.

Having argued that Luke does not aim here to eliminate eschatological features in Q, and having shown the shortcomings of the chief objections to the eschatological understanding of Luke 22:29-30, we may now strengthen the case for the eschatological view. It may be noted first that texts displaying the Lukan feasting image often carry eschatological overtones.[220] This is especially apparent in 12:37, 40, where the return of

---

[217]Neyrey, 27.

[218]The meal in Luke 24:30 is eucharistic (note the vocabulary of 22:19 [cf. Guillaume, 143]), and the eating in 24:41-43 has to do with verifying Jesus' bodily resurrection. Acts 1:4 and 10:41 probably recall the meals of Luke 24 (I. H. Marshall, *Acts*, 193).

[219]Bossuyt and Radermakers, 476; Sweetland, "Lord's Supper," 25; Wanke, 65. This is to be distinguished from the claim that Luke sees the future meal of 22:30a (and vv 16, 18) as being the fulfillment or completion of the Eucharist, as Bösen (76-7) and Guillaume (158-9) maintain.

[220]E.g., Luke 6:21a, 23; 12:37; 13:29; 14:15-24; 22:16, 18. So Behm, "ἐσθίω," 695;

the serving master symbolizes the Parousia of the Son of man. Luke's motif of an eschatological feast may reflect a tradition from Judaism which regarded banqueting as symbolic of everlasting bliss.[221] Luke 22:30a thus fits in with a line of Lukan and Jewish thought which anticipated a future banquet in the kingdom, in the age to come.[222]

Going beyond 12:37, 40, correspondences between 12:42-44 and 22:28-30 are also significant for the question at hand.[223] Both texts involve the conferring by the master/ king on faithful subordinate leaders of greater ruling authority (cf. 19:17-19). What is important here is that in 12:44 this authority is for the period following the return of the master, who clearly symbolizes the Son of man (v 40; cf. 22:30).

An additional problem with the present-age understanding of 22:29-30 is that it does not account for the pronounced shift of mood in Jesus' discourse beginning at v 31. With the prediction of Peter's denial (vv 31-34) and the forecast of an era of opposition (vv 35-36), Jesus markedly alters the tone of his farewell address from the hope of celebration and victory to the expectation of adversity and conflict.[224] Together with Acts 14:22 and Luke 9:23, 22:36 prompts the Lukan reader to suppose that living in the church age would involve significant struggle, and accordingly that 22:29-30 looks ahead to a decisively new era, i.e., the eschaton.

The similarities of the Lukan and Pauline Institution Narratives[225] may be important here as well. Following his counterpart to Luke 22:20

Esler, 192-3; Fitzmyer, *Gospel*, 2:1026, 1419; Guillaume, 146-9; Polag, 49, 52.

[221]Str-B 4:1154ff. On OT and Jewish background also note Isa 25:6-8; 55:1-2; 65:13-14; *1 Enoch* 62:14; *2 Apoc. Bar.* 29:4; *Pirqe ʾAbot* 3.20 (cited in Fitzmyer, *Gospel*, 2:1026). Cf. secs. 3.3 and 3.5.

[222]Here we may also note (with Bösen, 136) that the "eat and drink" formula is a preferred Lukan expression (of 17 usages of πίνω in Luke, 14 have "eat and drink"). Luke even includes it when it is not present in his sources (5:30, 33, 39; perhaps 10:7; 13:26; 17:28). This may suggest that in v 30a we are not merely reading a tradition passed on by Luke, but rather one that he has played a role in bringing to its final form.

[223]See D. Wenham, *Rediscovery*, 132. Indeed, there are noteworthy correspondences of 22:24-30 and 12:35-48 (see further secs. 2.5.2 and 8.3).

[224]Schlatter, *Markus und Lukas*, 381. Note the role of ἀλλὰ νῦν (v 36) in drawing a sharp contrast between the disciples' earlier mission (10:4) with its positive results (10:17-19), and the new, different period which is to follow in Jesus' absence. The contrast, however, must not be overstated; Peter will be able to turn and strengthen his brothers (22:32), and the Acts account reveals many mission successes amidst ongoing adversity.

[225]See sec. 3.4, n. 49.

(1 Cor 11:25), Paul adds that observance of the Lord's Supper proclaims the Lord's death *until he comes* (11:26). For Paul, eucharistic experience was clearly associated with eschatological expectation. Further, since Luke has no direct parallel to 1 Cor 11:26 but shows strong affinities to the Pauline Institution Narrative, Jesus' prediction in Luke (and the Synoptics) of a future meal/ drink in the kingdom of God (Luke 22:16, 18) coupled with Luke's inclusion of 22:30a may reflect the influence of Paul's eschatological expectation associated with the Last Supper (via his letters or the practice in Pauline churches).[226]

Some maintain that *both* church and eschatological ages are in view in Luke 22:29-30.[227] The question at hand, however, is not whether there is some thematic likeness between the apostles' actions in Acts and the depiction in Luke 22:29-30—clearly there is, for the apostles are leaders in Acts[228] and they observe a meal associated with the presence of Jesus—which may then allow the eschatological experience broadly to cover both the church age and the age to come, but whether careful analysis suggests that the language of 22:29-30, against the backdrop of Luke-Acts, can naturally encompass apostolic activity in Acts. It is here maintained that such an understanding is implausible.

Specific objections to the idea that 22:29-30 has both eras in view include the following: 1) Many of the preceding arguments against a church age fulfillment of 22:29-30 are not neatly accommodated to the church-and-eschaton view (e.g., there is no image in Acts of the apostles on thrones). 2) Luke does share the traditional concept of the overlapping

---

[226]Jervell supports the eschatological view when he maintains that the seemingly unusual phenomenon of replacing Judas (Acts 1:15-26) but not James (12:2) is due to the eschatological function of the apostles: "If a new apostle were elected, the eschatological Israel would have thirteen regents over the twelve tribes" (*Luke*, 82 [cf. A. Clark, 67; Kurz, *Farewell*, 66]). While agreeing that for Luke the eschatological role of the apostles is a primary one, it is necessary to note that they also have a present-era transitional function by which they bridge from the life of Jesus to the period of the church (cf. sec. 2.5.1). Accordingly, the failure to replace James may signal the beginning of the end of the apostolic transition era rather than imply an eschatological function for the Twelve (i.e., at some point it had to become necessary *not* to replace a dying apostle).

[227]See n. 211 above. Chance takes this view with a definition of "eschatological" as corresponding to the era which the Christ event inaugurates (139-40; see also 78-9; cf. York, 55). It remains difficult, however, to find a Lukan basis for the realization of Jesus' promise in 22:30 prior to the end-time.

[228]They were leaders in the pre-Easter period as well, according to 22:26 (cf. sec. 6.5.3).

of ages, but to see 22:29-30 as being fulfilled in the church era would be to blur the ages and to undermine the newness of the eschatological age.[229] 3) Luke speaks elsewhere of the conferral upon the apostles of power from God for their work in the church era (Luke 24:46-49; Acts 1:8).[230] If Luke 22:29-30 is made to apply to the church age, the Great Commission becomes largely redundant.[231]

The evidence of Lukan language, themes, the flow of thought in Luke 22:29-30, together with various relevant texts in Luke-Acts and beyond, therefore, support the view that these verses focus on the age to come, not the church age. The initial act of conferral takes place in the moment of Jesus' speech, but the fulfillment of that conferral is to be truly realized only in the eschaton. That is when the apostles will receive their reward of table fellowship with Jesus and enthronement to govern the twelve tribes of Israel.

In summary of vv 29-30, the conferral of kingship upon the apostles (v 29) is grounded in their faithful perseverance in Jesus' trials (v 28). This "kingship" or "royal authority" enables them, in the age to come, to rule over the people of God, reconstituted Israel (v 30b). But this reward and responsibility is to be accompanied by a banquet with Jesus at his table in his kingdom (v 30a). In this way the apostles are to experience the ultimate fulfillment of the Last Supper they presently share with Jesus, and the Lord's Supper they would yet share with each other. Various alternative interpretations have been discussed and found unsatisfactory (e.g., a testamentary sense for διατίθημι, a figurative meaning for the "twelve tribes of Israel" and a church-age fulfillment for vv 29-30). The following translation of vv 29-30 is offered: "And so, as my Father conferred kingship on me, I confer kingship on you, that you may eat and drink at my table in my kingdom; and you shall sit on thrones ruling the twelve tribes of Israel."

---

[229]Geiger (255-6) observes that Luke's conception of the end-time as set out in Luke 21 involves a wholly new order.

[230]The commissioning of the Twelve (9:1-5; cf. 10:19) may be relevant here as well.

[231]One notes that 22:29-30 is not without relevance for the apostles and other leaders in the church era. Though the text anticipates eschatological feasting and ruling, the hope of such grand events is a present experience—the apostles are to take courage now in the hope of a future reward for their faithfulness to Jesus (cf. sec. 8.4).

7.5 Conclusion

While Luke 22:24-27 narrates a descending movement from greatness to service, 22:28-30 describes the apostles' upward progression from the endurance of trials with the servant Jesus to the reception of both seats of honor at Jesus' eschatological banquet and seats of authority to rule the people of God. The details of vv 28-30 then fill out this broad movement from low to high, from the endurance of trials to the exercise of great authority.

A central feature of Luke 22:28-30 is its focus on the union of the apostles with Jesus. Not only does Jesus praise the Twelve for remaining at his side during trials, but he promises them a reunion around the banquet table in his eschatological kingdom. Further, Jesus' possession of kingship and a kingdom (vv 29-30a) implies that the apostles will rule with Jesus in the age to come.[232] When these points are seen together with v 27 ("I am in the midst of you...") and vv 19-20 (on the profound communion of the Last Supper which paves the way for the Lord's Supper), the great importance of Luke's solidarity motif stands out.

Since vv 28-30 emphasize union with Jesus (in trials and as coming king), and since vv 29-30 continue to develop and clarify the theme of authority from vv 24-27, it is important to keep Jesus' self-description in v 27 in mind. That is, it is unlikely that vv 28-30 are intended to be read without recalling that king Jesus is a ruler who serves his people.[233] Further, it is probable that the apostles are to anticipate a form of rule in the kingdom of Jesus that is likewise based on a radical commitment to the welfare of those ruled.[234]

The scale of exaltation for Jesus and the apostles implied in vv 28-30 is not to be missed. The above survey of patterns of authority and subordination in antiquity (ch. 2) reminds one that the acquisition of kingship by a servant who has been enduring trials represents a dramatic elevation which prevalent, rigid hierarchical structures of authority would

[232]This would seem to be one respect in which the mixed metaphors of v 30 overlap, i.e., both allow for the eschatological activity of the apostles in solidarity with Jesus.

[233]This suggests a nuanced Christology that emphasizes not only a lofty but also a lowly Jesus (cf. sec. 9.2).

[234]See further sec. 8.2 on the implications here for the unity of vv 24-30. Even the lowly aspect of servanthood is not to be forgotten in Jesus' kingdom.

have prevented the ordinary person from imagining. Thus the portrayal of the apostles' elevation to seats of privilege at the kingly banquet and to thrones for judging Israel breaks with all natural expectation in the NT world. We have seen that the Lukan Jesus offers a sharp critique of standard notions about authority (cf. esp. vv 25-27), but in vv 29-30 one is reminded that it is not authority itself that is rejected. Indeed, the fact that apostles will rule at the side of king Jesus in the eschatological age reveals Luke's positive valuation of authority properly understood.

Another prominent feature of vv 28-30 is the basis it provides for the theme of hope, in particular hope amidst or in spite of trouble (so the juxtaposition of vv 28 and 29-30 [and the context with v 36]). The apostles are prompted by Jesus to live during his absence in the hope of sharing his great destiny when he returns. Thus the challenges of life today must be informed by and enhanced by the expectation of great good which will come tomorrow (cf. secs. 8.4 and 9.3).

Chapter 8:
Luke 22:24-30: The Paradox of Discipleship

8.1 Introduction

As was the case with chapters 6 and 7, the present chapter is significantly informed by the background perspectives of Part One, particularly the reversal motifs in chapter 4. Further, chapter 8 is also able to build upon the detailed analysis of Luke 22:24-30 which chapters 6 and 7 present. The uniqueness within Part Two of the present chapter, however, lies in its concentration on 22:24-30 as a literary whole. Correspondingly, the chief aim will be to uncover aspects of meaning which surface when 22:24-30 is analyzed with attention to its unifying features.[1]

After attending to matters of definition and clarification (sec. 8.1), thematic and logical lines of unity in 22:24-30 will be put forward (8.2) to strengthen the basis for analyzing 22:24-30 as a literary whole. Two key aspects of discipleship as portrayed in the text before us will then be examined, namely the "pivot-point" feature (8.3) and the aspect of motivation (8.4). Finally, the conclusion (8.5) will address the question, What is the paradox of discipleship?

To speak of "discipleship" in Luke is to enter a stream of scholarship in which that term is used in different ways. Many tie the concept closely to a linguistic base (i.e., μαθητής and/ or ἀκολουθέω),[2] and some stress

[1]The unifying features of 22:24-30 set forth in secs. 1.1, 4.1 and 4.6 provisionally justify our pursuit here of the text's thought and expression as a literary whole (cf. also sec. 7.3.1). Sec. 8.2 below, however, extends and enhances the basis for this approach.

[2]So Beck, *Character*, 93-4; Kariamadam, 113-14; Ryan, 56-8; Sheridan, 252-4; et al. The shortcoming of this approach is that it overlooks texts and themes

that discipleship is restricted to the experience of Jesus' disciples during his lifetime.[3] Such understandings which emphasize specific terms or concentrate only on the period of Jesus make useful points, but they unduly narrow a concept that may, for Luke, be extended to any who have an attachment to Jesus which is characterized by allegiance to him.[4] It is this broader concept of discipleship as involving a relationship with and loyalty to Jesus that informs the present study.[5]

Given this broad approach, there can be no doubt that issues relating to discipleship surface in 22:24-30. The imperative of v 26 implies a relation of the apostles to Jesus involving allegiance and obedience. V 28 portrays the apostles loyally enduring trials in solidarity with Jesus, also a scenario suggesting the allegiance of disciple to master. Further, the implicit call for imitation of Jesus in v 27 fits well with a discipleship focus, as do the intimate setting of a shared meal with Jesus as Passover president and the "with Jesus" motif (cf. sec. 7.3.2). Although it will be proposed that other aspects of Lukan discipleship are in view here (see secs. 8.3 and 8.4), these suffice to show that the broad concept of discipleship is a prominent feature of 22:24-30.

Since the present study centers on the Lukan narrative rather than the evangelist's implicit proclamation to the church of his day (cf. sec. 1.2), it may seem apt in this chapter to speak of "apostleship" (22:14)

---

which are relevant for a concept of discipleship but lack "disciple" and such terms.

[3]E.g., H. Betz (*Nachfolge*, 40-1; ἀκολουθέω drops out in Acts for this reason). Betz elaborates, "Daß Lukas gewisse Parallelen zwischen der Verfolgungssituation des Stephanus, des Paulus und der Jesu hervorhebt, zeigt weniger ein Interesse am Nachfolgegedanken oder gar an der imitatio—wie etwa im Martyrium des Polykarp!—, sondern will dem in der Verfolgung stehenden christlichen Leser als Trost schildern, daß die Leidenzeit der Kirche seit ihrem Beginn andauert" (41). Conzelmann (*Theology*, 233) allows for a form of discipleship in Luke's time, but asserts that it is very different from what it was in Jesus' time; then it was literally a question of "following" (so the journey narrative). Fitzmyer (*Theologian*, 118) seeks to clarify the matter by distinguishing between Luke's depiction of Jesus' immediate disciples and his broader concept of discipleship.

[4]See e.g., Evans, 99-104; Fitzmyer, *Gospel*, 1:235, 241-51; Schürmann, "Jüngerkreis," 27-34; Talbert, "Discipleship," 62; cf. Monsarrat, 44-7.

[5]Crouzel's idea of "La »suite« du Christ" (19-21) is similar to discipleship as understood in this study. Following, however, may be distinguished from imitation in that the former necessarily involves a relationship between disciple and master while the latter does not (21; similarly Thysman, 147-8), though following may still involve imitation (on imitation and discipleship in Luke, also see Beck, *Character*, 93-126).

rather than "discipleship." The fact that certain concepts and themes in 22:24-30 are elsewhere in Luke made relevant to disciples or followers in general,[6] however, and the identification of the apostles as "disciples" (6:13; 22:11, 14), justify our use here of the broader term, "discipleship." Nonetheless, our concern will be limited largely to the form of discipleship which the Lukan Jesus commends to the Twelve in 22:24-30; it is not our aim to set out a Lukan discipleship which would correspond in general to church leaders or all Christians.

The term "paradox" in this chapter title directs attention to the unexpected and even ironic qualities of discipleship as portrayed in Luke 22:24-30 (see further sec. 8.5 below). Most important are the sharp and contrasting contours of the discipleship course along a literary path of reversal: the apostles want to be great but Jesus tells them to serve; they remain loyal during his trials and Jesus promises them exaltation (cf. secs. 4.1, 7.3.1 and 8.2). This progression from high ambitions to lowly roles and back to a final exaltation constitutes a paradoxical course, and represents a discipleship of reversal. Also significant are the paradoxes which operate within the two subsections of 22:24-30: the "great" are called to serve, but they remain leaders (vv 24-27); the persevering apostles are enthroned, but their rule does not involve an abandonment of the servanthood orientation (vv 28-30).[7]

It will be argued in the present chapter that crucial facets of the meaning of 22:24-30 may be discerned when the passage is viewed in terms of the "paradox of discipleship." Moreover, an attempt will be made to show that when 22:24-30 is seen from this perspective, and is viewed against the backdrop of similar Lukan texts and themes, the text makes a notable contribution to the literary and theological content of Luke-Acts.

---

[6]Imitation of Jesus is urged upon disciples (6:40; cf. 22:27), the preoccupation with greatness is rebuked (9:46-48; cf. 22:24-27), the importance of perseverance in adversity is stressed (12:35-46; 21:19; cf. 22:28), eschatological union with Jesus in the kingdom is offered to the penitent thief (23:42-43; cf. 22:30), and the eschatological banquet is made available to people from throughout the world (13:29; cf. 22:30) (that reward is a facet of Lukan discipleship will be argued below [sec. 8.4]).

[7]Cf. chs. 6 and 7 on the reversals within 22:24-27 and 22:28-30 respectively.

8.2 The Unity of Luke 22:24-30

Before exploring features of the discipleship reversal in 22:24-30, we may enhance the basis for analyzing the text as a literary whole by returning briefly to consider the text's unity. In section 1.1 certain verbal, conceptual and structural ties linking 22:24-27 to 22:28-30 were set out. The 360-degree reversal form of 22:24-30 discussed in sections 4.1 and 4.6 also constitutes a unifying feature of our text (see further sec. 8.4 below), and the closeness of service (v 27) and perseverance in trials (v 28) discussed in section 7.3.1 enhances the claim for a dovetailing of the reversal's descent and ascent elements. It remains, however, to note various logical, thematic and other links which have not been considered until now because they can be seen most clearly in the light provided by chapters 6 and 7, and which add yet more weight to the case for the unitary Lukan conception of 22:24-30.[8]

In spite of the arguments for unity that have been and will be made, however, vv 28-30 would come as something of a surprise to the first-time reader.[9] The two units differ in tone (rebuke then affirmation, humility then exaltation), and their juxtaposition may alarm or perplex the reader. Creed, however, goes too far when he asserts that there is no close connection between 22:28-30 and the preceding verses.[10] I. H. Marshall also overstates when he claims that 22:28-30 is in "sharp contrast to the previous section, which emphasized the need for lowly service without thought of reward,..."[11] Indeed, the idea that the admonitions of vv 25-27 are to be carried out without thought of reward may well clash with an important reason for which Luke allows vv 24-27 and 28-30 to stand side by side (see further sec. 8.4).[12]

---

[8]It is admitted that the tradition-historical backgrounds of the logia in 22:24-30 may be far from unified (so the emphasis of Otto [273], Schürmann [*Abschiedsrede*, 56-7, 62-3, et al.] and many others; see further secs. 6.2 and 7.2.). Since the chief focus of this study, however, is on the meaning of Luke's finished text (sec. 1.2), a mixed background for our material need not weigh against its unity in Luke's sight.

[9]So Eltester, 134; Lohfink, *Sammlung*, 80; Schürmann, *Abschiedsrede*, 57; et al. Lagrange (551) claims regarding vv 24-27 that "... le conseil sur l'attitude à prendre [i.e., humility] ne préparait pas à l'image des trônes."

[10]Creed, 268.

[11]I. H. Marshall, *Gospel*, 814. Kollmann (*Mahl*, 222-3) also emphasizes aspects of disunity in 22:24-30.

[12]It is useful here to note that Luke is quite capable of imposing a unity

G. Schneider approaches the text from a different angle and contends that vv 24-27 and 28-30 are linked by the duality of "Mahnung und Verheißung."[13] Such a duality gives incentive to meet a challenge: the call to give up the prizing of greatness and follow the path of leadership through service and trials (vv 25-28) is made more palatable by the realization that such a downward course leads to a lofty destination (vv 29-30) (cf. again sec. 8.4).

A different yet complementary perspective on 22:24-30 recognizes there a single concern with greatness—greatness prized and greatness realized. Godet makes the point, "After having thus contrasted the ideal of an altogether new greatness with the so different tendency of the natural heart, Jesus proceeds to satisfy what of truth there was in the aspiration of the disciples (vers. 28-30)."[14] Dupont similarly maintains, "Ils [the apostles] seront ainsi «les plus grands», mais dans le monde à venir, après s'être faits, dans le monde présent, les serviteurs des autres."[15] Lull also discerns throughout 22:24-30 the strand of thought having to do with greatness.[16] We may accordingly portray 22:24-30 in chiastic form:

A		The great ones (vv 24-25)
	B	are to become servants (vv 26-27);
	B'	the "servants" (v 28)
A'		will become "great" (vv 29-30)

In terms of the general thematic content of 22:24-30, then, we have this

upon disparate materials (e.g., the sayings in 13:22-30 [so Chilton, 184-5; Maddox, 124], in 22:14-38 [so Kurz, *Farewell*, 69; LaVerdiere, "Discourse," 1546-7], and in 12:13-21 [so Thériault, 222]; note also Lukan compositional activity in 12:35-46 [Fitzmyer, *Gospel*, 2:984]).

[13]G. Schneider, *Evangelium*, 2:451; cf. Rienecker, 504; Soards, 52.

[14]Godet, 297.

[15]Dupont, "Trônes," 380 (cf. Fitzmyer, *Gospel*, 2:1415; Schlatter, *Lukas*, 424). Along similar lines, many see 22:24-30 as centering on the subject of authority or leadership (e.g., Gooding, 333; Karris, *Gospel*, 716; Kurz, *Farewell*, 64; Sellew, 77; Tiede, *Luke*, 385; cf. Evans, 102; Fitzmyer, *Gospel*, 2:1412; Meynet, *Initiation*, 166). That the greatness prized (v 24) and the kingly authority received (vv 29-30) both involve dimensions of honor and status as well as power is apparent (cf. sec. 2.2). The Lukan Jesus clarifies, however, that the lofty outcome is reached only at the end of the downward course.

[16]Lull, 299, 301 (though for him the kings and benefactors [v 25] are positive examples ([contrast sec. 6.3]). Lull also maintains that both Jesus' self-sacrifice (v 27) and the apostles' loyalty (v 28) exemplify the servanthood of true greatness (300-1; cf. sec. 7.3.1).

reversal progression: greatness is esteemed (though misguidedly), lowly service is urged instead, servanthood involving perseverance in trials is commended, and a reward of true greatness is promised.[17]

On a different note, Léon-Dufour asserts, "Cette exhortation [22:24-30] comporte deux volets, correspondant au double aspect qu'a le mystère unique du Christ. A la mort correspond le service fraternel (22,24-27), à la résurrection la perspective de gloire qui réconforte les disciples de Jésus (22,28-30)."[18] That the death of Jesus is in view in vv 24-27 has been argued (secs. 5.3 and 6.5.3), and Jesus' resurrection is clearly implied in the prediction of the meal in his kingdom (v 30; cf. vv 16, 18). Further, the respective tone (humiliation and exaltation) and timing (present age and eschaton) of vv 24-27 and 28-30 correlate symbolically with Jesus' death and resurrection. We also may recall that Jesus' passion-resurrection predictions accompany reversal sayings which correspond to the disciples' experience (9:22-24; 18:29-34). Thus there are adequate grounds for seeing in 22:24-30 a unifying symbolism of Jesus' death and resurrection.

From another angle, Matera asserts that the presence of Jesus the testator's recollections of his past in both vv 24-27 and 28-30 serves to unify 22:24-30.[19] To be sure, only vv 27c and 28 retrace the past, and even these verses do not have only the past in view.[20] Nonetheless, there is a discernible element of reflection on the past in vv 27c and 28, and the fact that these recollections are at the seam between 22:24-27 and 22:28-30 adds weight to the claim that 22:24-30 is a unified pericope.[21]

---

[17]Cf. Grundmann (402), who claims, "Lukas fügt diese Wortfolge ohne Unterbrechung an die vorhergehenden Worte Jesu an und macht damit deutlich: Der Dienende wird von Gott erhöht" (similarly Wiefel, 371-2). Rienecker (504) summarizes 22:24-30 as follows: "Im Zusammenhang mit dem bisher Gesagten (Lk 22, 25-27) gedenkt der Herr auch der Erhöhung Seiner Jünger, die nach ihrer Demut folgt (Lk 23 [sic], 28-30)." Loisy (515) contends that Luke here wishes to connect service to its recompense.

[18]Léon-Dufour, "Testament," 273; cf. "Letzte Mahl," 47.

[19]Matera, *Passion*, 162; cf. ch. 5 on testamentary genre.

[20]The service of Jesus climaxes in his impending death (cf. sec. 6.5.3), and perfect διαμεμενηκότες encompasses the apostles' past action of remaining in solidarity with Jesus in his trials together with a present state resulting from that action (cf. sec. 7.3.2). V 35 also contains a recollection of the past (cf. 10:4), but it does not correspond to the pious past of the testator.

[21]Other arguments for unifying features in 22:24-30 have been proposed as well: L'Eplattenier makes the plausible claim (252) that, in response to the quarrel over rank (v 24), "Il [Jesus] les met à égalité dans une promesse qui les qualifie d'abord, malgré leur prochain abandon, comme «ceux qui sont demeurés avec

Together with verbal, conceptual and structural factors noted in section 1.1 and the unifying 360-degree reversal form of 22:24-30 (secs. 4.1 and 4.6; cf. 7.3.1), the above thematic, logical and other factors count strongly in favor of a Lukan unitary conception for 22:24-30. Although this is not an unprecedented claim, previous work has not produced an extended analysis such as that offered by the present study to demonstrate the unity of 22:24-30, nor has the unifying reversal form of our text previously been the subject of in-depth investigation. The unity of 22:24-30 justifies the pursuit of Lukan lines (or fields) of thought in which the constitutive elements of the pericope function together to form an integrated and coherent literary whole, so it is to that pursuit we turn in the remainder of this chapter.

8.3 Pivot-point Discipleship

In sections 8.3 and 8.4 we will seek to discern certain distinguishing, if not wholly unique, features of the discipleship reversal in Luke 22:24-30. The survey of reversal motifs presented in chapter 4 provides some useful perspectives from which to make such determinations, as do other background studies, and certain of these will be drawn upon in the following analysis.

---

moi dans mes épreuves»" (cf. Dillersberger, 512-13). Baumbach (193) sees the "trials" of v 28 as involving the temptation to defect from "service" (cf. LaVerdiere [*Luke*, 260-1], for whom the trials involve serving). For Roloff (*Apostolat*, 187) the διαθήκη motif (vv 29-30) interprets διακονία (v 27). We also note that the motif of union with Jesus is present in vv 27-30 (cf. sec. 7.3.2). In addition, Jesus' presence is closely related to the presence of the kingdom (cf. sec. 7.4.3), so 17:21 may imply that 22:27c leads naturally into the kingdom sayings of vv 29-30. Further, vv 24-27 and 28-30 overlap in terms of time frames (both encompass past, present and future [in v 27 Jesus' symbolized death is yet a future event]). It is also noteworthy that 12:37 speaks of the Son of man's eschatological table service (διακονέω), an image that may support a link of the servant Jesus (22:27) with his kingdom banquet (v 30). On a different note, Leaney's claim (269) may be oversubtle, but it is not implausible: "Luke's reason for bringing the passage [22:24-27] here is probably the thought that only in the imminent kingdom will the Apostles be accorded any position in which they will be tempted to exercise too much power over others (verse 29)." Tannehill contends that vv 24-27 and 28-30 are unified by their common reference to the death of Jesus ("Study," 200). That Jesus' death is in view in v 27c has been argued (see sec. 6.5.3), but Tannehill's claim (202) that διατίθεμαι in v 29 has the sense "to dispose of property by a will" and not "to confer" or "to covenant" has not been accepted (sec. 7.4.2). For further discussion of the unity question, see Fitzmyer, *Gospel*, 2:1412.

"Pivot-point discipleship" denotes the aspect of the apostles' position portrayed in vv 24-30 which places them, as Jesus' loyal followers, in the middle of a framework of authority. In short, this aspect of discipleship involves the combination of leading and following, ruling and serving (cf. sec. 2.5.2. on the Lukan stewardship motif). The Lukan apostles here stand both in and under authority.

This description of the pivot-point feature, however, overlooks some of the complexities involved and can lead to oversimplification, so we will seek a measure of clarification by examining the apostles' roles in relation to both Jesus and other people. In vv 24-27 the only reference to Jesus describes him as ὁ διακονῶν in the apostles' midst, so it may be inferred that, in some sense,[22] Jesus takes a subordinate role as one who humbly works to benefit them. It is essential to note, however, that the servant Jesus claims the right to issue commands (v 26), and his self-reference (v 27c) clearly sets him up as an exemplar to be imitated. Thus it is clear that Jesus remains the leader of the apostolic band in vv 24-27 (cf. sec. 6.5), even though his peculiar form of leadership does not exclude duties customarily assigned to subordinate figures.

In vv 28-30, though the apostles are given kingship and promised banquet seats and thrones for judging, Jesus is again their superior; he confers kingship on them, and it is in Jesus' kingdom that they will dine and rule. Jesus is the king, and he oversees the subordinate governing actions of the Twelve. So throughout 22:24-30 Jesus is portrayed as the apostles' leader; pivot-point discipleship thus involves being subject to Jesus' rule.

Pivot-point discipleship as depicted in both 22:24-27 and 22:28-30, however, also involves the ruling of the apostles as Jesus' authorized delegates within the larger community of disciples. It has been argued (sec. 6.5.3) that the injunction to become like the youngest and the servant (v 26) does not involve the elimination of the apostles' role (or the role of some among their circle) as "great" ones, as leaders. To be sure, their summons to become servant-leaders suggests a profound transformation of current ideas of "greatness," but it does not call for the removal of all forms of hierarchy or authority structures among them.

In vv 28-30 the role of the apostles as ones bearing authority to lead is made more explicit: Jesus confers kingship upon them (v 29), and he

[22]Cf. sec. 6.5.3 on the service of Jesus.

assures them that they will sit on thrones to govern the twelve tribes of Israel. To be sure, the injunction to the apostles to follow the pattern of Jesus' serving rule (vv 26-27) implies that a service orientation is not to be lacking in the rule described in vv 29-30.[23] Nonetheless, there can be no doubt that, while Jesus remains their king, the Twelve are entrusted with great powers to govern the people of God.

In the reversal texts surveyed in chapter 4 and other texts as well, one can find some precedent for the concept of pivot-point discipleship, though it is not a particularly widespread motif. Numerous texts commend the 360-degree reversal course to disciple-like figures, but typically the call to allegiance along a descent-ascent path is a call to follow the leader, and not to lead followers as well. Nevertheless, in the literature of Judaism one reads, for example, of the "righteous" (Wis 3:1-8) or the "saints" (Dan 7:18-22, 27) being given authority by God to judge the nations.[24] In the NT a similar line of thought surfaces in various texts including 1 Cor 6:2-3 (the saints will judge the world and angels), 2 Tim 2:12 ("if we endure, we shall also reign with him [Christ Jesus]") and Rev 3:21 (the one who conquers will sit with Jesus Christ on his throne).[25] In each NT text Christians are given a share in the eschatological ruling power of Jesus Christ, and thus they come to be in authority as well as under authority.

Luke, however, seems to be particularly fond of pivot-point discipleship, for, in addition to 22:24-30, the basic concept surfaces once without parallel in the Gospels (16:1-9), and in two other texts in which Luke gives special emphasis to multi-layered authority structures and focuses on the role of a "middle-man" (12:42-46; 19:11-27).[26] The similarities of Luke 22:24-30 and 12:42-46 as pivot-point discipleship texts are particularly noteworthy (cf. secs. 2.5.2 and 4.5.1).[27] In both there are

---

[23]So Moxnes, *Economy*, 158; Tiede, *Luke*, 385; cf. Meynet, *Parole*, 183.

[24]Cf. sec. 7.4.3; see also Pobee, 42. The pivot-point feature in Wis 3:1-8 is restricted to the afterlife (cf. Winston, 31, 129), so its parallels with the Lukan idea are limited (see also sec. 4.3). In this connection we may also note *T. Levi* 13:8-9 (teaching and doing good lead to being enthroned with kings [so Joseph]) and Epict. *Ench.* 15 (the humble person will assist the gods in governing).

[25]Cf. the discussion of Rev 3:20-21 in n. 160 of sec. 7.4.3.

[26]On 12:42-46 see n. 103 in sec. 2.5.2; on 19:11-27 see n. 106 in sec. 2.5.2.

[27]Moessner (181) argues that the journeying guest motif is the constitutive link between the traditions of Luke 12:32-48 and those of 22:21-34. While this claim may have some merit, it overlooks noteworthy similarities in the area of pivot-point discipleship.

representations of Jesus and the disciples as ruler and subordinates respectively,[28] yet in both the subordinates are also given leadership responsibilities. In both cases there is a strong interest in leadership that cares for and does good to the subjects, and does not follow the path of power which degenerates into tyranny (12:42, 45 [and cf. v 37]; 22:27). In both, the role of Jesus' delegates involves ruling in the present age as well as in the age to come.[29] And in both texts the extent of leadership responsibility assigned to Jesus' delegates is increased in the eschatological era (12:44; 22:29-30). It is noteworthy that Matthew's parallel to Luke 12:42-46 (Matt 24:45-51) does not portray the household as having a multi-tiered authority structure as clearly as the Lukan text does.[30]

In Luke 16:1-9 and 19:11-27 the similarities to 22:24-30 are not quite so extensive, but key points may be noted nonetheless. In both texts a subordinate figure is entrusted with authority while his master is away, and in both the returning master settles up with the servant on the basis of his performance (cf. sec. 2.5.2). These texts, then, together with 12:42-46, reveal an interest in a form of discipleship that involves not merely following, but following *and* leading. Although many studies of discipleship in general and Lukan discipleship in particular focus on the term "follow" (ἀκολουθέω),[31] a careful analysis of 22:24-30 against the backdrop of the above texts would imply that leading others in the course of following Jesus is an important expression of the apostles' discipleship.

The pivot-point portrayal places a certain emphasis on the communal dimensions of discipleship. That is, in addition to being a relationship between master and follower, pivot-point discipleship also emphasizes the apostles' contact with each other and with other followers of Jesus for whom they are to act as servant-leaders. Correspondingly, 22:24-30 stresses both "vertical" and "horizontal" dimensions of the apostles' discipleship.[32]

---

[28]Luke 12:35-40 (or a portion of it) is described as a "parable" (v 41), implying that the expansion in vv 42-46 is parabolic as well. This observation cautions us against over allegorizing, but Jesus' words of application in v 40 would seem to invite the measure of allegorizing which is proposed.

[29]The return of the "master" (v 43) symbolizes the anticipated future return of the Son of man (v 40), namely—in Luke's view—Jesus (e.g., 22:22).

[30]See n. 103 in sec. 2.5.2.

[31]Cf. n. 2 above.

[32]Other themes in Luke-Acts also imply a community dimension of discipleship (e.g., traveling with Jesus, shared meals, and the shared ownership seen in Acts 2:44 and 4:32). On the subject see Fitzmyer, *Gospel*, 1:251-7; Talbert,

In summary of pivot-point discipleship, it appears that in 22:24-30 Luke has taken up a traditional concept, yet the prevalence of this idea in his writings suggests a special emphasis. Since the pivot-point feature requires the apostles to look in two directions (toward both leader and followers), it is implied that, as leaders in the Jesus movement, the apostles must be aware that they are also subordinates.[33] This overlap of leading and following seems to reveal a certain defiance of the standard patterns of authority and subordination that were prevalent in antiquity. That is, Luke is perhaps calling into question the common assumption that, on the spectrums of power and status, superiors and inferiors are poles apart and hold positions which may be sharply distinguished from each other (cf. ch. 2). In this way the pivot-point framework opens the way for the apostles' exercise of servanthood as an expression of a transformed style of leadership.

Luke's pivot-point discipleship also appears to have a special relevance for the period of Jesus' absence (so too the orientation of a farewell discourse [ch. 5]). That is, Luke 22:24-30, with its implied concern for the period between Jesus' presence with the apostles (vv 24-28) and their future reunion at the eschatological banquet table (v 30), coincides with the interest of 12:42-46 and 19:11-27 (cf. 16:1-9) in faithful stewardship while the master is away. Such a depiction would support both a Lukan expectation of a potentially lengthy interim period in which life in this world would carry on as usual (i.e., long enough to accomplish significant duties [cf. Acts 1:8]), and the evangelist's certainty of Jesus' return following that period.[34] Pivot-point discipleship, however, continues into the eschatological era as well, as the extension of the disciples' subordinate ruling powers in 22:29-30 (cf. 12:44; 19:16-19) directly implies.

"Discipleship," 71-3.

[33]Not only are they under the authority of Jesus, but in following his example of servanthood (22:27), they would, in a certain sense, subordinate themselves to the community they lead.

[34]See further sec. 9.3 on 22:24-30 and the matrix of history. Gaventa (37-8) and Franklin (14, 26) are among those who recognize Luke's interest and confidence in the Parousia (features that do not vanish after Acts 2).

8.4 Reversal and Motivation for Discipleship

Another aspect of discipleship seen in the reversal portrayal of 22:24-30 is the possible function of the anticipation of ascent as a motivating force for enduring descent. To put it differently, the hope of reward may be seen as providing incentive for the apostles to follow or continue a downward movement in service and trials.[35] This line of thought is conceivable, of course, whenever a 360-degree reversal is commended to a "disciple," for a view of the whole cycle sees the positive outcome, and the notion that such an end would enhance the disciple's willingness to endure difficulty cannot be ruled out.[36]

A brief review of Luke's commended reversals reveals a close connection between admonitions to follow the way of the cross (etc.) and the expectation that good will eventually or finally come:[37] Rejoice when you are persecuted, "for" (γάρ) your reward in heaven will be great (6:22-23). If you love enemies and lend without hope of repayment, your reward will be great (6:35). If you take up your cross daily to follow Jesus, you will save your life (9:23-24). If you adopt the lowly status of a child and become the least, you will be truly great (9:46-48). Sell your possessions, give alms, and you will have treasure in heaven (12:33). If you are watchful and faithful servants, Jesus will reward you with a banquet and greater authority (12:35-48). Take the low seat "so that" (ἵνα) your host will bring you up; he who humbles himself will be exalted (14:7-11). Show hospitality to those who cannot reciprocate and you will be repaid at the resurrection of the just (14:12-14). Humbly confess your sin and you will be justified (18:9-14). Renounce possessions and receive earthly reward as well as eternal life (18:29-30; cf. v 22).[38] Thus the prospect of a "reward" for Jesus' disciples, often an eschatological one, is repeatedly linked directly to the commendation of self-denial, condescension or the endurance of suffering.[39] When we turn to 22:24-30, can we rule out the

[35]Cf. certain unifying features of 22:24-30 noted in sec. 8.2 above (e.g., the admonition-promise duality).

[36]York's "bi-polar" reversal, however, does not similarly link condescension with subsequent elevation (see the discussion in sec. 4.5).

[37]This is not to imply that the hope of reward functions for Luke *only* to give incentive for following Jesus and bearing the cross.

[38]Cf. 21:19, "By your endurance you will gain your lives."

[39]In some of these texts there is not so much a descent element as existence on a low plane (e.g., 6:22-23; 12:35-48; 21:19). Technically this suggests a 180-degree

idea that an anticipated reward (vv 29-30) would have the effect of giving the apostles strong incentive to take the downward path of service and trials (vv 25-27, 28)?

Much of the literature on discipleship in Luke, however, overlooks such a possibility; indeed, the notion that the ascent element of reversal may even be a part of discipleship is quite frequently bypassed. Discipleship for many consists essentially of meeting rigorous demands and following Jesus through trying circumstances.[40] Accordingly, Luke 9:57-62 and 14:25-33 are often cited as pillars of the Lukan concept of discipleship. Luke 9:23-27 is also noted frequently, though little is made of the ascent element in the discipleship reversal there (v 24; cf. sec. 4.5.1). Some see a more balanced portrayal in general, but even these interpreters tend to lay stress on the demand aspect of discipleship.[41] From a different angle, some who discern a pattern of reversal unifying 22:24-30 still do not develop the idea of anticipated ascent as giving incentive for descent,[42] and this particular reversal text is not connected with other Lukan texts undergirding the motif.

N. Richardson offers an exception to the drift of scholarship when he stresses that in Luke the cost of discipleship and the generosity of God must go hand in hand. "The demands of the gospel, by themselves, invite only despair or cynicism; but apart from them the generosity of God would be distorted into grace 'on the cheap'."[43] Although Richardson

---

reversal, but this point does not eliminate other notable similarities to 22:24-30.

[40]E.g., Aerts, 511-12; Beck, *Character*, 98-101; Fitzmyer, *Gospel*, 1:241-51; *Theologian*, 128-35 (disciples must "trudge along" the way of salvation in the Savior's steps [135]); Kariamadam, 115-30 (the Lukan concept of discipleship is "austere"); Kittel, "ἀκολουθέω"; O'Toole, "Parallels," 207-9; Pathrapankal, 538; Rengstorf, "μαθητής"; Schmahl, 33; Sheridan, 254-5; Schürmann, "Jüngerkreis," 27-34 (though maximum demands were not made of all disciples [30-31]); Senior, 64, 71; Talbert, "Discipleship," 62. In certain cases these and other writers qualify their descriptions and allow for some element of reward, but the focus is heavily on discipleship as meeting radical demands.

[41]E.g., Coulot, 122-4; Crouzel, 20-21 (though the Synoptic Gospels are approached without great concern for the particular interests of individual evangelists); R. Martin, 378-80 (parousia expectations give incentive for Christian conduct, but this is not understood in terms of hope for reward [379]); Ryan, 56-7; Schweizer, *Lordship*, 17-20 (an approach similar to Crouzel's); Seccombe, 97-134, 225; Sweetland, "Discipleship," 78-9.

[42]E.g., Dupont, "Trônes," 380; Easton, 325; Rienecker, 504.

[43]N. Richardson, 33. The Parable of the Prodigal Son and Jesus' frequent contacts with tax collectors and "sinners" (cf. sec. 3.5.1 above) offer crucial expres-

does not speak in terms of a descent-ascent progression and does not identify a challenge-incentive discipleship pattern in 22:24-30, his stress on the generosity of God as enabling a disciple to respond to demands[44] correlates with the emphasis here on a positive outcome of the reversal progression in 22:24-30 as giving the apostles incentive to remain true to Jesus while enduring lowly servanthood and trials.

The motivation aspect of the Lukan reversal motif is enhanced when seen in the light of the frequently mentioned passion-resurrection reversal of Jesus (cf. sec. 4.5). It may be recalled that in Luke 9:22 and 18:31-34, the reversal course of discipleship is commended in the immediate context of passion-resurrection predictions. The role of God in ensuring the eventual completion of Jesus' reversal course (stressed so often in Acts) would lend an element of certainty to the widespread discipleship reversal patterns.[45] If one must bear the cross, give up the pleasures of family life, etc., the assurance remains that trials will not be endless and reward will come. The widespread motif in Acts of threat and deliverance would support this claim as well; as the reader encounters numerous reversals, he becomes ever more sure that bad circumstances will yield good ends.

If we focus again more directly on 22:24-30, the challenge-incentive dimensions of Lukan discipleship shed light on this text. For instance, in sections 2.2.2 and 6.5.1 it was made clear that in antiquity benefaction was not normally a disinterested action; patrons/ benefactors gave gifts and did favors in order to win the praise and support of their clients/ beneficiaries. So given the connection of 22:24-27, 28 to 22:29-30 in which the hope of reward serves to inspire commendable behavior, it would probably be a misunderstanding of vv 25-26 to suppose that benefactors are being criticized because they do good for gain.[46] Rather, it may well be implied that they are put forward as negative examples because they do good for the *wrong kind* of gain—they seek elevation which is not rooted in prior condescension.[47] On this understanding of 22:24-30, the

sions of the generosity of God; also note esp. 14:12-14 diff. Matt (30-4).

[44]N. Richardson, 33.

[45]The sense of certainty would be strengthened as well by the frequent descriptions of the ascent element in which human participants are passive.

[46]That they function in the Lukan narrative as negative examples was demonstrated in secs. 6.3 and 6.5.1.

[47]Correspondingly, the implication of 14:12-14 is not that reciprocation is intrinsically negative, but that it is not nearly as valuable a gain as the reception of divine compensation at the "resurrection of the just" (cf. sec. 4.5.1).

apostles would be warned that there is no path to true greatness which does not pass through service and trials.

The sense of 22:24-30 as a reversal which motivates the apostles to follow Jesus is nuanced by the fact that they are portrayed negatively in v 24 (cf. secs. 6.3 and 6.4). That is, the apostles' failure to reckon with the gravity of the moment and their unacceptable preoccupation with greatness do not exclude them from "eligibility" for the sort of discipleship advocated by Jesus in which loyalty in service and trials are rewarded in the coming kingdom. Thus the Lukan Jesus does not hold out to them an unreachable ideal of discipleship. To be sure, Luke is not unaware of the tension which accompanies the promise of reward following so closely after a negative action and the rebuke for it,[48] but the significant connections between 22:24-27 and 22:28-30 would suggest that the apostles' path of discipleship remains open even when they have faltered. This suggests a Lukan anthropology that recognizes a human need for pull as well as push.

A further clarification concerns the timing of descent and ascent in the discipleship reversal of 22:24-30. To be specific, even though reward for condescension follows in the eschatological era, the anticipation of this future event is experienced in the present by the apostles amidst the endurance of lowly service and trials, thus allowing hope for "tomorrow" to provide a motivating force which is felt "today." In this way the present and the future are brought close together and made to influence one another (cf. sec. 9.3).[49]

In summary of section 8.4, Luke 22:24-30 reveals, as do a number of other Lukan texts (cf. sec. 4.5), a strand of thought which ties the descent and ascent elements of reversal closely together. In fact, 6:23 and 14:10 seem to make explicit what is probably implicit in 22:24-30 and several texts, namely that an anticipated elevation is set forth to give incentive

[48]Perhaps his awareness of this tension partially accounts for the presence of the many unifying features we have seen in 22:24-30. Cf. n. 9 above. Also note Moessner's view that the Lukan Jesus, like Moses, dies "on behalf of" those he has led through an exodus but who still reject his authority. This paradox explains the promise of rule in the midst of the apostles' rejection in 22:21-34 (181). While there is some merit in pursuing such Jesus-Moses parallels in Luke, it is quite difficult to be sure of the appropriateness of this approach in the post-journey section of the Gospel.

[49]Note the command to rejoice *now* in anticipation of a great reward *in heaven* (6:23).

for enduring necessary humiliation or adversity. A weakness of much scholarship on Lukan discipleship is that the elevation element—the hope of reward—is overlooked or understated.

How then is the apostles' discipleship portrayed in 22:24-30? It is a relationship with Jesus in which the apostles condescend to a lifestyle of service and faithful endurance of adversity in the course of remaining loyal to Jesus, which is inseparably linked with the vital element of anticipated final compensation and celebration. This balance of loss and gain implies that the discipleship in view is not merely a relationship between a ruling master and compliant subjects, but a relationship between a ruling *and wooing* master and compliant *and hopeful* subjects.

8.5 Conclusion

In this chapter it has been argued that the theme of discipleship and the form of reversal come together in Luke 22:24-30. The survey of texts and themes in chapter 4 set the stage for an analysis of the discipleship reversal in our text, and it revealed many lines of continuity between 22:24-30 and motifs elsewhere. The extension of prior claims for the unitary conception of Luke 22:24-30 enhanced the basis for seeking lines or fields of thought in the text as a literary whole. Two facets of the unifying reversal in 22:24-30—pivot-point discipleship and the hope of ascent as a motive for descent—were examined is some depth.

We may now bring together the key findings from the present chapter and ask, What is the paradox of discipleship in Luke 22:24-30? To answer this question, several points may be made. First, the discipleship in view is paradoxical in that it is a downward course that leads upward. The way for the apostles to be truly great and receive ultimate exaltation is to humble themselves and adopt the servant role. An implication of this claim is that one does not obtain an accurate representation of the apostles' discipleship by examining that relationship and lifestyle at any one point in time. For example, to concentrate on the demands involved and paint a picture of austerity minimizes the hope of eschatological reward, and to focus on glory without suffering only inverts the error. Such portrayals miss the element of paradox that the discipleship portrayed in 22:24-30 (and in many other Lukan texts) involves.

Second, the discipleship before us is also paradoxical in that it involves leaders who serve and servants who lead. For this reason the common idea of discipleship as "following" is inadequate for approaching 22:24-30, for the pivot-point feature there implies that the Twelve must both follow and be followed. Although a similar idea surfaces in certain non-Lukan texts, the development of pivot-point discipleship in 12:42-46, 16:1-9, 19:11-27 and 22:24-30 reveals a special interest which the scholarly discussion of Lukan discipleship has largely overlooked.[50]

Third, it has been proposed that the close connection of a commended downturn with a promised upturn in Luke 22:24-30 (as well as several other Lukan texts) is not without significance: the anticipated elevation serves to motivate the apostles to endure the difficulties of condescension. Moreover, the expected reward should not be sharply distinguished from a "pure" discipleship as meeting demands, for it has an important function not only in the future but also in the present for life in the face of trials; the apostles gain strength *in the present* because of the hope of reward to come. Studies of Lukan discipleship, however, have often overlooked or underemphasized the importance of reward. An implication of 22:24-30, which is supported by many other Lukan texts, is that Luke's anthropology involves an appreciation of the value of incentives to inspire positive conduct—the apostles need pull as well as push. This in turn suggests that Luke sanctions and commends the apostles' endurance of difficulty in the course of following Jesus (and leading Jesus' followers) on the basis of motivation drawn from the hope of future reward.

Fourth, given the conception of discipleship as involving not merely imitation but also a relationship with Jesus characterized by allegiance,[51] and given the close ties between Jesus' passion-resurrection and the descent-ascent reversal,[52] Luke's paradoxical discipleship may well be conceived of as a means of remaining in solidarity with the suffering and risen Jesus through trials in this age and on to celebration in the next. There is, in a sense, a sharing of the death and resurrection of Jesus in 22:24-30.[53] This of course coincides with key dimensions of the Last

[50]The emphasis on a discipleship which involves being both in and under authority probably suggests that Luke envisions a particular though not exclusive line of relevance for Christian leaders in his day.

[51]So Crouzel, 19-21, et al.; cf. n. 4 in sec. 8.1 above.

[52]Note the intersection of Jesus' passion-resurrection reversal and discipleship reversals in 9:22-24 and 18:29-34 (cf. 9:44-48; see sec. 4.5).

[53]Cf. the quotation from Léon-Dufour in sec. 8.2 above. On discipleship and sharing in the death and resurrection of Jesus, also see Goulder, *Type*, 38, 51;

Supper as providing for the apostles a means of ongoing communion with the departing Jesus (vv 19-20), and it is an emphasis that finds a natural setting in a farewell speech.[54]

Fifth, in light of the repeated trials and deliverances of Paul and the apostles in Acts (cf. sec. 4.5.2), the "daily" and "many" of Luke 9:23 and Acts 14:22, and the depiction in Luke 22:28 of the apostles' loyal perseverance during Jesus' trials (note the plural), it is arguable that Luke would nuance our portrayal of discipleship by including in its path a series of this-age falls (or falls and rises) within the single, overarching, era-bridging reversal course. Consequently, the prospect of repeated reversals makes it all the more hazardous to assess the nature of the apostles' discipleship by examining their experience at a single point in time.

Sixth, it is important not to overlook the issue of agency in the discipleship reversal of 22:24-30. Shared agency is seen in the combination of a commended humiliation and a promised exaltation: Jesus and the Father (v 29) effect the rise to power and glory, but disciples are called to humble themselves and adopt an attitude of service. Since Luke portrays God as the ultimate elevating agent and associates Jesus with him, the apostles' discipleship calls for a dimension of trust and hope. A perspective which equates discipleship with meeting demands, however, draws attention to human agency only.

In conclusion, on the basis of the preceding description it is arguable that the complex "paradox of discipleship" represents crucial aspects of Luke 22:24-30. This perspective allows for strong lines of continuity between 22:24-27 and 22:28-30, units that have sometimes been thought of merely as pearls on a string of sayings on the basis of tradition-historical factors and supposed contradictory emphases. Moreover, this viewpoint allows 22:24-30 to find a place within the larger Lukan framework in setting out a distinctive concept of discipleship along a course of reversal. Further, the mixing of allusions to death and resurrection in our text complements the Last Supper's combined anticipation of death

---

Kariamadam, 113; Talbert, "Discipleship," 66. Cosgrove claims, "The passion event (cross and resurrection/ ascension) expresses paradigmatically God's way of working in history as a providential pattern of reversal" (188). Dehandschutter (546) is hesitant on the idea of imitating the passion of Jesus.

[54]It may be that Luke would have disciples in his day find consolation in knowing that their trials may be thought of as Jesus' trials (cf. v 28), and that their reward will involve ongoing communion with the risen Jesus at his eschatological table (cf. v 30).

and hope of a future meal (vv 15-20). Accordingly, an attempt to discern the meaning of 22:24-30—whether focusing on 22:24-27 and 22:28-30 as distinguishable subsections or on 22:24-30 as a whole—which overlooks the paradox of discipleship will thus be significantly impoverished.

CONCLUSION

Chapter 9: Summary and Synthesis

9.1 Introduction

Now that background perspectives (Part One) and an analysis of Luke 22:24-30 (Part Two) have been presented, we are in a position to step back, overview the central claims of the dissertation as a whole, and draw certain conclusions as to the meaning of the text. The present chapter attempts this task by combining a summary and a synthesis of the major findings of this dissertation. Synthesis, however, takes priority over summary, for while it is useful to bring the key points of the work back to center stage at this point,[1] it is even more important to combine such points so as to form an integrated and reasonably concise statement of the meaning of the text.[2] Although we will draw upon the achievements of all chapters in the present work, the unitary conception of 22:24-30 as demonstrated in section 8.2 (cf. secs. 1.1, 4.1, 4.6 and 7.3.1) especially warrants the pursuit of this integrated and concise statement.

The chief aim of the present chapter is to substantiate and elaborate upon the implicit claim which the title of this dissertation constitutes, namely that leadership and discipleship are concepts central to Luke 22:24-30. The developing argument will include an exploration of the

[1]This will be done throughout the present chapter, though often not in an explicit manner.

[2]This is to be distinguished from ch. 8, which focuses on aspects of the thought and expression of 22:24-30 as a literary whole only. Here we will be concerned to bring all parts of the dissertation—background perspectives (chs. 2-5), the detailed analysis of the text's subsections (chs. 6-7) and the presentation of broader unifying features (ch. 8)—back into view.

interplay between the two concepts (sec. 9.2) and their outworking in the matrix of history (9.3). Subsequently, a relatively concise statement elucidating the meaning of Luke 22:24-30 will be offered (9.4).

Before turning to the interplay of leadership and discipleship in 22:24-30, however, a few explanatory comments about these concepts are in order. To describe the type of leadership[3] in view here, it is not adequate merely to point to the authority language of vv 24-30 (cf. sec. 1.1; ch. 2) as representing a general idea of leadership, for there are distinguishing features of the concept here. Jesus describes his life as one of service (see sec. 6.5.3) and aligns himself with children and domestic servants (see sec. 6.3), yet there can be no doubt that he remains the leader of the apostles (cf. secs. 6.5 and 8.3). And just as Jesus is a servant who leads, he calls the apostles who are "great" and "leaders" to lead as servants (vv 26-27).[4] The sharp distinction made between the ordinary form of leadership exercised by civil powers and the social elite, and that advocated by the Lukan Jesus (vv 25-27) implies that positive leadership involves adopting an extraordinary, counter-cultural form (though this does not reflect ambitions of political revolution).[5] Jesus thus urges the apostles to follow his example and lead "from below" as servants committed to the welfare of those they lead.

The picture of leadership in vv 24-30, however, is yet more complex, for it also involves a future elevation of the apostles to thrones in the eschatological kingdom (vv 29-30). Here too the apostles' leadership is modeled on Jesus' rule; they are granted kingship as he was (v 29), and they will be enthroned in his kingdom (v 30).[6] Although this expression of the apostles' leadership still lies in the future at this point in the Lukan story, however, their awareness and anticipation of it would provide motivation in the present for persevering service (cf. sec. 8.4).

[3]By way of a general working definition, leadership involves the exercise of authority in relation to followers which is made effective in support of a cause or in pursuit of a goal.

[4]Koenig, 118-19; Moxnes, *Economy*, 158-9.

[5]The critique of political authorities is not presented as a direct challenge to their rule. Rather, public rulers are taken as a negative example for the exercise of authority *in the community of Jesus' followers*. Against Cassidy (e.g., 39, 60) and others, 22:24-30 does not portray the Lukan Jesus is a political revolutionary (see sec. 6.6).

[6]The juxtaposition of the saying on thrones and the promise of a banquet in the kingdom (v 30) implies that it is still Jesus' kingdom that is described in v 30b: the apostles will rule with and under king Jesus.

Leadership in 22:24-30, then, is not simply a role or power or even a personal quality. More importantly, it amounts to a course which at points defies all that was expected of ordinary expressions of authority in the NT world (cf. ch. 2). This course changes directions (i.e., down then up [cf. chs. 4 and 8]), and involves both lowly and lofty roles. At root it is a course determined by a priority on meeting the needs of people, both in the present era (i.e., the church age) and in the eschatological kingdom.[7]

In the present work "discipleship" has been defined as more than meeting Jesus' demands and following in his steps; it is taken as a broad concept involving life in a relationship of allegiance to Jesus.[8] While facets of discipleship emphasized most often in scholarship are important in 22:24-30 (e.g., following Jesus, "bearing the cross," meeting demands, etc.), the relational element is perhaps the most constant aspect of discipleship in the text at hand:[9] the solidarity of Jesus and the apostles is threatened in v 24, in vv 25-27 Jesus calls for a return by the Twelve to share his posture of service among them, in v 28 the enduring union of the apostles with Jesus is commended, and in vv 29-30 a future reunion with Jesus and a sharing of his power is envisioned. Further, the setting at table and the hope for a future meal with Jesus heighten the emphasis on the solidarity of Jesus and the apostles (cf. secs. 3.3 and 3.5).[10]

9.2 The Interplay of Leadership and Discipleship

The prevalence of both leadership and discipleship in 22:24-30 provides a basis for exploring the interplay of the two concepts. Along these lines it may first be noted that both are relational concepts; i.e., it is not just discipleship that depicts the apostles and Jesus in a relationship.[11] Luke's motif of revelation at table—both the identity of Jesus as saving

[7]Many who see Luke 22:24-30 as centering on leadership and authority are listed in sec. 8.2, n. 15.

[8]Cf. sec. 8.1 (a number of issues relating to discipleship thus understood surface in 22:24-30).

[9]Among those who see a major emphasis on being and remaining in relation to Jesus in Luke 22:24-30, as in vv 14-38 as a whole, are Evans, 798-801; Feldkämper, 207-8; Monsarrat, 41.

[10]The table context also highlights the inappropriateness of defections from interpersonal harmony and solidarity (cf. secs. 3.4-6).

[11]Leadership would perhaps correspond to a more formal relational pattern, and discipleship to a more personal aspect or form of relations, but both presuppose a social context in which they are exercised.

host and the sinful secrets of his guests are revealed—gives some indication of the depth and significance of such relations. Additionally, both concepts have "vertical" as well as "horizontal" interpersonal dimensions. That is, both involve the relation of inferiors to a superior (the apostles to Jesus),[12] and relations within the sphere of the inferiors (the apostles as fellow subordinates or disciples). To be sure, the focus in 22:24-30 would seem to be on the vertical, but an interest in the horizontal dimension—the social aspect involving the apostles' interactions with one another—is clearly present: it is a problem which is manifested in the social sphere (v 24) that occasions Jesus' sayings here, it is to the social unit of the apostles that Jesus instructions and promises are directed (contrast vv 21-23; 31-34), and it is a plurality of thrones which is envisioned (i.e., there will be joint rule).

One notes as well that the interplay of the two concepts also becomes an overlap. Discipleship by nature involves an element of authority and subordination which is typical of teacher-student relationships. Correspondingly, Luke's pivot-point discipleship (sec. 8.3) places the apostles both in and under authority (cf. 12:42-44; 19:12-19). Therefore, it is neither necessary nor possible fully to separate the two concepts in this study.

This interplay and overlap of our two key concepts is representative of Luke's capacity to place thoughts and images in tension so as to alert readers to new possibilities for meaning. It probably reflects an impulse similar to the one behind his preference for reversals (cf. sec. 4.5): an element of surprise is introduced, the narrative is enlivened, and doors to new perspectives are opened. Such features in the Lukan writings reveal both a form of thought which grapples with paradox, and a significant level of literary skill, which together allow creative and striking perspectives to grip the attention of the reader.

We may focus here on certain of the specific tensions or ironies of 22:24-30 within the larger "paradox of discipleship." Jesus the testator (see ch. 5) surprisingly prophesies his coming life (v 30; cf. vv 16, 18).[13] Similarly, Jesus the testator bequeaths authority using an appropriate verb for a testamentary disposition (διατίθημι), yet comparative καθώς in v 29 weighs heavily against a testamentary sense for the term there (see

[12]One also notes the relation of the twelve tribes to their apostolic rulers.

[13]Further, vv 19-20 are also surprising in a farewell discourse in that they describe a mode of Jesus' presence for the coming time of his absence.

sec. 7.4.2).[14] Jesus is a servant (v 27), yet he is also king (vv 29-30).[15] Leadership is not eliminated,[16] but it is drastically transformed by an orientation toward service. Various arguments for the unity of 22:24-30 (cf. esp. sec. 8.2) further illustrate Luke's way of juxtaposing certain themes in a striking manner.

The background perspectives of chapter 2 underscore the radical nature of such Lukan paradoxes; there we saw the great "distance" in the life and thought of the NT world between ruler and subject, master and slave, father and child. For Luke to overturn concepts of authority and create such paradoxes is to startle the reader with his message. This striking quality in Luke 22:24-30, however, is greatly diminished by Lull who sees the kings and benefactors of v 25 as positive examples for the apostles (contrast the analysis set out in sec. 6.3).[17] Lull does not recognize the decisive importance of Jesus' alignment of his own life and mission with "Position B" in the antithetical structure of 22:25-27, and he thus reduces the sharp contrast the Lukan Jesus draws between the apostles' role and the prevalent patterns of authority in civil and social spheres.

The prominence of both leadership and discipleship throughout 22:24-30, together with their extensive interplay and overlap, makes possible the conclusion that in 22:24-30 the two concepts form a single, though complex, relational pattern involving Jesus and the Twelve. It is a relationship involving the exercise of the transformed authority of servant-leadership (by Jesus and the Twelve) and subordination to authority (by the Twelve [and those whom they govern]), and the experience of solidarity (with one another, and especially with Jesus). This conceptual linkage of leadership and discipleship as a single complex relational pattern seen in 22:24-30 has not been identified and analyzed in previous work on the text.

---

[14]The resurrection event probably accounts for this departure from the generic norm. Tannehill ("Study," 202) and others who favor a testamentary sense for διατίθημι in 22:29 (cf. sec. 7.4.2), however, overlook Luke's irony.

[15]Cf. 19:38. Note that the aorist διέθετο in v 29 implies Jesus' *past* reception of kingly authority (see further below in sec. 9.3 on christology).

[16]See above (sec. 9.1) on the fact that both Jesus and the apostles are leaders.

[17]Lull, 294-7. Although the scholarly consensus is against Lull's reading and takes the kings and benefactors of v 25 as negative examples, previous work on the text has not observed how the larger reversal form of 22:24-30, including the "descent" element which Jesus urges upon the apostles (vv 25-27), supports the consensus view.

9.3 The Matrix of History

It is important to observe that, according to Luke 22:24-30, these activities of Jesus and the Twelve are carried out over a great span of time. That is, Luke makes history—in the present age and into the eschaton—the matrix for experiencing leadership and discipleship. A historiographical portrayal gives continuity and the aura of unbreakable duration to these activities. To be sure, there are important shifts of style and form over time for the actions described in 22:24-30. The injunction to lead from the posture of service (vv 25-27), for instance, differs in tone from the picture of enthronement (v 30).[18] Nonetheless, it is argued that 22:24-30 portrays leadership and discipleship as characterizing the relations of Jesus and the Twelve in the era of Jesus' ministry, at the Passion, in the church age and into the eschaton.[19] Past, present and future together form a unified matrix for the ongoing, if varied, exercise of leadership and discipleship.

This historiographical portrayal invites an outlook of optimism for viewing the actions of Jesus or the Twelve at any particular point in time (cf. secs. 7.5 and 8.4). Despite Jesus' passion suffering, despite the apostles' anticipated period of trials and adversity (v 36), 22:24-30 creates a framework of hope. It provides a forward-looking perspective that anticipates the reversal of present or future adversities with an eventual positive outcome. Despite Jesus' imminent death, he will yet prevail as king, and the apostles will reign with him over the twelve tribes of Israel. Thus history is the matrix in which the reversal form of 22:24-30 depicts the transformation of a somber farewell into a joyous reunion for Jesus and the apostles.

It has been argued that such hope and anticipation would provide incentive for the apostles in the time of Jesus' absence to endure trials and carry out a ministry of service (sec. 8.4). The strength of such an incentive is underlined when we recall that the agent who effects the upward

[18]This is not to suggest that the eschatological rule of the apostles over the twelve tribes is seen by Luke as an abandonment of the service orientation. On the contrary, the juxtaposition of 22:24-27 with vv 28-30 suggests just the opposite: in keeping with the model of Jesus the servant-king, the apostles are to govern in a self-giving manner so as to benefit their subjects.

[19]Cf. the common concern of testamentary discourses with the passage of time (ch. 5).

movement in the reversal progression of vv 24-30 is Jesus, who acts in collaboration with the Father (v 29).[20] The many 360-degree reversals in Luke-Acts (see sec. 4.5) buttress this feature of 22:24-30. Luke's presentation of motivating factors of this sort reveals an anthropology of leadership and an ecclesiology which allow for or even expect that those in positions of authority in the church will need encouragement—pull as well as push—to accomplish their duties.[21]

By looking at the temporal aspects of 22:24-30 from other angles, we may gain additional insight into Luke's historiographical portrayal. First, it has been argued that the trials Jesus endured with the apostles referred to in v 28 transpired during the era of his pre-passion ministry (see secs. 7.3.2-3).[22] On the understanding of Conzelmann and others, however, the "trials" of Jesus in v 28 are restricted to the Passion.[23] This view severs an important section of Luke's time line, and overlooks his strong interest in the past and its value as a guide for life in the present and into the future.[24] A reverse error is made by those who argue for a church-age fulfillment of the conferral and promises in 22:29-30 (see sec. 7.4.4).[25] This view also restricts Luke's temporal spectrum and undermines the value of vv 29-30 as offering hope for a significantly new era of celebration and reward.

In contrast to these perspectives, it is here maintained that Luke's time line in vv 24-30 extends from the public ministry and life of Jesus (vv 27-28) to the Passion (v 27 [cf. sec. 6.5.3]) to the church era (the service commended in vv 25-27 is to characterize the apostles' leadership in the church, and after) and to the age to come (vv 29-30).[26] The time frame of

[20]Though the elevation assumes the apostles' commendable perseverance in trials (v 28, cf. sec. 7.4.1), it does not amount to an apostolic achievement.

[21]The final positive outcome (vv 29-30) for apostles who stooped to the low level of the quarrel in v 24 would support this "generous" anthropology, and an implication is that Luke envisions church leaders as people who experience failure in their walk of discipleship and who need to be encouraged to carry on with their service.

[22]Further, though Jesus' service (v 27c) is centered in his death, it probably also involves pre-passion humble actions to aid his followers (cf. sec. 6.5.3).

[23]Conzelmann, *Theology*, 80-1; so also e.g., Ott, 85-9; S. Schulz, 330.

[24]Recollections of a testator's past constitute an important element in many farewell discourses (cf. ch. 5).

[25]E.g., S. Brown, 64; Karris, *Gospel*, 716; Neyrey, 27-8; G. Schneider, *Theologe*, 84; Wanke, 65. See sec. 7.4.4, n. 211, for additional documentation.

[26]An implication of Luke's depiction here is that leadership and authority are not just necessary evils for the present era that can be eliminated in the ideal

vv 24-30 thus corresponds in general to that seen in Luke's motif of Jesus' table fellowship with his people (cf. sec. 3.5; cf. also the Passover [sec. 3.3]): Luke links the periods of history by the meals of Jesus earthly life, his Passion meal, the Lord's Supper in the church era, and the anticipated messianic banquet in the coming kingdom.[27]

Second, time is made the link between ethics and eschatology. That is, the clear ethical injunction in vv 25-27 and the commendation of past loyalty (v 28)[28] build to an eschatological reward of table fellowship and thrones (vv 29-30). More specifically, not only does the promise in vv 29-30 serve as a motivating force for the conduct enjoined and commended in vv 25-28, but the conduct of vv 25-28 is also made the ground for the promise of vv 29-30 (cf. sec. 7.4.1). Such a conception implies significant connections between the present and eschatological ages, and it weighs against the notion that Luke sees the eschaton as having become a remote future reality.[29]

Although it is true that for Luke the anticipation of an eschatological age remains vitally important for life in the present, the very writing of an account like Acts does reveal a keen interest in the developing history of the Jesus movement. Luke does not choose between salvation history and eschatological expectation, but, keeping the age to come in view, he is concerned to explain the continuing passing of time in a way that gives guidance for life in the world—life after Jesus' ministry but before his return. It is in line with this concern that the text before us takes an important place in Luke's theological interpretation of history.

Luke's historiographical portrayal in vv 24-30 also becomes the stage for christological expression. The most distinctive feature of Luke's

---

world of the eschaton (cf. secs. 7.4.3 and 7.4.4). The Lukan view is that a form of governance for the ordering of life in the eschatological kingdom is both appropriate and good.

[27]Cf. esp. Bösen, 75-7; Guillaume, 140-59.

[28]The existence of a christological dimension of the apostles' persevering loyalty to Jesus (cf. sec. 7.3.3) does not exclude an important ethical dimension.

[29]Conzelmann (*Theology*, 131-2, 135 etc.) is the one most commonly associated with a view that makes much of the delay of the Parousia, though he does not say that it has lost relevance for life in the present. While it is evident that Luke does wrestle with that delay (see e.g., Luke 9:27 diff. Mark 9:1; Luke 19:11 without a Matthean parallel), 22:24-30 implies that he sees a clear and important connection between the ages (cf. I. H. Marshall, *Historian*, 136; see also e.g., Francis [58-63], Franklin [14, 18] and Gaventa [38, 42] on the continuing importance and firm expectation of the Parousia for Luke).

christology here is the wide range of positions Jesus holds. His status is lowly (vv 27-28) yet lofty (vv 29-30), his tasks are menial yet exalted. This range of roles or positions for Jesus is clarified when one notes Luke's implication that Jesus holds them simultaneously: Jesus is already recognized in the Lukan framework as "king" in the pre-Passion narrative (19:38; and note the conferral of kingship on Jesus [22:29] is in past time), and yet Luke has implied that his status as servant carries on to the Parousia at which time he will wait on his faithful servants (12:37).[30] It is difficult to imagine how one could broaden the christological spectrum beyond the extremes of social and political images such as those of table servant and king.[31]

9.4 **Conclusion**

We may now draw together the elements of this chapter. The text before us represents a strand of Lukan thought reflecting a keen consciousness of the passage of time. For Luke the eras corresponding to Jesus' life, the Passion, the church age and the coming eschatological kingdom are linked together—one inevitably leads to another. History is moving inexorably toward a final outcome in which the condescension of Jesus and his followers will be reversed, and the apostles will participate in Jesus' reign and dine at his banquet table.

Within this perspective on time, then, Luke's description of leadership and discipleship finds its fullest sense. Jesus transforms the apostles' concept of power with the injunction to lead as servants, and they must expect to continue so to lead in the church era. Further, on the basis of the unified character of 22:24-30, the apostles as servant-leaders can be assured that they will one day rule in splendor and glory (though such a hope would hardly anticipate a return to the ruling style of worldly kings and benefactors). Solidarity with Jesus as his loyal disciples is also an experience to continue over the course of time. Although it is necessary for this too to be transformed in the period of Jesus' absence (i.e., through the Lord's Supper), the personal union involved in discipleship is lived

[30]This aspect of Lukan christology reflects the author's inclination to defy reader expectations through the use of paradox (cf. sec. 9.2 above).

[31]This juxtaposition corresponds in general terms to Luke's peculiar emphasis that Jesus was a suffering Messiah (cf. Fitzmyer, *Gospel*, 1:200; Franklin, 60-1; see 24:26, 46; Acts 3:18; 17:3; 26:23). See sec. 4.5 on the reversal course in the life of the Lukan Jesus.

out in the sure expectation of an eschatological celebration in the presence of Jesus.

In short, then, the core of thought and expression in Luke 22:24-30 concerns the ongoing relationship of Jesus and the apostles, which, though changing over time in terms of tone and form, remains one of leader and followers, teacher and disciples. It is a relationship in which there is a clear authority structure and a strong bond of personal union and solidarity. It is a relationship that critiques and transforms ordinary ideas of authority by its commendation of leadership from the posture of service. And it is a relationship shot through with hope for elevation and celebration in the age to come. In 22:24-30 Luke affirms the importance of Jesus' and the apostles' exercise of authority in solidarity with one another over the unbroken span of time.

Bibliography

Texts, Translations and Reference Works

Works in the LCL series which are cited in the present study are not listed in the bibliography.

Aland, K., ed., *Synopsis* Aland, Kurt, ed. *Synopsis Quattuor Evangeliorum.* 13th ed. Stuttgart: Deutsche Bibelgesellschaft, 1985.

———, et al., eds., UBS3 ———, et al., eds. *The Greek New Testament.* 3rd ed. Stuttgart: United Bible Societies, 1983.

———, et al., eds., NA26 ———, et al., eds. *Novum Testamentum Graece.* 26th ed. Stuttgart: Deutsche Bibelstiftung, 1979.

The American and British Committees of the International Greek New Testament Project, eds. *The New Testament in Greek. The Gospel According to St. Luke.* Part Two: *Chapters 13-24.* Oxford: Clarendon, 1987.

Aune, *Jesus* Aune, David E. *Jesus and the Synoptic Gospels: A Bibliographic Study Guide.* Madison: Theological Students Fellowship, 1980.

Bachmann, H., and Slaby, W. A., eds. *Computer Concordance to the Novum Testamentum Graece of Nestle-Aland, 26th Edition, and to The Greek New Testament, 3rd Edition.* 2nd ed. New York: de Gruyter, 1985.

Barrett, C. K., ed., *Documents* Barrett. Charles K., ed. *The New Testament Background: Selected Documents.* Rev. ed. London: SPCK, 1987.

Bauer, Walter. *A Greek-English Lexicon of the New Testament and Other Early Christian Literature.* 2nd ed. Trans. William F. Arndt and F. Wilbur Gingrich. Revised by F. Wilbur Gingrich and Frederick W. Danker. Chicago: University, 1979.

Berkowitz, Luci, and Squitier, Karl A., eds. *Thesaurus Linguae Graecae. Canon of Greek Authors and Works.* 2nd ed. New York: Oxford, 1986.

Bickford-Smith, R. A. H., ed. *Publilii Syri. Sententiae.* London: C. J. Clay, 1895.

Blass, F., and Debrunner, A. *A Greek Grammar of the New Testament and Other Early Christian Literature.* Trans. and edt. Robert W. Funk. Chicago: University, 1961.

Brooks, James A., and Winbery, Carlton L. *Syntax of New Testament Greek.* 2nd ed. Lanham, MD: University Press of America, 1988.

Brown, Francis, and Driver, S. R., and Briggs, Charles A. *A Hebrew and English Lexicon of the Old Testament.* Oxford: Clarendon, 1907.

Cartlidge, David R., and Dungan, David L. *Documents for the Study of the Gospels.* London: Collins, 1980.

Charlesworth, James H., ed. *The Old Testament Pseudepigrapha.* 2 vols. London: Darton, Longman and Todd, 1983, 1985.

Danby, H., ed. *The Mishnah.* London: Oxford, 1933.

Denis, Albert-Marie, ed. *Concordance greque des pseudépigraphes d' ancien testament.* Louvain: Université Catholique, 1987.

Dittenberger, W., ed. *Sylloge Inscriptionum Graecarum.* 4 vols. 3rd ed. Leipzig: Hirzelium, 1915-21.

Elliger, K., and Rudolph, W., eds. *Biblia Hebraica Stuttgartensia.* Stuttgart: Deutsche Bibelgesellschaft, 1984.

Epstein, Isidore, ed. *The Babylonian Talmud.* 18 vols. London: Soncino, 1961.

Fee, Gordon D. *New Testament Exegesis.* Philadelphia: Westminster, 1983.

Fitzmyer, *Bibliography* Fitzmyer, Joseph A. *An Introductory Bibliography for the Study of Scripture* (SubBib 3). Rome: Biblical Institute, 1981.

France, *Guide* France, R. T. *A Bibliographic Guide to New Testament Research.* Cambridge: Tyndale Fellowship for Biblical Research, 1974.

Funk, Robert W., ed. *New Gospel Parallels.* Vol. 1: *Synoptic Gospels* (FF). Philadelphia: Fortress, 1985.

Gordon, W. M., and Robinson, O. F., eds. and trans. *The Institutes of Gaius.* London: Duckworth, 1988.

Harvey, W. Wigan, ed. *Sancti Irenaei, episcopi lugenensis. Libros quinque adversus Haereses.* 2 vols. Cambridge: University, 1857.

Hatch, Edwin, and Redpath, Henry A., eds. *A Concordance to the Septuagint.* 2 vols. Oxford: Clarendon, 1897.

Hausrath, Augustus, ed. *Corpus Fabularum Aesopicarum* (Bibliotheca Scriptorum Graecorum et Romanorum Teubneriana 1/2). Leipzig: Teubneri, 1961.

Horsley, G. H. R., ed. *New Documents Illustrating Early Christianity.* 5 vols. North Ryde, Australia: Macquarie University, 1981-1990.

Ibycus Scholarly Computer. Designed by Thesaurus Linguae Graecae, University of California, Irvine, 1987.

De Jonge, ed., *Testamenta* De Jonge, M., ed. *Testamenta XII Patriarcharum Edited according to Cambridge University Library MS Ff 1.24 fol. 203a-261b* (PVTG 1). 2nd ed. Leiden: Brill, 1970.

———, ed., *Testaments* ———, ed. *The Testaments of the Twelve Patriarchs. A Critical Edition of the Greek Text* (PVTG 1/2). Leiden: Brill,

1978.

Kee, "Testaments" Kee, Howard C. "The Testaments of the Twelve Patriarchs. A New Translation and Introduction," 775-828. In *The Old Testament Pseudepigrapha.* Vol. 1. Edt. James H. Charlesworth. London: Dartman, Longman and Todd, 1983.

Kepple, R. J. *Reference Works for Theological Research.* Lanham, MD: University Press of America, 1981.

Lampe, ed., *Lexicon* Lampe, G. W. H, ed. *A Patristic Greek Lexicon.* Oxford: Clarendon, 1961-68.

Larfeld, W., ed. *Griechische Epigraphik.* 3rd ed. Munich: Beck, 1914.

Liddell, H. G., and Scott, R. *A Greek-English Lexicon.* 9th ed. Edt. H. Stuart Jones and R. McKenzie. Oxford: Clarendon, 1940.

Lohse, ed., *Die Texte* Lohse, Eduard, ed. *Die Texte aus Qumran Hebräisch und Deutsch.* 4th ed. Munich: Kösel, 1986.

Mattill, A. J., Jr., and Mattill, Mary B. *A Classified Bibliography of Literature on the Acts of the Apostles* (NTTS 7), Leiden: Brill, 1966.

Metzger, *Commentary* Metzger, Bruce M. *A Textual Commentary on the Greek New Testament.* London: United Bible Societies, 1971.

———, *Festschriften* ———. *Index of Articles on the New Testament and the Early Church Published in Festschriften* (SBLMS 5). Philadelphia: Society of Biblical Literature, 1951; Supplement, 1955.

———, *Index* ———. *Index to Periodical Literature on Christ and the Gospels* (NTTS 6). Leiden: Brill, 1966.

Mills, W. E. *A Bibliography of the Periodical Literature on Acts, 1962-84.* Leiden: Brill, 1986.

Morgenthaler, Robert. *Statistik des neutestamentlichen Wortschatzes.* Zurich: Gotthelf, 1958.

Moule, *Idiom Book* Moule, C. F. D. *An Idiom Book of the New Testament.* 2nd ed. Cambridge: University, 1959.

Moulton, James H., and Howard, Wilbert F. *A Grammar of New Testament Greek.* Vol. 2: *Accidence and Word-Formation.* Edinburgh: Clark, 1929.

Moulton, James H., and Milligan, G. *The Vocabulary of the Greek New Testament Illustrated from the Papyri and Other Non-Literary Sources.* London: Hodder and Stoughton, 1914-30.

Nunn, H. P. V. *A Short Syntax of New Testament Greek.* 5th ed. Cambridge: University, 1938.

Rahlfs, Alfred, ed. *Septuaginta.* 7th ed. Stuttgart: Würtembergische Bibelanstalt, 1935.

Rengstorf, ed., *Concordance* Rengstorf, Karl H., ed. *A Complete Concordance to Flavius Josephus.* 4 vols. Leiden: Brill, 1973-1983.

Robertson, A. T. *A Grammar of the Greek New Testament in the Light of Historical Research.* 4th ed. Nashville: Broadman, 1923.

Scholer, David M. *A Basic Bibliographic Guide for New Testament Exegesis.* 2nd ed. Grand Rapids: Eerdmans, 1973; Unpublished supplement, 1981.

Segbroeck, Frans Van. *The Gospel of Luke: A Cumulative Bibliography 1973-1988* (BETL 88). Leuven: University, 1989.

Smyth, Herbert W. *Greek Grammar.* Revised by Gordon M. Messing. Cambridge, MA: Harvard, 1956.

Strack, Hermann L, and Billerbeck, P. *Kommentar zum Neuen Testament aus Talmud und Midrasch.* 6 vols. Munich: Beck, 1922-61.

Turner, *Style* Turner, Nigel. *Style.* Vol. 4 of Moulton, James H. *A Grammar of New Testament Greek.* Edinburgh: Clark, 1976.

———, *Syntax* ———. *Syntax.* Vol. 3 of Moulton, James H. *A Grammar of New Testament Greek.* Edinburgh: Clark, 1963.

Vermes, G., ed. *The Dead Sea Scrolls in English.* 3rd ed. London: Penguin, 1987.

Wagner, Günter. *An Exegetical Bibliography of the New Testament.* Vol. 2: *Luke and Acts.* Macon, GA: Mercer, 1985.

Zerwick, Maximilian. *Biblical Greek.* Trans. Joseph Smith. Rome: Biblical Institute, 1963.

Commentaries and Studies

Aalen, S. "St. Luke's Gospel and the Last Chapters of I Enoch." *NTS* 13 (1966): 1-13.

Achtemeier, Paul J. "An Exposition of Mark 9:30-37." *Int* 30 (1976): 178-83.

Adams, David R. *The Suffering of Paul and the Dynamics of Luke-Acts.* PhD dissertation, unpublished. Yale University, 1979.

Aerts, T. "Suivre Jésus. Evolution d'un thème biblique dans les évangiles synoptiques." *ETL* 42 (1966): 476-512.

Aland, Kurt, and Aland, Barbara. *The Text of the New Testament.* Trans. Errol F. Rhoades. Grand Rapids: Eerdmans, 1987.

Albright, W. F., and Mann, C. S. *Matthew* (AB 26). New York: Doubleday, 1971.

Alter, Robert. *The Art of Biblical Narrative.* London: George Allen and Unwin, 1981.

Applebaum, Shimon. "Judea as a Roman Province; the Countryside as a Political and Economic Factor." *ANRW* 2/8:355-96.

Arens, Eduardo. *The* ΗΛΘΟΝ-*Sayings in the Synoptic Tradition* (Orbis Biblicus et Orientalis 10). Göttingen: Vandenhoeck und Ruprecht, 1976.

Arndt, William F. *The Gospel According to St. Luke.* St. Louis: Concordia, 1956.

Aune, "Septem" Aune, David E. "Septem Sapientum Convivium (Moralia 146B-164D)," 51-105. In *Plutarch's Ethical Writings and Early Christian Literature* (SCHNT 4). Edt. H. D. Betz. Leiden: Brill, 1978.

Baarda, T. "'... Als hij die bedient', Luc. 22:27. Marginalia bij een woord van Jezus in het verhaal van het avondmaal in het evangelie van Lucas," 11-22. In *De knechtsgestalte van Christus*. Edt. H. H. Grosheide et al. Kampen: Kok, 1978.

Badian, "Client Kings" Badian, E. "Client Kings." *OCD* 253.

———, *Clientelae* ———. *Foreign Clientelae (264-70 B.C.)*. Oxford: Clarendon, 1958.

Bahr, G. J. "The Seder of the Passover and the Eucharistic Words." *NovT* 12 (1970): 181-202.

Bailey, F. G. "The Peasant View of the Bad Life," 299-321. In *Peasants and Peasant Societies* (Penguin Modern Sociology Readings). Harmondsworth: Penguin, 1971.

Bailey, J. A. *The Traditions Common to the Gospels of Luke and John* (NovTSup 7). Leiden: Brill, 1963.

Balsdon, "Gaius" Balsdon, John P. V. D. "Gaius." *OCD* 452-3.

———, "Imperium" ———. "Imperium." *OCD* 542-3.

Baltzer, Klaus. *The Covenant Formulary in Old Testament, Jewish, and Early Christian Writings*. Trans. David E. Green. Philadelphia: Fortress, 1971.

Bammel, "Das Ende" Bammel, Ernst. "Das Ende von Q," 39-50. In *Verborum veritas: Festschrift für Gustav Stählin zum 70. Geburtstag*. Edt. O. Böcher and K. Haacker. Wuppertal: Brockhaus, 1970.

———, "πτωχός" ———. "πτωχός κτλ." *TDNT* 6:885-915.

———, "Testament" ———. "Das >Testament< Jesu (Luk 22.27ff)," 74-83. In *Jesu Nachfolger. Nachfolgeüberlieferungen in der Zeit des frühen Christentums* (Studia Delitzschiana 3/1). Heidelberg: Schneider, 1988.

Barclay, John M. G. "Paul, Philemon and the Dilemma of Christian Slave-Ownership." *NTS* 37 (1991): 161-86.

Barrett, "Background" Barrett, Charles K. "The Background of Mark 10.45," 1-18. In *New Testament Essays. Studies in Memory of Thomas Walter Manson*. Edt. A. J. B. Higgins. Manchester: University, 1959.

———, *John* ———. *The Gospel According to St. John*. 2nd ed. London: SPCK, 1978.

———, *Luke* ———. *Luke the Historian in Recent Study*. London: Epworth, 1961.

———, "Mark 10:45" ———. "Mark 10:45: A Ransom for Many," 20-6. In *New Testament Essays*. London: SPCK, 1972.

———, "Address" ———. "Paul's Address to the Ephesian Elders," 107-21. In *God's Christ and His People. Festschrift for Nils A. Dahl*. Edt. J. Jervell and W. Meeks. Oslo: Universitetsforlaget, 1977.

———, "Apostle" ———. "*Shaliaḥ* and Apostle," 88-102. In *Donum Gentilicum: New Testament Studies in honour of David Daube*. Edt E. Bammel et al. Oxford: Clarendon, 1978.

———, "Theologia Crucis" ———. "Theologia Crucis—in Acts?" 73-84. In *Theologia Crucis—Signum Crucis: Festschrift für Erich Dinkler zum 70.*

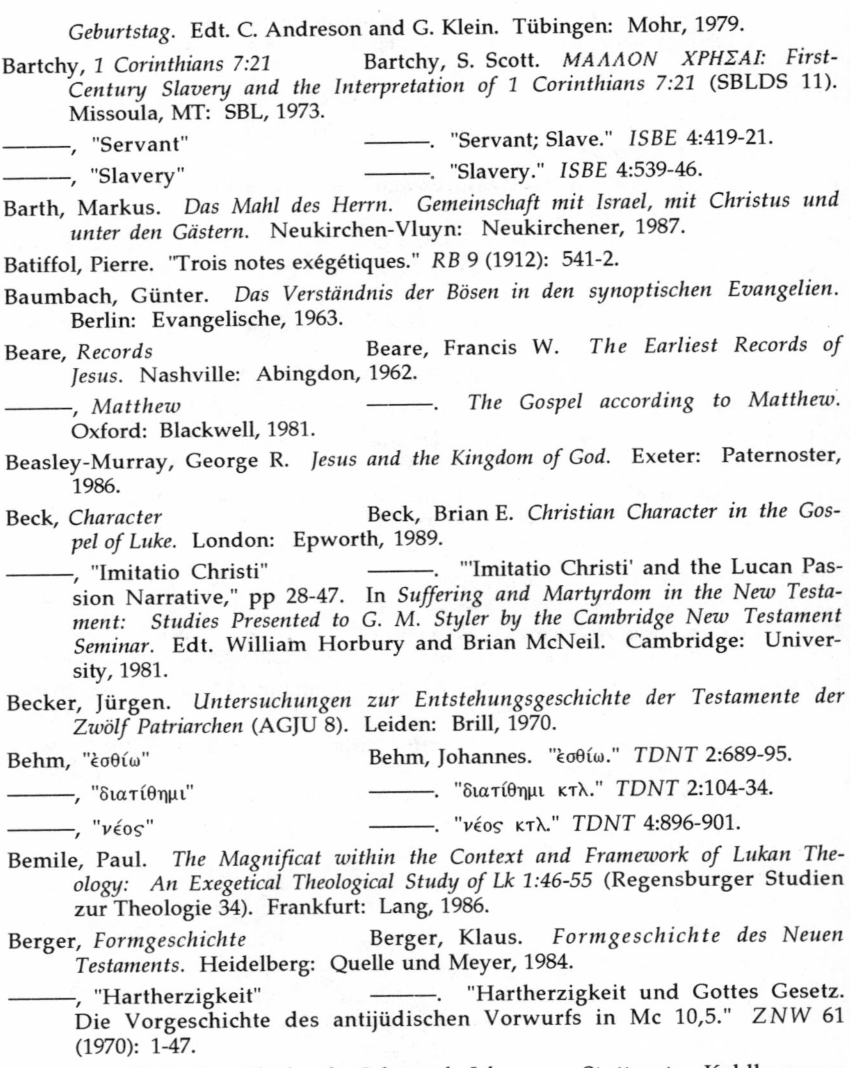

Geburtstag. Edt. C. Andreson and G. Klein. Tübingen: Mohr, 1979.

Bartchy, *1 Corinthians 7:21* Bartchy, S. Scott. *ΜΑΛΛΟΝ ΧΡΗΣΑΙ: First-Century Slavery and the Interpretation of 1 Corinthians 7:21* (SBLDS 11). Missoula, MT: SBL, 1973.

———, "Servant" ———. "Servant; Slave." *ISBE* 4:419-21.

———, "Slavery" ———. "Slavery." *ISBE* 4:539-46.

Barth, Markus. *Das Mahl des Herrn. Gemeinschaft mit Israel, mit Christus und unter den Gästern.* Neukirchen-Vluyn: Neukirchener, 1987.

Batiffol, Pierre. "Trois notes exégétiques." *RB* 9 (1912): 541-2.

Baumbach, Günter. *Das Verständnis der Bösen in den synoptischen Evangelien.* Berlin: Evangelische, 1963.

Beare, *Records* Beare, Francis W. *The Earliest Records of Jesus.* Nashville: Abingdon, 1962.

———, *Matthew* ———. *The Gospel according to Matthew.* Oxford: Blackwell, 1981.

Beasley-Murray, George R. *Jesus and the Kingdom of God.* Exeter: Paternoster, 1986.

Beck, *Character* Beck, Brian E. *Christian Character in the Gospel of Luke.* London: Epworth, 1989.

———, "Imitatio Christi" ———. "'Imitatio Christi' and the Lucan Passion Narrative," pp 28-47. In *Suffering and Martyrdom in the New Testament: Studies Presented to G. M. Styler by the Cambridge New Testament Seminar.* Edt. William Horbury and Brian McNeil. Cambridge: University, 1981.

Becker, Jürgen. *Untersuchungen zur Entstehungsgeschichte der Testamente der Zwölf Patriarchen* (AGJU 8). Leiden: Brill, 1970.

Behm, "ἐσθίω" Behm, Johannes. "ἐσθίω." *TDNT* 2:689-95.

———, "διατίθημι" ———. "διατίθημι κτλ." *TDNT* 2:104-34.

———, "νέος" ———. "νέος κτλ." *TDNT* 4:896-901.

Bemile, Paul. *The Magnificat within the Context and Framework of Lukan Theology: An Exegetical Theological Study of Lk 1:46-55* (Regensburger Studien zur Theologie 34). Frankfurt: Lang, 1986.

Berger, *Formgeschichte* Berger, Klaus. *Formgeschichte des Neuen Testaments.* Heidelberg: Quelle und Meyer, 1984.

———, "Hartherzigkeit" ———. "Hartherzigkeit und Gottes Gesetz. Die Vorgeschichte des antijüdischen Vorwurfs in Mc 10,5." *ZNW* 61 (1970): 1-47.

Bergmeier, Roland. *Glaube als Gabe nach Johannes.* Stuttgart: Kohlhammer, 1980.

Bertram, Georg. "ἔργον κτλ." *TDNT* 2:635-55.

Best, *Disciples* Best, Ernest. *Disciples and Discipleship.*

Studies in the Gospel according to Mark. Edinburgh: Clark, 1986.

———, *Following* ———. *Following Jesus. Discipleship in the Gospel of Mark* (JSNTSup 4). Sheffield: JSOT, 1981.

———, *Temptation* ———. *The Temptation and the Passion: The Markan Soteriology* (SNTSMS 2). Cambridge: University, 1965.

Betz, H. "De laude" Betz, Hans D. "De laude ipsius (Moralia 539A-547F)," 367-93. In *Plutarch's Ethical Writings and Early Christian Literature* (SCHNT 4). Leiden: Brill, 1978.

———, *Nachfolge* ———. *Nachfolge und Nachahmung Jesu Christi im Neuen Testament* (BHT 37). Tübingen: Mohr, 1967.

Betz, Otto. "Jesu Evangelium vom Gottesreich," 55-77. In *Das Evangelium und die Evangelien. Vorträge vom Tübinger Symposium 1982* (WUNT 28). Edt. Peter Stuhlmacher. Tübingen: Mohr, 1983.

Beyer, Hermann. "διακονέω κτλ." *TDNT* 2:81-93.

Bietenhard, Hans. *Die himmlische Welt im Urchristentum und Spätjudentum* (WUNT 2). Tübingen: Mohr, 1951.

Black, C. Clifton. *The Disciples according to Mark. Markan Redaction in Current Debate* (JSNTSup 27). Sheffield: JSOT, 1989.

Blevins, J. L. "The Passion Narrative: Luke 19:28-24:53." *RevExp* 64 (1967): 513-22.

Blinzler, Josef. "Passionsgeschehen und Passionsbericht des Lukasevangeliums." *BK* 24 (1969): 1-4.

Bock, Darrell, L. *Proclamation from Prophecy and Pattern* (JSNTSup 12). Sheffield: JSOT, 1987.

Boismard, M. E. "Saint Luc et la rédaction du quatrième évangile." *RB* 69 (1962): 185-211.

Borg, Marcus J. *Conflict, Holiness and Politics in the Teachings of Jesus* (Studies in the Bible and Early Christianity 5). New York: Mellen, 1984.

Borgen, P. "John and the Synoptics in the Passion Narrative." *NTS* 5 (1958-59): 246-59.

Boring, M. Eugene. *Sayings of the Risen Jesus: Christian Prophecy in the Synoptic Tradition* (SNTSMS 46). Cambridge: University, 1982.

Borsch, *Son of Man* Borsch, Frederick H. *The Christian and Gnostic Son of Man* (SBT 2/14). London: SCM, 1970.

———, *Power* ———. *Power in Weakness: New Hearing for Gospel Stories of Healing and Discipleship.* Philadelphia: Fortress, 1983.

Bösen, Willibald. *Jesusmahl. Eucharistisches Mahl. Endzeitmahl. Ein Beitrag zur Theologie des Lukas* (StBib 97). Stuttgart: Katholisches Bibelwerk, 1980.

Bossuyt, Philippe, and Radermakers, Jean. *Jésus, Parole de la Grâce selon saint Luc.* Vol. 2. 2nd ed. Brussels: Institut d'Etudes Théologiques, 1984.

Bouhours, J. F. "Une étude de l'ordonnance de la triple tradition." *RSR* 60 (1972):

595-614.

Boulton, P. H. "Διακονέω and its Cognates in the Four Gospels." SE I (1959): 415-22.

Bousset, *Kyrios* Bousset, W. *Kyrios Christos: A History of the Belief in Christ from the Beginning of Christianity to Irenaeus.* Trans. John E. Steely. Nashville: Abingdon, 1970.

———, *Religion* ———. *Die Religion des Judentums im Spät-hellenistischen Zeitalter* (HNT 21). Tübingen: Mohr, 1926.

Bovon, *Lukas* Bovon, François. *Das Evangelium nach Lukas. Lk 1,1-9,50* (EKKNT 3/1). Zurich: Benziger; Neukirchen-Vluyn: Neukirchener, 1989.

———, *Vingt-cinq ans* ———. *Luc le théologien. vingt-cinq ans de recherches (1950-1975).* 2nd ed. Geneva: Labor et Fides, 1988.

———, *Thirty-three years* ———. *Luke the Theologian. Thirty-three years of research (1950-1983)* (Princeton Theological Monograph Series 12). Trans. Ken McKinney. Allison Park, PA: Pickwick, 1987.

Boyer, J. L. "The Classification of Subjunctives: A Statistical Study." *GTJ* 7 (1986): 3-19.

Braumann, G. "Das Mittel der Zeit. Erwägungen zur Theologie des Lukasevangeliums." *ZNW* 54 (1963): 117-45.

Braund, D. C. *Rome and the Friendly King: the Character of the Client Kingship.* London: Croom Helm, 1984.

Brawley, Robert L. *Luke-Acts and the Jews. Conflict, Apology, and Conciliation* (SBLMS 33). Atlanta: Scholars, 1987.

Bright, John. *A History of Israel.* 3rd ed. London: SCM, 1981.

Broer, Ingo. "Das Ringen der Gemeinde um Israel. Exegetischer Versuch über Mt 19, 28," 148-65. In *Jesus und der Menschensohn. Festschrift für A. Vögtle.* Edt. R. Pesch and R. Schnackenburg. Freiburg: Herder, 1975.

Brown, R., *Birth* Brown, Raymond E. *The Birth of the Messiah.* Garden City, NY: Doubleday, 1977.

———, *John* ———. *The Gospel According to John XIII-XXI* (AB 29A). Garden City, NY: Doubleday, 1970.

Brown, Schuyler. *Apostasy and Perseverance in the Theology of Luke* (AnBib 36). Rome: Biblical Institute, 1969.

Bruce, *Greek Text* Bruce, F. F. *The Acts of the Apostles. The Greek Text with Introduction and Commentary.* London: Tyndale, 1951.

———, *Commentary* ———. *Commentary on the Book of Acts* (NICNT). Rev. ed. Grand Rapids: Eerdmans, 1988.

———, "Speeches" ———. "The Speeches in Acts—Thirty Years After," 53-68. In *Reconciliation and Hope.* Edt. R. Banks. Grand Rapids: Eerdmans, 1975.

Büchle, Anton. *Der Tod Jesu im Lukasevangelium. Eine redaktionsgeschichtliche Untersuchung zu Lk 23* (Frankfurter Theologische Studien). Frankfurt: Knecht, 1978.

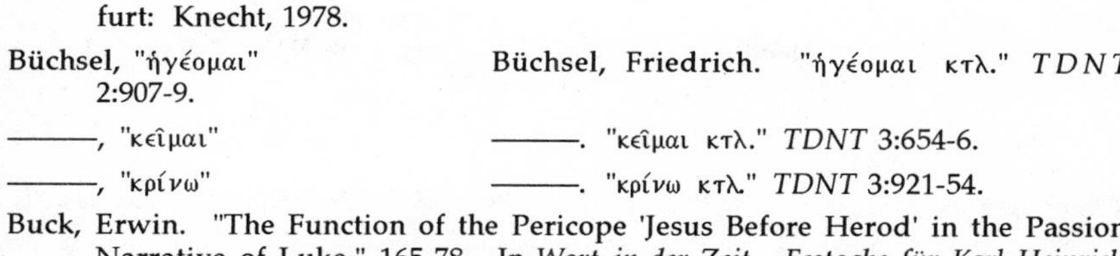

Büchsel, "ἡγέομαι" Büchsel, Friedrich. "ἡγέομαι κτλ." *TDNT* 2:907-9.

———, "κεῖμαι" ———. "κεῖμαι κτλ." *TDNT* 3:654-6.

———, "κρίνω" ———. "κρίνω κτλ." *TDNT* 3:921-54.

Buck, Erwin. "The Function of the Pericope 'Jesus Before Herod' in the Passion Narrative of Luke," 165-78. In *Wort in der Zeit. Festgabe für Karl Heinrich Rengstorf zum 70. Geburtstag.* Edt. W. Haubeck and M. Bachmann. Leiden: Brill, 1980.

Budesheim, Thomas L. "Paul's Abschiedsrede in the Acts of the Apostles." *HTR* 69 (1976): 9-30.

Bultmann, *History* Bultmann, Rudolf. *The History of the Synoptic Tradition.* Trans. John Marsh. Oxford: Blackwell, 1963.

———, *Theology* ———. *Theology of the New Testament.* 2 vols. Trans. Kendrick Grobel. London: SCM, 1952, 1955.

Burnett, Fred W. "Παλιγγενεσία in Matt. 19:28: A Window on the Matthean Community?" *JSNT* 17 (1983): 60-72.

Buse, S. I. "St. John and the Passion Narratives of St. Matthew and St. Luke." *NTS* 7 (1960-61): 65-76.

Cadbury , *Luke-Acts* Cadbury, Henry J. *The Making of Luke-Acts.* London: SPCK, 1958.

———, *Style* ———. *The Style and Literary Method of Luke* (HTS 6). Cambridge, MA: Harvard University, 1920.

———, et al., "History" ———, et al. "The Greek and Jewish Traditions of Writing History," 7-29. In *The Beginnings of Christianity.* Vol. 2. Edt. F. J. Foakes-Jackson and Kirsopp Lake. London: Macmillan, 1922.

Cadoux, C. J. *The Early Church and the World.* Edinburgh: Clark, 1925.

Caird, *Language* Caird, George B. *The Language and Imagery of the Bible.* London: Duckworth, 1980.

———, *Luke* ———. *Saint Luke* (PGC). Middlesex: Penguin, 1963.

Caragounis, Chrys C. *The Son of Man. Vision and Interpretation* (WUNT 38). Tübingen: Mohr, 1986.

Carroll, John T. *Response to the End of History. Eschatology and Situation in Luke-Acts* (SBLDS 92). Atlanta: Scholars, 1988.

Casey, Maurice. *Son of Man. The Interpretation and Influence of Daniel 7.* London: SPCK, 1979.

Cassidy, Richard. *Jesus, Politics and Society. A Study of Luke's Gospel.* Maryknoll, NY: Orbis, 1978.

Catchpole, "Matthew xxv. 31-46" Catchpole, David R. "The Poor on Earth and the Son of Man in Heaven. A Re-Appraisal of Matthew xxv. 31-46." *BJRL* 61 (1979): 355-97.

———, "Tradition History" ———. "Tradition History," 165-80. In *New Testament Interpretation. Essays on Principles and Methods.* Edt. I. Howard Marshall. Exeter: Paternoster, 1977.

Chance, J. Bradley. *Jerusalem, the Temple, and the New Age in Luke-Acts.* Macon, GA: Mercer, 1988.

Charlesworth, Martin P. "*Providentia* and *Aeternitas.*" *HTR* 29 (1936): 107-33.

Chilton, Bruce D. *God in Strength. Jesus' Announcement of the Kingdom* (SNTSU B/1). Plöchl: Freistadt, 1979.

Clark, Andrew C. "Apostleship: Evidence from the New Testament and Early Christian Literature." *VE* 19 (1989): 49-82.

Clark, Kenneth W. "The Meaning of [κατα] κυριεύειν," 207-12. In *The Gentile Bias and other Essays* (NovTSup 54). Leiden: Brill, 1980.

Clarke, Andrew D. "The Good and the Just in Romans 5:7." *TynBul* 41 (1990): 128-42.

Coffey, Michael. "Symposium Literature." *OCD* 1028-9.

Collins , "Literature" Collins, John J. "The Testamentary Literature in Recent Scholarship," 268-78. In *Early Judaism and its Modern Interpreters.* Edt. R. Kraft and G. Nickelsburg. Philadelphia: Fortress; Atlanta: Scholars, 1986.

———, "Testaments" ———. "Testaments," 325-55. In *Jewish Writings of the Second Temple Period.* Edt. Michael E. Stone. Philadelphia: Fortress, 1984.

Conzelmann, *Acts* Conzelmann, Hans. *Acts of the Apostles* (Hermenia). Trans. James Limburg, A. Thomas Kraabel and Donald H. Juel. Philadelphia: Fortress, 1987.

———, *Theology* ———. *The Theology of St. Luke.* Trans. Geoffrey Buswell. London: Faber and Faber, 1960.

———, and Lindemann, Andreas. *Interpreting the New Testament. An Introduction to the Principles and Methods of N. T. Exegesis.* Trans. Sigfried S. Schatzmann. Peabody, MA: Hendrickson, 1988.

Cosgrove, Charles H. "The Divine Δεῖ in Luke-Acts." *NovT* 26 (1984): 168-90.

Cotterell, Peter, and Turner, Max. *Linguistics and Biblical Interpretation.* London: SPCK, 1989.

Coulot, Claude. *Jésus et le disciple. Étude sur l'autorité messianique de Jesus* (EBib NS 8). Paris: Gabalda, 1987.

Cousar, Charles B. "An Exposition of Luke 5.29-35." *Int* 40 (1986): 58-63.

Cranfield, C. E. B. *The Gospel According to Mark* (CGTC). Cambridge: University, 1959.

Creed, J. M. *The Gospel According to St. Luke.* London: Macmillan, 1965.

Cribbs, "St. Luke" Cribbs, F. L. "St. Luke and the Johannine Tradition." *JBL* 90 (1971): 422-50.

———, "Study" ———. "A Study of the Contacts That Exist

between St. Luke and St. John," 1-93. In *SBL 1973 Seminar Papers*. Vol. 2. Edt. G. W. MacRae. Cambridge, MA: SBL, 1973.

Cross, Frank M. *The Ancient Library of Qumran and Modern Biblical Studies*. 2nd ed. Garden City, NY: Doubleday, 1961.

Crossan, *Fragments* Crossan, John D. *In Fragments: The Aphorisms of Jesus*. San Francisco: Harper & Row, 1983.

———, *In Parables* ———. *In Parables: The Challenge of the Historical Jesus*. New York: Harper and Row, 1973.

Crouzel, H. "L'imitation et la 'suite' de Dieu et du Christ dans les premiers siècles chrétiens, ainsi que leurs sources gréco-romaines et hebraïques." *JAC* 21 (1978): 7-41.

Crump, David M. *Jesus the Intercessor: Prayer and Christology in Luke-Acts*. PhD dissertation, unpublished. University of Aberdeen, 1988.

Culley, Robert C. "Structural Analysis: Is it Done with Mirrors?" *Int* 28 (1974): 165-81.

Daane, James. "Father." *ISBE* 2:284-6.

Dahl, "Purpose" Dahl, Nils A. "The Purpose of Luke-Acts," 87-98. In *Jesus in the Memory of the Early Church*. Minneapolis: Augsburg, 1976.

———, "Abraham" ———. "The Story of Abraham in Luke-Acts," 139-58. In *Studies in Luke-Acts. Essays Presented in Honor of Paul Schubert*. Edt. Leander E. Keck and J. Louis Martyn. London: SPCK, 1968.

Dahood, Mitchell. *Psalms I. 1-50* (AB 16). Garden City, NY: Doubleday, 1966.

Dalman, Gustaf. *Jesus-Jeshua. Studies in the Gospels*. Trans. Paul P. Levertoff. London: SPCK, 1929.

Danker, *Benefactor* Danker, Frederick W. *Benefactor: Epigraphic Study of a Graeco-Roman and New Testament Semantic Field*. St. Louis: Clayton, 1982.

———, "Endangered Benefactor" ———. "The Endangered Benefactor in Luke-Acts," 39-48. In *SBL 1981 Seminar Papers*. Edt. Kent H. Richards. Chico, CA: Scholars, 1981.

———, "Accommodation" ———. "Graeco-Roman Cultural Accommodation in the Christology of Luke-Acts," 391-414. In *SBL 1983 Seminar Papers*. Edt. Kent H. Richards. Chico, CA: Scholars, 1983.

———, *Jesus* ———. *Jesus and the New Age According to St. Luke: A Commentary on the Third Gospel*. Rev. ed. Philadelphia: Fortress, 1988.

———, *Luke* ———. *Luke* (PC). 2nd ed. Philadelphia: Fortress, 1987.

———, "Stones" ———. "On Stones and Benefactors." *CurTM* 8 (1981): 351-6.

———, "Paul's Debt" ———. "Paul's Debt to the *De Corona* of Demosthenes: A Study of Rhetorical Techniques in Second Corinthians,"

262-80. In *Persuasive Artistry. Studies in New Testament Rhetoric in Honor of George A. Kennedy* (JSNTSup 50). Edt. Duane F. Watson. Sheffield: JSOT, 1991.

Daube, David. "Shame Culture in Luke," 355-72. In *Paul and Paulinism. Essays in honour of C. K. Barrett.* Edt. Morna D. Hooker and S. G. Wilson. London: SPCK, 1982.

Davies, R. E. "Christ in our Place—The Contribution of the Prepositions." *TynBul* 21 (1970): 71-91.

Davies, W. D. *The Gospel and the Land.* Berkeley: University of California, 1974.

Davis, E. C. *The Significance of the Shared Meal in Luke-Acts.* Ann Arbor: University Microfilms, 1967.

Dawsey, "Unity" Dawsey, James M. "The Literary Unity of Luke-Acts: Questions of Style—A Task for Literary Critics." *NTS* 35 (1989): 48-66.

———, *Voice* ———. *The Lucan Voice.* Macon, GA: Mercer, 1986.

Degenhardt, H. -J. *Lukas Evangelist der Armen. Besitz und Besitzverzicht in der lukanischen Schriften. Eine traditions- und redaktionsgeschichtliche Untersuchung.* Stuttgart: Katholisches Bibelwerk, 1965.

Dehandschutter, B. "La persécution des chrétiens dans les Actes des Apôtres," 541-6. In *Les Actes des Apôtres. Traditions, rédaction, théologie* (BETL 48). Edt. J. Kremer. Gembloux: Duculot, 1979.

Deismann, Adolf. *Light from the Ancient East.* Trans. L. Strachan. London: Doran, 1927.

Delobel, J. "L'onction par la pecheresse." *ETL* 42 (1966): 415-75.

Derrett, *Audience.* Derrett, J. Duncan M. *Jesus' Audience. The Social and Psychological Environment in which He Worked.* London: Darton, Longman and Todd, 1973.

———, *Resolutions* ———. *New Resolutions of Old Conundrums: A Fresh Insight into Luke's Gospel.* Shipston-on-Stour: Drinkwater, 1986.

———, "Palingenesia" ———. "Palingenesia (Matthew 19:28)." *JSNT* 20 (1984): 51-8.

———, "Parable" ———. "The Parable of the Profitable Servant (Luke xvii. 7-10)," 157-66. In *Studies in the New Testament.* Vol. 4. Leiden: Brill, 1986.

DeVine, C. F. "The Blood of God in Acts 20:28." *CBQ* 9 (1947): 381-408.

Dibelius, Martin. *Studies in the Acts of the Apostles.* Trans. Mary Ling. Edt. Heinrich Greeven. London: SCM, 1956.

Dillersberger, Joseph. *The Gospel of St. Luke.* Cork: Mercier, 1958.

Dillon, Richard J. *From Eye-Witnesses to Ministers of the Word* (AnBib 82). Rome: Biblical Institute, 1978.

De Dinechin, Olivier. "Καθώς: La similitude dans l'évangile selon saint Jean."

RSR 58 (1970): 195-236.

Dodd, C. H. *Historical Tradition in the Fourth Gospel.* Cambridge: University, 1963.

Drury, John. *Tradition and Design in Luke's Gospel: A Study in Early Christian Historiography.* Atlanta: John Knox, 1977.

Dumm, Demetrius. "Luke 24:44-49 and Hospitality," 231-39. In *Sin, Salvation, and the Spirit: Commemorating the Fiftieth Year of the Liturgical Press.* Edt. Daniel Durken. Collegeville, MN: Liturgical, 1979.

Dunn, *Jesus* Dunn, James D. G. *Jesus and the Spirit* (NTL). London: SCM, 1975.

———, *Unity* ———. *Unity and Diversity in the New Testament.* London: SCM, 1977.

Dupont, "L'après-mort" Dupont, Jacques. "L'après-mort l'œuvre de Luc." *RTL* 3 (1972): 3-21.

———, "Construction" ———. "La construction du discours de Milet," 424-45. In *Nouvelles Études sur les Actes des Apôtres* (LD 118). Paris: Cerf, 1984.

———, *Discours* ———. *Le discours de Milet: Testament pastoral de Saint Paul (Actes 20,18-36)* (LD 32). Paris: Cerf, 1962.

———, "Trônes" ———. "Le logion des douze trônes (Mt 19,28; Lc 22,28-30)." *Bib* 45 (1964): 355-92.

———, "Ministères" ———. "Les ministères de l'Église naissante d'après les Actes des Apôtres," 133-85. In *Nouvelles Études sur les Actes des Apôtres* (LD 118). Paris: Cerf, 1984.

Eades, Keith L. "Testament." *ISBE* 4:796-7.

Easton, B. S. *The Gospel According to St. Luke.* Edinburgh: Clark, 1926.

Elliott, "Patronage" Elliott, John H. "Patronage and Clientism in Early Christian Society. A Short Reading Guide." *Forum* 3 (1987): 39-48.

———, "Criticism" ———. "Social-Scientific Criticism of the New Testament: More on Methods and Models." *Semeia* 35 (1986): 1-33.

Ellis, *Eschatology* Ellis, E. Earle. *Eschatology In Luke* (FBBS 30). Philadelphia: Fortress, 1972.

———, "La fonction" ———. "La fonction de l'eschatologie dans l'évangile de Luc," 141-55. In *L'evangile de Luc. Problèmes littéraires et théologiques. Mémorial Lucien Cerfaux* (BETL 32). Edt. F. Neirynck. Gembloux: Duculot, 1973.

———, *Gospel* ———. *The Gospel of Luke* (NCB). London: Nelson, 1966.

———, "Present" ———. "Present and Future Eschatology in Luke." *NTS* 12 (1965): 27-41.

Eltester, W. "Israel im Lukanischen Werk und die Nazarethperikope," 76-147. In *Jesus in Nazareth* (BZNW 40). Edt. Erich Grässer et al. Berlin: de Gruyter,

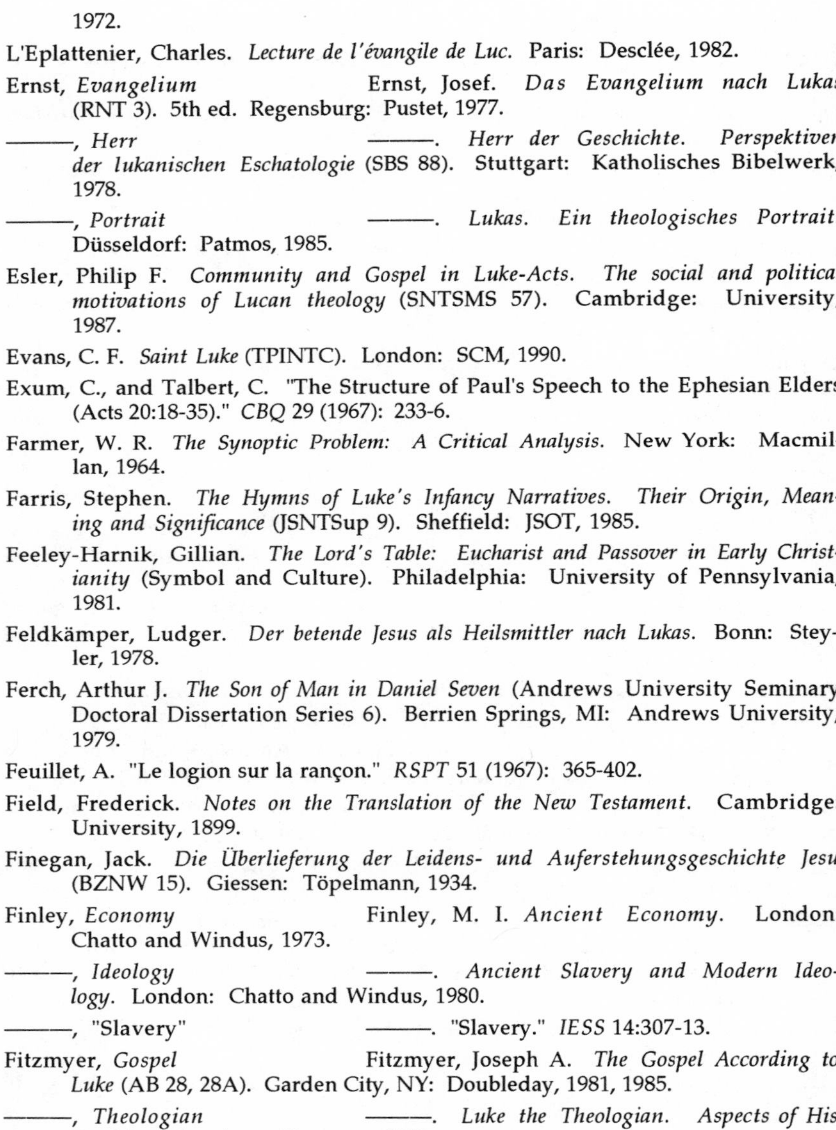

1972.

L'Eplattenier, Charles. *Lecture de l'évangile de Luc.* Paris: Desclée, 1982.

Ernst, *Evangelium* Ernst, Josef. *Das Evangelium nach Lukas* (RNT 3). 5th ed. Regensburg: Pustet, 1977.

———, *Herr* ———. *Herr der Geschichte. Perspektiven der lukanischen Eschatologie* (SBS 88). Stuttgart: Katholisches Bibelwerk, 1978.

———, *Portrait* ———. *Lukas. Ein theologisches Portrait.* Düsseldorf: Patmos, 1985.

Esler, Philip F. *Community and Gospel in Luke-Acts. The social and political motivations of Lucan theology* (SNTSMS 57). Cambridge: University, 1987.

Evans, C. F. *Saint Luke* (TPINTC). London: SCM, 1990.

Exum, C., and Talbert, C. "The Structure of Paul's Speech to the Ephesian Elders (Acts 20:18-35)." *CBQ* 29 (1967): 233-6.

Farmer, W. R. *The Synoptic Problem: A Critical Analysis.* New York: Macmillan, 1964.

Farris, Stephen. *The Hymns of Luke's Infancy Narratives. Their Origin, Meaning and Significance* (JSNTSup 9). Sheffield: JSOT, 1985.

Feeley-Harnik, Gillian. *The Lord's Table: Eucharist and Passover in Early Christianity* (Symbol and Culture). Philadelphia: University of Pennsylvania, 1981.

Feldkämper, Ludger. *Der betende Jesus als Heilsmittler nach Lukas.* Bonn: Steyler, 1978.

Ferch, Arthur J. *The Son of Man in Daniel Seven* (Andrews University Seminary Doctoral Dissertation Series 6). Berrien Springs, MI: Andrews University, 1979.

Feuillet, A. "Le logion sur la rançon." *RSPT* 51 (1967): 365-402.

Field, Frederick. *Notes on the Translation of the New Testament.* Cambridge: University, 1899.

Finegan, Jack. *Die Überlieferung der Leidens- und Auferstehungsgeschichte Jesu* (BZNW 15). Giessen: Töpelmann, 1934.

Finley, *Economy* Finley, M. I. *Ancient Economy.* London: Chatto and Windus, 1973.

———, *Ideology* ———. *Ancient Slavery and Modern Ideology.* London: Chatto and Windus, 1980.

———, "Slavery" ———. "Slavery." *IESS* 14:307-13.

Fitzmyer, *Gospel* Fitzmyer, Joseph A. *The Gospel According to Luke* (AB 28, 28A). Garden City, NY: Doubleday, 1981, 1985.

———, *Theologian* ———. *Luke the Theologian. Aspects of His Teaching.* London: Chapman, 1989.

———, "Priority" ———. "The Priority of Mark and the 'Q'

Source in Luke," 3-40. In *To Advance the Gospel: New Testament Studies.* New York: Crossroad, 1981.

Fleddermann, "Cross" Fleddermann, Harry. "The Cross and Discipleship in Q," 472-82. In *SBL 1988 Seminar Papers.* Edt. David Lull. Atlanta: Scholars, 1988.

———, "Discourse" ———. "The Discipleship Discourse (Mark 9:33-50)." *CBQ* 43 (1981): 57-75.

Flender, Helmut. *St Luke. Theologian of Redemptive History.* Trans. Reginald H. and Ilse Fuller. Philadelphia: Fortress, 1967.

Flew, R. N. *Jesus and His Church.* London: Epworth, 1938.

Flory, Marleen B. "Family in *Familia.* Kinship and Community in Slavery." *American Journal of Ancient History* 3 (1978): 78-95.

Foakes-Jackson, F. J., and Lake, Kirsopp, eds. *The Beginnings of Christianity.* 5 vols. London: Macmillan, 1920-1933.

Foerster, "ἔξεστιν" Foerster, Werner. "ἔξεστιν κτλ." *TDNT* 2:560-75.

———, "κύριος" ———. "κύριος κτλ." *TDNT* 3:1039-98.

Ford, Josephine M. *My Enemy Is My Guest. Jesus and Violence in Luke.* Maryknoll, NY: Orbis, 1984.

Foster, George M. "Peasant Society and the Image of the Limited Good." *AAnth* 67 (1965): 293-315.

Fowl, Stephen. "The Ethics of Interpretation, or What's Left Over After the Elimination of Meaning," 69-81. In *SBL 1988 Seminar Papers.* Edt. David J. Lull. Atlanta: Scholars, 1988.

Fox, Robin L. *Pagans and Christians in the Mediterranean World from the Second Century A.D. to the Conversion of Constantine.* London: Viking, 1987.

France, *Jesus* France, R. T. *Jesus and the Old Testament.* London: Tyndale, 1971.

Francis, Fred O. "Eschatology and History in Luke-Acts." *JAAR* 37 (1969): 49-63.

Franklin, Eric. *Christ the Lord. A Study in the Purpose and Theology of Luke-Acts.* London: SPCK, 1975.

Fransen, Irénée. "Cahier de Bible: Le baptême de sang (Luc 22,1-23,56)." *BVC* 25 (1959): 20-8.

Frend, W. C. H. *Martyrdom and Persecution in the Early Church. A Study of a Conflict from the Maccabees to Donatus.* Oxford: Blackwell, 1965.

Friedrich, G. "Das Problem der Autorität im Neuen Testament," 374-415. In *Auf das Wort kommt es an.* Göttingen: Vandenhoeck und Ruprecht, 1978.

Fuller, Reginald H. "Luke and Theologia Crucis," 214-20. In *Sin, Salvation, and the Spirit: Commemorating the Fiftieth Year of the Liturgical Press.* Edt. Daniel Durken. Collegeville, MN: Liturgical, 1979.

Gager, John G. *Kingdom and Community. The Social World of Early Christian-*

ity. Englewood Cliffs, NJ: Prentice-Hall, 1975.

Garrett, Susan R. *The Demise of the Devil. Magic and the Demonic in Luke's Writings*. Minneapolis: Augsburg, 1989.

Gasque, *History* Gasque, W. Ward. *A History of the Interpretation of the Acts of the Apostles*. Peabody, MA: Hendrickson, 1989.

———, "Study" ———. "Recent Study of the Acts of the Apostles." *Int* 42 (1988): 117-31.

Gaventa, Beverly. "The Eschatology of Luke-Acts Revisited." *Encounter* 43 (1982): 27-42.

Geiger, Ruthild. *Die lukanischen Endzeitreden: Studien zur Eschatologie des Lukas-Evangeliums* (Europäische Hochschulschriften 23/16). Bern: Lang, 1973.

Geldenhuys, Norval. *Commentary on the Gospel of Luke* (NLNTC). London: Marshall, Morgan & Scott, 1950.

Gempf, Conrad. "To Christians: The Miletus Speech," 268-340. In *Historical and Literary Appropriateness in the Mission Speeches of Paul in Acts*. PhD dissertation, unpublished. University of Aberdeen, 1988.

George, *Lecture* George, Augustin. *L'annonce du salut de Dieu: Lecture de l'évangile de Luc*. Paris: Équipes enseignantes, 1963.

———, *Études* ———. *Études sur l'œuvre de Luc* (SB). Paris: Gabalda, 1978.

———, "Israël" ———. "Israël dans l'œuvre de Luc." *RB* 75 (1968): 481-525.

———, "Jésus" ———. "Jésus Fils de Dieu dans l'évangile selon saint Luc." *RB* 72 (1965): 185-209.

———, "Royauté" ———. "La royauté de Jésus selon l'évangile de Luc." *ScEccl* 14 (1962): 57-69.

———, *Mort* ———. "Le sens de la mort de Jesus pour Luc," 185-212. In *Études sur l'œuvre de Luc*. Paris: Gabalda, 1978.

———, "Service" ———. "Le service du royaume." *BVC* 25 (1959): 15-19.

Gerhardsson, B. "Die Boten Gottes und die Apostel Christi." *SEÅ* 27 (1962): 89-131.

Gerth, H. H., and Mills, C. Wright, eds. and trans. *From Max Weber: Essays in Sociology*. London: Routledge and Kegan Paul, 1948.

Gillman, John. "A Temptation to Violence: The Two Swords in Lk 22:35-38." *LS* 9 (1982): 142-53.

Gilmour, S. M. *The Gospel According to St. Luke*. In *IB* 8:1-434.

Girardet, Giorgio. "Le pain qui nous accompagne sur la route de la liberation (22, 1-20. 24-27)," 203-11. In *Lecture politique de l'évangile de Luc*. Brussels: Vie Ouvriere, 1978.

Glasson, T. Francis. "The Speeches in Acts and Thucydides." *ExpTim* 76 (1964-65): 165.

Glöckner, R. *Die Verkündigung des Heils beim Evangelisten Lukas.* Mainz: Matthias-Grünewald, 1975.

Gnilka, Joachim. "Die neuetestamentliche Hausgemeinde," 229-42. In *Freude am Gottesdienst. Festschrift für J. Ploger.* Edt. J. Schreiner. Stuttgart: Katholisches Bibelwerk, 1983.

Godet, Frédéric. *A Commentary on the Gospel of St. Luke.* 4th ed. Vol. 2. Trans. E. W. Shalders. Edinburgh: Clark, 1889.

Gooding, D. *According to Luke: A New Exposition of the Third Gospel.* Grand Rapids: Eerdmans, 1987.

Goppelt, "πίνω" Goppelt, Leonhard. "πίνω κτλ." *TDNT* 6:135-60.

———, *Theology* ———. *Theology of the New Testament.* 2 vols. Edt. Jürgen Roloff. Trans. J. E. Alsup. Grand Rapids: Eerdmans, 1981, 1982.

———, "τράπεζα" ———. "τράπεζα." *TDNT* 8:209-15.

Gormley, Joan F. *The Final Passion Prediction: A Study of Lk. 22:35-38.* PhD dissertation, unpublished. Fordham University, 1974.

Goulder, *Luke* Goulder, Michael D. *Luke: A New Paradigm* (JSNTSup 20). 2 vols. Sheffield: JSOT, 1989.

———, *Type* ———. *Type and History in Acts.* London: SPCK, 1964.

Grassi, Joseph A. *God Makes Me Laugh. A New Approach to Luke* (GNS 17). Wilmington, DE: Glazier, 1986.

Green, *Death* Green, Joel B. *The Death of Jesus. Tradition and Interpretation in the Passion Narrative* (WUNT 2/33). Tübingen: Mohr, 1988.

———, "Passover" ———. "Preparation for Passover (Luke 22:7-13): a Question of Redactional Technique." *NovT* 29 (1987): 305-19.

Gregory, James R. "Image of Limited Good, or Expectation of Reciprocity?" *Current Anthropology* 16 (1975): 73-92.

Grundmann, Walter. *Das Evangelium nach Lukas* (THKNT 3). 2nd ed. Berlin: Evangelische, 1961.

Guillaume, Jean-Marie. *Luc interprète des anciennes traditions sur la résurrection de Jésus* (EBib). Paris: Gabalda, 1979.

Guillet, Jacques. "Luc 22,29: Une formule johannique dans l'évangile de Luc?" *RSR* 69 (1981): 113-22.

Gundry, Robert H. *Matthew. A Commentary on his Literary and Theological Art.* Grand Rapids: Eerdmans, 1982.

Gutbrod, Walter. "Ἰσραήλ κτλ." *TDNT* 3:356-91.

Haenchen, *Acts* Haenchen, Ernst. *The Acts of the Apostles.* Trans. Hugh Anderson. Oxford: Blackwell, 1971.

———, "History" ———. "The Book of Acts as Source Material

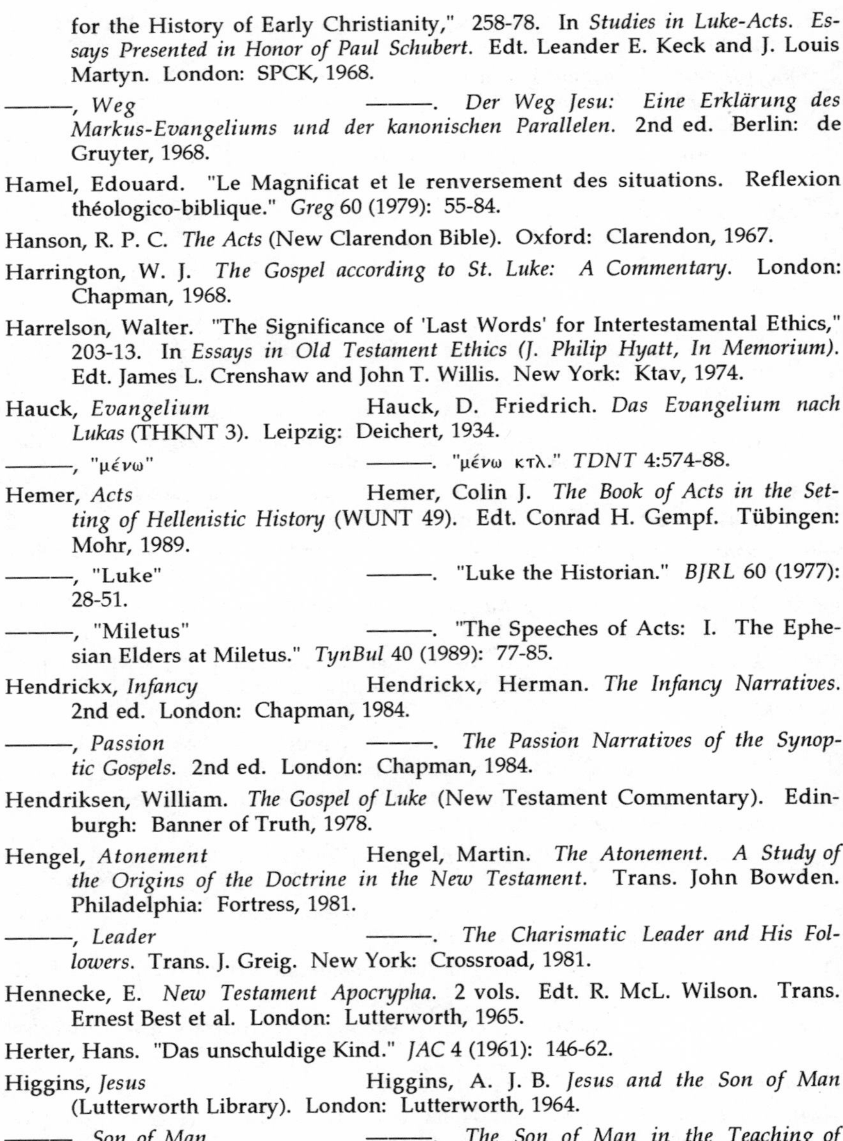

for the History of Early Christianity," 258-78. In *Studies in Luke-Acts. Essays Presented in Honor of Paul Schubert.* Edt. Leander E. Keck and J. Louis Martyn. London: SPCK, 1968.

———, *Weg* ———. *Der Weg Jesu: Eine Erklärung des Markus-Evangeliums und der kanonischen Parallelen.* 2nd ed. Berlin: de Gruyter, 1968.

Hamel, Edouard. "Le Magnificat et le renversement des situations. Reflexion théologico-biblique." *Greg* 60 (1979): 55-84.

Hanson, R. P. C. *The Acts* (New Clarendon Bible). Oxford: Clarendon, 1967.

Harrington, W. J. *The Gospel according to St. Luke: A Commentary.* London: Chapman, 1968.

Harrelson, Walter. "The Significance of 'Last Words' for Intertestamental Ethics," 203-13. In *Essays in Old Testament Ethics (J. Philip Hyatt, In Memorium).* Edt. James L. Crenshaw and John T. Willis. New York: Ktav, 1974.

Hauck, *Evangelium* Hauck, D. Friedrich. *Das Evangelium nach Lukas* (THKNT 3). Leipzig: Deichert, 1934.

———, "μένω" ———. "μένω κτλ." *TDNT* 4:574-88.

Hemer, *Acts* Hemer, Colin J. *The Book of Acts in the Setting of Hellenistic History* (WUNT 49). Edt. Conrad H. Gempf. Tübingen: Mohr, 1989.

———, "Luke" ———. "Luke the Historian." *BJRL* 60 (1977): 28-51.

———, "Miletus" ———. "The Speeches of Acts: I. The Ephesian Elders at Miletus." *TynBul* 40 (1989): 77-85.

Hendrickx, *Infancy* Hendrickx, Herman. *The Infancy Narratives.* 2nd ed. London: Chapman, 1984.

———, *Passion* ———. *The Passion Narratives of the Synoptic Gospels.* 2nd ed. London: Chapman, 1984.

Hendriksen, William. *The Gospel of Luke* (New Testament Commentary). Edinburgh: Banner of Truth, 1978.

Hengel, *Atonement* Hengel, Martin. *The Atonement. A Study of the Origins of the Doctrine in the New Testament.* Trans. John Bowden. Philadelphia: Fortress, 1981.

———, *Leader* ———. *The Charismatic Leader and His Followers.* Trans. J. Greig. New York: Crossroad, 1981.

Hennecke, E. *New Testament Apocrypha.* 2 vols. Edt. R. McL. Wilson. Trans. Ernest Best et al. London: Lutterworth, 1965.

Herter, Hans. "Das unschuldige Kind." *JAC* 4 (1961): 146-62.

Higgins, *Jesus* Higgins, A. J. B. *Jesus and the Son of Man* (Lutterworth Library). London: Lutterworth, 1964.

———, *Son of Man* ———. *The Son of Man in the Teaching of Jesus* (SNTSMS 39). Cambridge: University, 1980.

Hill, David. *Greek Words and Hebrew Meanings. Studies in the Semantics of Soteriological Terms* (SNTSMS 5). Cambridge: University, 1967.

Hirsch, E. D. *Validity in Interpretation.* New Haven: Yale, 1967.

Hoffmann, P. *Studien zur Theologie der Logienquelle.* Münster: Aschendorf, 1972.

———, and Eid, V. *Jesus von Nazareth und eine christliche Moral. Sittliche Perspektivien der Verkündigung Jesu* (QD 66). Freiburg: Herder, 1975.

Hofius, Otfried. *Jesu Tischgemeinschaft mit den Sündern.* Stuttgart: Calwer, 1967.

Hollander, Harm W. *Joseph as an Ethical Model in the Testaments of the Twelve Patriarchs* (SVTP 6). Leiden: Brill, 1981.

———, and de Jonge, M. *The Testaments of the Twelve Patriarchs. A Commentary* (SVTP 8). Leiden: Brill, 1985.

Holmberg, Bengt. *Paul and Power. The Structure of Authority in the Primitive Church as Reflected in the Pauline Epistles* (Coniectanea Biblica New Testament Series 11). Lund: Gleerup, 1978.

Hooker, *Jesus* Hooker, Morna D. *Jesus and the Servant.* London: SPCK, 1959.

———, *Son of Man* ———. *The Son of Man in Mark.* London: SPCK, 1967.

Horbury, William. "The Twelve and the Phylarchs." *NTS* 32 (1986): 503-27.

Horn, Friedrich W. *Glaube und Handeln in der Theologie des Lukas* (GTA 26). Göttingen: Vandenhoeck und Ruprecht, 1983.

Howard, "Jesus" Howard, Virgil P. "Did Jesus Speak About His Own Death?" *CBQ* 39 (1977): 515-27.

———, *Das Ego* ———. *Das Ego Jesu in den synoptischen Evangelien. Untersuchungen zum Sprachgebrauch Jesu.* Marburg: Elwert, 1975.

Hubbard, Benjamin J. "Commissioning Stories in Luke-Acts: A Study of their Antecedents, Form and Content." *Semeia* 8 (1977): 103-26.

Hug, "Symposion" Hug, August. "Symposion." PW 2/4:1266-70.

———, "Symposion-Literatur" ———. "Symposion-Literatur." PW 2/4:1273-82.

Hultgren, A. J. "Interpreting the Gospel of Luke." *Int* 30 (1976): 353-65.

Hunt, Leslie. "Family." *ISBE* 2:279-81.

Hurtado, Larry. "Jesus as Lordly Example in Philippians 2:5-11," 113-26. In *From Jesus to Paul. Studies in Honour of Francis Wright Beare.* Edt. Peter Richardson and John C. Hurd. Waterloo, Ontario: Wilfrid Laurier University, 1984.

Jacobson, Richard. "The Structuralists and the Bible." *Int* 28 (1974): 146-64.

Jeremias , *Words* Jeremias, Joachim. *The Eucharistic Words of Jesus* (NTL). 3rd ed. Trans. N. Perrin. London: SCM, 1966.

———, *Promise* ———. *Jesus' Promise to the Nations* (SBT 24). Trans. S. H. Hooke. London: SCM, 1958.

———, "Lösegeld" ———. "Das Lösegeld für Viele," 216-29. In *Abba. Studien zur neutestamentlichen Theologie und Zeitgeschichte.* Göttingen: Vandenhoeck und Ruprecht, 1966.

———, *Theology* ———. *New Testament Theology* (NTL). Vol. 1. Trans. John Bowden. London: SCM, 1971.

———, *Parables* ———. *The Parables of Jesus* (NTL). Rev. ed. Trans. S. H. Hooke. London: SCM, 1963.

———, "Umstellungen" ———. "Perikopen-Umstellungen bei Lukas?" *NTS* 4 (1958): 115-19.

———, *Sprache* ———. *Die Sprache des Lukasevangeliums.* Göttingen: Vandenhoeck und Ruprecht, 1980.

Jervell, "Interpolator" Jervell, Jacob. "Ein Interpolator interpretiert. Zu der christlichen Bearbeitung der Testamente der zwölf Patriarchen," 30-61. In *Studien zu den Testamenten der zwölf Patriarchen* (BZNW 36). Edt. W. Eltester. Berlin: Töpelmann, 1969.

———, *Luke* ———. *Luke and the People of God.* Minneapolis: Augsburg, 1972.

Johnson, L., *Possessions* Johnson, Luke T. *The Literary Function of Possessions in Luke-Acts* (SBLDS 39). Missoula, MT: Scholars, 1977.

———, "Kingship" ———. "The Lukan Kingship Parable." *NovT* 24 (1982): 139-59.

Johnson, S., "Manual" Johnson, Sherman E. "The Dead Sea Manual of Discipline and the Jerusalem Church of Acts," 129-42. In *The Scrolls and the New Testament.* Edt. Krister Stendahl. London: SCM, 1958.

———, "Message" ———. "The Message of Jesus to the Poor and the Powerful." *ATR Supplementary Series* 11 (1990): 16-28.

Jones, Donald L. "The Title 'Servant' in Luke-Acts," 148-65. In *Luke-Acts: New Perspectives from the Society of Biblical Literature Seminar.* Edt. Charles H. Talbert. New York: Crossroad, 1984.

De Jonge, *Studies* De Jonge, M. *Studies on the Testaments of the Twelve Patriarchs* (SVTP 3). Leiden: Brill, 1975.

Joüon, P. "Notes philologiques sur les évangiles." *RSR* 18 (1928): 345-59.

Jüngel, Eberhard. *Paulus und Jesus.* 4th ed. Tübingen: Mohr, 1972.

Kaestli, Jean-Daniel. *L'Eschatologie dans l'œuvre de Luc. Ses charactéristiques et sa place dans le développement du christianisme primitif* (Nouvelle série théologique 22). Geneva: Labor et Fides, 1969.

Kany, Roland. "Der lukanische Bericht von Tod und Auferstehung Jesu aus der Sicht eines hellenistischen Romanlessers." *NovT* 28 (1986): 75-90.

Kaplan, D., and Saler, B. "Foster's 'Image of Limited Good': An Example of Anthropological Explanation." *AAnth* 68 (1966): 202-6.

Kariamadam, Paul. "Discipleship in the Lucan Journey Narrative." *Jeevadhara*

10 (56, 1980): 111-30.

Karris, *Gospel* Karris, Robert J. *The Gospel According to Luke*, 675-721. In *The New Jerome Biblical Commentary*. Edt. Raymond E. Brown et al. London: Chapman, 1989.

———, *Invitation* ———. *Invitation to Luke: A Commentary on the Gospel of Luke with the Complete Text from the Jerusalem Bible* (Image Books). Garden City, NY: Doubleday, 1977.

———, "Soteriology" ———. "Luke's Soteriology of With-ness." *CurTM* 12 (1985): 346-52.

———, "Poor" ———. "Poor and Rich: the Lukan *Sitz im Leben*," 112-25. In *Perspectives on Luke Acts* (Special Studies Series 5). Danville, VA: Association of Baptist Professors of Religion, 1978.

———, "Food" ———. "The Theme of Food," 47-78. In *Luke: Artist and Theologian. Luke's Passion Account as Literature* (TI). New York: Paulist, 1985.

Käsemann, *Versuch* Käsemann, E. *Exegetische Versuch und Besinnungen*. 4th ed. Vol. 1. Göttingen: Vandenhoeck und Ruprecht, 1964.

———, *Testament* ———. *The Testament of Jesus*. Trans. G. Krodel. Philadelphia: Fortress, 1968.

Kealy, S. P. *The Gospel of Luke*. Denville, NJ: Dimension Books, 1979.

Keck, Leander E., and Martyn, J. Louis, eds. *Studies in Luke-Acts. Essays Presented in Honor of Paul Schubert*. London: SPCK, 1968.

Kee, *The Truth* Kee, Howard C. *Knowing the Truth. A Sociological Approach to New Testament Interpretation*. Minneapolis: Fortress, 1989.

Kertelge, "Menschensohn" Kertelge, Karl. "Der dienende Menschensohn (Mk 10,45)," 225-39. In *Jesus und der Menschensohn*. Edt. R. Pesch and R. Schnackenburg. Freiburg: Herder, 1975.

———, "Aussagen" ———. "Die soteriologischen Aussagen in der urchristlichen Abendmahlsüberlieferung und ihre Beziehung zum geschichtliche Jesus." *TTZ* 4 (1972): 193-202.

Kiddle, M. "The Passion Narrative in St. Luke's Gospel." *JTS* 36 (1935): 267-80.

Kim, Seyoon. *The "Son of Man" as the Son of God* (WUNT 30). Tübingen: Mohr, 1983.

Kingsbury, Jack D. *Jesus Christ in Matthew, Mark, and Luke* (PC). Philadelphia: Fortress, 1981.

Kittel, "ἀκολουθέω" Kittel, Gerhard. "ἀκολουθέω κτλ." *TDNT* 1:210-16.

———, "δοκέω" ———. "δοκέω κτλ." *TDNT* 2:232-55.

Klappert, "Arbeit" Klappert, Bertold. "Arbeit Gottes und Mitarbeit des Menschen (Phil 2,6-11)," 84-134. In *Recht auf Arbeit—Sinn der Arbeit*. Edt. J. Moltmann. Munich: Kaiser, 1979.

———, "King" ———. "King, Kingdom." *NIDNTT* 2:372-90.

Klausner, Joseph. *The Messianic Idea in Israel from Its Beginning to the Completion of the Mishnah.* Trans. W. F. Stinespring. London: George, Allen and Unwin, 1956.

Klein, Günter. *Die zwölf Apostel: Ursprung und Gehalt einer Idee* (FRLANT 77). Göttingen: Vandenhoeck und Ruprecht, 1961.

Klein, Hans. "Die lukanisch-johanneische Passionstradition." *ZNW* 67 (1976): 155-86.

Kleinknecht, Hermann. "βασιλεύς in the Greek World." *TDNT* 1:564-5.

Klostermann, Erich. *Das Lukasevangelium* (HNT 5). 3rd ed. Tübingen: Mohr, 1975.

Knight, G. A. F. "Feet-washing," 814-23. In *Encyclopedia of Religion and Ethics.* Vol. 5. Edt. James Hastings. Edinburgh: Clark, 1912.

Knoch, O. "Tut das zu meinem Gedächtnis!' (Lk 22, 20; 1 Kor 11, 24f). Die Feier der Eucharistie in den urchristliche Gemeinden," 31-42. In *Freude am Gottesdienst. Festschrift für J. G. Ploger.* Edt. J. Schreiner. Stuttgart: Katholisches Bibelwerk, 1983.

Knoche, U. "Der römische Ruhmesgedanke," 420-45. In *Römische Wertbegriffe.* Edt. H. Oppermann. Darmstadt: Wissenschaftliche, 1983.

Knox, Wilfred L. *The Sources of the synoptic Gospels.* Vol. 1. Cambridge: University, 1953.

Koch, Robert. "Die Wertung des Besitzes im Lukasevangelium." *Bib* 38 (1957): 159-69.

Kodell, "Children" Kodell, Jerome. "Luke and the Children: The Beginning and the End of the Great Interpolation (Luke 9:46-56; 18:9-23)." *CBQ* 49 (1987): 415-30.

———, "Death" ———. "Luke's Theology of the Death of Jesus," 221-30. In *Sin, Salvation, and the Spirit: Commemorating the Fiftieth Year of the Liturgical Press.* Edt. Daniel Durken. Collegeville, MN: Liturgical, 1979.

Koenig, John. *New Testament Hospitality* (OBT). Philadelphia: Fortress, 1985.

Kolenkow, "Genre" Kolenkow, Anitra B. "The Genre Testament and Forecasts of the Future in the Hellenistic Jewish Milieu." *JSJ* 6 (1975): 57-71.

———, "Testaments" ———. "Testaments: the Literary Genre 'Testament'," 259-67. In *Early Judaism and its Modern Interpreters.* Edt. R. Kraft and G. Nickelsburg. Philadelphia: Fortress, 1986.

Kollmann, "Gleichnis" Kollmann, Bernd. "Lk 12,35-38—ein Gleichnis der Logienquelle." *ZNW* 81 (1990): 254-62.

———, *Mahl* ———. *Ursprung und Gestalten der frühchristlichen Mahl Feier* (GTA 43). Göttingen: Vandenhoeck und Ruprecht, 1990.

Kötting, B. "Euergetes." *RAC* 6:848-60.

Krause, G. *Die Kinder im Evangelium.* Stuttgart: Klotz, 1973.

Kreissig, Heinz. *Die sozialen Zusammenhänge des jüdischen Krieges. Klassen und Klassenkampf im Palästina des 1. Jahrhunderts v. u. Z.* (Schriften zur Geschichte und Kultur der Antike 1). Berlin: Akademie, 1970.

Kremer, J. *Lukasevangelium* (Die Neue Echter Bibel, Kommentar zum Neuen Testament mit der Einheitsübersetzung 3). Wurzburg: Echter, 1988.

Krodel, Gerhard. *Acts* (PC). Philadelphia: Fortress, 1981.

Kuhn, Heinz-Wolfgang. "Nachfolge nach Ostern," 105-32. In *Kirche. Festschrift für Gunther Bornkamm zum 75. Geburtstag.* Edt. D. Lührmann and G. Strecker. Tübingen: Mohr, 1980.

Kuhn, K., "Lord's Supper" Kuhn, Karl G. "The Lord's Supper and the Communal Meal at Qumran," 65-93. In *The Scrolls and the New Testament.* Edt. Krister Stendahl. London: SCM, 1958.

———, "New Light" ———. "New Light on Temptation, Sin and Flesh in the New Testament," 94-113. In *The Scrolls and the New Testament.* Edt. Krister Stendahl. London: SCM, 1958.

Kümmel, "Accusations" Kümmel, Werner G. "Current Theological Accusations Against Luke." *ANQ* 16 (1975): 131-45.

———, *Promise* ———. *Promise and Fulfillment: The Eschatological Message of Jesus.* 3rd ed. Trans. Dorothea M. Barton. London: SCM, 1969.

———, *Theology* ———. *The Theology of the New Testament According to its Major Witnesses: Jesus - Paul - John.* Trans. John E. Steely. London: SCM, 1974.

Kurz, *Farewell* Kurz, William S. *Farewell Addresses in the New Testament* (Zacchaeus Studies: New Testament). Collegeville, MN: Liturgical, 1990.

———, "Rhetoric" ———. "Hellenistic Rhetoric in the Christological Proof of Luke-Acts." *CBQ* 42 (1980): 171-95.

———, "Luke 22:14-38" ———. "Luke 22:14-38 and Greco-Roman and Biblical Farewell Addresses." *JBL* 104 (1985): 251-68.

Lacey, W. K. "*Patria Potestas,*" 121-44. In *The Family in Ancient Rome. New Perspectives.* Edt. Beryl Rawson. London: Croom Helm, 1986.

Ladd, *Theology* Ladd, George E. *A Theology of the New Testament.* Grand Rapids: Eerdmans, 1974.

———, *Presence* ———. *The Presence of the Future.* London: SPCK, 1974.

Lagrange, M. -J. *Évangile selon Saint Luc* (EBib). 8th ed. Paris: Gabalda, 1948.

Lake, Kirsopp. "The Twelve and the Apostles," 37-59. In *Beginnings of Christianity.* Vol. 5. Edt. F. J. Foakes-Jackson and Kirsopp Lake. London: Macmillan, 1933.

Lambrecht, J. "Paul's Farewell-Address at Miletus (Acts 20,17-38)," 307-37. In *Les Actes des Apôtres. Traditions, rédaction, théologie* (BETL 48). Edt. J.

Kremer. Gembloux: Duculot, 1979.

Lampe, *Luke* Lampe, G. W. H. *Luke*, 820-43. In *Peake's Commentary on the Bible*. Rev. ed. Edt. M. Black and H. H. Rowley. London: Nelson, 1962.

Lane, William L. *The Gospel According to Mark* (NLNTC). London: Marshall, Morgan & Scott, 1974.

De Lange, Nicholas. *Judaism*. Oxford: University, 1986.

Laub, *Sklaverei* Laub, Franz. *Die Begegnung des frühen Christentums mit der antiken Sklaverei* (StBib 107). Stuttgart: Katholisches Bibelwerk, 1982.

———, "Autorität" ———. "Verkündigung und Gemeindeamt. Die Autorität der ἡγούμενοι Hebr 13,7.17.24." *Studien zum Neuen Testament und seiner Umwelt* 6/7 (1981-82): 169-90.

LaVerdiere, "Discourse" LaVerdiere, Eugene. "A Discourse at the Last Supper." *Bible Today* 71 (1974): 1540-8.

———, *Luke* ———. *Luke* (New Testament Message 5). Dublin: Veritas, 1980.

———, "Passion" ———. "The Passion-Resurrection of Jesus according to St. Luke." *Chicago Studies* 25 (1986): 35-50.

———, "Testament" ———. "The Testament of Christ," 8-18. In *Bread from Heaven*. Edt. P. Bernier. New York: Paulist, 1977.

Leaney, *Gospel* Leaney, A. R. C. *The Gospel According to St. Luke* (BNTC). London: Adam & Charles Black, 1958.

———, "Child" ———. "Jesus and the Symbol of the Child (Luke ix. 46-48)." *ExpTim* 66 (1954-55): 91-2.

Lebram, J. C. H. "Jüdische Martyrologie und Weisheitsüberlieferung," 88-126. In *Die Entstehung der jüdischen Martyrologie* (SPB 38). Edt. J. W. van Henten et al. Leiden: Brill, 1989.

Légasse, "L'enfant" Légasse, S. "L'enfant dans l'evangile." *VSpir* 570 (1970): 409-21.

———, *Jésus* ———. *Jésus et l'enfant: "Enfants," "petits" et "simples" dans la tradition synoptique* (EBib). Paris: Gabalda, 1969.

Leivestad, R. *Christ the Conqueror. Ideas of Conflict and Victory in the New Testament*. London: SPCK, 1954.

Lenski, R. C. H. *The Interpretation of St. Luke's Gospel*. Minneapolis: Augsburg, 1961.

Leonard, Paul E. *Luke's Account of the Lord's Supper Against the Backdrop of Meals in the Ancient Semitic World and More Particularly Meals in the Gospel of Luke*. PhD dissertation, unpublished. University of Manchester, 1976.

Léon-Dufour, "Mort" Léon-Dufour, Xavier. *Face à la mort. Jésus et Paul* (PD). Paris: Seuil, 1979.

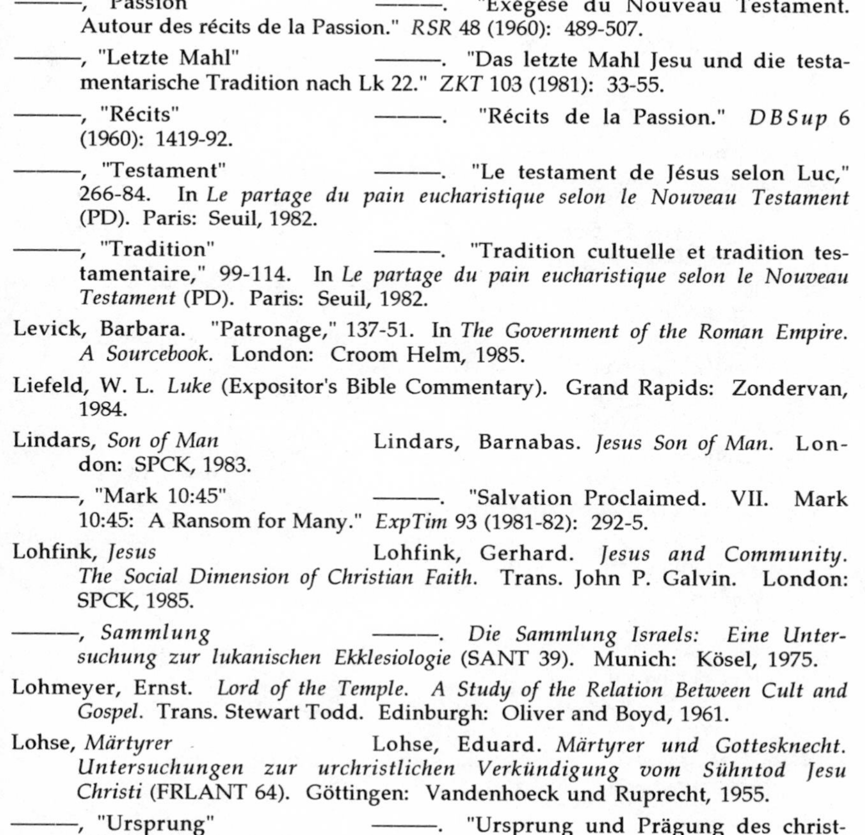

———, "Jésus" ———. "Jésus devant sa mort à la lumière des textes de l'Institution eucharistique et des discours d'adieu," 141-68. In *Jésus aux origines de la christologie* (BETL 40). Edt. Jacques Dupont. Gembloux: Duculot, 1975.

———, "Passion" ———. "Exégèse du Nouveau Testament. Autour des récits de la Passion." *RSR* 48 (1960): 489-507.

———, "Letzte Mahl" ———. "Das letzte Mahl Jesu und die testamentarische Tradition nach Lk 22." *ZKT* 103 (1981): 33-55.

———, "Récits" ———. "Récits de la Passion." *DBSup* 6 (1960): 1419-92.

———, "Testament" ———. "Le testament de Jésus selon Luc," 266-84. In *Le partage du pain eucharistique selon le Nouveau Testament* (PD). Paris: Seuil, 1982.

———, "Tradition" ———. "Tradition cultuelle et tradition testamentaire," 99-114. In *Le partage du pain eucharistique selon le Nouveau Testament* (PD). Paris: Seuil, 1982.

Levick, Barbara. "Patronage," 137-51. In *The Government of the Roman Empire. A Sourcebook.* London: Croom Helm, 1985.

Liefeld, W. L. *Luke* (Expositor's Bible Commentary). Grand Rapids: Zondervan, 1984.

Lindars, *Son of Man* Lindars, Barnabas. *Jesus Son of Man.* London: SPCK, 1983.

———, "Mark 10:45" ———. "Salvation Proclaimed. VII. Mark 10:45: A Ransom for Many." *ExpTim* 93 (1981-82): 292-5.

Lohfink, *Jesus* Lohfink, Gerhard. *Jesus and Community. The Social Dimension of Christian Faith.* Trans. John P. Galvin. London: SPCK, 1985.

———, *Sammlung* ———. *Die Sammlung Israels: Eine Untersuchung zur lukanischen Ekklesiologie* (SANT 39). Munich: Kösel, 1975.

Lohmeyer, Ernst. *Lord of the Temple. A Study of the Relation Between Cult and Gospel.* Trans. Stewart Todd. Edinburgh: Oliver and Boyd, 1961.

Lohse, *Märtyrer* Lohse, Eduard. *Märtyrer und Gottesknecht. Untersuchungen zur urchristlichen Verkündigung vom Sühntod Jesu Christi* (FRLANT 64). Göttingen: Vandenhoeck und Ruprecht, 1955.

———, "Ursprung" ———. "Ursprung und Prägung des christlichen Apostolates." *TZ* 9 (1953): 259-75.

Loisy, A. *L'Evangile selon Luc.* Paris: Nourry, 1924.

Lövestam, Evald. "Paul's Address at Miletus." *ST* 41 (1987): 1-10.

Luce, H. K. *The Gospel According to S. Luke* (Cambridge Greek Testament). Cambridge: University, 1949.

Lull, David J. "The Servant-Benefactor as a Model of Greatness (Luke 22:24-30)." *NovT* 28 (1986): 289-305.

Maccoby, Hyam. "Paul and the Eucharist." *NTS* 37 (1991): 247-67.

McDonald, Alexander H. "Historiography, Roman." *OCD* 523.

McDonald, James I. H. *Kerygma and Didache* (SNTSMS 37). Cambridge: University, 1980.

MacMullen, *Social Relations* MacMullen, Ramsay. *Roman Social Relations, 50 B.C. to A.D. 284.* New Haven: Yale, 1974.

———, "Peasants" ———. "Peasants, during the Principate." *ANRW* 2/1:253-61.

Maddox, Robert. *The Purpose of Luke-Acts.* Edinburgh: Clark, 1982.

Malamat, Abraham. "The Period of the Judges," 129-63. In *The World History of the Jewish People.* Vol. 3: *Judges.* Edt. Benjamin Mazar. Tel-Aviv: Massada, 1971.

Malherbe, Abraham J. *Social Aspects of Early Christianity.* 2nd ed. Philadelphia: Fortress, 1983.

Malina, *World* Malina, Bruce J. *The New Testament World. Insights from Cultural Anthropology.* Atlanta: John Knox, 1981.

———, "Wealth" ———. "Wealth and Poverty in the New Testament and Its World." *Int* 41 (1987): 354-67.

Mánek, "New Exodus" Mánek, J. "The New Exodus in the Books of Luke." *NovT* 2 (1957): 8-23.

———, "Umwandlung" ———. "Vier Bibelstudien zur Problematik der sozialen Umwandlung." *Communio Viatorium* 10 (1967): 61-70.

Mann, C. S. *Mark* (AB 27). Garden City, NY: Doubleday, 1986.

Manson, T. W., *Ministry* Manson, T. W. *The Church's Ministry.* London: Hodder and Stoughton, 1948.

———, *Sayings* ———. *The Sayings of Jesus.* London: SCM, 1949.

———, *Teaching* ———. *The Teaching of Jesus,* 2nd ed. Cambridge: University, 1935.

Manson, William. *The Gospel of Luke* (MNTC). London: Hodder and Stoughton, 1930.

Marshall, I. H., *Acts* Marshall, I. Howard. *The Acts of the Apostles* (TNTC). Leicester: Inter-Varsity, 1980.

———, *Gospel* ———. *The Gospel of Luke. A Commentary on the Greek Text* (NIGTC). Exeter: Paternoster, 1978.

———, *Jesus* ———. *Jesus the Saviour. Studies in New Testament Theology.* London: SPCK, 1990.

———, *Perseverance* ———. *Kept by the Power of God: A Study of Perseverance and Falling Away.* London: Epworth, 1969.

———, *Last Supper* ———. *Last Supper and Lord's Supper.* Exeter: Paternoster, 1980.

———, *Historian* ———. *Luke: Historian and Theologian.* 3rd

ed. Exeter: Paternoster, 1988.

———, "Lucan Studies" ———. "The Present State of Lucan Studies." *Themelios* 14 (1989): 52-7.

Marshall, Peter. *Enmity in Corinth: Social Conventions in Paul's Relations with the Corinthians* (WUNT 2/23). Tübingen: Mohr, 1987.

Martin, Dale B. *Slavery as Salvation. The Metaphor of Slavery in Pauline Christianity.* New Haven: Yale, 1990.

Martin, Josef. *Symposion. Die Geschichte einer literarischen Form* (Studien zur Geschichte und Kultur des Altertums 17/1-2). 2 vols. Paderborn: Schöningh, 1931.

Martin, Ralph P. "Salvation and Discipleship in Luke's Gospel." *Int* 30 (1976): 366-80.

Matera, "Death" Matera, Frank J. "The Death of Jesus according to Luke: A Question of Sources." *CBQ* 47 (1985): 469-85.

———, *Passion* ———. *Passion Narratives and Gospel Theologies. Interpreting the Synoptics Through Their Passion Stories* (TI). New York: Paulist, 1986.

Matthews, Victor H. *Manners and Customs in the Bible.* Peabody, MA: Hendrickson, 1988.

Mattill, A. J., Jr., *Luke and the Last Things.* Dillsboro, NC: Western North Carolina, 1979.

Mau, August. "Convivium." PW 4:1201-8.

Maurer, Christian. "φυλή." *TDNT* 9:245-50.

Mealand, David L. *Poverty and Expectation in the Gospels.* London: SPCK, 1980.

Mearns, Chris. "Realized Eschatology in Q? A Consideration of the Sayings in Luke 7.22, 11.20 and 16.16." *SJT* 40 (1987): 189-210.

Meeks, *Urban Christians* Meeks, Wayne A. *The First Urban Christians: The Social World of the Apostle Paul.* New Haven: Yale, 1983.

———, *Moral World* ———. *The Moral World of the First Christians.* London: SPCK, 1986.

De Meeûs, X. "Composition de *Lc.*, XIV et genre symposiaque." *ETL* 37 (1961): 847-70.

Mendelsohn, I. *Slavery in the Ancient Near East.* New York: Oxford, 1949.

Merk. Otto. "Das Reich Gottes in den lukanischen Schriften," 201-20. In *Jesus und Paulus: Festschrift für Werner Georg Kümmel.* Edt. E. Earle Ellis and Erich Grässer. Göttingen: Vandenhoeck und Ruprecht, 1975.

Meynet, *Luc* Meynet, Roland. *L'Évangile selon saint Luc. Analyse rhétorique.* 2 vols. Paris: Cerf, 1988.

———, *Initiation* ———. *Initiation à la rhétorique biblique. Qui donc est le plus grand?* (Initiations). 2 vols. Paris: Cerf, 1982.

———, *Parole* ———. *Quelle est donc cette parole? Lecture «rhetorique» de l'évangile de Luc (1-9, 22-24)* (LD 99A, 99B). 2 vols. Paris:

Cerf, 1979.

Michaelis, Wilhelm. "μέγας κτλ." *TDNT* 4:529-44.

Michel, H. -J. *Die Abschiedsrede des Paulus an die Kirche Apg 20,17-38* (SANT 35). Munich: Kösel, 1973.

Milik, J. T. *Ten Years of Discovery in the Wilderness of Judea* (SBT 26). Trans. J. Strugnell. London: SCM, 1959.

Mills, Mary E. "The Apostles According to Luke," 109-23. In *Human Agents of Cosmic Power in Hellenistic Judaism and the Synoptic Tradition* (JSNTSup 41). Sheffield: JSOT, 1990.

Minear, *Commands* Minear, Paul S. *Commands of Christ.* Nashville: Abingdon, 1972.

———, *Heal* ———. *To Heal and to Reveal: The Prophetic Vocation according to Luke.* New York: Seabury, 1976.

———, "Birth Stories" ———. "Luke's Use of the Birth Stories," 111-30. In *Studies in Luke-Acts. Essays Presented in Honor of Paul Schubert.* Edt. Leander E. Keck and J. Louis Martyn. London: SPCK, 1968.

———, "Note" ———. "A Note on Luke xxii 36." *NovT* 7 (1964): 128-34.

———, "Glimpses" ———. "Some Glimpses of Luke's Sacramental Theology." *Worship* 44 (1970): 322-31.

Moessner, David P. *Lord of the Banquet. The Literary and Theological Significance of the Lukan Travel Narrative.* Minneapolis: Fortress, 1989.

Momigliano, "Augustus" Momigliano, Arnaldo. "Augustus." *OCD* 149-51.

———, "Cliens" ———. "Cliens. " *OCD* 252.

———, "Patronus" ———. "Patronus." *OCD* 791.

Monsarrat, Violaine. "Le récit de la passion: un enseignment pour le disciple fidèle (Luc 22-23)." *Foi et vie* 81 (1982): 40-7.

Montgomery, James A. *The Book of Daniel* (ICC). Edinburgh: Clark, 1927.

Moo, Douglas J. *The Old Testament in the Gospel Passion Narratives.* Sheffield: Almond, 1983.

Moore, George F. *Judaism in the First Centuries of the Christian Era. The Age of the Tannaim.* 3 vols. Cambridge, MA: Harvard University, 1927.

Moore, Stephen G. *Literary Criticism and the Gospels: the Theoretical Challenge.* New Haven: Yale, 1989.

Morgan, Robert, with Barton, John. *Biblical Interpretation* (OBS). Oxford: University, 1988.

Morris, Leon. *The Gospel According to St. Luke: An Introduction and Commentary* (TNTC). Rev. ed. London: Inter-Varsity, 1988.

Mosley, A. W. "Historical Reporting in the Ancient World." *NTS* 12 (1965): 10-26.

Mott, Stephen C. *Biblical Ethics and Social Change.* New York: Oxford, 1982.

Moulder, W. J. "The Old Testament Background and the Interpretation of Mark x. 45." *NTS* 24 (1977-78): 120-27.

Moule, "Christology" Moule, C. F. D. "The Christology of Acts," 159-85. In *Studies in Luke-Acts. Essays Presented in Honor of Paul Schubert.* Edt. Leander E. Keck and J. Louis Martyn. London: SPCK, 1968.

Mowinckel, S. *The Psalms in Israel's Worship.* 2 vols. Trans. D. R. Ap-Thomas. Oxford: Blackwell, 1962.

Moxnes, *Economy* Moxnes, Halvor. *The Economy of the Kingdom. Social Conflict and Economic Relations in Luke's Gospel* (OBT). Philadelphia: Fortress, 1988.

———, "Honor" ———. "Honor, Shame, and the Outside World in Paul's Letter to the Romans," 207-18. In *The Social World of Formative Christianity and Judaism. Essays in Tribute to Howard Clark Kee.* Edt. Jacob Neusner et al. Philadelphia: Fortress, 1988.

———, "Meals" ———. "Meals and the new community in Luke." *SEÅ* 51-52 (1986-87): 158-67.

Muddiman, John. "The Glory of Jesus, Mark 10:37," 51-8. In *The Glory of Christ in the New Testament. Studies in Christology in Memory of George Bradford Caird.* Edt. L. D. Hurst and N. T. Wright. Oxford: Clarendon, 1987.

Muhlack, Gudrun. *Die Parallelen von Lukas-Evangelium und Apostelgeschichte* (Theologie und Wirklichkeit 8). Frankfurt: Lang, 1979.

Müller, P. -G. *Lukasevangelium* (Stuttgarter kleiner Kommentar, Neues Testament 3). Stuttgart: Katholisches Bibelwerk, 1984.

Mullins, Terence. "New Testament Commission Forms, Especially in Luke-Acts." *JBL* 95 (1976): 603-14.

Munck, *Acts* Munck, Johannes. *The Acts of the Apostles* (AB 31). Garden City, NY: Doubleday, 1967.

———, "Discours" ———. "Discours d'adieu dans le Nouveau Testament et dans la litérateur biblique," 155-70. In *Aux sources de la tradition Chrétienne: Mélanges offert à M. Maurice Goguel.* Edt. J. J. von Allmen. Paris: Delachaux et Niestle, 1950.

Mussner, Franz. "Das Wesen des Christentums ist συνεσθίειν," 92-102. In *Mysterium der Gnade: Festschrift für Johann Auer.* Edt. H. von Rossmann and J. Ratzinger. Regensburg: Pustet, 1975.

Navone, "Banquet" Navone, John. "The Lukan Banquet." *Bible Today* 51 (1970): 155-61.

———, *Themes* ———. *Themes of St. Luke.* Rome: Gregorian University, 1970.

Neirynck, "Argument" Neirynck, Frans. "The Argument from Order and St. Luke's Transpositions." *ETL* 49 (1973): 784-815.

———, *Agreements* ———. *Minor Agreements of Matthew and Luke Against Mark.* Gembloux: Duculot, 1975.

Neusner, *Judaism* Neusner, Jacob. *Judaism in the Beginning of*

Christianity. London: SPCK, 1984.

———, "Eating Club" ———. "Two Pictures of the Pharisees: Philosophical Circle or Eating Club." *ATR* 64 (1982): 525-38.

Neyrey, Jerome. *The Passion According to Luke: A Redaction Study of Luke's Soteriology* (TI). New York: Paulist, 1985.

Nickels, P. *Targum and New Testament*. Rome: Biblical Institute, 1967.

Nickelsburg, *Resurrection* Nickelsburg, George W. E. *Resurrection, Immortality, and Eternal Life in Intertestamental Judaism* (HTS 26). Cambridge, MA: Harvard University, 1972.

———, "Riches" ———. "Riches, the Rich, and God's Judgement in I Enoch 92-105 and the Gospel according to Luke." *NTS* 25 (1979): 324-44.

Nilsson, M. P. "Saturnalia." PW 2/2A:201-11.

Nock, Arthur D. "*Soter* and *Euergetes*," 720-35. In *Essays on Religion and the Ancient World*. Vol. 2. Edt. Zeph Stewart. Oxford: Clarendon, 1972.

Nolland , *Luke* Nolland, John. *Luke 1-9:20* (WBC 35a). Waco, TX: Word, 1989.

———, *Luke's Readers* ———. *Luke's Readers: a study of Luke 4:22-8; Acts 13:46; 18:6; 28:28 and Luke 21:5-36*. PhD dissertation, unpublished. Cambridge University, 1977.

Nordheim, *Die Lehre I* Nordheim, Eckhard von. *Die Lehre der Alten I: Das Testament als Literaturgattung im Judentum der hellenistisch-römischen Zeit* (ALGHJ 13). Leiden: Brill, 1980.

———, *Die Lehre II* ———. *Die Lehre der Alten II: Das Testament als Literaturgattung im Alten Testament und im Alten Vorderen Orient* (ALGHJ 18). Leiden: Brill, 1985.

Oepke, A. "παῖς κτλ." *TDNT* 5:636-54.

Opperwall, Nola J. "Foot Washing." *ISBE* 2:333.

Osty, *Évangile* Osty, E. *L'Évangile selon Saint Luc* (Bible de Jérusalem). 3rd ed. Paris: Cerf, 1961.

———, "Points" ———. "Les points de contact entre le récit de la Passion dans saint Luc et dans saint Jean." *RSR* 39 (1951): 146-54.

Otomo, Yoko. *Nachfolge Jesu und Anfänge der Kirche im Neuen Testament. Eine exegetische Studie*. DrTheol dissertation, unpublished. Johannes Gutenberg-Universität zu Mainz, 1970.

O'Toole, "Highlights" O'Toole, Robert F. "Highlights of Luke's Theology." *CurTM* 12 (1985): 353-60.

———, "Parallels" ———. "Parallels between Jesus and His Disciples in Luke-Acts." *BZ* 27 (1983): 195-212.

———, *Unity* ———. *The Unity of Luke's Theology: An Analysis of Luke-Acts* (GNS 9). Wilmington, DE: Glazier, 1984.

Ott, Wilhelm. *Gebet und Heil. Die Bedeutung der Gebetsparänese in der lukan-*

ischen Theologie. Munich: Kösel, 1965.

Otto, Rudolph. *The Kingdom of God and the Son of Man. A Study in the History of Religion.* Trans. Floyd V. Filson and Bertram L. Woolf. London: Lutterworth, 1938.

Page, Sydney H. T. "The Authenticity of the Ransom Logion (Mark 10:45b)," 137-61. In *Studies of History and Tradition in the Four Gospels* (GP 1). Edt. R. T. France and David Wenham. Sheffield: JSOT, 1980.

Parker, Pierson. "Luke and the Fourth Evangelist." *NTS* 9 (1962-63): 317-66.

Parkin, V. "Συνεσθίειν in the New Testament." SE III (1964): 250-3.

Parsons, Mikeal. *The Departure of Jesus in Luke-Acts. The Ascension Narratives in Context* (JSNTSup 21). Sheffield: JSOT, 1987.

Pathrapankal, J. "Christianity as a 'Way' according to the Acts of the Apostles," 533-9. In *Les Actes des Apôtres. Traditions, rédaction, théologie* (BETL 48). Edt. J. Kremer. Gembloux: Duculot, 1979.

Patsch, *Abendmahl* Patsch, Hermann. *Abendmahl und historischer Jesus* (Calwer Theologische Monographien A/1). Stuttgart: Calwer, 1972.

———, "Terminologie" ———. "Abendmahlsterminologie ausserhalb der Einsetzungsberichte." *ZNW* 62 (1971): 210-31.

Patte, Daniel. *The Gospel According to Matthew.* Philadelphia: Fortress, 1987.

Patterson, Orlando. *Slavery and Social Death. A Comparative Study.* Cambridge, MA: Harvard, 1982.

Peabody, Robert L. "Authority." *IESS* 1:473-7.

Pecota, D. B. "Young(er) (Man)." *ISBE* 4:1165-6.

Percy, Ernst. *Die Botschaft Jesu. Eine traditionskritische und exegetische Untersuchung* (Lunds Universitets Årsskrift 49/5). Lund: Gleerup, 1953.

Perrin, *Kingdom* Perrin, Norman. *The Kingdom of God in the Teaching of Jesus* (NTL). London: SCM, 1963.

———, "Wisdom" ———. "Wisdom and Apocalyptic in the Message of Jesus," 543-72. In *SBL 1972 Seminar Papers.* Vol. 2. Edt. Lane C. McGaughy. Los Angeles: SBL, 1972.

Perry, "Passion-Source" Perry, Alfred M. "Luke's Disputed Passion-Source." *ExpTim* 46 (1934-35): 256-60.

———, *Sources* ———. *The Sources of Luke's Passion Narrative.* Chicago: University, 1920.

Pesch, R., *Abendmahl* Pesch, Rudolf. *Das Abendmahl und Jesu Todesverständnis* (QD 80). Freiburg: Herder, 1978.

———, *Apostelgeschichte* ———. *Die Apostelgeschichte* (EKK 5). 2 vols. Zurich: Benziger, 1986.

———, "Last Supper" ———. "The Last Supper and Jesus' Understanding of His Death." *Bible Bhashyam* 3 (1977): 58-75.

———, "Kleine Herde" ———. "»Sei getrost, kleine Herde« (Lk 12,

32). Exegetische und ekklesiologische Erwagüngen," 85-118. In *Krise der Kirche—Chance des Glaubens. Die "Kleine Herde" heute und morgen.* Edt. K. Faerber. Frankfurt: Knecht, 1968.

———, "Structures" ———. "Structures du ministère dans le Nouveau Testament." *Istina* 16 (1971): 437-52.

———, and Kratz, R. *So liest man synoptisch: Anleitung und Kommentar zum Studium der synoptischen Evangelien, VI & VII. Passionsgeschichte: Erster Teil & zweiter Teil.* Frankfurt: Knecht, 1979, 1980.

Pesch, Wilhelm. *Der Lohngedanke in der Lehre Jesu, verglichen mit der religiösen Lohnlehre des Spätjudentums* (Münchener Theologische Studien 1/7). Munich: Zink, 1955.

Petzer, Kobus. "Style and Text in the Lucan Narrative of the Institution of the Lord's Supper (Luke 22.19b-20)." *NTS* 37 (1991): 113-29.

Pilgrim, Walter E. *Good News to the Poor. Wealth and Poverty in Luke-Acts.* Minneapolis: Augsburg, 1981.

Piper, Ronald A. *Wisdom in the Q Tradition. The Aphoristic Teaching of Jesus* (SNTSMS 62). Cambridge: University, 1989.

Pitt-Rivers, *Fate* Pitt-Rivers, Julian. *The Fate of Shechem or the Politics of Sex: Essays in the Anthropology of the Mediterranean.* Cambridge: University, 1977.

———, "Honor" ———. "Honor," 503-11. In *Encyclopedia of the Social Sciences.* 2nd ed. New York: Macmillan, 1968.

———, "Status" ———. "Honour and Social status," 19-78. In *Honour and Shame. The Values of Mediterranean Society* (The Nature of Human Society). Edt. J. G. Peristiany. London: Weidenfeld and Nicolson, 1965.

———, *People* ———. *The People of the Sierra.* London: Wiedenfeld and Nicolson, 1954.

Plummer, Alfred. *The Gospel According to St. Luke* (ICC). 4th ed. Edinburgh: Clark, 1901.

Pobee, John S. *Persecution and Martyrdom in the Theology of Paul* (JSNTSup 6). Sheffield: JSOT, 1985.

Polag, Athanasius. *Die Christologie der Logienquelle.* Neukirchen-Vluyn: Neukirchener, 1977.

Porteous, Norman. *Daniel* (OTL). Trans. W. Beyerlin. London: SCM, 1965.

Porter, Stanley E. "Thucydides 1.22.1 and Speeches in Acts: Is there a Thudydidean View?" *NovT* 32 (1990): 121-42.

Prast, F. *Presbyter und Evangelium in nachapostolischer Zeit: Die Abschiedsrede des Paulus in Milet (Apg 20, 17-38) im Rahmen der lukanischen Konzeption der Evangeliumsverkündigung.* Stuttgart: Katholisches Bibelwerk, 1979.

Price, J. L. "The Servant Motif in the Synoptic Gospels." *Int* 12 (1958): 28-38.

Quesnell, Quentin. "The Women at Luke's Supper," 59-79. In *Political Issues in*

Luke-Acts. Edt. Richard J. Cassidy and Philip J. Scharper. Maryknoll, NY: Orbis, 1983.

von Rad, Gerhard. "מֶלֶךְ and מַלְכוּת in the OT." *TDNT* 1:565-71.

Radl, *Lukas* Radl, Walter. *Das Lukasevangelium* (Erträge der Forschung 261). Darmstadt: Wissenschaftliche Buchgesselschaft, 1988.

———, *Paulus* ———. *Paulus und Jesus im lukanischen Doppelwerk: Untersuchung zu Parallelmotiven im Lukasevangelium und in der Apostelgeschichte* (Europäische Hochschulschriften 22/49). Frankfurt: Lang, 1975.

Rasmussen, Larry. "Luke 22:24-27." *Int* 37 (1983): 73-6.

Ravens, D. A. S. "St. Luke and Atonement." *ExpTim* 97 (1986): 291-4.

Rawson, "Children" Rawson, Beryl. "Children in the Roman *Familia*," 170-200. In *The Family in Ancient Rome. New Perspectives.* London: Croom Helm, 1986.

———, "Family" ———. "The Roman Family," 1-57. In *The Family in Ancient Rome. New Perspectives.* London: Croom Helm, 1986.

Rehkopf, Friedrich. *Die lukanische Sonderquelle: Ihr Umfang und Sprachgebrauch* (WUNT 5). Tübingen: Mohr, 1959.

Reicke, Bo. *Diakonie, Festfreude und Zelos in Verbindung mit der altchristlichen Agapefeier* (Uppsala Universitets Årsskrift 5). Uppsala: Lundequistka, 1951.

Reiling, J., and Swellengrebel, J. L.. *A Translator's Handbook on the Gospel of Luke* (UBS Helps for Translators 10). Leiden: Brill, 1971.

Rengstorf, "ἀποστέλλω" Rengstorf, Karl H. " ἀποστέλλω." *TDNT* 1:398-447.

———, "δοῦλος" ———. "δοῦλος κτλ." *TDNT* 2:261-80.

———, "δώδεκα" ———. "δώδεκα." *TDNT* 2:321-8.

———, *Evangelium* ———. *Das Evangelium nach Lukas* (NTD 3). 8th ed. Göttingen: Vandenhoeck und Ruprecht, 1958.

———, "μαθητής" ———. "μαθητής κτλ." *TDNT* 4:415-61.

Rese, Martin. *Alttestamentliche Motive in der Christologie des Lukas* (SNT 1). Gütersloh: Mohn, 1969.

Rice, George. "Luke's Thematic Use of the Call to Discipleship." *AUSS* 19 (1981): 51-8.

Richard, Earl. "Luke—Writer, Theologian, Historian: Research and Orientation of the 1970's." *BTB* 13 (1983): 3-15.

Richardson, Alan. *An Introduction to the Theology of the New Testament*. London: SCM, 1958.

Richardson, Neil. *The Panorama of Luke*. London: Epworth, 1982.

Richter, G. *Die Fusswaschung im Johannesevangelium. Geschichte ihrer Deutung* (Biblische Untersuchungen 1). Regensburg: Pustet, 1967.

Rickards, R. R. "Luke 22:25—They Are Called 'Friends of the People.'" *BT* 28

(1977): 445-6.

Rienecker, Fritz. *Das Evangelium des Lukas* (Wuppertaler Studienbibel 4). Wuppertal: Brockhaus, 1974.

Rigaux, Beda. "Die 'Zwolf' in Geschichte und Kerygma," 468-86. In *Der historische Jesus und der kerygmatische Christus.* Edt. H. Ristow-K. Matthiae. Berlin: Evangelische, 1960.

Robinson, J. A. T. "The Significance of the Footwashing," 144-7. In *Neotestamentica et Patristica. Festschrift für Oscar Cullmann* (NovTSup 6). Edt. W. C. van Unnik. Leiden: Brill, 1962.

Rodd, Cyril S. "On Applying a Sociological Theory to Biblical Studies." *JSOT* 19 (1981): 95-106.

Roetzel, Calvin. *The World that Shaped the New Testament.* London: SCM, 1987.

Rollin, B. "'Quittant tout, ils le suivirent' (Lc 5,11)." *Vie Consacrée* 53 (1981): 104-15.

Roloff, "Amt" Roloff, Jürgen. "Amt/ Ämter/ Amtverstandnis." *TRE* (1978): 2:500-622.

———, "Anfänge" ———. "Anfänge der soteriologischen Deutung des Todes Jesu (Mk. x. 45 und Lk. xxii. 27)." *NTS* 19 (1972-73): 38-64.

———, "Apostel" ———. "Apostel/ Apostolat/ Apostolizität." *TRE* (1978): 3:430-83.

———, *Apostelgeschichte* ———. *Die Apostelgeschichte* (NTD 5). Göttingen: Vandenhoeck und Ruprecht, 1981.

———, *Apostolat* ———. *Apostolat—Verkündigung—Kirche. Ursprung, Inhalt und Funktion des kirchlichen Apostelamtes nach Paulus, Lukas und den Pastoralbriefen.* Gütersloh: Mohn, 1965.

Ruppert, Lothar. "Der leidende (bedrängte, getötete) Gerechte nach den Spätschriften des Alten Testaments (inclusive Septuaginta) und der (nichtrabbinischen) Literatur des Frühjudentums unter besonderer Berücksichtigung des Gottesbildes," 76-87. In *Die Entstehung der jüdischen Martyrologie* (SPB 38). Edt. J. W. van Henten et al. Leiden: Brill, 1989.

Ryan, Rosalie. "The Women from Galilee and Discipleship in Luke." *BTB* 15 (1985): 56-9.

Sabbe, M. "The Footwashing in Jn 13 and its Relation to the Synoptic Gospels." *ETL* 58 (1982): 279-308.

Sabourin, "Eschatology" Sabourin, L. "The Eschatology of Luke." *BTB* 12 (1982): 73-6.

———, *Luc* ———. *L'évangile de Luc. Introduction et commentaire.* Rome: Gregorian University, 1985.

de Ste. Croix, *Class Struggle* de Ste. Croix, G. E. M. *The Class Struggle in the Ancient Greek World from the Archaic Age to the Arab Conquests.* London: Duckworth, 1981.

———, "Attitudes" ———. "Early Christian Attitudes to Property and Slavery," 1-38. In *Church, Society and Politics* (Studies in Church History). Edt. Derek Baker. Oxford: Blackwell, 1975.

Saller, *Patronage* Saller, Richard. *Personal Patronage under the Early Empire.* Cambridge: University, 1982.

———, "Slavery" ———. "Slavery and the Roman Family," 65-87. In *Classical Slavery.* Edt. M. I. Finley. London: Frank Cass, 1987.

Salmon, Marilyn. "Insider or Outsider? Luke's Relationship with Judaism," 76-82. In *Luke-Acts and the Jewish People.* Edt. Joseph B. Tyson. Minneapolis: Augsburg, 1988.

Sanders, E. P. *Jesus and Judaism.* London: SCM, 1985.

———, and Davies, Margaret. *Studying the Synoptic Gospels.* London: SCM, 1989.

Sanders, Jack T. *The Jews in Luke-Acts.* London: SCM, 1987.

Sandmel, S. "Herod (Family)." *IDB* 2:585-94.

Savage, Timothy B. *Power Through Weakness. An Historical and Exegetical Examination of Paul's Understanding of the Ministry in 2 Corinthians.* PhD dissertation, unpublished. Cambridge University, 1986.

Schenker, A. *Substitution du châtiment ou prix de la paix? Le don de la vie du Fils de l'homme en Mc 10, 45 et par. à la lumière de l'Ancien Testament. La Pâque du Christ, mystère de salut* (LD 112). Paris: Cerf, 1982.

Schillebeeckx, E. *Die Auferstehung Jesu als Grund der Erlösung. Zwischenbericht über die Prolegomena zu einer Christologie* (QD 78). Trans. Hugo Zulauf. Freiburg: Herder, 1979.

Schlatter, *Markus und Lukas* Schlatter, Adolf. *Die Evangelien nach Markus und Lukas* (Erläuterungen zum Neuen Testament 2). Stuttgart: Calwer, 1987.

———, *Lukas* ———. Schlatter, Adolf. *Das Evangelium des Lukas.* 3rd ed. Stuttgart: Calwer, 1975.

Schlosser, Jacques. "La genèse de *Luc,* XXII, 25-27." *RB* 89 (1982): 52-70.

Schmahl, Günther. *Die Zwölf im Markus-evangelium. Eine redaktionsgeschichtliche Untersuchung* (Trierer Theologische Studien 30). Trier: Paulinus, 1974.

Schmeichel, Waldemar. "Does Luke Make a Soteriological Statement in Acts 20:28?" 501-14. In *SBL 1982 Seminar Papers.* Edt. Kent Richards. Chico, CA: Scholars, 1982.

Schmid, Josef. *Das Evangelium nach Lukas* (RNT 3). 4th ed. Regensburg: Pustet, 1960.

Schmidt, Karl L. "βασιλεύς κτλ." *TDNT* 1:564-93.

Schmidt, Thomas E. *Hostility to Wealth in the Synoptic Gospels* (JSNTSup 15). Sheffield: JSOT, 1987.

Schmitz, Otto. "θρόνος." *TDNT* 3:160-7.

Schmithals, *Lukas* Schmithals, Walter. *Das Evangelium nach*

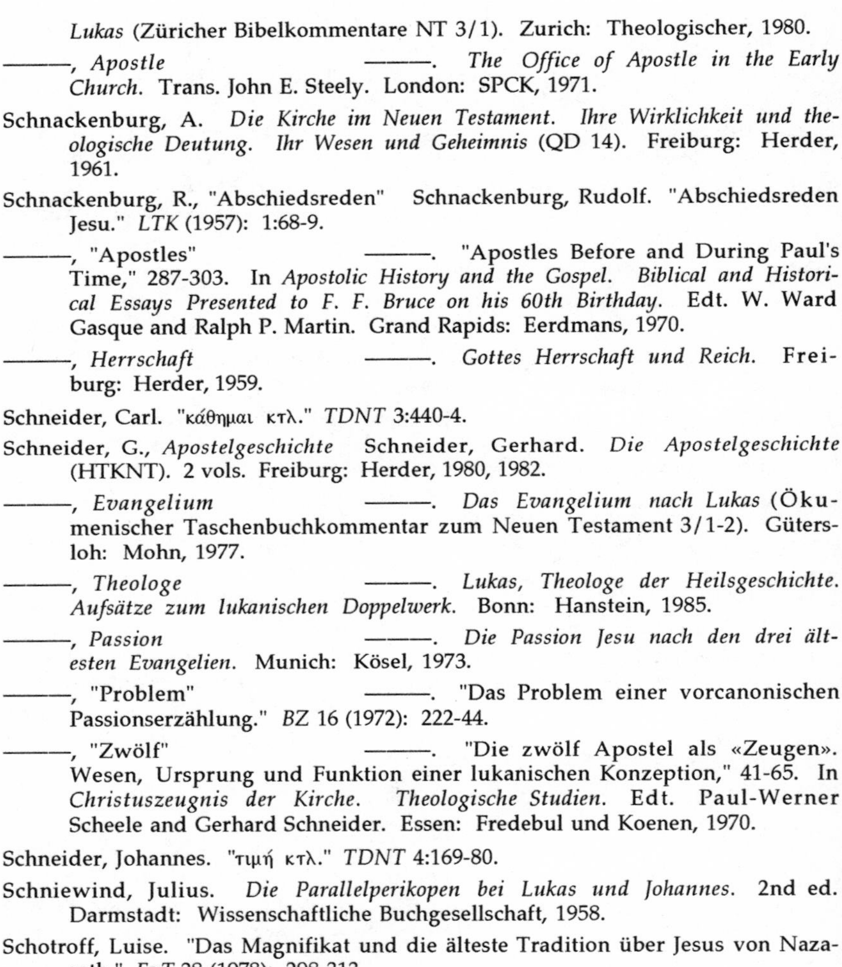

Lukas (Züricher Bibelkommentare NT 3/1). Zurich: Theologischer, 1980.

———, *Apostle* ———. *The Office of Apostle in the Early Church*. Trans. John E. Steely. London: SPCK, 1971.

Schnackenburg, A. *Die Kirche im Neuen Testament. Ihre Wirklichkeit und theologische Deutung. Ihr Wesen und Geheimnis* (QD 14). Freiburg: Herder, 1961.

Schnackenburg, R., "Abschiedsreden" Schnackenburg, Rudolf. "Abschiedsreden Jesu." *LTK* (1957): 1:68-9.

———, "Apostles" ———. "Apostles Before and During Paul's Time," 287-303. In *Apostolic History and the Gospel. Biblical and Historical Essays Presented to F. F. Bruce on his 60th Birthday*. Edt. W. Ward Gasque and Ralph P. Martin. Grand Rapids: Eerdmans, 1970.

———, *Herrschaft* ———. *Gottes Herrschaft und Reich*. Freiburg: Herder, 1959.

Schneider, Carl. "κάθημαι κτλ." *TDNT* 3:440-4.

Schneider, G., *Apostelgeschichte* Schneider, Gerhard. *Die Apostelgeschichte* (HTKNT). 2 vols. Freiburg: Herder, 1980, 1982.

———, *Evangelium* ———. *Das Evangelium nach Lukas* (Ökumenischer Taschenbuchkommentar zum Neuen Testament 3/1-2). Gütersloh: Mohn, 1977.

———, *Theologe* ———. *Lukas, Theologe der Heilsgeschichte. Aufsätze zum lukanischen Doppelwerk*. Bonn: Hanstein, 1985.

———, *Passion* ———. *Die Passion Jesu nach den drei ältesten Evangelien*. Munich: Kösel, 1973.

———, "Problem" ———. "Das Problem einer vorcanonischen Passionserzählung." *BZ* 16 (1972): 222-44.

———, "Zwölf" ———. "Die zwölf Apostel als «Zeugen». Wesen, Ursprung und Funktion einer lukanischen Konzeption," 41-65. In *Christuszeugnis der Kirche. Theologische Studien*. Edt. Paul-Werner Scheele and Gerhard Schneider. Essen: Fredebul und Koenen, 1970.

Schneider, Johannes. "τιμή κτλ." *TDNT* 4:169-80.

Schniewind, Julius. *Die Parallelperikopen bei Lukas und Johannes*. 2nd ed. Darmstadt: Wissenschaftliche Buchgesellschaft, 1958.

Schotroff, Luise. "Das Magnifikat und die älteste Tradition über Jesus von Nazareth." *EvT* 38 (1978): 298-313.

Schramm, Tim. *Der Markus-Stoff bei Lukas. Eine literarkritische und redaktionsgeschichtliche Untersuchung* (SNTSMS 14). Cambridge: University, 1971.

Schulz, A., *Jünger* Schulz, Anselm. *Jünger des Herrn. Nachfolge Christi nach dem Neuen Testament*. Munich: Kösel, 1964.

———, *Nachfolge* ———. *Nachfolge und Nachahmen. Studien über das Verhältnis der neutestamentlichen Jüngerschaft zur urchrist-*

lichen Vorbildethik (SANT 6). Munich: Kösel, 1962.

Schulz, Siegfried. *Q: Die Spruchquelle der Evangelisten.* Zurich: Theologischer, 1972.

Schürer, Emil. *The History of the Jewish People in the Age of Jesus Christ (175 B.C. - A.D. 135): A New English Version Revised and Edited.* 3 vols. Edt. G. Vermes et al. Edinburgh: Clark, 1973.

Schürmann, "Dienst" Schürmann, Heinz. "Der Dienst des Petrus und Johannes." *TTZ* 60 (1950): 99-101.

———, "Dubletten" ———. "Die Dubletten im Lukasevangelium." *ZKT* 75 (1953): 338-45.

———, "Vermeidungen" ———. "Die Dublettenvermeidungen im Lukasevangelium." *ZKT* 76 (1954): 83-93.

———, *Einsetzungsbericht* ———. *Der Einsetzungsbericht Lk 22,19-20. II. Teil einer quellenkritischen Untersuchung des lukanischen Abendmahlsberichtes Lk 22,7-38* (NTAbh 20/4). Münster: Aschendorff, 1955.

———, "Jüngerkreis" ———. "Der Jüngerkreis Jesu als Zeichen für Israel." *Geist und Leben* 16 (1963): 21-35.

———, "Textüberlieferung" ———. "Lk 22,19b-20 als ursprüngliche Textüberlieferung." *Bib* 32 (1951): 364-92; Fortsetzung, 522-41.

———, *Lukasevangelium* ———. *Das Lukasevangelium: Erster Teil: Kommentar zu Kap. 1, 1-9, 50* (HTKNT 3/1). Freiburg: Herder, 1969.

———, *Abschiedsrede* ———. *Jesu Abschiedsrede Lk 22,21-38. III. Teil einer quellenkritischen Untersuchung des lukanischen Abendmahlsberichtes Lk 22,7-38* (NTAbh 20/5). Münster: Aschendorff, 1957.

———, *Paschamahlbericht* ———. *Der Paschamahlbericht Lk 22,(7-14) 15-18. I. Teil einer quellenkritischen Untersuchung des lukanischen Abendmahlsberichtes Lk 22,7-38* (NTAbh 19/5). Münster: Aschendorff, 1953.

———, "Testament" ———. "Das Testament Paulus für die Kirche Apg 20,18-35," 310-40. In *Traditionsgeschichtliche Untersuchungen zu den synoptischen Evangelien.* Düsseldorf: Patmos, 1968.

———, *Ursprung* ———. *Ursprung und Gestalt: Erörterungen und Besinnungen zum Neuen Testament.* Düsseldorf: Patmos, 1970.

———, "Tod" ———. "Wie hat Jesus seinen Tod bestanden und verstanden? Eine methodkritische Besinnung" 325-63. In *Orientierung an Jesus. Zur Theologie der Synoptiker. Festschrift Josef Schmid.* Edt. P. Hoffmann et al. Freiburg: Herder, 1973.

Schütz, Frieder. *Der leidende Christus. Die angefochtene Gemeinde und das Christuskerygma der lukanischen Schriften* (BWANT 9). Stuttgart: Kohlhammer, 1969.

Schütz, John H. *Paul and the Anatomy of Apostolic Authority* (SNTSMS 26). Cambridge: University, 1975.

Schweizer, *Church Order* Schweizer, Eduard. *Church Order in the New Testament* (SBT 32). Trans. Frank Clarke. London: SCM, 1961.

———, "Speeches" ———. "Concerning the Speeches in Acts," 208-16. In *Studies in Luke-Acts. Essays Presented in Honor of Paul Schubert.* Edt. Leander E. Keck and J. Louis Martyn. London: SPCK, 1968.

———, *Erniedrigung* ———. *Erniedrigung und Erhöhung bei Jesus und seinen Nachfolgern.* Zurich: Zwingli, 1955.

———, *Luke* ———. *The Good News According to Luke.* Trans. David E. Green. Atlanta: John Knox, 1984.

———, *Mark* ———. *The Good News According to Mark.* Trans. Donald H. Madvig. London: SPCK, 1971.

———, *Matthew* ———. *The Good News According to Matthew.* Trans. David E. Green. London: SPCK, 1976.

———, *Lordship* ———. *Lordship and Discipleship* (SBT 28). London: SCM, 1960.

Scott, James C. *The Moral Economy of the Peasant.* New Haven: Yale, 1976.

Scroggs, Robin. "The Sociological Interpretation of the New Testament: The Present State of Research." *NTS* 26 (1979-80): 164-79.

Scullard, Howard H. "Rome." *OCD* 925-35.

Seccombe, David P. *Possessions and the Poor in Luke-Acts* (SNTSU B/6). Linz: Fuchs, 1982.

Seeley, David. "Rulership and Service in Mark 10:41-45." *NovT* 35 (1993): 234-50.

Seesemann, Heinrich. "πεῖρα κτλ." *TDNT* 6:23-36.

Segovia, F. F. "John 13,1-20, The Footwashing in the Johannine Tradition." *ZNW* 73 (1982): 31-51.

Sellew, Philip H. "The Last Supper Discourse in Luke 22:21-38." *Forum* 3 (1987): 70-95.

Senior, Donald. *The Passion of Jesus in the Gospel of Luke* (The Passion Series 3). Wilmington, DE: Glazier, 1989.

Shepherd, M. H., Jr. "Deacon." *IDB* 1:785-6.

Sheridan, M. "Disciples and Discipleship in Matthew and Luke." *BTB* 3 (1973): 235-55.

Sherwin-White, A. N. *Roman Society and Roman Law in the New Testament.* Oxford: Clarendon, 1978.

Skard, Eiliv. "Zwei religiös-politische Begriffe: Euergetes Concordia." *Norske Videnskaps Akademi i Oslo, Avhandlinger* 2 (1932): 6-66.

Skehan, Patrick W., and Di Lella, Alexander A. *The Wisdom of Ben Sira* (AB 39). New York: Doubleday, 1987.

Smart, James D. "Mark 10:35-45." *Int* 33 (1979): 288-93.

Smith, Dennis E. "Table Fellowship as a Literary Motif in the Gospel of Luke." *JBL* 106 (1987): 613-38.

Soards, Marion L. *The Passion according to Luke. The Special Material of Luke 22* (JSNTSup 14). Sheffield: JSOT, 1987.

Sparks, H. F. D. "St. Luke's Transpositions." *NTS* 3 (1956-57): 219-22.

Speiser, E. A. "The Manner of the King," 280-7. In *The World History of the Jewish People.* Vol. 3: *Judges.* Edt. Benjamin Mazar. Tel-Aviv: Massada, 1971.

Spivey, Robert A. "Structuralism and Biblical Studies: The Uninvited Guest." *Int* 28 (1974): 133-45.

Stager, L. "The Archaeology of the Family in Ancient Israel." *BASOR* 260 (1985): 1-35.

Stählin, Gustav. *Die Apostelgeschichte* (NTD 5). 16th ed. Göttingen: Vandenhoeck und Ruprechet, 1980.

Stambaugh, John, and Balch, David. *The Social World of the First Christians.* London: SPCK, 1986.

Stanton, Graham N. *The Gospels and Jesus* (OBS). Oxford: University, 1989.

Stauffer, "Abschiedsreden" Stauffer, E. "Abschiedsreden." *RAC* 1 (1950): 29-35.

———, "Farewell Speeches" ———. "Valedictions and Farewell Speeches," 344-7. In *New Testament Theology.* Trans. John Marsh. London: SCM, 1955.

Steele, E. Springs. "Luke 11:37-54—A Modified Hellenistic Symposium?" *JBL* 103 (1984): 379-94.

Stein, Robert H. *The Synoptic Problem: An Introduction.* Grand Rapids: Baker, 1987.

Stöger, A. "Eigenart und Botschaft der lukanischen Passionsgeschichte." *BK* 24 (1969): 4-8.

Stonehouse, Ned B. *The Witness of Luke to Christ.* London: Tyndale, 1951.

Streeter, B. H. *The Four Gospels.* 2nd ed. London: Macmillan, 1930.

Stuhlmacher, Peter. "Existenzstellvertretung für die Vielen: Mk 10,45 (Mt 20,28)," 412-27. In *Werden und Wirken des Alten Testaments. Festschrift für Claus Westermann zum 70. Geburtstag.* Edt. Fainer Albertz et al. Göttingen: Vandenhoeck und Ruprecht; Neukirchen-Vluyn: Neukirchener, 1980.

Sweetland, "Discipleship" Sweetland, Dennis M. "Discipleship and Persecution: A Study of Luke 12,1-12." *Bib* 65 (1984): 61-80.

———, "Lord's Supper" ———. "The Lord's Supper and the Lukan Community." *BTB* 13 (1983): 23-27.

Talbert, "Discipleship" Talbert, Charles H. "Discipleship in Luke-Acts," 62-75. In *Discipleship in the New Testament.* Edt. Fernando F. Segovia. Philadelphia: Fortress, 1985.

———, *Patterns* ———. *Literary Patterns, Theological Themes and the Genre of Luke-Acts* (SBLMS 20). Missoula, MT: Scholars, 1974.

———, ed., *Luke-Acts* ———, ed. *Luke-Acts: New Perspectives from the Society of Biblical Literature Seminar.* New York: Crossroad, 1984.

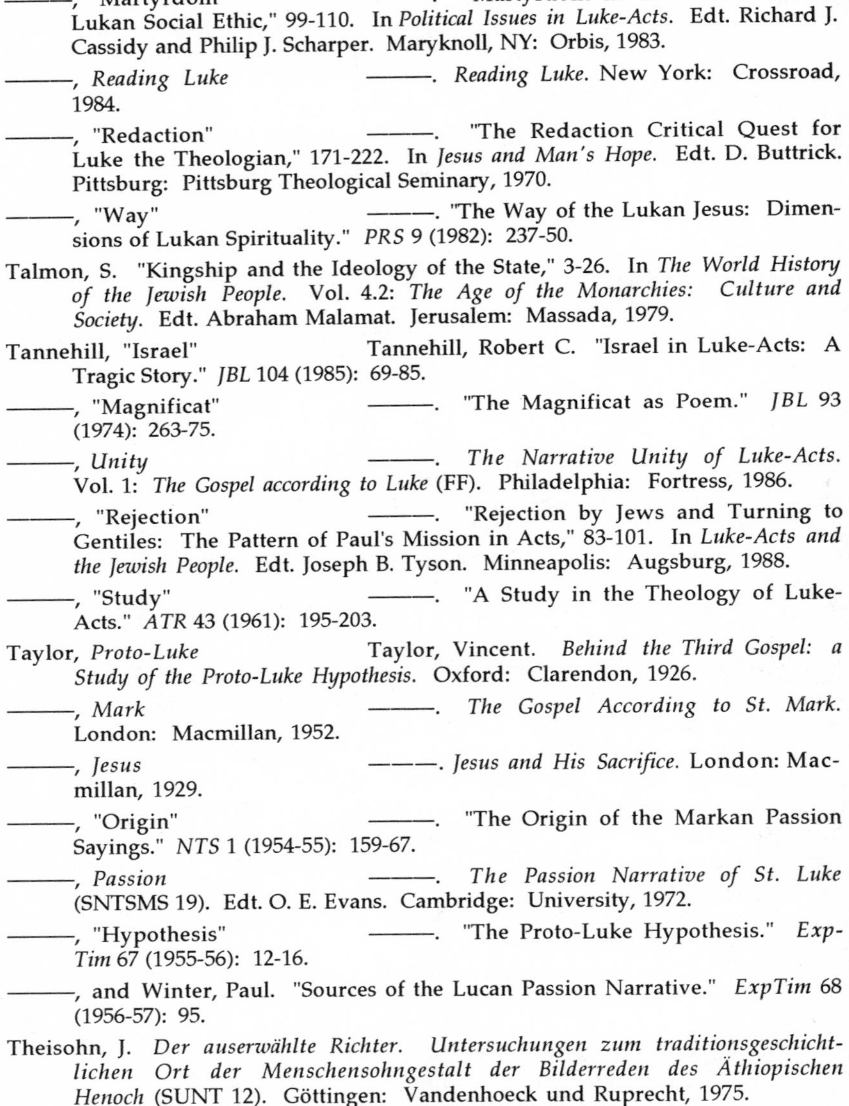

———, "Martyrdom" ———. "Martyrdom in Luke-Acts and the Lukan Social Ethic," 99-110. In *Political Issues in Luke-Acts*. Edt. Richard J. Cassidy and Philip J. Scharper. Maryknoll, NY: Orbis, 1983.

———, *Reading Luke* ———. *Reading Luke*. New York: Crossroad, 1984.

———, "Redaction" ———. "The Redaction Critical Quest for Luke the Theologian," 171-222. In *Jesus and Man's Hope*. Edt. D. Buttrick. Pittsburg: Pittsburg Theological Seminary, 1970.

———, "Way" ———. "The Way of the Lukan Jesus: Dimensions of Lukan Spirituality." *PRS* 9 (1982): 237-50.

Talmon, S. "Kingship and the Ideology of the State," 3-26. In *The World History of the Jewish People*. Vol. 4.2: *The Age of the Monarchies: Culture and Society*. Edt. Abraham Malamat. Jerusalem: Massada, 1979.

Tannehill, "Israel" Tannehill, Robert C. "Israel in Luke-Acts: A Tragic Story." *JBL* 104 (1985): 69-85.

———, "Magnificat" ———. "The Magnificat as Poem." *JBL* 93 (1974): 263-75.

———, *Unity* ———. *The Narrative Unity of Luke-Acts*. Vol. 1: *The Gospel according to Luke* (FF). Philadelphia: Fortress, 1986.

———, "Rejection" ———. "Rejection by Jews and Turning to Gentiles: The Pattern of Paul's Mission in Acts," 83-101. In *Luke-Acts and the Jewish People*. Edt. Joseph B. Tyson. Minneapolis: Augsburg, 1988.

———, "Study" ———. "A Study in the Theology of Luke-Acts." *ATR* 43 (1961): 195-203.

Taylor, *Proto-Luke* Taylor, Vincent. *Behind the Third Gospel: a Study of the Proto-Luke Hypothesis*. Oxford: Clarendon, 1926.

———, *Mark* ———. *The Gospel According to St. Mark*. London: Macmillan, 1952.

———, *Jesus* ———. *Jesus and His Sacrifice*. London: Macmillan, 1929.

———, "Origin" ———. "The Origin of the Markan Passion Sayings." *NTS* 1 (1954-55): 159-67.

———, *Passion* ———. *The Passion Narrative of St. Luke* (SNTSMS 19). Edt. O. E. Evans. Cambridge: University, 1972.

———, "Hypothesis" ———. "The Proto-Luke Hypothesis." *ExpTim* 67 (1955-56): 12-16.

———, and Winter, Paul. "Sources of the Lucan Passion Narrative." *ExpTim* 68 (1956-57): 95.

Theisohn, J. *Der auserwählte Richter. Untersuchungen zum traditionsgeschichtlichen Ort der Menschensohngestalt der Bilderreden des Äthiopischen Henoch* (SUNT 12). Göttingen: Vandenhoeck und Ruprecht, 1975.

Theissen, *Followers* Theissen, Gerd. *The First Followers of Jesus. A Sociological Analysis of the Earliest Christianity*. Trans. John Bowden.

London: SCM, 1978.

———, *Shadow* ———. *The Shadow of the Galilean.* Trans. John Bowden. London: SCM, 1987.

———, *Social Setting* ———. *The Social Setting of Pauline Christianity.* Trans. John H. Schütz. Philadelphia: Fortress, 1982.

Thériault, J. Y. "Les dimensions sociales, économiques, et politiques dans l'œuvre de Luc." *ScEs* 26 (1974): 205-31.

Thiselton, "Meaning" Thiselton, Anthony C. "Meaning," 435-8. In *A Dictionary of Biblical Interpretation.* Edt. R. J. Coggins and J. L. Houlden. London: SCM, 1990.

———, "Semantics" ———. "Semantics and New Testament Interpretation," 75-104. In *New Testament Interpretation. Essays on Principles and Methods.* Edt. I. Howard Marshall. Exeter: Paternoster, 1977.

———, *Two Horizons* ———. *The Two Horizons. New Testament Hermeneutics and Philosophical Description with Special Reference to Heidegger, Bultmann, Gadamer, and Wittgenstein.* Exeter: Paternoster, 1980.

Thompson, G. H. P. *The Gospel according to Luke* (New Clarendon Bible). Oxford: Clarendon, 1972.

Thysman, R. "L'Ethique de l'imitation du Christ dans le Nouveau Testament: Situation, notations et variations du thème." *ETL* 42 (1966): 138-75.

Tiede, "Exaltation" Tiede, David L. "The Exaltation of Jesus and the Restoration of Israel in Acts 1." *HTR* 79 (1986): 278-86.

———, "Glory" ———. "'Glory to Thy People Israel!': Luke-Acts and the Jews," 142-51. In *SBL 1986 Seminar Papers.* Edt. Kent H. Richards. Atlanta: Scholars, 1986.

———, "Kings" ———. "The Kings of the Gentiles and the Leader Who Serves: Luke 22:24-30." *WW* 12 (1992): 23-8.

———, *Luke* ———. *Luke* (Augsburg Commentary on the New Testament). Minneapolis: Augsburg, 1988.

———, *Prophecy* ———. *Prophecy and History in Luke-Acts.* Philadelphia: Fortress, 1980.

Tinsley, E. J. *The Cambridge Bible Commentary in the New English Bible: The Gospel according to Luke.* Cambridge: University, 1965.

Tödt, H. E. *The Son of Man in the Synoptic Tradition* (NTL). London: SCM, 1965.

Toy, C. H. *The Book of Proverbs* (ICC). Edinburgh: Clark, 1904.

Trautmann, Maria. *Zeichenhafte Handlungen Jesu. Ein Beitrag zur Frage nach dem historischen Jesus* (FB 37). Würzburg: Echter, 1980.

Tresmontant, C. *Évangile de Luc. Traduction et notes.* Paris: O.E.I.L., 1987.

Treves, Piero. "Historiography, Greek." *OCD* 521-3.

Trilling, W. "Zur Entstehung des Zwölferkreises. Eine geschichtskritische Überlegung," 201-22. In *Die Kirche des Anfangs. Festschrift für Heinz Schür-*

mann zum 65. Geburtstag. Edt. R. Schnackenburg et al. Freiburg: Herder, 1978.

Troadec, H. *L'évangile selon saint Luc* (Paroles de vie). Paris: Mame, 1969.

Trocmé, Étienne. *The Passion as Liturgy: A Study in the Origin of the Passion Narratives in the Four Gospels.* London: SCM, 1983.

Tuckett, Christopher. *Reading the New Testament: Methods of Interpretation.* London: SPCK, 1987.

Tyson, *Death of Jesus* Tyson, Joseph B. *The Death of Jesus in Luke-Acts.* Columbia, SC: University of South Carolina, 1986.

———, ed., *Jewish People* ———, ed. *Luke-Acts and the Jewish People.* Minneapolis: Augsburg, 1988.

———, "Food" ———. "The Problem of Food in Acts: A Study of Literary Patterns with Particular Reference to Acts 6:1-7," 69-85. In *SBL 1979 Seminar Papers.* Edt. Paul Achtemeier. Missoula, MT: Scholars, 1979.

van Unnik, "Book of Acts" Unnik, W. C. van. "'The Book of Acts,' the Confirmation of the Gospel." *NovT* 4 (1960): 26-59.

———, "Historiography" ———. "Luke's Second Book and the Rules of Hellenistic Historiography," 37-60. In *Les Actes des Apôtres. Traditions, rédaction, théologie* (BETL 48). Edt. J. Kremer. Gembloux: Duculot, 1979.

Untergassmair, *Kreuzweg* Untergassmair, Franz G. *Kreuzweg und Kreuzigung Jesu: Ein Beitrag zur lukanischen Redaktionsgeschichte und zur Frage nach der lukanischen "Kreuzestheologie"* (Paderborner Theologische Studien 10). Paderborn: Schöningh, 1980.

———, "Thesen" ———. "Thesen zur Sinndeutung des Todes Jesu in der lukanischen Passionsgeschichte." *TGl* 70 (1980): 180-93.

Urbach, E. E. "The Laws Regarding Slavery as a Source for Social History of the Period of the 2nd Temple, the Mishnah and Talmud," 1-94. In *Papers of the Institute of Jewish Studies, London.* Vol. 1. Edt. J. G. Weiss. Oxford: University, 1964.

de Vaux, Roland. *Ancient Israel: Its Life and Institutions.* London: Darton, Longman and Todd, 1961.

Verhey, Allen. *The Great Reversal. Ethics and the New Testament.* Grand Rapids: Eerdmans, 1984.

Veyne, Paul. *Bread and Circuses. Historical Sociology and Political Pluralism.* Trans. Brian Pearce. London: Penguin, 1990.

Via, E. Jane. "Women, the Discipleship of Service, and the Early Christian Ritual Meal in the Gospel of Luke." *Saint Luke's Journal of Theology* 29 (1985): 37-60.

Vielhauer, "Gottesreich" Vielhauer, Philipp. "Gottesreich und Menschensohn in der Verkündigung Jesu," 55-91. In *Aufsätze zum Neuen Testament* (Theologische Bücherei 31 NT). Munich: Kaiser, 1965.

———, "Paulinism" ———. "On the 'Paulinism' of Acts," 33-50.

In *Studies in Luke-Acts. Essays Presented in Honor of Paul Schubert.* Edt. Leander E. Keck and J. Louis Martyn. London: SPCK, 1968.

Vogt, J. *Ancient Slavery and the Ideal of Man.* Trans. Thomas Wiedemann. Oxford: Blackwell, 1974.

Vögtle, *Neue Testament* Vögtle, A. *Das Neue Testament und die Zukunft des Kosmos* (Kommentare und Beiträge zum Alten und Neuen Testament). Düsseldorf: Patmos, 1970.

———, "Einladung" ———. "Die Einladung zum Großen Gastmahl und zum königlichen Hochzeitsmahl. Ein Paradigma für den Wandel des geschichtlichen Verständnis-horizonts," 171-218. In *Das Evangelium and die Evangelien. Beiträge zur Evangelienforschung.* Düsseldorf: Patmos, 1971.

Völkel, M. "Zur Deutung des 'Reiches Gottes' bei Lukas." *ZNW* 65 (1974): 57-70.

Vööbus, "Text" Vööbus, Arthur. "A New Approach to the Problem of the Shorter and Longer Text of Luke." *NTS* 15 (1968-69): 457-63.

———, *Prelude* ———. *The Prelude to the Lukan Passion Narrative: Tradition-, Redaction-, Cult-, Motif-Historical and Source-Critical Studies* (Papers of the Estonian Theological Society in Exile 17). Stockholm: ETSE, 1968.

Voss, P. Gerhard. *Die Christologie der lukanischen Schriften in Grundzügen* (StudNeot 2). Paris: Desclée de Brouwer, 1965.

Wainwright, Arthur. "Luke and the Restoration of the Kingdom to Israel." *ExpTim* 89 (1977-78): 76-9.

Wainwright, Geoffrey. *Eucharist and Eschatology.* 2nd ed. London: Epworth, 1978.

Walasky, Paul W. *"And so we came to Rome." The Political Perspective of St. Luke* (SNTSMS 49). Cambridge: University, 1983.

Wallace-Hadrill, Andrew, ed. *Patronage in Ancient Society* (Leicester-Nottingham Studies in Ancient Society 1). London: Routledge, 1989.

Wanke, Joachim. *Beobachtungen zum Eucharistieverständnis des Lukas, auf Grund der lukanischen Mahlberichte* (Erfurter Theologische Schriften 8). Leipzig: St. Benno, 1973.

Weatherly, J. A. "The Jews in Luke-Acts." *TynBul* 40 (1989): 107-17.

Weber, Hans-Ruedi. *Jesus and the Children.* Geneva: World Council of Churches, 1979.

Wedderburn, Alexander J. M. "Paul and Jesus: Similarity and Continuity," 117-44. In *Paul and Jesus. Collected Essays* (JSNTSup 37). Sheffield: JSOT, 1989.

Weeden, Theodore J. *Mark—Traditions in Conflict.* Philadelphia: Fortress, 1971.

Weiss, Herold. "Foot Washing in the Johannine Community." *NovT* 21 (1979): 298-325.

Weiss, Johannes. *Jesus' Proclamation of the Kingdom of God.* Trans. Richard H. Hiers and David L. Holland. London: SCM, 1971.

Weiss, Konrad. "πούς." *TDNT* 6: 624-31.

Welch, John W., ed. *Chiasmus in Antiquity: Structures, Analyses, Exegesis*. Hildesheim: Gerstenberg, 1981.

Wellhausen, J. *Das Evangelium Lucae übersetzt und erklärt*. Berlin: Reimer, 1904.

Wenham, D., "Note" Wenham, David. "A Note on Mark 9:33-42/ Matt. 18:1-6/ Luke 9:46-50." *JSNT* 14 (1982): 113-18.

———, *Rediscovery* ———. *The Rediscovery of Jesus' Eschatological Discourse* (GP 4). Sheffield: JSOT, 1984.

Wenham, John. *Redating Matthew, Mark and Luke: A Fresh Assault on the Synoptic Problem*. London: Hodder and Stoughton, 1991.

Westermann, Claus. *Isaiah 40-66* (OTL). Trans. David Stalker. London: SCM, 1969.

Whitelam, K. W. "The Symbols of Power: Aspects of Royal Propaganda in the United Monarchy." *BA* 49 (1986): 166-73.

Whybray, R. N. *Isaiah 40-66* (NCB). London: Marshall, Morgan and Scott, 1975.

Wiedemann, *Children* Wiedemann, Thomas. *Adults and Children in the Roman Empire*. London: Routledge, 1989.

———, *Greek* ———. *Greek and Roman Slavery*. London: Croom Helm, 1981.

———, *Slavery* ———. *Slavery* (Greece and Rome: New Surveys in the Classics 19). Oxford: Clarendon, 1987.

Wiefel, Wolfgang. *Das Evangelium nach Lukas* (THKNT 3). 3rd ed. Berlin: Evangelische, 1988.

Wikan, Unni. "Shame and Honour: A Contestable Pair." *Man* 19 (1984): 635-52.

Wilckens, Ulrich. *Die Missonsreden der Apostelgeschichte. Form- und traditiongeschichtliche Untersuchungen* (WMANT 5). 3rd ed. Neukirchen-Vluyn: Neukirchener, 1974.

Wilson, S. G. *The Gentiles and the Gentile Mission in Luke-Acts* (SNTSMS 23). Cambridge: University, 1973.

Wimsatt, William K., Jr., and Beardsley, Monroe C. "The Intentional Fallacy," 3-18. In *The Verbal Icon: Studies in the Meaning of Poetry*. Lexington: University of Kentucky, 1954.

Winston, David. *The Wisdom of Solomon* (AB 43). New York: Doubleday, 1979.

Winter, B., "Benefactors" Winter, Bruce W. "The Public Honouring of Christian Benefactors. Romans 13.3-4 and 1 Peter 2.14-15." *JSNT* 34 (1988): 87-103.

———, "Welfare" ———. "'Seek the welfare of the city': social ethics according to 1 Peter." *Themelios* 13 (1988): 91-94.

Winter, Paul. "The Treatment of His Sources by the Third Evangelist in Luke xxi-xxiv." *ST* 8 (1955): 138-172.

Winton, Alan P. *The Proverbs of Jesus. Issues of History and Rhetoric* (JSNTSup

35). Sheffield: JSOT, 1990.

Wolf, C. U. "Servant." *IDB* 4:291-2.

Wolff, Christian. "Humility and Self-Denial in Jesus' Life and Message and in the Apostolic Existence of Paul," 145-60. In *Paul and Jesus* (JSNTSup 37). Edt. A. J. M. Wedderburn. Sheffield: JSOT, 1989.

York, John O. *The Last Shall Be First. The Rhetoric of Reversal in Luke* (JSNT-Sup 46). Sheffield: JSOT, 1991.

Young, Edward J. *The Book of Isaiah* (NICOT). Vol. 3. Grand Rapids: Eerdmans, 1972.

Zahn, Theodor. *Das Evangelium des Lucas ausgelegt* (Kommentar zum Neuen Testament). 2nd ed. Leipzig: Deichert, 1913.

Zehnle, Richard. "The Salvific Character of Jesus' Death in Lucan Soteriology." *TS* 30 (1969): 420-44.

Ziesler, John. *Paul's Letter to the Romans* (TPINTC). London: SCM, 1989.

Zmijewski, Josef. *Die Eschatologiereden des Lukas-Evangeliums. Eine traditions- und redaktionsgeschichtliche Untersuchung zu Lk 21,5-36 und Lk 17, 20-37* (BBB). Bonn: Hanstein, 1972.

Index of Subjects

Index of Authors

Index of References

NEW TESTAMENT

Matthew

Mark

Luke

John

Acts

PATRISTIC WRITINGS